CW00742722

THE DOMESDAY BOOK OF
GIANT SALMON

THE DOMESDAY BOOK OF
GIANT SALMON

A Record of the Largest Atlantic Salmon Ever Caught

Fred Buller

CONSTABLE

For my lady – Margaret

First published by Constable, an imprint of
Constable & Robinson Ltd
3 The Lanchesters
162 Fulham Palace Road
London W6 9ER
www.constablerobinson.com

Copyright © Fred Buller 2007

The right of Fred Buller to be identified as the author of this work has been asserted by him in accordance with the Copyright, Designs and Patents Act, 1988.

All rights reserved. This book is sold subject to the condition that it shall not, by way of trade or otherwise, be lent, re-sold, hired out or otherwise circulated in any form other than that in which it is published and without a similar condition including this condition being imposed on the subsequent purchaser.

A copy of the British Library Cataloguing in Publication Data is available from the British Library.

ISBN 13: 978 1 84529 598 1

Printed and bound in the EU

PREVIOUS PAGE: *The enormous salmon of 60lb or more caught on a dry fly and an 8lb test leader by Mike Crosby on the Restigouche River in 1988 and released to continue its journey upriver*

CONTENTS

Acknowledgements 6

Foreword 8

Introduction 10

THE LISTS 18
List 1   Salmon over 50lb caught on fly 23
List 2   Salmon between 50 and 60lb method uncertain 35
List 3   Salmon over 60lb caught by any method 45

Maps 54

SALMON OVER 50LB CAUGHT ON FLY 59

SALMON BETWEEN 50 AND 60LB METHOD UNCERTAIN 211

SALMON OVER 60LB CAUGHT BY ANY METHOD 257

TALES OF LOST FISH 415

NOT STRICTLY SPEAKING... 439

APPENDICES

1   Salmon fishing in Norway 452
2   Fishing in Norway by 'Rugde' 459
3   Big salmon caught in Finland and Sweden 465
4   Decline of the River Rhine 469
5   Number of salmon caught weighing over 60lb since 1700 471
6   The top twelve giant salmon caught on fly since the end of World War II 472
7   Sturdy's table 473

Bibliography 474

Picture Credits and Acknowledgements 477

Index 478

ACKNOWLEDGEMENTS

Most historians of British angling history rely to a great extent on two main tools – the *Fishing Gazette* and *The Field*. Both were founded a very long time ago but, sadly, in the 1960s we lost the *F.G.*, as it was affectionately called by all who wrote or spoke about it.

The *F.G.*, in the capable hands of its long-standing editor R.B. Marston, set a standard in angling journalism that is unlikely to be reached ever again. During my writing career I have spent more Mondays than I care to remember (which will be self-evident after you have read this book) perusing copies of the *Fishing Gazette* in the reading room of the British Museum's Newspaper Library at Colindale. Styles of expression, punctuation and indeed language change, and I have made no attempt to standardise any of these in the copious quotes and extracts that appear throughout the book, from the *F.G.* or from any other source for that matter.

I am sure that I have thanked the *Fishing Gazette* and its editors in every one of my eight books but in this instance I do not wish to check the validity of this statement for fear of finding that my previous thanks have been inadequate. The *Fishing Gazette* is an institution that contains a huge volume of raw, and pre-digested, material for many as yet unwritten books and it will continue to give leads into rich seams of research for those who delve with intent.

The Field – necessarily because by definition it has to cover all field sports – has never competed with the *F.G.* on the fishing side. Nevertheless, since its angling editors were often famous angling authors in their own right, it has documented much that is of inestimable value.

Last of all so far as institutions go, I must add the British Library, especially the Newspaper Library, which in a way is like a bank that unbelievably allows you to go on drawing out knowledge free of charge.

When I was three quarters of the way through the slog of producing the manuscript for this book, I suddenly found myself being helped out by two stalwarts. David Hatwell very kindly converted my handwritten lists of fish, which are a feature of this book, into readable form, which meant – with the frequent arrival of more data – that he needed constantly to shuffle the previous entries in order to correct the sequences.

My other assistant was Dutchman Jan Eggers, who, because of our long friendship and because of his unique knowledge of the continental angling scene and his mastery of European languages, was able to document quite a significant number of post-war catches of big salmon. Sadly, these catches are no longer reported in the British angling press as they had been for the previous one hundred and fifty years.

Lastly, but inevitably, an author/compiler always needs to thank those who have worked the machinery that translates thoughts into print. In this instance, Kay Varney, my secretary, is on my list as is my friend Marion Paull, who always casts a critical eye over some but not all of my work. I thank them both.

As I was nearing the end of this quest, my old friend Dr Malcolm Greenhalgh, who made a study of large salmon for his own book *The Complete Salmon Fisher* (1996), submitted some data that had arrived too late for inclusion in his own published list. I am grateful to him for these – as I am for a number of very good photographs of Norwegian rivers.

When I thought I had come close to finishing the manuscript, I looked for somebody who would undertake to read it and lay bare as many faults as he could find. Naturally, I looked for someone who had considerable experience of salmon fishing both in Britain and abroad. I was very lucky indeed to find Dr Roy Flury, who had not only jumped these fences but had himself co-authored two books about his favourite Norwegian salmon river, the Alten. Now I thank him for his critique, which proved to be *extremely* valuable, and for providing relevant photographs.

The information recorded in this book stems from notes that I have patiently collected over forty years. The facts are necessarily incomplete but at least they will create a base for big-fish statistics that can be built up as time goes by.

FOREWORD

This is truly a work of awesome research, scholarship and extraordinary dedication. Considering that the book is mainly composed of stories about salmon so huge that the majority of us will never see one, it is also written with commendable discipline. Fred Buller has given his all and achieved something that anyone who has tried to research the history of notable salmon will readily admit is extremely difficult.

Since first meeting Fred Buller in the summer of 2005 to discuss some Norwegian salmon, he has never ceased to amaze me, both with the contents of this book and his remarkable knowledge of all things angling. I learned that as a young man he worked in Windermere for two years, studying the ecology of the lake and local becks. He has always retained this interest and here frequently refers to the ecology of the fish as much as its weight.

Angler, historian, author, ecologist and detective – Buller really enjoys the hunt for a few crumbs of evidence to solve a problem. In the autumn of 2006 the manuscript was almost complete when he received an old photograph of a gentleman sitting on a chair with a huge fish at his feet. Could he identify the man? This was just his cup of tea. All was put on hold while he went to work and, in a surprisingly short time, with a little help from his old friend the *Fishing Gazette*, he duly named his man.

Buller is also blessed with an uncanny knack of being able to make things happen. I was surprised when, during a cold and miserable week at the end of November 2005, he set off for Scotland, not to fish but to take photographs and investigate two reports of large salmon. On his return he was in good spirits. The sun had come out at convenient moments, and thanks to a chance meeting when he stopped to ask the way, he learned of another huge fish caught on the River Ewe.

On the way home he had called in at Bemersyde on the River Tweed, where a monster salmon had been lost around 1905 by the then laird, Colonel Haig. He needed a picture of the pool so, parking his car, he walked down to the river. There, as if waiting by appointment, was the present laird, Earl Haig, son of the Colonel who had lost the fish and who, with promotion, as Buller instantly grasped, became Field Marshal Sir Douglas Haig of Great War fame. A conversation ensued, the photograph was permitted and he was on his way – another demonstration of the remarkable serendipity so characteristic of Buller.

Certainly, more problems are inherent in researching big salmon from Scandinavian countries than from Scotland. Fish over 50lb have been caught in Norway in each of the past fifty years, except the odd one, and good numbers have also been caught in Sweden and Finland, but we hear little news of these. Details of many of the big fish caught in earlier years are misty, and the occasional fish shows a weight increase at intervals after it was caught! A prime example of this is a fish from the Aaro caught by Count Denissoff and well described here.

Nearly thirty years ago Hugh Falkus wrote in the foreword to *The Domesday Book of Mammoth Pike*: 'It is the most remarkable piece of research in the history of angling.' Here is a serious challenger. What was achieved for pike has now been done for salmon.

This is an important book. It may be opened where you please as there is no particular beginning or end. It is a book to browse through, to discuss or argue over with a friend. Above all, it is an appreciation and a fine tribute to the salmon and the rivers to which they return to spawn.

Roy Flury
Oxford
2007

INTRODUCTION

To judge by accounts concerning the capture of large salmon published in the local, national and sporting press over the last two centuries, it is obvious that the public is interested, perhaps morbidly so, when one of these leviathans is taken by rod, net or gaff from its natural element, where hitherto it had been invisible.

At the present time in most countries apart from Norway, Sweden and Finland, the landing of a 50lb specimen of *Salmo salar*, the Atlantic salmon, would cause a stir and the landing of a 60-pounder, a sensation. In times gone by, a good number of fish weighing over 60lb was caught; not so many as would make a researcher spend a lifetime documenting them all, but enough so far as I am concerned for the present undertaking.

The chart on page 471 shows that whereas only twenty-two fish exceeding a weight of 60lb were caught during the period 1700–1875, twenty-four fish are documented for the period 1876–1900, which may reflect improved transport facilities, the opening up of the Norwegian fisheries or the development of suitable tackle for both anglers and commercial net fishermen – more probably a combination of all three. The chart also shows that the golden age for landing these giant specimens was between 1901 and 1925, when fifty-four were caught. During the next fifty years, a rapid decline in numbers caught set in, but from 1976 the decline slowed down. This unlikely rally may be due to the development of deep-water rod fishing for *feeding* fish in the Baltic Sea.

In R. Sutterby and Malcolm Greenhalgh's book *Atlantic Salmon* (2005), mention is made of a recovery in the populations of herring and sprat in the Baltic. These in turn attract salmon, which prey on the smaller fish, and the increased food supply has had an effect on the number of large salmon being caught on rod and line. Kenneth Olsson's 60lb 10oz Baltic salmon (No. 335), which won first prize in a salmon angling festival, provides hard evidence of this. Indeed, two other fish of over 60lb have been caught in previous competitions.

A few years ago, when I was fishing as a guest of Alan Lane (the Coventry tackle dealer) on a beat on the North Esk, I met Jesper Fohrmann, a Danish angling correspondent. Jesper had read and enjoyed *The Domesday Book of Mammoth Pike* and my co-authored book *Falkus & Buller's Freshwater Fishing*, and in September 2005 he wrote to me because he had heard I was researching a book on big salmon. He described how he caught his best fish, 45½lb:

I have fished for salmon every year since the age of five, which has given me 33 years of salmon fishing. Through all these years I have only seen two fish on the bank weighing more than 20kg. I was lucky enough to catch one of these fish. It was a beautiful silver 20.5kg fish – silver right to the tail. A true predator in its natural environment. The fish was caught in the Baltic Sea on a dead herring trolled at 2 knots 60 feet down in 250 feet of water. It took me 50 minutes of hard battle to get it in my boat.

The fact that Jesper was fishing down to sixty feet reflects the depth at which the herring and sprat shoals swim. Doubtless echo sounders are used to locate them in the same way that they are used on Lake Superior, or indeed in the Pacific. Interestingly, the trolling (I prefer the term trailing) speed used by Jesper is the same as that used by charr fishermen on Windermere and Coniston.

So this is the method that is now being employed in the Baltic to catch feeding salmon – the deep-water trolling method pioneered on Lake Superior to catch Coho salmon is now being used to catch Atlantic salmon. To get back to where this is all leading us – perhaps to salmon fishermen going to the Greenland feeding ground to chance their luck?

All is not lost elsewhere, however. After the serious declines of the twentieth century, the River Rhine in Germany now holds salmon again, and those who pursue their fishing in Scotland can only marvel at the following report:

The River Tweed Commissioners have announced that there was a 46 per cent increase in rod-caught salmon numbers in 2003. Almost 14,000 fish were recorded, the most since accurate record-keeping began in 1963.

Chairman John Lovett said "Many people have told us we would be better investing in artificial stocking measures but they were wrong. We have committed huge resources to pay for the improvements but the fish have done it for themselves."

Nick Yonge, director of the Tweed Foundation, added, "There is little doubt our initiative to reduce exploitation by nets has played its part too. Reduced coastal and estuary netting and now the substantial closure of the North-east drift-net fishery have helped a great deal."

Andrew Wallace, director of the Association of Salmon Fishery Boards added, "I really do believe the Tweed is probably now the best salmon river in the world."

Uncovering the dramas behind the capture of these huge salmon has been as fascinating and rewarding as coming across another 50lb-plus fish. The relevant lines of

enquiry, together with what I have been able to discover, are collected in this book, although I have been unable to find out anything other than the bare facts about some of the fish, and these remain tantalisingly in the lists with, as yet, no added story to tell.

While I was reading, or more precisely re-reading, the big-fish accounts, I was surprised to discover how young the salmon – approximately 98 per cent of which are cock fish – were at the time of capture. On further investigation, another surprise was the relative accuracy of the weight/length scale for salmon that was invented by W.H. Sturdy (see page 473) in contrast to the best-known weight/length scale for pike, invented by 'Mona', which is useless. I daresay the pike scale is hardly practical because it takes no account of the possibility of the pike having taken a recent meal or of weight loss due to spawning (all big pike are female), both of which events could account for 20 per cent of body weight. Sturdy had the good fortune to do his calculations knowing that salmon stop feeding once they enter freshwater and do not spawn until sometime after the fishing season has closed. Big cock fish are rarely, if ever, more than six years old, having spent two years in freshwater and four years at sea. J. Arthur Hutton spent a lifetime studying fish scales – cleaning, mounting, reading and indexing them – and was the top British expert on the subject, regularly consulted by the *Fishing Gazette*, and often quoted in this book. His evidence is always important and he made a very clear statement on the age of big male salmon in his book *Wye Salmon and Other Fish* (1949):

> People, when they see a really big Salmon, say of 40 or 50lb, would naturally think that it was a comparatively old fish, whereas, as a matter of fact, it would probably be not more than five or six years old. The salmon is a rapid-growing but comparatively short-lived animal. Most of the Wye salmon spend two years of their childhood in the river and then migrate to the sea when they weigh only two or three ounces. It is the rich feeding in salt water, which enables them to grow so rapidly. Some return to the river as grilse weighing about 6lb after a year and a half's feeding in the sea, but the great majority will continue feeding for another one or two years. Their ultimate weight depends entirely on the length of time they have spent in salt water without returning to spawn. A few will not return until they have spent four complete years 'guzzling and gorging' in the sea, and these are the really heavy fish weighing 30 or 40lb or more. A very few may remain in the sea for a fifth year, but such Salmon are very rare.
>
> After spawning, the great majority of the fish die, so it will be realized

Jesper Fohrmann with his big salmon caught in the Baltic, trolling a dead herring at 2 knots 60 feet down in 250 feet of water. It took 50 minutes before it was brought into the boat

that very few Wye Salmon live for any great length of time, and that most of all these big fish are only about six years old.

However, further research has been carried out since Hutton's era. As Roy Flury has pointed out, scales of fish caught in northern Norwegian rivers show that there smolting often lasts for four years. He gives Bozo Ivanovic's fish as an example (No. 20). That 50lb fish had spent four years in freshwater and four years at sea. Sutterby and Greenhalgh's *Atlantic Salmon* includes up-to-date research that confirms the subject is more complex than Hutton suggests. We now know that salmon populations in specific rivers can have different spawning strategies from the one Hutton describes. An extreme example is found on the Tana River, which flows between Norway and Finland and is called the Teno in Finland. Salmon parr may remain for up to eight years before smolting and may not return to spawn for five years. Even more surprisingly, when compared with salmon populations in other rivers, a small percentage of Tana salmon may make as many as three spawning runs, with necessary intervals spent feeding at sea. Greenhalgh calculates that salmon behaving in this way could reach the age of seventeen years and advises that 'this relatively small number of multiple spawners has been estimated to attain weights in the 44–66lb range.'

Very little seems to be known about why such insignificant numbers of male salmon return to sea after their spawning activities, where they could regain their strength in order to spawn a second time. As Hutton noted, the majority of them die. P.D. Malloch, whose classic study *Life-History and Habits of the Salmon, Sea-Trout, Trout and Other Freshwater Fish* (1910) is referred to several times in this book, made an relevant statement after he had read a scale taken from the shoulder of a 14lb cock fish that had been netted from the River Tay.

> The scale is a very interesting one, as it is taken from the only male salmon I have ever seen in our fish-house on its second return from the sea. Going down as a smolt, it came up a grilse in 1910; descending as a kelt in the spring of 1911, it returned to the river and was caught in our nets on the 20th August. This fish was fresh from the sea, and had sea-lice clinging to it.
>
> During its sojourn in the sea ten rings were added to the scale beyond the kelt-grilse mark. The mortality amongst male fish entering a river must be very great, few surviving, as I must have examined 100,000 fish before I came across this specimen.

Exhaustion is frequently cited as the cause of death, although there is little evidence to support this. If it is the case, it seems likely that male competition for a hen fish rather

Malloch's 14lb cock salmon, which descended the river as a kelt in Spring 1911 and was caught on 20 August of the same year. Malloch had never seen a cock fish ascending the river for the second time, although, as he said, 'I must have examined 100,000 fish before I came across this specimen'

than the spawning act itself is the reason for the weariness. In *Wye Salmon and Other Fish* Hutton reported a visit to a salmon spawning redd at Brynwern Bridge on the River Wye in November 1924, where he witnessed many rounds of fighting between male fish that could have lead to their deaths.

> On the same day we saw a most interesting fight between two Cock-fish. When we first saw them they had evidently been at it for some time, for they were like two "prize-fighters" who had got to their 17th round. They would occasionally make a lunge at each other and then would drop a yard or two down-stream quite exhausted with the struggle. Each one's principal effort seemed to be to try and get hold of the other by the tail, and so give him the knock-out blow by pulling him up-stream. No salmon can stand being held with his head down-stream for he would "drown" in a very short time, as the water would pass the wrong way through his gills. We watched them for over ten minutes and we left them still at it. Probably both would die, for they seemed very much exhausted. This may partly explain why so many Cock-fish die after spawning.

A first-hand account of a duel between two male salmon was published in *The Scotsman* (11 January 1930):

> While walking along the banks of a salmon river in the neighbourhood of Campbeltown [The unnamed river is almost certainly the Conieglen Water

in Kyntyre] I was attracted to the peculiar movements of fish in a shallow pool. On moving to the edge of the water I witnessed a remarkable spectacle. Two salmon were behaving in an extraordinary manner. Both buried their snouts in the gravel, facing each other and about two feet apart, and being in a vertical position, their tails showed above the surface. In this attitude they remained motionless for about a minute and a half, then resumating the horizontal, suddenly and at great speed they rushed at each other, colliding head on. Then they chased one another in a succession of circles and semi-circles, causing a commotion of swirls and eddies in the pool. After this display they once more assumed their former position – their noses on the bottom with their tails sticking out if the water, and in a short time the fight was renewed. For about twenty minutes they carried on in this fashion, and I was further astonished, that beyond shifting the focus of the struggle a few yards up stream from where I was standing, they ignored my presence. I was able to identify them as two male fish which were evidently engaged in a battle royal for a specific female, which was not to be seen. At last one of the combatants, evidently beaten, set off at speed down stream. Shortly afterwards his conqueror made a dash underneath the bank, and next moment a salmon leapt out of the water on to the side grass and rolled back again. Presumably this was the female fish for which this intense battle was fought. I have never before observed a phenomenon of this nature. Apparently the male salmon, like the male grey seal, has at times to fight hard for a mate. – N. M.

Female salmon rarely attain the heavyweight status that some males reach. According to H.D. Turing in *Where to Fish* (1937), the heaviest female salmon recorded at that time weighed 52lb and was caught by Major C.W. Wallace in the Vefsen River in Norway on 2 August 1928. It was 50½in long and had a girth of 28in. Fourteen years later, a 54lb hen fish was caught in Norway on the Nausta River by Trygue Kleiva. A 54lb salmon caught on the Grand Cascapedia River in 1920 is the heaviest hen fish from North America.

Major B.D. Corbet, following up an article about the 'Weight of Female Salmon' that was published in the *Fishing Gazette* on 1 December 1923, had the following comment to make (*Fishing Gazette*, 29 December 1923):

DEAR SIR – Since writing with reference to Major Morrison's 51lb. hen fish, I have seen in the shop of Forrest & Son, of Kelso, at Thomas Street, Oxford Street, the cast of a hen fish weighing 58lb. This fish was killed on the

Evanger River before the war. I could not get the date, as Mr. Forrest was out. The measurements are: Length 50½in.; girth 29in.

Yours faithfully

B.D. CORBETT (MAJOR)

Finally, as a little but important digression, I think that the best advice about playing all salmon, let alone the biggest of the tribe, comes from J.R. Holden. I found it on page 11 of Arthur Oglesby and Lucy Money-Coutts' book *The Big Fish*. Holden, who had just described the hooking, playing and landing of a 59½lb salmon on Norway's Evanger River on 23 June 1949, goes on to say: 'So far as my own fish was concerned, it was never on less than 25 yards of line until it was well beaten and it was not gaffed until it was completely spent – both points due to the keeper's skill. One of the signs of inexperience is a dreadful battle under the rod tip.

Holden gave us another gem, which he in turn had learned from the angling writer 'Lemon Gray', 'Dinner is the angler's enemy; high tea and late supper is the answer, so far as fishing is concerned.' I couldn't agree more.

THE LISTS

I believe that to catch a salmon weighing over 50lb on fly is the highest distinction that a salmon fisherman can hope to achieve in his or her lifetime. I have therefore made them the subject of List 1. However, because so many 50-pounders have been documented without mention of the method used to catch them, the list can only be tentative and, accordingly, I have included a subsidiary list (List 2) of fish that *may* have been caught on fly weighing between 50 and 60lb. This list of rod-caught fish, I have labelled 'method uncertain'. This list does not contain any fish from North America, perhaps because of the almost universal use of fly-fishing for Atlantic Salmon there. It is important to note that I have *not* explored the catch records of fish between 50lb and 60lb caught on bait, simply because if their numbers were added to the task that I have just completed, the book could not have been published in my lifetime.

Salmon of 60lb are so spectacular and rare that I have recorded them in a third list which disregards the method used for their capture. Incorporated in List 3 are 150 or so of the largest Atlantic salmon. I suspect that not too many fish of such a weight have escaped my attention unless they were caught in saltwater or in the River Rhine, before industrial pollution and netting ruined it as a salmon fishery.

The book is principally historical in method. For each fish, there may have been several sources of information, and corroboration. Those given in these lists are generally the first chronologically that I have found and others may be detailed in the stories behind the catching of these big salmon.

Weights used to be recorded using the Dutch system of pounds, but in 1826, during the reign of George IV, the Imperial Weights and Measures Act brought about the change to what is known as the avoirdupois system. This introduced the current system throughout Britain. To convert Dutch to English pounds it is necessary to divide by 1.085. I have mentioned this where necessary in the accounts of the big fish. Interestingly, it is perhaps because of the confusion caused by retaining the name but changing the value that the one-time record rod-caught salmon, caught by Lord Home during the eighteenth century, is no longer recognised as such.

A major problem faces anyone researching the many big fish caught in Norway, especially on very large rivers, such as the Alten (also known at the Alta – I have used the older spelling throughout), Namsen, Tana and Vosso, because detailed records are few and far between. However, old photographs may be found and many wooden models of the fish. Photographs often show a fisherman holding a long fly rod with a large reel at the butt end, a combination that suggests the angler was fly-fishing. It does not necessarily mean that he was casting a fly, though, because he may well have been harling with a fly, and even using a small spinner or fly spoon.

To some extent, the same difficulty exists with regard to fish caught in Scotland. John Ashley-Cooper, who made a study of these matters, reckoned that we can safely say that most big salmon caught in Scottish rivers before 1900 were caught on fly, although that may mean that some fish were caught harling with fly – especially fish caught on the Tay.

Following the lists I have included as many of the stories of capture of these giant salmon as I have been able to find.

A final word is needed about 'catch and release'. I have not included any of the very large salmon that have been caught and released without being weighed in recent years, although sometimes these have been supported by plausible estimates and photographs. As I show in the main text, photographs are hopelessly unreliable means of estimating size, and the difficulties of estimating weight from hastily gathered information about length and girth are too great for the results to merit inclusion.

I am told that on the Alten River in Norway, a scheme was tried where boatmen were issued with special lightweight weighing-nets with powerful and accurate spring balances and tape measures – that would enable them to 'process' a beaten fish so that it could be returned to the water quickly and without harm. Experience in Britain has shown that special mats are also needed so that fish do not harm themselves on the ground or in the bottom of a boat. Experience with this experiment has revealed that the provision and storage of these instruments is unsustainable in practical terms.

The problem with 'catch and release' would appear to be insoluble when it comes to records. Even if you have taken fine supportive photographs, you cannot put a weight to a fish that has been released that will be acceptable or classifiable in any form. Does it matter? I have included as a frontispiece a photograph of an enormous salmon caught on a dry fly (and an 8lb test leader!) in New Brunswick's Restigouche River. Mike Crosby wrote an account of its capture, which originally appeared in the magazine *Eastern Woods and Waters* in October 1988:

> I thought the guide was going to have a heart attack. The first time it rose
> for the fly it was just like a big shadow. The second and third time he came,
> I knew he had it and I pulled, but I didn't connect. I found out why later
> when I saw that big hook [kype].

The fourth time he came, he just showed deep under the fly and I started to get worried. So I changed the fly. It took me two or three minutes to find him again and I was starting to panic... but the fifth time he came for the fly it didn't travel three feet and he had it! The only way I can describe what happened when he took off downriver was that it was like looking inside a washing machine, he churned the river up that much.... The 250 yards of backing was just gone in one run so we had to pull the anchor and start up the motor and go after him. I would gather my line back and we would get downriver of him... Then he would strip the reel again and we would go upriver.... We did that for an hour... I only had an 8lb test leader so I couldn't do much with him.... He was taking line so fast I couldn't go ashore to play with him....

When we got him to the boat, all I could think about was getting him loose before we hurt him so we didn't get any scale samples or measurements... But I don't really care whether he was a North American record or not. I know I caught a salmon that no-one else will probably ever catch again and I'm happy with that.

Harling on the Namsen

Low water conditions on the Grand Cascapedia River

LIST 1
SALMON OVER 50lb
CAUGHT ON FLY

Number	Weight lb oz	Length (in)	Girth (in)	Location	Country	Captor
1	50			River Spey	Scotland	Duncan Grant
2	50			Grand Cascapedia	Canada	General Chester A. Arthur
3	50			River Tay	Scotland	H. Clarke-Jervoise
4	50			River Ewe	Scotland	Mr Grant
5	50	49½	28	River Spey	Scotland	Lord Winterton
6	50	48	28	River Shannon	Ireland	Mr Archibald Kirker's Keeper
7	50			River Ewe	Scotland	Mr Dugdale's Keeper
8	50	51½	28½	River Awe	Scotland	Dr C. Child
9	50	49	33	River Beauly	Scotland	Major Piper Fraser
10	50			Grand Cascapedia	Canada	Irving Bonbright
11	50	51	27½	Grand Cascapedia	Canada	J.T. Spaulding
12	50	52	27	Eira River	Norway	Neville Bostock
13	50	51¾	27½	River Tay	Scotland	Miss Lettice Ward
14	50	48½	28	Alten River	Norway	Major B.D. Corbet
15	50			Alten River	Norway	Hans Kjeldsberg
16	50			Alten River	Norway	Admiral W.A. Read
17	50			Alten River	Norway	Torleif Leinan
18	50			Alten River	Norway	Dagfinn Storvann
19	50			Matepedia River	Canada	Dr Rodolphe Coigney
20	50			Alten River	Norway	Bozo Ivanovic
21	50			Alten River	Norway	Peter Stroh
22	50			Alten River	Norway	Tor Arne Olaussen
23	50 4			Alten River	Norway	Jacqueline Vernes
24	50 8	52		Grand Cascapedia	Canada	Dr William Drummond
25	50 8	54½	29½	River Annan	Scotland	Peter Loudon
26	50 8	50½	27½	River Tweed	Scotland	J.D. Rudd
27	50 8			Tana (Teno) River	Finland	Eino Kukkonen
28	50 8	47½	28½	Morrum River	Sweden	Christer Lundquist
29	50 8			Morrum River	Sweden	P. Bjorklund
30	50 12			Gaula River	Norway	Magnar Lilleler
31	50 12			Tana (Teno) River	Finland	Esko Ovaska
32	50 12	51¼		Tana (Teno) River	Finland	Pekka Heiskanen
33	51			Grand Cascapedia	Canada	Edmond W. Davis
34	51			Grand Cascapedia	Canada	Charles Barnes
35	51			River Tay	Scotland	Sir Stuart Coates
36	51			Grand Cascapedia	Canada	Henry C. Phipps
37	51	54	24½	River Tweed	Scotland	Howard St George
38	51			Alten River	Norway	Major Morrison
39	51			River Awe	Scotland	Major A.W. Huntington

Date	Source
c1813	*Days and Nights of Salmon Fishing in the Tweed* Scrope (1843)
1878	*Grand Cascapedia Giants* Swanson (2005); in *Observations on a Salmon River* (1922) Griswold gives a weight of 52lbs
1883	*The Great Salmon Rivers of Scotland* Ashley-Cooper (1980)
1885	*Salmon Rivers and Lochs of Scotland* page 292 Calderwood (1909)
1892	*Daily Mail* 7 September 1904; *The Salmon Rivers of Scotland* Grimble (1913)
1895	*Fishing Gazette* 9 February 1895
1902	*British Freshwater Fish* page 224 (1904)
1907	*Fishing Gazette* 9 November 1907
1909	Newspaper cutting
1912	*Grand Cascapedia Giants* Swanson (2005)
1922	*Observations on a Salmon River* Griswold (1922)
1927	*The Fisherman's Bedside Book* 'BB' (1945)
1928	*Where to Fish* (1937)
1928	*Where to Fish* (1937)
1947	Tormod Leinan's list
1959	Letter from Roy Flury, September 2005
1976	Tormod Leinan's list
1981	Tormod Leinan's list
1983	*Flyfishers Journal* (Summer 1993)
1994	Letter from Roy Flury, 13 July 2005
1999	Tormod Leinan's list
2000	Tormod Leinan's list
1956	Roxburghe Records
1890	*Grand Cascapedia Giants* Swanson (2005)
1893	*Game Fish Records* page 151 Scott (1936)
1925	*The Big Fish* Oglesby and Money-Coutts (1992)
1969	*ABu's Nyt Nappaa* ('Tight Lines') (1970); Optic fly
1979	*Fiske Journalen Yearbook No. 2* (1979)
June 1991	Note to Nils-Erik Tornquist from Anders Sorensson (2006)
1981	*Fiske Journalen Yearbook No. 4* page109
July 1991	*Urheilu Kalastus* ('Sportfishing') magazine (March 1993)
Aug 1996	*Urheilu Kalastus* ('Sportfishing') magazine (March 1997)
1900	*Salmon Fishing on the Grand Cascapedia* Davis (1904, 2001)
1906	*Grand Cascapedia Giants* Swanson (2005)
1913	*Where to Fish* page 390 (1937)
c1920	*Grand Cascapedia Giants* page 34 Swanson (2005)
1921	*The Big Fish* Oglesby and Money-Coutts (1992)
1923	Roxburghe Records. Caught second 51lb fish three days later
1930	*The Field*, 14 June 1930

Number	Weight lb oz	Length (in)	Girth (in)	Location	Country	Captor
40	51			Alten River	Norway	Hans Kjeldsberg
41	51	52		Aaro River	Norway	Richard Waddington
42	51			Alten River	Norway	Jens Jensen
43	51			Alten River	Norway	Duke of Roxburghe
44	51			Alten River	Norway	Odd Hansen
45	51			Alten River	Norway	Hans Lie
46	51			Alten River	Norway	Morton Seaman
47	51			Alten River	Norway	Espen Ottem
48	51 6			Morrum River	Sweden	R. Johnsson
49	51 8			River Tay	Scotland	John Gellatly
50	51 8	51	28	River Tweed	Scotland	Colonel W. Home
51	51 8			River Tweed	Scotland	General W. Home
52	51 8	50¾	27	River Tweed	Scotland	Dr E. Fison
53	51 8			Namsen River	Norway	Mr Bainbridge (Junior)
54	51 8			Tana (Teno) River	Finland	Sakari Leppakases
55	51 12			Tana (Teno) River	Finland	Pauli Ja Jorma
56	51 12			Stryn River	Norway	Otto Grieg Tiedenman
57	51 14			Morrum River	Sweden	O. Andreasson
58	52			Stryn River	Norway	Captain 'C'
59	52			River Derwent	England	L. Ferguson
60	52			River Awe	Scotland	Colonel James Thorpe
61	52			Grand Cascapedia	Canada	Edmond W. Davis
62	52			Grand Cascapedia	Canada	Henry C. Phipps
63	52			Alten River	Norway	Colonel N. Dalrymple Hamilton
64	52	48½	26½	Grand Cascapedia	Canada	Mr O'Neill Ryan
65	52			Alten River	Norway	Didrik Heitmann
66	52			Alten River	Norway	Geir Zakariassen
67	52			Alten River	Norway	Morton Seaman
68	52 8	42	30	Margaree River	Canada	Cecil McKenzie
69	52 10			Morrum River	Sweden	M. Svensson
70	52 10			Morrum River	Sweden	K. Hakkansson
71	52 14			Tana (Teno) River	Finland	Jouko Nousianen
72	52 14			Orkla	Norway	Stig Hansen
73	52 14			Tana (Teno) River	Finland	Tuomo Inget
74	53			Namsen River	Norway	Viscount Dungarvan
75	53			Namsen River	Norway	Hon. D. Leigh
76	53			River Tay	Scotland	Lord Blythswood
77	53	49½	29	River Spey	Scotland	W.G. Craven
78	53			North Esk	Scotland	J.M. Oldham
79	53	50	29	Grand Cascapedia	Canada	Charles B. Barnes

Date	Source
1945	Tormod Leinan's list
c1955	*The Big Fish* page 31 Oglesby and Money-Coutts (1992)
1978	Tormod Leinan's list
1979	Personal communication
1983	Tormod Leinan's list
1984	Tormod Leinan's list
1992	Alten Records
1996	Tormod Leinan's list
April 1992	Note to Nils-Erik Tornquist from Anders 1992 Sorensson (2006)
1875	*Where to Fish* (1937)
1892	*British Freshwater Fishes* Maxwell (1904)
1902	*Where to Fish* (1937)
1922	Game Fish Records page 211 Scott (1936)
1937	Letter from Malcolm Greenhalgh, 9 December 2005; harling with a fly?
July 1991	*Urheilu Kalastus* ('Sportfishing') magazine 1991 (March 1992)
Unknown	*Urheilu Kalastus* ('Sportfishing') magazine (March 1998)
1981	*Fiske Journalen Yearbook No. 4* page 109
Sept 1995	Note to Nils-Erik Tornquist from Anders Sorensson (2006)
c1860	*Reminiscences of Halsten Muri Hutton* (1907)
1885	*Game Fish Records* page 15 Scott (1936)
c1890	*The Salmon Rivers of Scotland* page 88 Grimble (1913)
1901	*Salmon Fishing on the Grand Cascapedia* Davis (1904, 2001)
c1920	*Grand Cascapedia Giants* page 30 Swanson (2005)
1926	*Alten: The Story of a Salmon River* Flury and Dalenson (1991)
1954	*Grand Cascapedia Giants* Swanson (2005)
1976	Tormod Leinan's list
1983	Tormod Leinan's list
1994	Alten Records
1927	*Fishing Gazette* 1 October 1927
May 1995	Note to Nils-Erik Tornquist from Anders Sorensson (2006)
May 2000	Note to Nils-Erik Tornquist from Anders Sorensson (2006)
Aug 1985	*Urheilu Kalastus* ('Sportfishing') magazine (March 1986); Black Doctor fly
1987	*Fiske Journalen Yearbook* No. 10 page 87
c1994	*Metsastys Ja Kalastus* magazine (January 1995)
1888	Letter from Roy Flury, 13 July 2005; harling with a fly?
1888	Letter from Roy Flury, 13 July 2005; harling with a fly?
1889	*The Salmon Rivers of Scotland* page 296 Grimble (1913)
1897	*Daily Mail* 7 September 1904
c1901	*Game Fish Records* page 168 Scott (1936)
1911	*Grand Cascapedia Giants* Swanson (2005)

Number	Weight lb oz	Length (in)	Girth (in)	Location	Country	Captor
80	53			River Awe	Scotland	Angus McCall
81	53	49	29	River Tay	Scotland	Sir Stuart Coates
82	53			Alten River	Norway	Major B.D. Corbet
83	53	51¼	29	River Tay	Scotland	O.M. Pritchard
84	53	49	30	Alten River	Norway	Duke of Roxburghe
85	53			Alten River	Norway	Margaret Du Bois
86	53	52	29	Alten River	Norway	Clare De Burgh
87	53			Alten River	Norway	Kare Jorgensen
88	53			Alten River	Norway	Odd Hansen
89	53			Alten River	Norway	Olafe Lampe
90	53			Alten River	Norway	William Caine
91	53 3			Morrum River	Sweden	C. Palm
92	53 10			River Em	Sweden	J. Derehed
93	53 12			River Em	Sweden	L.P. Gustafsson
94	54	50	30	River Tay	Scotland	Lord Ruthven
95	54	54	28	Grand Cascapedia	Canada	Robert Dun
96	54			River Awe	Scotland	The schoolmaster
97	54			River Shannon	Ireland	Fred Milburn
98	54	48		Grand Cascapedia	Canada	Henry Nadeau
99	54			Alten River	Norway	Duke of Westminster
100	54			Alten River	Norway	Mr Black
101	54			Alten River	Norway	Gunnar Kristensen
102	54			Alten River	Norway	Alistair Ballantine
103	54			Alten River	Norway	Einar Anthonsen
104	54 3			River Em	Sweden	L. Postonen
105	54 7			Morrum River	Sweden	M. Bjorkman
106	54 8			River Tay	Scotland	Alexander Mackintosh
107	54 8			River Awe	Scotland	Sir John Bennett Lawes
108	55			River Garry	Scotland	Alexander Grant
109	55		25	River Tweed	Scotland	Mr Brereton
110	55			Grand Cascapedia	Canada	Hon. Victor Stanley R.N.
111	55	50	30	River Tay	Scotland	Marquis of Zetland
112	55			River Tweed	Scotland	W.A. Kidson
113	55			Rauma River	Norway	Sir W. Bromley-Davenport
114	55			Laerdal River	Norway	Ola Sviggum
115	55	52	27¾	Fusta River	Norway	Major H.H.R. White
116	55			Tana River	Norway	A Lapp
117	55			Alten River	Norway	Antti Parkkinen
118	55 2			Tana (Teno) River	Finland	Mr Hirvonen
119	55 2			Tana (Teno) River	Finland	Kosti Linder

Date	Source
1913	*Game Fish Records* page 153 Scott (1936)
1923	*Where to Fish* (1926); *Fishing Gazette* 1 December 1923
1923	Roxburghe Records
1924	*Where to Fish* (1926)
1928	*Where to Fish* page 391 (1937); Roxburghe Records
1965	Roxburghe Records
1968	*Salmon Stories* Chance (1983)
1980	Tormod Leinan's list
1983	Tormod Leinan's list
1989	Tormod Leinan's list
1998	Tormod Leinan's list
July 1992	Note to Nils-Erik Tornquist from Anders Sorensson (2006)
Oct 1992	Note to Nils-Erik Tornquist from Goran Ulfsparres (2006)
May 2000	Note to Nils-Erik Tornquist from Goran Ulfsparres (2006)
1883	*Fishing Gazette* 14 November 1903
1886	*Game Fish Records* page 273 Scott (1936)
1887	*The Salmon Rivers of Scotland* page 88 Grimble (1913)
1903	*Fishing Gazette* 14 November 1903
1920	*Game Fish Records* page 273 (1936)
1950	*Salmon Fishing in Norway* Prag (1953)
1954	Tormod Leinan's list
1984	Tormod Leinan's list
1992	*Alten Reflections* Flury and Dalenson (1993)
2000	Tormod Leinan's list
Sept 1992	Note to Nils-Erik Tornquist from Goran Ulfsparres (2006)
May 1992	Note to Nils-Erik Tornquist from Anders Sorensson (2006)
1765	*The Driffield Angler* Mackintosh (1806, 1994)
1887	*The Salmon Rivers of Scotland* page 88 Grimble (1913); *Fishing Gazette* 14 November 1903
1887	*Game Fish Records* Scott (1936)
1889	*Fishing Gazette* 14 November 1903
1892	*A Memoir* (1880–1893) Victor Stanley (unpublished)
1895	*Fishing Gazette* 19 October1895 and 14 November 1903
1913	*A Line on Salmon* Ashley-Cooper (1983)
1926	*Fishing Gazette* 26 June 1926
c1930	*Angling in Laerdal River* J. Bruvoli (1970s)
1932	*Where to Fish* (1937)
c1965	*Flyfishers Journal* (Summer 1970); harling with a fly?
1985	*Alten Reflections* Flury and Dalenson (1993)
c 1950	*Metsastys Ja Kalastus* magazine hen fish page 308 (1951)
Unknown	*Tenon Tarinat* ('Stories of Tana') page 136 Ronkainen (1999); Brown Mallard fly

Number	Weight lb oz	Length (in)	Girth (in)	Location	Country	Captor
120	55 6			Morrum River	Sweden	E. Nedergaar
121	55 8			River Derwent	England	Unknown
122	55 8			River Tay	Scotland	P.M. Coates
123	55 8	49¾	30¼	Grand Cascapedia	Canada	Esmond Bradley Martin
124	55 9			Alten River	Norway	Einar Suhr
125	55 12			Tana (Teno) River	Finland	Heino and Satu Sirkka
126	56			Grand Cascapedia	Canada	R.G. Dun
127	56			River Eden	England	George Mackenzie
128	56	50	29	River Deveron	Scotland	Colonel A.E. Scott
129	56	52½	27½	River Awe	Scotland	Major A.W. Huntington
130	56	52	29	River Awe	Scotland	H.G. Thornton
131	56			Alten River	Norway	Age Helgesen
132	56			Alten River	Norway	Frode Danielsen
133	56 4			Alten River	Norway	Ola Seppanen
134	57			River Suir	Ireland	M. Maher
135	57			Namsen River	Norway	Miss Wheen
136	57			River Awe	Scotland	Unknown
137	57			Alten River	Norway	Colonel N. Dalrymple Hamilton
138	57	48½	30¾	Fusta River	Norway	Major H.H.R. White
139	57			Alten River	Norway	Agnar Johansen
140	57 6			Dalalven- Alvkarlaby	Sweden	Jurgen Reppening
141	57 8		26	Namsen River	Norway	Hannah Covington
142	57 8	53	28½	River Tweed	England	Arthur Pryor
143	57 8			Namsen River	Norway	G.B. Bainbridge
144	57 9			Tana (Teno) River	Finland	Jouko Lukkari
145	58			Alten River	Norway	Colonel N. Dalrymple Hamilton
146	58			Alten River	Norway	Torleif Leinan
147	58			Alten River	Norway	Admiral W.A. Read
148	58			Alten River	Norway	Kare Bull
149	58 8	52	29	Evanger	Norway	J. Arthur Hutton
150	58 8			Paatsjoki River	Finland	Kalle Karhunen
151	58 8			Eira River	Norway	Percy Tarbutt
152	58 13			Morrum River	Sweden	Per Brugmann
153	59			River Shannon	Ireland	Captain Cotter
154	59 4			Indalsalven River	Sweden	Kristian Stiemstrom
155	60	48	31	Namsen River	Norway	Sir Hyde Parker
156	60	54	27	River Eden	England	Lowther Bridger
157	60	53		Alten River	Norway	Colonel N. Dalrymple Hamilton
158	60			Alten River	Norway	Hans Kjeldsberg

Date	Source
July 1992	Note to Nils-Erik Tornquist from Anders Sorensson (2006)
1874	*Fishing Gazette* 14 November 1903
1903	*Life-History and Habits of the Salmon Sea-Trout, Trout and Other Freshwater Fishes* Malloch (1910)
1939	*Atlantic Salmon and the Fly Fisherman* pages 37-38 Anderson (1985)
1985	*I Storlaksens Rike* ('A Big Fish Empire') published by Alta Association (2001)
1995	*Urheilu Kalastus* ('Sportfishing') magazine (March 1996))
1878	*Grand Cascapedia Giants* Swanson (2005)
1892	*Fishing Gazette* 14 November 1903
1920	*The Illustrated London News* 11 November 1922
1921	*The Illustrated London News* 11 November 1922
1923	*Fishing Gazette* 23 June and 28 July 1923
1975	Tormod Leinan's list
1992	Letter from Roy Flury
Unknown	*Urheilu Kalastus* ('Sportfishing') magazine (January 1982)
1874	*Fishing Gazette* 14 November 1903
1899	*Laksefisket í Namsen och de andere Elvene í Namdalen* ('Salmon Fishing in the Namsen and Other Rivers in the Nam Valley') page 69; harling with a fly?
1909	*The Salmon Rivers of Scotland* page 96 Grimble (1913)
1923	*Alten Reflections* Flury and Dalenson (1993)
1925	*Where to Fish* page 391 (1937)
1982	*Alten Reflections* Flury and Dalenson (1993)
1991	*Dar Laxen Vandrar* page 62 Benney Lindgren (1991)
1885	*Fishing Gazette* 7 January 1911; harling with a fly?
1886	*Fishing Gazette* 6 November 1886
1937	*Namdelens Folkeblad* 21 August 1953; harling with a fly?
c 1954	*Urheilu Kalastus* & Lehji (March 1974)
1913	*Alten: The Story of a Salmon River* Flury and Dalenson (1991)
1947	Tormod Leinan's list
1962	*Alten Reflections* Flury and Dalenson (1993)
1980	Tormod Leinan's list
1922	*The Illustrated London News* 11 November 1922
1928	*Metsastys Ja Kalastus* magazine page 181 (1933)
1931	*Where to Fish* (1937)
June 1992	Note to Nils-Erik Tornquist from Anders Sorensson (2006)
1840	*The Practice of Angling* O'Gorman (1845)
1999	*F.J. Fiskearet* page 8 (January 2000)
c1840	Jones's *Guide to Norway* Tolfrey (1848)
1888	*Fishing Gazette* 2 December 1922
1929	*Alten Reflections* Flury and Dalenson (1993)
1948	Tormod Leinan's list

Number	Weight lb oz	Length (in)	Girth (in)	Location	Country	Captor
159	60			Alten River	Norway	Earl of Dudley
160	60 8			Alten River	Norway	Ole Andreas Mosesen
161	60 10			Petsamo Paats River	Finland	Kalle Karhunen
162	61	53	33	River Deveron	Scotland	Mrs Morison
163	61			Alten River	Norway	General Joseph Laycock
164	61 12	53½	31½	Tana (Teno) River	Finland	Wiljo Saaristo
165	64	53		River Severn	England	Thomas Allen
166	64			Alten River	Norway	Anton Pedersen
167	64			River Awe	Scotland	Henry Willes
168	69 12			River Tay	Scotland	Earl of Home
169	70			Tana River	Norway	Major Ivar Hauge
170	72			River Tay	Scotland	A member of the Athole family

Date	Source
1949	*Alten: The Story of a Salmon River* Flury and Dalenson (1991)
1948	*Alten Reflections* Flury and Dalenson (1993)
c 1966	*Metsastys Ja Kalastus* magazine (April 1967))
1924	*Fishing Gazette* 1 November 1924
1934	Roxburghe Records
Unknown	*Tenon Tarinat* ('Stories of Tana') page 142 Ronkainen (1999)
1912	*The Times* 29 October 1997
c1920	*Alten Reflections* Flury and Dalenson (1993)
c1945	Flyfishers Journal (Autumn 1946)
1730	*The History of British Fishes* Yarrell (1841)
1952	*Out of the Mainstream* Crowe (1970); harling with a fly
c1820	*Fishing Gazette* 8 March 1902

Spring fishing on the Tay

LIST 2
SALMON BETWEEN 50 AND 60lb
METHOD UNCERTAIN

Number	Weight lb oz	Length (in)	Girth (in)	Location	Country	Captor
171	50			Namsen River	Norway	W.M. Owen
172	50			River Towy	Wales	Dr Alexander Lindsay
173	50			Loch Tay	Scotland	Unknown
174	50			River Wye	England	Mr Wells-Ridley
175	50			Namsen River	Norway	Fred Shaw
176	50			River Shannon	Ireland	Major W.P. Jones
177	50			River Shannon	Ireland	G.C. Williams
178	50			River Ness	Scotland	G. Thomas
179	50	51	27	River Wye	England	Dr Cyril Marson
180	50			Vefsen River	Norway	Unknown
181	50			River Annan	Scotland	D.J.W.
182	50			Leardal River	Norway	Miss Phyllis Schwabe
183	50			Vosso River	Norway	R.J. Colman
184	50			Bjora River	Norway	Unknown
185	50			River Tay	Scotland	Major F. Pullar
186	50			River Shannon	Ireland	M. Tuohy
187	50			Sundal River	Norway	Unknown
188	50			Vosso River	Norway	C.M. Wells
189	50			Vosso River	Norway	C.M. Wells
190	50			Vosso River	Norway	C.M. Wells
191	50			Vosso River	Norway	C.M. Wells
192	50	49	27	River Wye	England	Professor T. Merton
193	50	51	26¼	River Wye	England	Captain Yates
194	50			Loch Ness	Scotland	Angus MacGruer
195	50			River Suir	Ireland	M. Donoghue
196	50			Vosso River	Norway	Raymond J. Moonens
197	50 4			River Awe	Scotland	D. Fraser
198	50 8			River Tay	Scotland	Dr Marshall
199	50 8			River Shannon	Ireland	D. Slattery
200	50 8	49	27½	River Wye	England	Col. Heywood's Keeper
201	50 8	48	30	River Blackwater	Ireland	J. Latham
202	50 8			River Shannon	Ireland	Lliam Ford
203	50 8			Namsen River	Norway	C. Bainbridge
204	50 8			Aaro River	Norway	W.E. Dale Shaw
205	50 8			Rauma River	Norway	Mr Tabor
206	50 12			Vosso River	Norway	Karl Bjørge
207	50 12			Alten River	Norway	Arne Soderholm
208	51			River Derwent	England	Unknown
209	51			Forde River	Norway	T. Beyer
210	51			River Tay	Scotland	Mr Fletcher

Date	Beat	Source
1842		*Med Karjolog Laksestenger* ('With Carriole and Salmon Rod') Gulbrandsen (1994)
		A Salmon Fisherman's Notebook J. Hughes-Parry (1949)
1880		*The Complete Salmon Fisher* Greenhalgh (1996)
1897		*Where to Fish* (1926)
1897		*Where to Fish* (1926)
1906		*Game Fish Records* page 79 Scott (1936)
1909	Castleconnell	*Game Fish Records* page 78 Scott (1936); *Daily Mail* 3 December 1909
1909	Inverness	*Daily Mail* 3 December 1909
Apr 1915		*Fishing for Salmon* Marson (1929)
1919		*Where to Fish* (1926)
Nov 1919		Auction notice, Neil Freeman, 23 March 1999
1921		*Where to Fish* (1926)
1921		*Where to Fish* (1926)
1928		*Game Fish Records* page 222 Scott (1936)
Jul 1928	Stobhall	*The Great Salmon Rivers of Scotland* page 96 Ashley-Cooper (1980)
1928	Hermitage	*The Big Fish* Oglesby and Money-Coutts (1992)
1929		*Game Fish Records* page 223 Scott (1936)
1920-1950		*Salmon Stories* Chance (1983)
1920-1950		*Salmon Stories* Chance (1983)
1920-1950		*Salmon Stories* Chance (1983)
1920-1950		*Salmon Stories* Chance (1983)
Apr 1930		*Game Fish Records* page 47 Scott (1936)
Mar 1935	Ballingham	*Game Fish Records* page 198 Scott (1936)
Mar 1944		*Inverness Courier*
Feb 1951		*Ireland Angler's Guide* (1957)
c1975		*Giant Salmon in Norway* Haraldsen's Tours, Oslo
Oct 1909	Taynuilt	*Daily Mail* 18 October 1909
Oct 1893		*Fishing Gazette* 21 October 1893
1928		*Game Fish Records* page 78 Scott (1936)
Feb 1930	Caradoc	*Game Fish Records* page 47 Scott (1936)
Feb 1930		*Game Fish Records* page 88 Scott (1936); *Fishing Gazette* 22 February 1930
1933		*The Complete Salmon Fisher* Greenhalgh (1996)
1932	Gartland beat	*Where to Fish* (1937)
Jul 1935		*Where to Fish* (1937)
1954		*Fishing Gazette* 31 July 1954
		Giant Salmon in Norway Haraldsen's Tours, Oslo
1981		*Fiske Journalen Yearbook No. 4* page 109
1872		*The Big Fish* Oglesby and Money-Coutts (1992)
1894		*Fishing Gazette* page 23 23 March 1895
1903	Freewater	*Where to Fish* (1937)

Number	Weight lb oz	Length (in)	Girth (in)	Location	Country	Captor
211	51			River Blackwater	Ireland	Mr Bowles' Gillie
212	51			River Tay	Scotland	E. Fieldhouse
213	51			River Awe	Scotland	A. Lees Milne
214	51	49	29	River Wye	England	Wyndham Smith
215	51			Fusta River	Norway	H. O'Hagen
216	51	52	28	River Shannon	Ireland	F. McDonnell
217	51			River Shannon	Ireland	Major W. McDonnell
218	51			River Blackwater	Ireland	Brigadier General E.C. Walthall
219	51			River Usk	Wales	Captain Llewelyn
220	51			River Awe	Scotland	Harold de Pass
221	51			Hellisylt River	Norway	Anton Larssen
222	51			Vosso River	Norway	C.M. Wells
223	51			Tana (Teno) River	Finland	Errki Reponen
224	51 8			River Thames	England	Unknown
225	51 8	51		River Rhine	Germany	Unknown
226	51 8			River Blackwater	Ireland	Mr O'Mahony
227	51 8	51	28½	River Annan	Scotland	John J. Varrie
228	51 8			River Lune	England	Unknown
229	51 12	50½	29	Namsen River	Norway	Miss Annie Oldfield
230	52			River Erne	Ireland	E.P. Bates
231	52			River Tay	Scotland	A. Macbeth
232	52			Aberdeenshire Dee	Scotland	Moses Ewen
233	52	54	26	River Wye	England	Colonel Tilney
234	52		28½	Aaro River	Norway	Count Denissoff
235	52			River Don	Scotland	J.P. McGowan
236	52	49	28½	Evanger River	Norway	S.M. Barlow
237	52	50½	28	River Vefsen	Norway	Major C.W. Wallace
238	52			River Earn	Scotland	J. Miller
239	52			Vosso River	Norway	Murray Sowerby
240	52			Vosso River	Norway	C.M. Wells
241	52			Vosso River	Norway	C.M. Wells
242	52			River Bandon	Ireland	Unknown
243	52			Vosso River	Norway	Egil Larsen
244	52			Stryn River	Norway	An American Lady
245	52 6			Tana River	Norway	Unknown
246	52 8	52½	28½	River Wye	England	R. Devereux
247	52 12			Namsen River	Norway	Scott Isachsen
248	52 14			Alten River	Norway	Hans Lie
249	53	48		River Tay	Scotland	Unknown
250	53			Namsen River	Norway	Lord Vane- Tempest-Stewart

Date	Beat	Source
1903		*Game Fish Records* page 88 Scott (1936)
1905		*Where to Fish* (1937)
1913		*The Big Fish* Oglesby and Money-Coutts (1992)
Mar 1914	Hoarwithy	*Wye Salmon and Other Fish* page 8 Hutton (1949)
1922		*Where to Fish* (1952)
1928		*The Big Fish* Oglesby and Money-Coutts (1992)
1929	Woodlands	*Game Fish Records* page 78 Scott (1936)
1930		*Game Fish Records* page 87 Scott (1936)
Apr 1936		*Where to Fish* page 304 (1952)
1936	Little Verie	*The Big Fish* Oglesby and Money-Coutts (1992)
1948	9 hour fight	*Salmon Fishing in Norway* Prag (1953)
1920-1950		*Salmon Stories* Chance (1983)
1988		ABu's *Nyt Nappaa* ('Tight Lines') (1989)
Unknown		Sir Tufton Beamish quoted in an article in *Trout and Salmon* 31 March 1961
c1879		*The Natural History of British Fishes* Buckland (1881)
1929		*Game Fish Records* page 87 Scott (1936); *Fishing Gazette* 13 April 1929
Nov 1929		*Game Fish Records* page 150 Scott (1936)
		Where to Fish page xxxii (1926)
Sept 1921	Moum beat	*Where to Fish* (1952)
1883		*Game Fish Records* page 80 Scott (1936)
1917	Kinnaird	*Where to Fish* (1937)
1918		*Game Fish Records* page 161 Scott (1936)
Mar 1920	Whitney	*Game Fish Records* page 46 Scott (1936)
Jul 1921	Letter from Denissoff	*Where to Fish* (1937)
1924		*Where to Fish* (1937)
May 1923		*Where to Fish* (1937)
Aug 1928	A female fish	*Where to Fish* (1937)
Oct 1944		*Where to Fish* page 303 (1952)
c1947		*Salmon Stories* Chance (1983)
1920-1950		*Salmon Stories* Chance (1983)
1920-1950		*Salmon Stories* Chance (1983)
c1950		Personal communication
		Giant Salmon in Norway Haraldsen's Tours, Oslo
1981		*Fiske Journalen Yearbook No. 5* page 54
1935		*The Complete Salmon Fisher* Greenhalgh (1996)
Apr 1928	Above Hay	*Game Fish Records* page 46 Scott (1936)
Jul 1921		*Where to Fish* (1937)
1981		*Fiske Journalen Yearbook No. 4* page 109
Jul 1868	Kinfauns	Cast of fish in Scottish Fisheries Museum
1898		Letter from Roy Flury, 13 July 2005; *Daily Mail* 7 September 1904

Number	Weight lb oz	Length (in)	Girth (in)	Location	Country	Captor
251	53			River Awe	Scotland	A. McCall
252	53			River Shannon	Ireland	W. Ivis
253	53			River Tay	Scotland	Mr Dow
254	54			River Shannon	Ireland	Fred Milburn
255	53			Evanger River	Norway	J.S. Phillips
256	53			Vosso River	Norway	M.A. Wallendahl
257	53			Vosso River	Norway	Mr Christensen
258	53			Namsen River	Norway	Major Whimper
259	53			Vosso River	Norway	C.M. Wells
260	53 8			Namsen River	Norway	Mrs Radclyffe
261	53 12			Laerdal River	Norway	Unknown
262	54			Aaro River	Norway	W.J. Smith
263	54	49	29	Evanger River	Norway	E.M. Corbett
264	54			River Don	Scotland	W. Henry
265	54			River Tay	Scotland	J.T. Ness
266	54			Nausta River	Norway	Trygue Kleiva
267	54			Vosso River	Norway	C.M. Wells
268	54			River Tay	Scotland	V. Ianetta
269	54			Leardal River	Norway	Unknown
270	54 8			Namsen River	Norway	Mrs Williams
271	55			River Garry	Scotland	A. Grant
272	55			River Tweed	Scotland	W.A. Kidson
273	55			Vosso River	Norway	Unknown
274	55			Sand River	Norway	Unknown
275	55			Namsen River	Norway	Odd Heia
276	55 2			Unknown	Sweden	Pentii Salmela
277	55 2			Vosso River	Norway	Odd Haraldsen
278	55 2			Tana (Teno) River	Finland	Pirko Sepponen
279	55 2			Tana (Teno) River	Finland	Heikki Ylamononen
280	55 5			Tana (Teno) River	Finland	Jukka Helenios
281	55 8			River Eden	England	E. Francis
282	56			Vosso River	Norway	C.M. Wells
283	56 6			Pasvik River	Norway	Lord Dudley
284	56 8			Bjora River	Norway	Unknown
285	56 11			Tana (Teno) River	Finland	Reino Johansson
286	57			River Dee	Scotland	C. Gordon
287	57			Vosso River	Norway	B. Wallendahl
288	57			Namsen River	Norway	Major Green
289	57			Eira River	Norway	Capt. Hon. R. Leigh
290	57			Vosso River	Norway	C.M. Wells

Date	Beat	Source
1913		*Where to Fish* (1937)
1914		*Game Fish Records* page 78 Scott (1936)
1915	Perth water	*Where to Fish* (1937)
Feb 1903		*British Freshwater Fishes* Maxwell (1904)
Jul 1920		*Where to Fish* (1937)
Jun 1920	Bolstad beat	*Where to Fish* (1952)
Jun 1921	Bolstad beat	*Where to Fish* (1952)
1932		*Where to Fish* (1952)
1950		*Salmon Stories* Chance (1983)
1901		*Where to Fish* (1937)
Aug 1921		*Where to Fish* (1937)
1920		*Where to Fish* (1937)
July 1923	Caught on bait?	*Where to Fish* (1937)
Oct 1939		*Where to Fish* page 303 (1952)
Oct 1942	Almondmouth	*The Great Salmon Rivers of Scotland* page 96 Ashley-Cooper (1980)
1942		*Fiske Journalen Yearbook No. 8* page 98
1950		*Salmon Stories* Chance (1983)
Sep 1969	Ballathie	*The Great Salmon Rivers of Scotland* page 96 Ashley-Cooper (1980)
1973		*The Complete Salmon Fisher* Greenhalgh (1996)
1928	Gartland beat	*Where to Fish* (1937)
Sep 1887		*The Complete Salmon Fisher* Greenhalgh (1996)
Nov 1913		*Where to Fish* (1937)
1961		*The Complete Salmon Fisher* Greenhalgh (1996)
c 1966	Stavanger	*Salmon Stories* Chance (1983)
1984		*Fiske Journalen Yearbook No. 17*
1977		ABu's *Napp och Nytt* ('Tight Lines')
1981		*Fly Fishing for Salmon and Sea Trout* Oglesby (1986)
1984		*Urheilu Kalastus* ('Sportfishing') magazine (March 1985)
c1992		Matti Kettunen's list (March 1993)
1988		ABu's *Nyt Nappaa* ('Tight Lines')
1888	Cons Nab pool	*Fishing Gazette* 14 November 1903; *Rod & Gun* 19 November 1892
1950		*Salmon Stories* Chance (1983)
1882		*The Complete Salmon Fisher* Greenhalgh (1996)
Jun 1913		*Where to Fish* page xxx (1926)
1986		ABu's *Nyt Nappaa* ('Tight Lines')
c1886	Ardoe pool	*Where to Fish* (1937); *Fishing Gazette* 14 November 1903
Aug 1922	Bolstad beat	*Where to Fish* (1952)
Jun 1921		*Norwegian Fishing Rights & Shooting* Andun Koren (1929)
Jun 1933		*Where to Fish* (1937)
1950		*Salmon Stories* Chance (1983)

Number	lb	oz	Weight (in)	Length (in)	Girth	Location	Country
291	57				River Tay	Scotland	D.O.H.
292	57				Vosso River	Norway	J. Graham Parsons
293	57	5			Namsen River	Norway	Ola Seim
294	57	6	53	27	Otra River	Norway	Per Mørch
295	57	6			River at Bergsche Maas	Holland	Gijsbert Struik
296	57	6			Tana (Teno) River	Finland	Iivari Dieski
297	57	6	52½	29	Evanger River	Norway	Mrs P. Barlow
298	57	8	53½	28½	River Tay	Scotland	Unknown
299	57	8			Rauma River	Norway	Friend of John Oates
300	58		48	28½	River Tweed	Scotland	Unknown
301	58				River Shannon	Ireland	Unknown
302	58				Namsen River	Norway	An Assistant
303	58		50	29	Evanger River	Norway	Unknown
304	58		51	30	Vosso River	Norway	G.C. Waud
305	58				Vosso River	Norway	F.L. Kronow
306	58		51	28½	Vosso River	Norway	G.D. Atkinson
307	58				Vosso River	Norway	C.M. Wells
308	58				Tana (Teno) River	Finland	Jouni V. Helander
309	58	6	50	33	Torridal	Norway	Halvor Ugland
310	58	6			Skjern A	Denmark	D.C. Dinesen
311	58	6	49½	30¼	Vosso River	Norway	E.M. Corbett
312	58	6	49½	29¾	Vosso River	Norway	Lady Haworth
313	58	10			Unknown	Sweden	Matti Heiskanen
314	59		53	28	South Esk	Scotland	Mr Somerville
315	59		52½	29	Vosso River	Norway	R.J. Bristowe
316	59		52	30½	Vosso River	Norway	G.D. Atkinson
317	59	8			Vosso River	Norway	Odd Haraldsen

Captor	Date	Beat	Source
1957			Letter from Alan Barker
Jun 1965			*Out of the Mainstream* Crowe (1970)
1924			*Namdelens Folkeblad* (21 August 1953)
Jul 1899		Foss of Vigeland	*Vigeland i Vennesla* Krogstad (1999)
1910			*Zalm Vernomen* Piet Hartman (1995)
			Teno – Saamen ja Lehen Virta ('The River of Lapland and its Salmon') Kojo (1984)
Jun 1923			*Where to Fish* (1937)
May 1907			*Life-History and Habits of the Salmon Sea-Trout, Trout and Other Freshwater Fishes* Malloch (1910)
1949			*The Field* (27 May 1950)
1826			*British Fishes* Volume IV page 198 Couch (1877)
1872			*Where to Fish* (1937)
Sept 1909			*Where to Fish* (1937)
c1910			*Fishing Gazette* 29 December 1923
Jun 1920	Evanger beat		*Where to Fish* (1937); *Fishing Gazette* 16 July 1921
Jun 1925	Bolstad beat		*Where to Fish* (1952)
1929			*Where to Fish* (1937)
1950			*Salmon Stories* Chance (1983)
1978			ABu's *Nyt Nappaa* ('Tight Lines')
Jul 1950			*Vigeland i Vennesla* Krogstad (1999)
Apr 1954			*Guinness Angling Records* (1988)
Jul 1902	Evanger beat		*Fishing Gazette* 15 November 1902
May 1911	Evanger beat		*Where to Fish* (1937)
1991			ABu's *Napp och Nytt* ('Tight Lines')
1922			*Where to Fish* (1937)
Jun 1922			*Where to Fish* (1937)
Jun 1928			*Where to Fish* (1937)
Jul 1965			*The Big Fish* Oglesby and Money-Coutts (1992)

This 73lb 14oz salmon was caught in nets at the mouth of the Alten River, Norway in 1923

LIST 3
SALMON OVER 60lb
CAUGHT BY ANY METHOD

Number	Weight lb oz	Length (in)	Girth (in)	Location	Country	Captor
318	59 8	52½	29	River Wye	England	Miss D. Davey
319	60			River Annan	Scotland	Reverend A. Cook
320	60	53	29	River Spey	Scotland	Netsmen
321	60			River Tay	Scotland	Tay netsmen
322	60			Namsen River	Norway	An Englishman
323	60			River Tweed	Scotland	Taken out of season
324	60	53	29	Vosso River	Norway	Major W.H.S. Alston
325	60	57	26	River Wye	England	Unknown
326	60			River Usk	Wales	Unknown
327	60			Alten River	Norway	Bjarne Mannsverk
328	60			Alten River	Norway	Reidar Jorgensen
329	60 4			Vosso River	Norway	F. Rieber
330	60 6			Tana (Teno) River	Finland	Unknown
331	60 6			Tana (Teno) River	Finland	Kirsti Guttorm
332	60 8			Rauma River	Norway	Lord Davenport
333	60 8			Baltic Sea	Unknown	
334	60 10	52¼	28½	River Vefsen	Norway	An invited guest
335	60 10	50½	33⅞	Baltic Sea	Sweden	Kenneth Olsson
336	61			Gefle River	Sweden	Unknown
337	61	54	31	Namsen River	Norway	An Englishman
338	61			Vosso River Bolstad	Norway	H.C. Charrington
339	61	61		Alten River	Norway	Paul Aas
340	61 4	54	29	River Exe	England	Richard Voysey and crew
341	61 4			Tana (Teno) River	Norway	Per Walle
342	61 8			River Tay	Scotland	J. Haggart
343	61 8			Unknown	Scotland	Unknown
344	61 8	56		River Taw	England	Unknown
345	61 8	54		River Tay	Scotland	Thomas Stewart
346	61 8	51	24¾	River Lyon	Scotland	Found dead
347	61 8	51	31½	North Sea	England	Messrs Fenwick Ltd
348	61 8			Dahl River	Sweden	Jarmo Virkkunen
349	61 11			Dahl River	Sweden	Jarmo Virkkunen
350	61 12			Tana (Teno) River	Finland	Samuli Dorsanger
351	61 12			Unknown	Finland	Tauno Karjalainen
352	61 12			Tana(Teno) River	Finland	Uula Guttorm
353	62	55½	29	River Tay	Scotland	Unknown
354	62			River Stinchar	Scotland	Unknown
355	62			Olden River	Norway	Henry Willes
356	62	54		Forth Estuary	Scotland	Mr Anderson's netsman

Date	Method	Source
1923	Spinning	*Game Fish Records* Scott (1936); *Wye Salmon and Other Fish* Hutton (1949)
c1852	Rod and line	*Game Fish Records* page 150 Scott (1936)
1894	Netted	Letter from Roy Flury, June 2005
1902	Netted	*British Freshwater Fishes* Maxwell (1904)
1903	Rod and line	Letter from Roy Flury, 12 July 2005; a Rowland Ward carved model of this fish, at Hollandsoi
1907	Netted	*Fishing Gazette* 14 January and 22 August 1908
1920-50	Rod and line	*Salmon Stories* page 53 Chance (1983)
1920	Found dead	*Fishing Gazette* 10 July 1920
1924	Trammel net	*Game Fish Records* page 39 Scott (1936)
Aug 1960	Spinning	Tormod Leinan's list
Jun 1967	Spinning	Tormod Leinan's list
1919	Rod and line	*Salmon Fishing in Norway* Prag (1953)
1984	Rod and line	Letter from Matti Kettunen, 29 July 2006
1994	Spinning	ABu's *Nyt Nappaa* ('Tight Lines') (1995)
1926	Rod and line	*Where to Fish* (1937)
1995	Unknown	*Atlantic Salmon* Sutterby and Greenhalgh (2005)
1921	On spoon	*Fishing Gazette* 3 November 1923
1995	Trailing	*Outdoor Sportfish News* Laxfestvalen
1901	Unknown	*Where to Fish* (1926)
1910	Rod and line	Letter from Roy Flury, 12 July 2005; carved Hardy model in existence
1924	Unknown	*Game Fish Records* page 222 Scott (1936)
1956	Spinning	Letter from Roy Flury, 2005
1924	Netted	*Fishing Gazette* 23 March 1924
1983	Abu wobbler	*Fiske Journalen Yearbook No. 6* page 63
1870	On minnow	*Angler's News* 28 January 1939; *Fishing Gazette* 14 November 1903
1879	Netted	*The Natural History of British Fishes* Buckland (1881)
1890	Netted	*Where to Fish* (1923); *Fishing Gazette* 24 March 1924
1907	On worm	*Fishing Gazette* 9 November 1907
1922	Killed by otter	*Dundee Courier* 21 November 1922
1934	Netted	*Fishing Gazette* 16 June 1934
1970	Wobbler	*Metsastys Ja Kalastus* magazine (November 1996)
1955/6	Plug fishing	Abu's *Napp och Nytt* ('Tight Lines') (1997)
Aug 1950	Plug fishing	*Metsastys Ja Kalastus* magazine (May 1973)
1974	Unknown	Abu's *Nyt Nappaa* ('Tight Lines') (1975)
Unknown	Unknown	*Teno – Saamen ja Lehen Virta* ('The River of Lapland and its Salmon') Kojo (1984)
1892	Netted	*Rod & Gun* 30 January 1892
1897	Netted	*Salmon Rivers and Lochs of Scotland* Calderwood (1909)
1907	Rod and line	*Fishing Gazette* 9 November 1907
1908	Bag net	*Fishing Gazette* 14 January 1908

Number	Weight lb oz	Length (in)	Girth (in)	Location	Country	Captor
357	62	43	29	Berriedale Estuary	Scotland	Unknown
358	62	48½	29½	River Shannon	Ireland	Unknown
359	62			Nether Don	Scotland	Unknown
360	62			River Shannon	Ireland	Abbey fishermen
361	62 8			Pasvik River	Norway	Sir Henry Gore Booth
362	62 9			Gaula River	Norway	Villey Letnes
363	62 12			River Usk	Wales	Unknown
364	62 14			Petsamo/Paats River	Finland	Unknown
365	62 14			Tana (Teno) River	Finland	Hannu Juntunen
366	62 14			Tana(Teno) River	Norway	Antoro Simpanen
367	62 14			Tana(Teno) River	Finland	Piera Guttorm
368	63	55½	28	River Wye	England	T. Miller
369	63			River Tay	Scotland	W. Stewart
370	63			Vosso River	Norway	Major W.H.S. Alston
371	63	57½	26	Namsen River	Norway	Erik and Svein Moum
372	63			Sand River	Norway	Charles Bergesen
373	63			Baltic Sea	Sweden	Unknown
374	63 1			Tana (Teno) River	Finland	T. Haataja
375	63 2			Unknown	Norway	Kent Sundstrom
376	63 5			Tana (Teno) River	Finland	Mr.T. Juhani
377	63 6			Unknown	Norway	Olaf Sotkajaervi
378	63 6			Baltic Sea	Sweden	Veikko Halunen
379	63 8			River Wye	England	Unknown
380	63 8			River Tay	Scotland	Unknown
381	63 9	50½	31½	Tana (Teno) River	Finland	Marti Remes
382	63 14			Namsen River	Norway	Ola Seem
383	63 14	57½		Namsen River	Norway	Unknown
384	64			River Severn	England	Unknown
385	64			River Tay	Scotland	Unknown
386	64			Namsen River	Norway	Merthyr Guest
387	64			River Tay	Scotland	Unknown
388	64	54	28½	River Tay	Scotland	Georgina Ballantine
389	64			Vefsen River	Norway	Unknown
390	64			North Esk	Scotland	Unknown
391	64			Vosso River	Norway	Georg Stromme
392	64 4			River Thames	England	Unknown
393	64 12			Unknown	Finland	Ilmari Tapiola
394	65	53½	25¾	River Tay	Scotland	Unknown

Date	Method	Source
1919	Netted	*Fishing Gazette* 1 May 1920
1921	Netted	*Fishing Gazette* 13 August 1921
1924	Netted	*Where to Fish* (1926)
1925	Netted	*The Angler's Guide to the Irish Free State* (1930)
1876	Rod and line	*Fishing Gazette* 18 December 1920
1972	Rod and line	*Fiske Journalen Yearbook* (1979)
1782	Netted?	*The Big Fish* Oglesby and Money-Coutts (1992)
Sep 1924	Unknown	*Metsastys Ja Kalastus* magazine page 98 (1925)
Aug 1987	Wobbler	*Urheilu Kalastus* ('Sportfishing') magazine (January 1988)
1990	Rod and line	Abu's *Napp och Nytt* ('Tight Lines') page 53 (1991)
Unknown	Heddon plug	*Metsastys Ja Kalastus* magazine (August 1998)
1895	Netted	*Fishing Gazette* page 408 8 June 1895
1903	Unknown	Engraved on plaque sold at Bonham's, Edinburgh 2005
1939	Rod and line	*Fishing Gazette* 18 November 1950
1946	Harling	Per Olav Moum via letter from Roy Flury, January 2006
1953	Rod and line	*Angler's Cavalcade* Horsfall Turner (1966)
1990	Trolling	Jan Olsson's website www.outdoor.se/sportfishnews/articles/laxfestival
1983		Abu's *Nyt Nappaa* ('Tight Lines') page 5 (1984)
1997	Rod and line	Abu's *Napp och Nytt* ('Tight Lines') (1999)
1982	Rod and line	Abu's *Nyt Nappaa* ('Tight Lines') (1983)
1979	Spinning	Abu's *Napp och Nytt* ('Tight Lines') pages 10 and 11 (1980)
1992	Trolling	*F.J. Fiskearet* 1 February 1999
1905	Netted	*Game Fish Records* page 46 Scott (1936)
1908	Netted	*Life-History and Habits of the Salmon Sea-Trout, Trout and Other Freshwater Fishes* Malloch (1910)
1984	Nils Master plug	*Urheilu Kalastus* ('Sportfishing') magazine (March 1985)
1914	Rod and line (harling)	*Laksefisket í Namsen och de andere Elvene í Namdalen* ('Salmon Fishing in the Namsen and Other Rivers in the Nam Valley') page 52
1935	Found dead	*Fishing Gazette* 4 January 1936
1873	Netted	*The Salmon Rivers of England and Wales* Grimble (1913)
c1880	Unknown	*The Natural History of British Fishes* Buckland (1881)
1899	Harling?	Letter from Roy Flury
1903	Unknown	*Fishing Gazette* 14 November 1903
1922	On bait	*Fishing Gazette* 2 December 1922
1929	Unknown	*Game Fish Records* Scott (1936)
1932	Netted	*Fishing Gazette* 12 June 1937
1954	Rod and line	*The Big Fish* Oglesby and Money-Coutts (1992)
1789	Netted	*The Angler Naturalist* Cholmondeley-Pennell (1863)
1976	Unknown	Abu's *Nyt Nappaa* ('Tight Lines') (1977)
1879	Netted	*The Natural History of British Fishes* Buckland (1881)

Number	Weight lb oz	Length (in)	Girth (in)	Location	Country	Captor
395	65	54	30	Vosso River	Norway	Finn Isdahl
396	65	53½	30	River Tweed	Scotland	Unknown
397	65			Sodal River	Norway	Unknown
398	65			Vosso River	Norway	Murray Sowerby
399	65			Drammen River	Norway	Unknown
400	65 14			Unknown	Norway	Per Iversen Porsanger
401	66	55		The Baltic Sea	Sweden	Herr Sjodin
402	66 2			Forde River	Norway	Unknown
403	66 2			Kemi River	Finland	Customerman Vahajarvi
404	66 2			Tana (Teno) River	Finland	Juha-Pekka Lievonen
405	66 2			Tana (Teno) River	Finland	Jahuni Tapiola
406	66 6			Kemi River	Finland	Unknown
407	67			River Tay	Scotland	Unknown
408	67	54		Lulea River	Sweden	Unknown
409	67 4			Oulu River	Finland	Unknown
410	67 8			River Nith	Scotland	Jock Wallace
411	68	54	29½	Aaro River	Norway	Wilfred Kennedy
412	68			Vosso River	Norway	Unknown
413	68			Namsen River	Norway	Fridgeir Sagmo
414	68			Bjora	Norway	K. Jacobsen
415	68 4	55¼	30	Aaro River	Norway	Count Denissoff
416	69	55½		Corrib River	Ireland	Unknown
417	69	56	32	River Rhine	Germany	Unknown
418	69 7	54	31¾	Namsen River	Norway	Svein Kjolstad
419	69 7			Nid River	Norway	Gunnar Kjelas
420	69 8	48	36	Unknown	England	Unknown
421	69 8			Aaro River	Norway	Johann Aarven
422	69 8	56¾		Evanger River	Norway	Jens Grimestad
423	69 9			Dalalven River	Sweden	Jarmo Virkkunen
424	69 15			Stolta Guldrullevinnare	Sweden	George Hagglund
425	70	52	31	River Tay	Scotland	Bishop Browne
426	70			River Severn	England	Unknown
427	70			River Tay	Scotland	Unknown
428	70			Tengs River	Norway	Local fisherman
429	70	60		River Wye	England	Unknown
430	70 8			Alten River	Norway	Unknown
431	70 8			Vosso River	Norway	Unknown
432	70 8			Aaro River	Norway	Unknown
433	70 8			Vosso River	Norway	Jakob Vassenden
434	70 8			Neiden River	Norway	Unknown

Date	Method	Source
1920	Rod and line	*Fishing Gazette* 17 December 1921
1922	Netted	*Fishing Gazette* 24 June 1922
1938	Unknown	*Vigeland í Vennesla* Krogstad (1999)
1951	Rod and line	*Salmon Stories* page 56 Chance (1983)
1955	Netted	*Flyfishers Journal* page 121 (September 1962)
1968	Plug fishing	Abu's *Napp och Nytt* ('Tight Lines') page 10 (1969)
1913	Rod and line	*Fishing Gazette* 7 June 1913
1931	Found dead	*Salmon Fishing in Norway* Prag (1953)
1945	Unknown	*Metsastys Ja Kalastus* magazine page 31 (1946)
1975	Unknown	Abu's *Nyt Nappaa* ('Tight Lines') (1976)
1981	Plug	*Fiske Journalen Yearbook No.4* page 109
1924	Unknown	*Metsastys Ja Kalastus* magazine (March 1993)
1877	Netted	*Angling Diversions* Courtney Williams page 144 (1945)
1914	Netted	*Fishing Gazette* 19 September 1914
1915	Unknown	*Metsastys Ja Kalastus* magazine (March 1993)
1812	On fly?	*Galloway News* 30 June 1922
1894	Prawn	*Fishing Gazette* 13 August 1921; *Fishing Gazette* page 251 30 March 1895
1919	Netted	*Atlantic Salmon* Sutterby and Greenhalgh (2005)
1931	Spinning	*Namsen i Vare Minner* Ola Hjulstad (1985)
1955	Spinning	*Namsen i Vare Minner* Ola Hjulstad (1985)
1921	Prawn	*Fishing Gazette* 13 August 1921
1866	Netted	*The Natural History of British Fishes* Buckland (1881)
1880	Unknown	*The Natural History of British Fishes* Buckland (1881)
1924	Spinning	*Fishing Gazette* 5 July 1924
1950	Spinning	*Salmon Fishing in Norway* Prag (1953)
1795	Unknown	*Rural Sports* volume II part II page 10 Daniel (1801)
1921	Rod and line	*Game Fish Records* (1936)
1922	Rod and line	*Fishing Gazette* 2 September 1922
1996	Spinn-fly	*Sportfiske* magazine (January/February 1997)
1992	Plug fishing	Abu's *Napp och Nytt* ('Tight Lines') (1993)
1870	Netted	*Land and Water* journal 25 June 1870
1873	Netted	*British and Irish Salmonidae* pages 141–2 Day (1887)
1877	Netted	*Angling Diversions* Courtney Williams (1945)
1900	On worm	*Flood, Fell and Forest* Pottinger (1905)
1950	Found dead	*The Shooting Times* 22 September 1951
c1880	Rod and line	*Alten: The Story of a Salmon River* Flury (1991)
1919	Unknown	*Fishing Gazette* 14 September 1929
1929	Rod and line	*Fishing Gazette* 14 September 1929
1931	Spinning	Letter from Norvald Vik, librarian of Norges Fiskers Museum, Bergen
1954	Netted	*Finnmarksposten* 23 June 1954; *Flyfishers Journal* (September 1962)

Number	Weight lb oz	Length (in)	Girth (in)	Location	Country	Captor
435	70 8			Tana(Teno) River	Finland	Joosef and Jouni Guttorm
436	70 9			Vefsna River	Norway	Angler from Mosjoen
437	70 10	55¾	31¾	Tana River	Norway	Nils Valle
438	72			River Tay	Scotland	Unknown
439	72			Shannon Estuary	Ireland	Unknown
440	72 9	55	33¼	Vosso River	Norway	Poacher
441	73 13	56		Lilleburgen	Norway	Unknown
442	73 14			Alten River	Norway	Ostlyngen and Rasmussen
443	74			Unknown	Unknown	Unknown
444	74	54	34¼	Unknown	Norway	Unknown
445	74 3			Tana (Teno) River	Russia	The Magistrate of Utsjok
446	75			Baltic Sea	Sweden	Unknown
447	75			Pasvik River	Norway	An Englishman
448	75			Tana(Teno) River	Finland	Hans E. Laiti
449	75 8	63¼		Drammen River	Norway	Poacher
450	76			River Blackwater	Ireland	Unknown
451	77			Namsen River	Norway	Unknown
452	77 2			Kymi River	Finland	Unknown
453	77 2			Tana (Teno) River	Finland	Nilo Porsanger
454	79 6			Pasvik River	Norway	Magnus Klerck
455	79 6			Tana River	Norway	Henrik Henriksen
456	79 6			Tana(Teno) River	Finland	Jouni Guttorm's father
457	80			Spittal Beach	England	Unknown
458	80	59½	29	River Tay	Scotland	Tay netsmen
459	82			Baltic Sea	Germany	Unknown
460	82 14	54		River Eden	England	Unknown
461	83			Unknown	Scotland	Unknown
462	83 12			Tana(Teno) River	Finland	Ville Alaollitervo
463	84			River Tay	Scotland	Wullie Walker
464	84			Moray Firth	Scotland	Unknown
465	84 12			Unknown	Ireland	Unknown
466	84 14			River Spey	Scotland	Unknown
467	88			Lake Liekovedessä	Finland	Pekka Rutuna
468	94 14			Tornio River	Finland	Unknown
469	103			River Forth	Scotland	Poachers

Date	Method	Source
Unknown	Spinning or fly fishing	*Teno – Saamen ja Lehen Virta* ('The River of Lapland and its Salmon') Kojo (1984)
1953	Rod and line	*Salmon Fishing in Norway* Prag (1953)
1951	Caught on krocodil bait	*Salmon Fishing in Norway* Prag (1953)
1877	Netted	*Angling Diversions* Courtney Williams (1945)
1886	Netted	*The Angler's Notebook and Naturalist's Record* (1888)
1919	Netted	*Fishing Gazette* 23 January 1926
1923	Bag-net	*Fishing Gazette* 9 June 1923
1923	Netted	*Alten: The Story of a Salmon River* Flury and Dalenson
c1776	Netted	*British Zoology* Pennant (1776)
1937	Netted	*Fishing Gazette* 9 May 1937
c1878	Rod and line	*Game Fish Records* page 220 Scott (1936)
1887	Netted	*Fishing Gazette* 7 June 1913
1905	Rod and line	*Nordnorske Lakseelver* Magnus Berg (1964)
1959 or 1960	Netted	*Lohiyō Tenolla* ('Salmon Nights on Tana') page 42 Kettunen (2000)
1925	Trapped	*Fishing Gazette* 15 August 1925
1880	Netted	*The Field* volume 55 page 224 (1880)
1936	Found dead	*Salmon Fishing in Norway* Prag (1953)
1896	Unknown	*Metsastys Ja Kalastus* magazine (March 1993)
1993	Netted	*Metsastys Ja Kalastus* magazine (September 1993)
1863	Fly fishing?	Letter from Roy Flury, 1 November 2005
1928	Spinning	*Game Fish Records* page 22 Scott (1936)
Unknown	Spinning	*Teno – Saamen ja Lehen Virta* ('The River of Lapland and its Salmon') Kojo (1984)
1906	Netted	*Daily Mail* 24 October 1906
Unknown	Netted	*Fishing Gazette* 15 April 1911
1938	Stake net	*Fishing Gazette* 25 June 1938
1881	Netted	*The Field* 16 July 1881
1821	Rod and line	*Fishing Gazette* 15 April 1911
1943	Netted	*Metsastys Ja Kalastus* magazine (March 1993)
1869	Netted	*Game Fish Records* Scott (1936)
Unknown	Netted	*Fishing Gazette* 1 May 1920
1881	Netted	*The Fishes of Great Britain and Ireland* Day (1880–84)
1778	Found dead	*Aberdeen Journal* 9 February 1778
1953	Spinning	*Flyfishers Journal* (September 1962); *Fishing Gazette* 26 September 1953
1940/5	Netted	*Metsastys Ja Kalastus* magazine (March 1993)
1907	Netted	*Daily Mail* 7 August 1908

MAPS

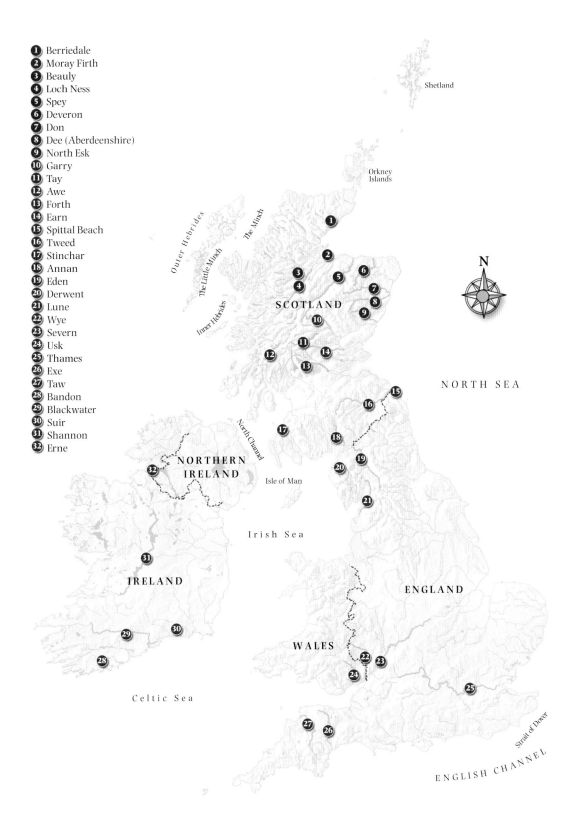

1 Berriedale
2 Moray Firth
3 Beauly
4 Loch Ness
5 Spey
6 Deveron
7 Don
8 Dee (Aberdeenshire)
9 North Esk
10 Garry
11 Tay
12 Awe
13 Forth
14 Earn
15 Spittal Beach
16 Tweed
17 Stinchar
18 Annan
19 Eden
20 Derwent
21 Lune
22 Wye
23 Severn
24 Usk
25 Thames
26 Exe
27 Taw
28 Bandon
29 Blackwater
30 Suir
31 Shannon
32 Erne

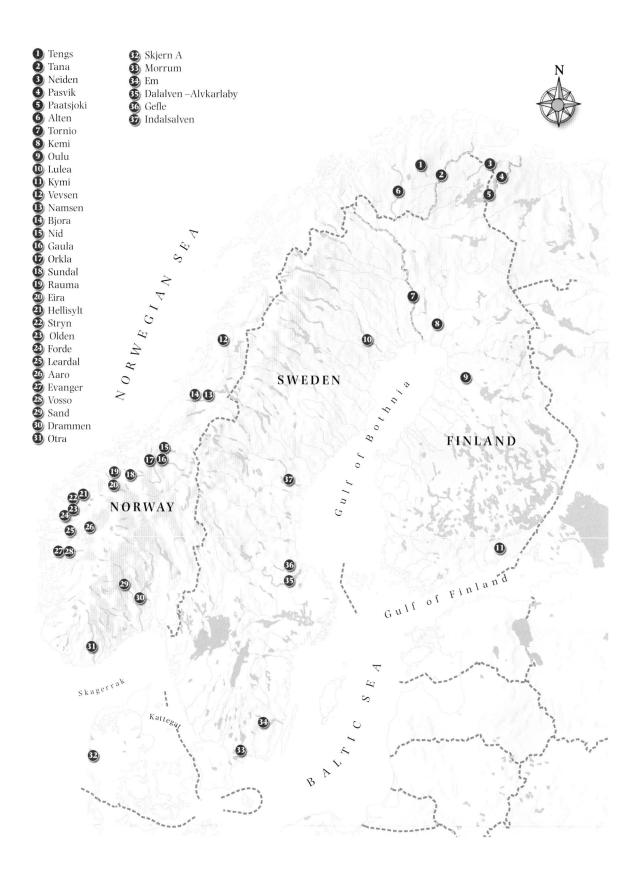

1 Tengs
2 Tana
3 Neiden
4 Pasvik
5 Paatsjoki
6 Alten
7 Tornio
8 Kemi
9 Oulu
10 Lulea
11 Kymi
12 Vevsen
13 Namsen
14 Bjora
15 Nid
16 Gaula
17 Orkla
18 Sundal
19 Rauma
20 Eira
21 Hellisylt
22 Stryn
23 Olden
24 Forde
25 Leardal
26 Aaro
27 Evanger
28 Vosso
29 Sand
30 Drammen
31 Otra

32 Skjern A
33 Morrum
34 Em
35 Dalalven –Alvkarlaby
36 Gefle
37 Indalsalven

NORWEGIAN SEA

SWEDEN

NORWAY

FINLAND

Gulf of Bothnia

Gulf of Finland

BALTIC SEA

Skagerrak

Kattegat

N

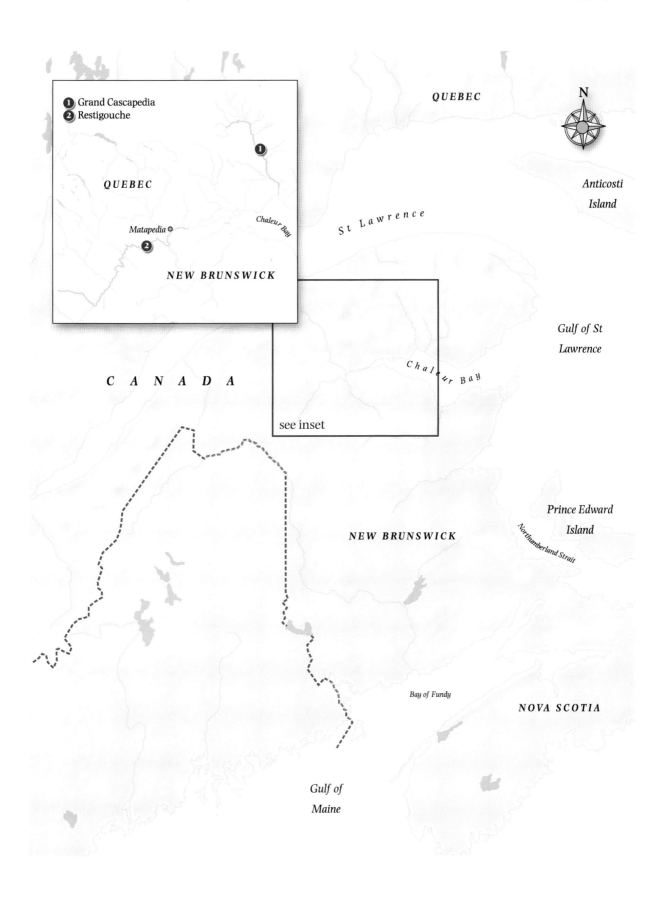

Grand Cascapedia
Restigouche

QUEBEC

Matapedia

Chaleur Bay

NEW BRUNSWICK

CANADA

see inset

QUEBEC

N

Anticosti
Island

St Lawrence

Chaleur Bay

Gulf of St
Lawrence

Prince Edward
Island

Northumberland Strait

NEW BRUNSWICK

Bay of Fundy

NOVA SCOTIA

Gulf of
Maine

Spey casting at Castleconnell

SALMON OVER 50lb
CAUGHT ON FLY

DUNCAN GRANT'S 12-HOUR BATTLE WITH A 50lb SPEY SALMON
No. 1

A strange but well-written account of Duncan Grant's battle with a giant Spey salmon appeared in William Scrope's *Days and Nights of Salmon Fishing in the Tweed* (1843), starting on page 187:

First you must understand that what is called 'preserving the river' was formerly unknown, and every one who chose to take a cast did so without let or hindrance.

In pursuance of this custom in the month of July, some thirty years ago, one Duncan Grant, a shoemaker by profession, who was more addicted to fishing than to his craft, went up the way from the village of Aberlour, in the north, to take a cast in some of the pools above Elchies-water. He had no great choice of tackle, as may be conceived; nothing, in fact, but what was useful, and scant supply of that.

Duncan tried one or two pools without success, till he arrived at a very deep and rapid stream facetiously termed the Mountebank: here he paused, as if meditating whether he should throw his line or not. 'She is very big,' said he to himself, 'but I'll try her; if I grip him he'll be worth the hauding.' He then fished it, a step and a throw, about way down, when a heavy splash proclaimed that he had raised him, though he missed the fly. Going back a few paces, he came over him again, and hooked him. The first tug verified to Duncan his prognostication, that if he was there 'he would be worth the hauding'; but his tackle had thirty plies of hair next the fly, and he held fast, nothing daunted. Give and take went on with dubious advantage, the fish occasionally sulking. The thing at length became serious; and, after a succession of the same tactics, Duncan found himself at the Boat of Aberlour, seven hours after he had hooked his fish, the said fish fast under a stone, and himself completely tired. He had some thought of breaking his tackle and giving the thing up; but he finally hit upon an expedient to rest himself, and at the same time to guard against the surprise and consequence of a sudden movement of the fish.

He laid himself down comfortably on the banks, the butt end of his rod in front; and most ingeniously drew out part of his line, which he held in his teeth. 'If he rugs when I'm sleeping,' said he, 'I think I'll find him noo'; and no doubt it is probable that he would. Accordingly after a comfortable nap of three or four hours, Duncan was awoke by a most unceremonious tug at his jaws. In a moment he was on his feet, his rod well up, and the fish swattering down the stream. He followed as best he could, and was beginning to think of the rock at Craigellachie, when he now found to his great relief that he could 'get a pull on him.' He had comparatively easy work; and exactly twelve hours after hooking him, he cleiked him at the head of Lord Fife's water: he weighed fifty-four pounds, Dutch, and had the tide lice upon him."

Dutch 54lb equals just over English 49¾lb. Since it is likely that the true weight was rounded off, it would be unkind to assume that it weighed slightly less when it might well have weighed slightly more than 54lb Dutch. I have therefore settled for 50lb.

In seven hours Grant's fish took him from the Mountebank pool through the Aberlour water to the Boat pool just above Craigellachie, where both fish and rod rested for three or four hours. The struggle then recommenced and continued for another hour or so. The fish was finally gaffed on Lord Fife's water. This view of Arndilly water faces upstream to where the action took place

GENERAL C.A. ARTHUR'S
50lb GRAND CASCAPEDIA SALMON
—— No. 2 ——

In 1873 General Arthur, a highly experienced and competent salmon fisher, teamed up with his friend R.C. Dun to explore and extensively fish Canada's Grand Cascapedia River. General Arthur, who subsequently became the 21st President of the United States (1881), killed a 50lb fish in June 1878. This fish, a record at the time, generated a great deal of interest in the Cascapedia as a producer of exceptionally large salmon. When Dun quickly followed with a 56-pounder in the same year, the river's reputation grew. Today we know the Cascapedia to be the number one river in North America for large Atlantic salmon, and it draws anglers who fish with the fly from all points of the compass.

COMMANDER H. CLARKE-JERVOISE'S
50lb TAY SALMON
—— No. 3 ——

The Commander caught his fish on a size 2/0 Jock Scott fly on 23 September 1883 at Findford Head on the Taymount beat of the lower River Tay, a beat I have fished on many occasions as a guest of Mr and Mrs John Apthorp. The fish was recorded and set up by P.D. Malloch of Perth.

A fellow taxidermist, A.J. Hall of Romford, has a collection of cased fish and he very kindly sent me photographs of three individual salmon weighing 50lb or more. One of them, although lacking in provenance, weighs between 50lb and 52lb and was caught *circa* 1885. It is a real fish in a bow case that was set up by P.D. Malloch of Perth. Judging from existing records, it could well be the Commander's 50lb fish.

This picture of the River Ewe in Ross-shire, above Pool Ewe Bridge, shows the flats above Ladies' pool, where Grant, 'the Pool House keeper', probably caught his fish

KEEPER GRANT'S 50lb EWE SALMON
No. 4

W.L. Calderwood, in *Salmon Rivers and Lochs of Scotland* (1909), describes the River Ewe and Lochs Maree, Clair and Coulin in these terms:

> It is doubtfull if any district in Scotland surpasses this for grandeur, combined with singular beauty. Seen under almost any weather conditions the picturesqueness on every hand is most striking. Let the rain pour in torrents, and the bare buttresses of rock are covered with a filigree of cascades. Let the mists wreathe the tops of the great mountain masses, and the colours of the old red sandstone, the schists, and the venerable gneiss only glow with greater intensity. Let the wind lash Loch Maree into foam, it is in perfect harmony. Let the sunshine play upon the woodland islets, and a vista of fairyland is disclosed. On every hand the eye and the imagination are captivated.

When discussing the fishing, Calderwood wrote:

> If the number of fish taken is small, the size of individual fish is sometimes great, and the 'playing' proclivities remarkably active. The second fish is one of 50lb, killed on the fly, by Grant the Pool House keeper.

Sadly, Calderwood does not give us any more details of this spectacular catch.

LORD WINTERTON'S
50lb SPEY SALMON
No. 5

Lord Winterton caught his big salmon in the Rock pool on the Gordon Castle water on the River Spey in the autumn of 1892. It is fairly certain that the fish was taken on a fly since, as that respected authority on all matters relating to salmon fishing, John Ashley-Cooper, says when speaking of salmon fishing in Victorian times, 'Then they used fly only, while nowadays this is far from being the case.'

Fortunately, Gordon Castle, seat of the Dukes of Gordon and Richmond, is near Fochabers, where Scotland's most famous fish painter and carver, John Buckland Russell, and his family of assistants had set up in business. Lord Winterton's fish is recorded on page 202 of Augustus Grimble's book *The Salmon Rivers of Scotland*, first published in 1900. He writes:

The ambition of every guest at Gordon Castle is to 'get into the smoking room' for there on the walls are hung casts or models of all fish of forty pounds or over, together with the date, the pool and the name of the lucky captor. Small wonder, then, that Gordon Castle visitors are keen to get a smoking-room fish for at the present there are but nine winners of this Gordon Castle Cross.

The Duke of Gordon and Richmond, whose seat was at
Gordon Castle near Fochabers

The Rock pool on the Gordon Castle water of the Spey where Lord Winterton caught his 50lb fish on 11 October 1892

Lord Winterton's fish, fourth to be hung, was the first 50lb fish caught on the Spey. The inscription read '50 lbs killed by Earl Winterton in the Rock Pool Oct 11th 1892. Length 4 ft 1½ ins / Girth 2 ft 4 inch.'

The person who has done most to research carvings of fish made at Fochabers by John Russell and then John Tully is Simon Brett. He and his wife Edwina spent years painstakingly looking into the provenance of these models, appreciating them as an art form and giving credit to the artist. The carvings were previously listed as a Farlow, Hardy or Fochabers fish. John Baxter of Fochabers remembers the day when one of these carvings could be bought for between £1 and £5.

In 1988, Simon Brett held an important exhibition at his gallery in Moreton in Marsh, and the model of Winterton's fish was number one in his catalogue. Simon quoted from John Russell's obituary, published in the *Banffshire Journal* on 9 May 1893 – 'At one time during the past winter, a visitor to the studio would have discovered several important fish paintings, including two models of a 50 lb Spey salmon' – and commented that his carving 'may' be one of those. The other might have been a second carving of the same fish or, less likely, a model of the other 50lb fish taken from the river that year, caught in the nets.

John Tully (1862–1931) and his wife Isabella (Dhuie) (?1864–1950). They worked in a studio in Fochabers Castle and later moved into their own studio in Fochabers itself

A KEEPER'S
50lb SHANNON SALMON
—— No. 6 ——

Whice recording Ireland's 50lb and over salmon, I have noticed that the reports rarely specify the method used to catch the fish. *The Fishing Gazette* of 9 February 1895 is an exception:

> MR. J. S. HAMMILL (of Belfast) writes: "On Feb. 4 there was on exhibition in Messrs. Meenan's establishment a salmon weighing 50lb., 4ft. in length, and 28in. in circumference at the broadest point. On Friday last, the opening day of the season, it was caught by rod and fly in the preserves of Mr. Archibald Kirker (of Belfast), in the Shannon, near Limerick, by that gentleman's keeper."

ANOTHER KEEPER'S
50lb FISH ON THE EWE
—— No. 7 ——

The Ladies' Pool, River Ewe

Sir Herbert Maxwell, on page 224 of *British Freshwater Fish* (1904), noted the capture of a 50lb salmon from the River Ewe, which connects Loch Maree (it used to be called Loch Ewe) to the sea. His actual words were: 'On June 16th, 1902, a salmon weighing 50 lbs was taken by Mr Dugdale's keeper with fly on the River Ewe, Rosshire.' Since I have an entry (No. 4) for another 50lb salmon taken on the River Ewe with fly by another keeper, this time Grant the Pool House keeper, it seems to me we are left with the impression that successive riparian owners of the fishing rights on the River Ewe were generous to their keepers.

DR C. CHILDS'
50-POUNDER FROM THE AWE
—— No. 8 ——

On 9 November 1907 the *Fishing Gazette* published C.J.H. Cassel's article 'Large Scottish Salmon of 1907' in which he described the capture of a 50lb salmon caught on 12 September by Dr Christopher Childs on the River Awe:

This time the fish was a 50lb one. It was killed on the Taynuilt Hotel water by Dr. Christopher Childs, of Looe, Cornwall and measured 51½in. by 28½in.; breadth of tail, 15in.; and head and upper jaw, 12½in. It was in fine condition, and had evidently been in the fresh water for about three weeks. Hooked in a strong stream, it took a medium-sized Blue Doctor well beneath the surface, and after a swift dart upstream leapt high out of the river. After this pretty acrobatic performance it was by degrees persuaded to return to midstream, and there kept for some time under the powerful strain of an 18ft Castleconnell rod, while the gillie went back a quarter of a mile to get the gaff, which had been left with another angler. Gradually playing the fish towards the shore, after various forcible piscine arguments on its part, and an attempt to make for the rapids below, the fisherman eventually checked it, and the reel having recovered nearly all the line out, this splendid specimen was at last gaffed by John MacNiven, gillie. The battle – as exciting a one as the heart of any angler could desire – lasted for forty-five minutes, and the strain of the rod was maintained during the whole of that time. A cast of this monster was taken by Mr. Malloch, and a photograph of the fish is reproduced.

Blue Doctor

The Taynuilt Hotel water consisted of ten pools and was notorious for being over-fished. 'It is not unusual,' Augustus Grimble noted, 'to find eight rods and six ghillies crowded on the hotel water', with the ghillies expected to fish as soon as the rods tired. The fishing, however, was free to guests staying in the hotel.

MAJOR PIPER FRASER AND CHEF LAGRUE'S 50lb BEAULY SALMON

No. 9

David Hatwell sent me the following valuable information. Malcolm Thorne, an avid collector of angling books and angling memorabilia, purchased a book at auction and discovered a press cutting glued to one of the end sheets. The caption read:

A FIFTY POUND SALMON

Mr. E. Savoure, who sends us this photograph, writes 'This salmon, weighing 50lb and in length 4ft 1in., with a circumference round the middle 2ft. 9in., was caught by Major Piper Fraser and G. Lagrue last month with a fly on the River Beauly, near the Black Bridge, Beaufort Castle, in Mr. Ogden's water. It took no less than three hours to land.'

Since there was no date on the press cutting, nor any indication of which newspaper or magazine it came from, I had no date for the capture of the fish. Luckily, I found another reference that allowed me to fill in the blanks. On 3 December 1909, the *Daily Mail*, reviewing 'notable captures of the season', reported that:

> ... a 49lb salmon which took four hours to land was captured on the Falls beat on the Beauly by Henry Frazier, fisherman to Mr. C. W. Ogden. The killing lure was the fly known as the Silver Grey, and this monster salmon is believed to be the largest of its species ever caught in the Beauly.

This report created a few problems. 1) We now have two weights for the fish. 2) Is the correct spelling Frazier or Fraser? 3) Did it take three or four hours to land? The *Daily Mail's* version is satisfying, however, because it identifies the fly used to capture this terrific fish.

In October 2005 I met Malcolm Fraser, who works in the rooms of Lord Lovat's

(Lord Simon Lovat, 19th baron of Lovat) factor at Beauly, and was shown a plaster cast of the head of the fish caught by Major Piper Fraser. I was also able to settle on the correct spelling (the same as his own). Malcolm Fraser directed me to the River Beauly where the fish was caught so that I could take my photograph.

After closing the Fraser file, and accepting that I was unlikely ever to resolve the anomaly of the time it took to land the fish, I had another note from David Hatwell. He had been re-reading BB's *The Fisherman's Bedside Book* (1945). Sure enough, BB re-tells a story told to him in 1944 by a Mrs Cameron Clunes, who had heard it from a Mr Mackintosh, who had witnessed the event in 1909.

From the first press cutting, we know that a Mr Lagrue was involved in the capture of the fish – but how? It turns out that Mr Lagrue was a chef at Beauly Castle and, although he was not a fisherman, he had picked up Mr Fraser's rod while the latter was raising the anchor 'and rashly hurled the lure [a fly] upon the bosom of the river.'

You can imagine what happened next. Yes, a huge salmon took the fly and Lagrue played it all morning and part of the afternoon before he killed it – but not before he had broken Fraser's rod and the landing net. My verdict, having taken a careful look at the photograph and noting the type of dress, is that it is Mr Lagrue the chef and not Fraser who is (quite rightly) standing up beside the fish, but as the first account suggests, that the playing of the fish may have been a joint effort.

River Beauly, looking downstream near the Black Bridge, Beaufort Castle, where Major Piper Fraser and M. Lagrue, the chef at the castle, landed their 50lb fish after a four-hour struggle in which both Fraser's rod and landing net were broken. The fish was hooked by Lagrue as Fraser was raising the anchor.

As to the time it took to land the salmon, I favour the four-hour version because in BB's account, Lagrue played the fish all morning (three hours) and at that juncture the rod and the net were as yet unbroken. The weight of the fish in the BB version is confirmed at 50lb.

E. Savoure's heavily retouched photograph showing what is undoubtedly Chef Lagrue holding the 50lb salmon caught by both himself and Major Piper Fraser with Silver Grey fly on the River Beauly in 1909

J.T. SPAULDING'S
50lb GRAND CASCAPEDIA SALMON
—— No. 11 ——

According to Frank Griswold in *Observations on a Salmon River* (1922), Spaulding caught his salmon on 17 June 1922 on a Baron fly. A carved wooden model of it hangs in Lorne Cottage, a famous camp for Cascapedia fishermen.

Ron Swanson in his *Grand Cascapedia Giants* (2005) elaborates by giving us the fish's length, 51in, and girth, 27½in, and he notes that it was a cock fish caught on a Baron fly. He also notes that the tradition of having undecorated wooden models of large salmon displayed on the walls of Lorne Cottage started in 1879–80.

NEVILLE BOSTOCK'S
50lb EIRA SALMON
—— No. 12 ——

In August 1927 Neville Bostock fished the Eira River in Norway with a 14ft Grant Vibration rod, which he knew in his heart was too small for such a big river. The rod was fitted with a reel and a greased fly line – an outfit that he had last used on the Aberdeenshire Dee.

He was fishing a very deep pool with a fly called Tilbouries, named after a beat on the Dee, but because the line floated he poked the top of his rod into the water in an attempt to make his fly fish at a greater depth. As he was watching the line gradually sink, a huge salmon surfaced just beyond, slowly revealing its head, back fin and tail. Instantly aware that his line was running out, he gripped it to the rod, which he raised and the fish was hooked.

Bostock landed his fish in twenty-seven minutes, which is extraordinary considering its huge size, a fact brought home to him by his gillie's refusal to carry it back until a pony and trap was fetched. Bostock sent scales of the fish to Arthur Hutton, the scale-reading expert, whose reply revealed that the fish had enjoyed two years of river life and four years feeding at sea. It was a cock fish weighing just over 50lb, length 52in and girth 27in. The above information comes from Neville Bostock's piece in BB's *The Fisherman's Bedside Book*.

CAUGHT BY MISS LETTICE WARD, ALDERNS, 12TH OCTOBER 1928. LENGTH 51¾". GIRTH 27½". WEIGHT 50LBS.

MISS LETTICE WARD'S
50lb TAY SALMON
No. 13

Although *Where to Fish* (1937) gives us the basic facts of Miss Lettice Ward's catch, John Ashley-Cooper's *The Great Salmon Rivers of Scotland* (1980) adds important details – it was caught on a fly on 12th October 1928 and taken from the River Tay at

Kinnaird. In August 2005, thanks to my friend Robert Walker I discovered the location of the cast of Miss Lettice Ward's big fish in Kinnaird House Hotel and it was not caught on the Kinnaird water as noted by Ashley-Cooper, but some seventeen beats farther down the river at Stobhall. Through the indulgence of the proprietors of the hotel, I was allowed to disorganise the billiard room and have ladders fetched, so that I could get close enough to photograph the salmon. The fly that caused the fish's demise is also mounted in the case. The fish is one of several very large cased salmon on show, all caught by members of the Ward family.

ABOVE *Kinnaird House, now one of the finest fishing hotels in Britain, where several large cased salmon are on show all caught by the Ward family*

LEFT *Alderns stream at Stobhall runs from left to right along the far bank. This is where Miss Lettice Ward caught her 50lb salmon. The pool is wadeable for almost its whole length and must be one of the most prolific pools on the whole river*

Major Bertie Corbet, on the left, and the 8th Duke of Roxburghe pose by their catch. This may be the only photograph of the two 50-pounders caught on the same day on a fly. The 8th Duke was a great fisher and a true lover of Alten. His were the golden years of fishing: he made 16 visits to Alten each lasting about a month. He caught 1091 salmon including one of 53 lbs and seven others over 40 lbs, all on fly

MAJOR B.D. CORBET'S
50lb ALTEN SALMON
——— No. 14 ———

In 1928, Major Corbet joined the Duke of Roxburghe on a fishing trip to the Alten River in Norway and, on 23 July, both were successful. *Where to Fish* (1937) gives details of Major Corbet's 50lb salmon, including girth and length. He caught his fish on a 1/0 Red Dusty Miller and his companion caught a 53-pounder on a fly of the same size and pattern.

'HERE'S TO TOMORROW'
ADMIRAL READ'S
50lb ALTEN SALMON
—— No. 16 ——

On September 2005 I received a letter from Roy Flury with the following most interesting account of Admiral William A. Read's success with large salmon:

Ole also told me about Read who came to Alten in 1954. He usually fished the upper beats and stayed at Sautso. He would fish the last week of June and all July, staying 5 or 6 weeks. He often fished with his wife, Edith and occasionally his boys Bill and Fred. He also fished with Vice Admiral E. McDonnel. His boatman was Ole Mosesen, one of the most experienced. Confusingly he was father to the Ole I know! (His father had caught a 60½ lb salmon himself in 1948.) Ole junior joined his father in the boat in 1958 and said that Admiral Read was fanatical about catching a 50 lb fish. After fishing every night he would thank the boatmen and enjoy a drink with them. He would always raise his glass and say, "Here's to tomorrow when we will certainly catch a 50 pounder." By 1959 Read was in his 6th year on Alten. On a July day they were coming to the end of the night's fishing and were on a pool called Valliniva. Read wanted to pack up but Ole suggested that each choose a fly and just fish the tail of the pool. Read chose a 3/0 Silver Wilkinson and Ole a 5/0 Black Dose. Read fished first with his choice of fly and then changed to the Black Dose. Almost on the last cast, a fish took. It was the long awaited 50 pounder. Ole said that after this Read caught several 50 pounders and then his big fish of 58 lb in 1962. They became good friends and when Ole told him that his ambition was to go to the United States to Manhattan, he offered to help him on the condition he took serious English lessons. Ole departed after the fishing season of 1961 and by 1972 was running his own ski school in Vermont. His place in the boat was taken by his brother Tormod Mosesen.

Black Dose

'CLEAR OF THE WATER'
DR COIGNEY'S
50lb MATAPEDIA SALMON
—— No. 19 ——

D r Rodolphe Coigney, who died on 6 June 2001, was an overseas member of the Flyfishers' Club for twenty years. He contributed an article to the Summer 1993 issue of the *Flyfishers Journal*, describing how, in 1983, he caught what is probably the record rod-caught fish for the River Matapedia in the province of Quebec:

> I had just cast about 25 yards towards the middle of the river and said to the guide: "I must check my leader again, I believe I made a knot." I mended the line because of the strong current while my fly was coming around. At that moment there was a large swish ten feet from the canoe and I immediately felt the strong pull of the salmon. He was hooked and felt heavy, a big fish.

Coigney, who was a very experienced angler, described his technique for playing a big fish, which in practice meant giving it as much line as it wanted, within reason.

> Ready for battle, I started winding up the line while putting some brake on the reel. The result was immediate and, as I had anticipated, the salmon took off in the opposite direction to the pressure, upriver against that very strong water. He was taking the backing nylon from the reel, but little by little I put more and more brake on the reel. Fighting both the reel and the current, the salmon went slower and slower, gaining little ground. When he was approximately 400 feet away he stopped and, in a desperate effort, the salmon jumped clear out of the water – a rare feat for a large fish which filled us all with awe. None of us, fishermen and guides, had ever seen such a big salmon.'

Coigney continued to play the fish while instructing his guide to wade into the water with the landing net.

> Reeling fast I was already back in my line. I held him firmly; he went down to the bottom of the pool and started shaking his head left and right, trying

This photograph of Rodolphe Coigney and his Matapedia fish was kindly given to me by his widow Martha who wrote: 'He was thrilled with the catch and the fact that it was almost the same day as my fiftieth birthday. The year was 1983. Rudy had a special pocheoux (to cook the fish) made in Paris. It looked like a railroad car on the back of my stove.'

to get rid of the fly. That was a critical moment. As I was determined not to lose him, I increased the brake and pulled as much as I dared, knowing that my leader was fairly strong. The end was near. The salmon started circling slowly in front of the canoe, but we could not see him because of the coloured water. Finally, the leader emerged from the water. I was standing up, holding my rod high as I could, and at last his large tail fin appeared on the surface. I led him towards Bill's net.

The fish was duly landed by Bill, the guide, and weighed, but Bill, like so many before him, had a problem converting kilos into pounds.

When we were on firm ground, we admired and measured the fish: 48 inches long, 25 inches in girth, and we weighed it on my Chatillion scale which Bill was holding. It went all the way and I announced "22.5 kilos!" "That's 45 pounds!" shouted Bill, congratulating me. So, I went back to the hotel announcing proudly that I had caught a 45 pounds salmon. It was only after dinner, when I recalled the whole affair with friends, that one of them exclaimed: "22.5 kilos, that's not 45 pounds. You don't double the kilos, you have to multiply by 2.2, you therefore took a 50-pound monster!" We rushed to the freezer to verify on the hotel scale and he was right, the fish weighed just over 50 pounds.

Coigney's 50-pounder was caught while using a weight forward No. 9 floating line. He added, 'For the record, I was fishing with a 10½ feet Fenwick graphite rod, my faithful Bogdan reel and a Silver Rat wet fly on a double hook No. 2.'

Rodolphe L. Coigney's name is familiar to serious angling book collectors for his comprehensive and definitive bibliography *Isaak Walton, A New Bibliography 1653–1987*, published by James Cummins, New York (1989). While he was researching the book, a fascinating correspondence built up with the late Ron Coleby, the esteemed English angling bibliophile, much of which is now in David Hatwell's possession. He also has a collection of correspondence between Coleby and other angling authors whom Coleby generously assisted.

DROPPED BACK IN – BOŽO IVANOVIC'S 50lb ALTEN SALMON
─── No. 20 ───

Brook's Sun Ray Shadow

The Nielo pool on Norway's Alten River lies between two small lakes through which the river passes as it enters a very deep gorge. This is where Bozo Ivanovic caught his big fish on a Brook's Sun Ray Shadow fly. The beat is called Sautso, as is the camp that accommodates the fishermen.

Ivanovic sent an admirably clear account of the capture of his 50-pounder, in a letter dated 7 September 1994, to his friend Nathaniel Reed in Florida. Reed had been a member of the team the previous year.

Dear Nathaniel,

It was a great loss that you were not with us on the Alta this year. The season did not appear to be late – it was warmish and the water was quite low but few fish had appeared and we arrived to find that 33 had been landed in the previous six days. I started at the lower camp accompanied by David, Mark, Jim and George. The first three days were slow with perhaps 13 fish for the five rods. I had one in Slingerplassen, one in Bollo and two from Upper Gognes (the main Gognes, so great in 1993, was too low).

Off to the upper river and with great hopes I started at Steinfossen and, although there were a few fish there, no takers – a blank was saved by a fish from Barilla very high up under the left bank cliff. All these fish were on Brooks or Collie Dogs with floating line and short sink tip. We saw Alan Russell's 42 pounder when Harald brought it down. Hopes rose! I had a lovely blank night at Toppen catching a biggish trout from the tunnel and savouring the peace, the wildflowers and the mosquitoes. As we came down to finish off we saw David at Nielo fishing from the left bank just before it widened into the lower lake. He was clearly having some sort of action and came back shortly to tell of three fish risen there of which I think two were on for a while. Three offers in Nielo is very unusual as you know and I feared the fish would have moved on by the time I got there the next evening. Well they hadn't!

We started off at Nielo with Jan letting the boat down on the rope from the bank: that gave me just the right angle from which to cover the water. Half way down we saw a movement – a sort of hump – not really a surface break. "A big one" said Tormod and the next 3 or 4 casts were nail-biters. We reached the spot – no rise – as the fly came in close to the bank another fish took the Ally shrimp and luckily, very luckily, turned downstream at once.

I let it run on down into the lake and we slid down past the "spot" as quietly as possible, landed the standard 10 kilo hen and paused for a confer-ence. Tormod thought we had better go straight back as fish don't stay long in Nielo especially if disturbed. Jan was for giving it a rest and I gave the cast-ing vote to go down to Valliniva. We saw a fish move by the big rock, so on with the Brooks and we got it on the third rise. With two fish under our belts we were ready for anything. Hasty checking of leaders, re-tying the fly and carefully starting Jan with the same length of rope from exactly the same place I began to cover the pool. After about 20 casts Tormod said "This is the place" and with a small surface break the fish rose and was on. It immedi-ately jumped clear out of the water and we knew we had a very big one. It tore up and down stream in Nielo, jumped and broached five times and then set off for the lake. Here the real battle began. Tormod was in agonies over all sorts of hidden rock outcrops, imagining every possible disaster. The fish was very hard to move even when stationary and took out yards of line with each flick of the tail. Inch by inch I worked it in and after 20 minutes we had it near the boat in 6 feet of water – no current – and seemingly no chance of lifting it. I asked Jan to row to the only hopeful spot about 80 yards away where there was a shallower part about two feet deep. The shore was covered with trees to the water – water, water everywhere and not a beach in sight. Finally the fish rose as the gravel bottom rose and my heart sank as Tormod produced the Sautso gaff – a 6 foot knobbly wooden pole with an old hook lashed to the top. Anyhow, in it went and Tormod lifted the fish out of the water. As he got it up it arched its back, snapped the gaff like matchwood and fell on the gunwale, 50/50 in the boat or in the water. You can guess: in the water, under the boat, line around the engine, but still thank God a good hold. More horsing of the fish and after a total fight of about 45 minutes both the boys got into the shallow water. Tormod grabbed the 12 inches of gaff handle still sticking out of the fish, Jan grabbed the tail and between them they heaved it over the side whereupon it set about smashing the boat. 50lbs and beautifully fresh – no sea lice. I expect it had been in a week and that David had risen it the previous evening. I had the scales read: 4 years in the river and 4 years at sea, a first time spawner. Lucky me!

The week ended with still falling water; down to a foot or so, and 56 salmon and few, very few grilse. I gather the August week produced about 75 fish half salmon and half grilse with the water at least a foot minus and the boats unable to negotiate the rapids without the fisherman walking.

All the very best

Bo

Bozo (his friends call him Bo) Ivanovic with his magnificent cock salmon from the Nielo Pool on the Sautso Beat on the Alten, caught on a Brooks Sun Ray Shadow. The gaff broke in the first attempt to land the fish and it fell back into the water

JACQUELINE VERNES'
50¼lb ALTEN SALMON
—— No. 23 ——

This photograph of the Alten River when it is in a hurry to get to the sea would soon unnerve a fisherman with a nervous disposition. Equally, it shows what playing a fish for three and a half hours could be like

In 1956, Jacqueline Vernes was a guest of the Pulizer family, who took over the lease of the Alten River after the previous leaseholder, the Duke of Westminster, died in 1954. On 28 June she hooked a fish in the Forbygnygen pool. It played for three-and-a-half hours and was finally landed three miles down river at Aronnes, one of the last pools before the sea. Mrs Vernes' stamina must have been considerable because the fly had hooked the fish under one of the pectoral fins and, as every experienced salmon fisherman knows, a fish hooked other than in the mouth usually fights twice as hard. I personally believe that the merit of landing a foul-hooked fish is no different from landing a properly hooked fish. On the other hand, deliberate foul-hooking and stroke-hauling are despicable. I have no doubt whatsoever that properly hooked fish sometimes throw the hook, only to be re-hooked almost instantly.

WEIGHT 50½lbs. CAUGHT IN THE ANNAN NOV. 1895 BY PETER LOUDON. LENGTH 54½ ins. GIRTH 29½ ins.

PETER LOUDON'S
50½lb ANNAN SALMON
—— No. 25 ——

Some details of the three largest salmon ever caught on the River Annan in Scotland appear in Jock Scott's *Game Fish Records* (1936), on pages 150–1. The record rod-caught fish, weighing 51½lb, was caught by John Varrie in 1929 but no information on the method of capture is included. A 60lb salmon caught circa 1850 by the Reverend A. Cook of St John's Church, Annan, is recorded but with no substantive catch details. However, about a 50½-pounder that was caught on a fly, Jock Scott writes:

> It was killed by the late Mr. Peter Loudoun [sic] of Port St Anna, at the head of the Black Pool below Mount Annan Island in the autumn of 1895. It was a cock fish and was killed on a Brown Turkey fly. My informant actually saw this fish. A cast was made, and painted by the late Mr. George Wright, a well-known artist. Mr. Loudoun [sic] had the fish cased and it was subsequently bought by Mr. Brook, of Hoddom Castle, and I understand that it is still in the possession of the Brook family.

Jock Scott added a note on two more portmanteaux salmon that were taken in the nets:

> Three years later [1898] a 57lb salmon was taken by an Annan poke-net. In 1934, after the expiration of the netting season, a salmon described as "fully 60lb. in weight" was "found" by two fishermen at Seafield, Annan. In all probability this fish was making for the Annan. As the affair occurred in the close season details are, not unnaturally, lacking!

The Loudon family were tailors and clothiers. They also sold fishing rods, fishing tackle and river licenses from this house, 25 Port Street. The plaster cast of the salmon was made from a 50½ pound (22.9kg) fish caught in the River Annan in 1893 by Peter Loudon. Miss Jean Loudon is on the left of the photograph and Peter is in the centre with his brother Jim on the right. Peter was the manager of Hardy Brothers' Edinburgh fishing tackle shop. He was drowned in the River Earn near Crieff in the 1930s when playing a large fish

On Monday, 18 April 2005 I visited the Newbie Fishery on the River Annan in Dumfriesshire just above the town of Annan, a beat that I last fished in the early 1950s. In those days I was a member of a shooting party who annually took the last week of the shooting season to flight geese and ducks at first light and at dusk on the Solway Firth. This routine left the rest of the day for the few salmon fishers in the party to fish the River Annan and the Border Esk during what was then the opening week of the fishing season.

I soon discovered when I met Russell Frank, the river keeper in charge, that the beat is now controlled by a syndicate. Moreover, it had just enjoyed an all-time catch record of 320 salmon. When I explained that the purpose of my visit was to find out more information about a number of huge salmon that had been caught on the lower Annan, he suggested that I return the next morning, leaving him time (after I had named some pools on the river) to make some enquiries.

The next day, because heavy overnight rain had caused a big brown flood and made the river unfishable, he was able to take time off to show me the Sand pool, Cook's Rock and the Island pool, or Black pool, below Mount Annan Island, so that I could photograph places that in the past had been the scene of dramatic events.

Working on another of my snippets of information, he confirmed that a cast of a big salmon made in 1893 still existed. The head gillie and river keeper of Hoddom Castle Estate had told him so and, to our great pleasure, Frank had obtained permission for us to go to the castle and take a photograph. Soon we were looking at Peter Loudon's magnificent 50½lb salmon. It adorns the wall of the main hall in what is left of Hoddom Castle. Some time during the 1950s the castle's roof was removed together with two storeys so as to avoid the payment of rates (a similar fate befell Kenmure Castle, which famously once housed the world-record rod-caught Kenmure pike). The Hoddom Estate has now become a five-star caravan site and the main hall is a restaurant.

The legend on the case revealed that the correct spelling of the captor's surname is Loudon, not Loudoun as he was named in the original catch report. Likewise, the fish was caught in 1893 and not 1895. It was 54½in long and the girth was 29½in.

Despite having seen a good many large salmon in his lifetime, Russell Frank was not quite prepared for the shock of seeing such a colossal salmon at close quarters – I had asked him to stand on a chair that was placed on top of a table so that he could photograph Loudon's fish for me.

After I had closed the file on Peter Loudon's salmon, I received a letter from Russell Frank enclosing a photocopy of a photograph of the Loudon brothers and their sister posing with the plaster cast of Peter's big fish. The photograph came from a book, *Through the Lens: Glimpses of Old Annan Burgh*, published by Dumfries & Galloway Libraries. The caption to the photograph on page 12 reveals a tragic ending to Peter Loudon's success as a fisherman and his career in the tackle trade.

J.D. RUDD'S
50½lb TWEED SALMON
— No. 26 —

Mr Rudd's great catch was recorded in Arthur Oglesby and Lucy Money-Coutts' book *The Big Fish* (1992). From their account we know that it was caught in Birgham Dub in November 1925. Although at first I listed Rudd's fish in my list of fish caught by unspecified methods, I moved it into the fly-caught section when I realised that it was caught during that part of the season, i.e. after 14 September, when the fly-only rule operates.

CHRISTER LUNDQUIST'S
50½lb MÖRRUM SALMON
— No. 28 —

When fishing the Mörrum River in Sweden on 18 May 1979, Christer Lundquist caught this big fish. I gleaned the information from Fiske Journalen Yearbook No. 2 and wrote to Jan Eggers for help in identifying large European-caught salmon. In September 2005 I received the following note:

> Christer Lundquist from the city of Lund caught a salmon of 22,9 kilo on the 18th of May 1979 in the Mörrum river pool, Sweden, with the fly. There is a nice picture of him with this fish salmon in *Fiske Journalen Yearbook 2*, printed at the end of 1979. The fly he used when he caught this big salmon was a Thunder and Lightning on a double hook size 1/0, his favourite fly. The length of the salmon was 121 cm and the girth 72 cm. For a long time the Swedish record.

Thunder and Lightning –
Lundquist's favourite fly which
he fished as a size 1/0 double

Davis' first 50-pounder actually weighed 50¹/₂lb. The fish is being held up by James Harrison, his guide, gillie and boatman, who was later to invent the famous Lady Amherst fly. Incidentally, Davis always preferred to tie his flies on double hooks

EDMOND W. DAVIS'
51lb GRAND CASCAPEDIA SALMON
No. 33

In a piece written for *Classic Angling* (January 2002), David Zincavage, who wrote the introduction for a reprint of Edmond Davis' *Salmon Fishing on the Grand Cascapedia* (Flyfisher's Classic Library, 2001), had this to say about North America's finest Atlantic salmon river:

> Catches on the Cascapedia River in Canada are legendary. Almost every North American salmon weighing more than 50lb has been taken from the Cascapedia's pools, from the long standing North American record RG Dun's 54lb fish taken on June 20, 1886, to the still unsurpassed 57 pounder killed by Mr Kirby on July 11, 1928.

Edmond Davis caught two salmon that weighed over 50lb, one in 1900 and the other in 1901. Zincavage believes that these two successes and the associated celebrity that followed led to an undertaking to prepare and publish the book, which is not only famous but, in its original 1904 form, now extremely valuable. Zincavage tells us that Davis had his salmon flies tied by Forrest of Kelso in Scotland but used a 15ft greenheart rod made by Dalzell of St John in New Brunswick.

The full account of the hooking, playing and killing of the first portmanteau salmon that Davis was pleased to call 'The River Goddess' (notwithstanding that it was a cock fish) is full of tension:

Drifting a short distance downstream, a few casts are made to the right, when, suddenly, something enormous rises from the bottom, and, as it disappears beneath the surface, the delicate dark leader is carefully watched. Gradually it begins to sink. Now the hook is sent home, for I know the fly has been seized...

"Keep the canoe as it is, James, until you know what he intends to do. I cannot move him. Quick! Up-stream. He's off! Whew! A run of forty yards without a stop. There he jumps! Faster, James!" I cry. "He is among the rocks! The leader will surely be cut."...

The rod bends and "He has gone!" I cry. "No, he is on; he is coming back!" Down the river he rushes; darting across the current and disappearing to sulk in thirty feet of water.

Dropping below the fish, we cross to the other side, and, paddling upstream, hold the canoe in readiness beside the ledge...

"He can't stand that strain much longer, Mr. Davis."

"Nor I, either, James. Look at the tip, it is three feet under water."

"Don't let up, sir; he will soon give in. Yes, there he comes now!" Slowly the rod is raised, and, looking down into the depths of that deep pool, I see a bright form boring steadily downward.

"Now he's coming up, sir; pull a little harder." Gradually the huge fish comes to the surface and, with a tremendous leap, tries for the current; but the struggle has been too severe: the spark of life has fled. So, gently drawing this beautiful creature towards me, I thrill with joy when the river-goddess finds a safe resting-place in my canoe.

"Have you ever seen so large a salmon, James?"

"None that was killed with a fly, sir: but my father tells of one which was speared many years ago weighing over sixty pounds."

Davis continued his chapter by describing the response of the other members of his party as each of them in turn spotted the huge fish for the first time. He ended with an apology for catching his second 50-pounder:

I will not weary my readers with the story of my other large salmon, taken the following year. It weighed fifty-one and one half pounds fifteen hours after it had been killed. The salmon was hooked about eight-thirty o'clock at night, but owing to the lateness of the hour we were unable to gaff the fish until a few minutes after nine.

SIR STUART COATES' FIRST PORTMANTEAU TAY SALMON, 51lb
No. 35

Sir Stuart Coates caught his 51-pounder at Ballathie on the Tay in 1913 at a time when not many fishermen fished for salmon with bait. I feel quite sure that this fish was taken on a fly (a feeling which is supported by John Ashley-Cooper in *A Line on Salmon*, page 220) especially as Sir Stuart subsequently became a member of that very exclusive club of fishermen (I believe there were three) who have caught two 50-pounders in their lifetime. His second fish was certainly caught on a fly. It was taken in 1923 and weighed 53lb (No. 81).

This railway bridge marks the upper limit of Ballathie and Cargill water and the lower limit of the Islamouth beat. Fish often lie under the bridge, attracting fishermen such as the two at work in a boat under the far span

HENRY C. PHIPPS'
51lb GRAND CASCAPEDIA SALMON
—— No. 36 ——

enry C. Phipps, who built and co-owned Camp Chaleur by Canada's Grand
Cascapedia River with his two brothers and two sisters, caught his 51-pounder in
Swallow's Nest pool in July, circa 1920. He also caught a 52-pounder from the same
pool (No. 62). According to Ronald Swanson in his *Grand Cascapedia Giants* (2005),
models of both fish were displayed with other giant salmon in the dining-room at Camp
Chaleur, but were lost when the camp burned down in 1977. Swanson also notes that
Phipps' first name was Henry, not Howard, as had previously been thought.

*Henry Phipps and his children pose with the first giant salmon he caught on the Grand Cascapedia. Judging by
the salmon's damaged flank, it appears that the fish has been eviscerated before being photographed, or perhaps
badly injured by a seal or other predator*

HOWARD ST GEORGE'S
51lb TWEED SALMON
—— No. 37 ——

oward St George's 51lb cock salmon was caught on the Tweed in the spring of 1921. This was the sum of the information that I managed to glean from *Where to Fish* (1937). Fortunately, a fine photograph of the fish was published in *The Illustrated London News* of 11 November 1922 and, according to John Ashley-Cooper in *The Great Salmon Rivers of Scotland* (1980):

> The fish was killed on a 'Jock Scott' fly in the Spring of 1921 (this is a very large fish for a Springer; large Tweed salmon are almost always Autumn fish). It was 54ins. long and had a girth of 24½ins.

John Ashley-Cooper's remark about Howard St George's salmon being large for a springer aroused my curiosity. Richard Waddington's fish (number 41) was of the same weight but two inches shorter and much fatter – a typical fresh-run autumn salmon. I suspect that Howard St George's fish was a fresh-run autumn fish in 1920. I think that it was a kelt when it was caught in the following spring, and probably weighed 60–65lb when it was fresh-run. Indeed, Sturdy's scale predicts a weight of 67½lb for a 54in fish.

Like many of his Victorian and Edwardian contemporaries, Howard St George was a skilful and wide-ranging fisherman, as the following note from page 89 of *Game Fish Records* (1936) illustrates:

> The Ministry officials have also mentioned to me a catch of 18 salmon in one day by Mr Howard St. George. This bag was made on June 30th 1903 and all the fish were taken on a fly. The River was the Screebe.

Boatman Bjorvlff Mikklesen rows up to Sautso from Valliniva on the River Alten at 4 a.m.

MAJOR MORRISON'S BRACE OF 51lb ALTEN SALMON
No. 38

When Major Morrison fished several beats on the Alten River in 1923, he caught two fish of over 50lb on fly in the space of three days. On 28 July he caught a 51-pounder from Upper Sautso and on 31 July another 51-pounder from Lower Sandia. This information comes courtesy of the Roxburghe Records.

Boatmen on the Alten in the 1920s

MAJOR A.W. HUNTINGTON'S
51lb AWE SALMON
—— No. 39 ——

The Huntington family, Major A.W. and his wife Gladys, caught several large salmon in the River Awe in Scotland. The Major landed a 51-pounder in 1930, from the Stepping Stone pool on a 5/0 Green Highlander. His bigger fish – 56lb – is No. 129 on this list. *The Field* of June 14th 1930 contains an illustration of a splendid salmon weighing 51lb and the following letter.

Sir – I enclose you a photograph of a 51lb salmon killed on the Awe on May 22. It was hooked in the Stepping Stone pool and eventually gaffed in the Fishing Field just above the boat, after a strenuous fight lasting two hours and twenty minutes. It was caught on a fly, and the distance from the Stepping Stone to where the fish was gaffed would be about a mile and a half.

Yours truly

A.W. Huntington
Bonawe House,
Taynuilt,
Argyle

Green Highlander

RICHARD WADDINGTON'S
51lb AARO SALMON
—— No. 41 ——

I daresay that every salmon fisher dreams of catching a 50lb salmon on a fly. Even the most famous of all British salmon fishers, Richard Waddington, said, when he at last caught such a fish, 'To me this fish represented the fulfilment of a dream, for it was caught on a fly, played and tailed entirely alone, and in a tremendous river, the Aaro in Norway. Such luck occurs but once in a lifetime.' This extract is from his *Salmon Fishing Philosophy and Practice*.

Thanks to a good friend, Waddington was able to fish on an exclusive beat on Norway's Aaro River, where he hooked, on a 9/0 Thunder and Lightning, and landed a 51lb cock salmon. In a very interesting piece published in Arthur Oglesby and Lucy Money-Coutts' *The Big Fish* (1992), Waddington referred to the difficulty of fishing the Aaro:

> I went by myself to fish a pool known as 'Solsken' off one of the platforms which are built right across this un-wadeable, un-boatable river Aaro. I had hardly got my line out when a fish took and very quickly came to the surface as he tried to turn away with the fly.

Waddington completed his account of playing this fish in his autobiography, *Richard Waddington 1910–1999* published by Janet Waddington in 2004:

> If one of these big fish is ever allowed to turn side-on in these powerful streams of the Aaro a breakage is certain. The only way in which they can be killed is by the angler getting directly straight above them and pulling them so hard that they cannot turn side-on.
>
> This I proceeded to do. I quickly ran along the platform until I was directly above the fish and then, with a sixteen-foot greenheart bent nearly double, began to pull as hard as possible. For about forty minutes the salmon struggled to get turned sideways but I had sufficient strength to keep him directly below me as I edged along the platform towards the shore. Happily the river here lapped on to a shingle beach and with little difficulty I got the fish to swim up almost on to it. He was far too big to catch by the tail so I slid my fingers into his gills and pulled him up on the beach and killed him with a big stone.

Richard Waddington with his 51lb Aaro salmon. He wrote in his autobiography, 'If one of these big fish is ever allowed to turn side-on in these powerful streams of the Aaro a breakage is certain. The only way in which they can be killed is by the angler getting directly straight above them and pulling them so hard that they cannot turn side-on.'

Very big fish suffer from being too big. The gills are comparatively too small for their body size and weight. Unable to acquire sufficient oxygen in their bloodstream they cannot utilise the latent energy stored in their tissues. It is this, not tiredness, which causes them to give up the struggle. It always sounds very grand to say. 'I caught a fish of over fifty pound on a fly and landed it alone without a gaff.' In truth when once you understand the technique of playing big fish in heavy water it is really quite simple.

Richard Waddington was a very experienced salmon fisherman and greatly influenced his own generation of salmon anglers. He was a forthright individual, and sure of himself. Who else could write the following about his favourite river, the Spey?

> This is the king of all the Scotch rivers. Compared to the Spey the Dee is trivial, the Tay lacking in fish, and the Tweed tedious.

Waddington pondered on the fact that, when he was fishing for spring fish on the lower Pitchroy beat of the Spey in the late 1940s, for every four pulls or takes, on flies tied on a single iron (size 8/0), he landed one fish, lost one fish, and failed to hook the other two. Subsequently, he developed the Waddington series of flies with a hinged treble hook and put them to the test. He noted on page 97 of his autobiography:

> I kept a record of my first year using these on my river, the Inverness-shire Garry. Using 8/0 flies tied on single 8/0 irons the results to the end of March were forty-seven caught with fly, 124 lost and pulled. In April and early May, in big water using the first properly made 8/0 and 6/0 Waddington's fifty-five fish were killed, four were lost (broken), one was lost (came off hooks), three pulls. Friends fishing my other rods in the same week, but using standard flies, registered thirteen fish killed and twenty-seven lost or pulled.

THE 10th DUKE OF ROXBURGHE'S 51lb ALTEN SALMON
No. 43

The Duke of Roxburghe owns two of the most famous salmon beats in Scotland – the Upper and Lower Floors beats on the Tweed, where the river flows through his Floors Castle Estate. Nevertheless, he caught this giant in Norway. Alerted to the existence of the salmon by a passage in *The Big Fish* by Arthur Oglesby and Lucy Money-Coutts, I wrote to the Duke asking for more details and, if possible, a photograph of the fish. In his reply he said, 'The fish was caught on the Sandia beat of the Alta River on 10th July 1979; it was 51lbs and caught on an 8/0 Silver Rat [fly] with a single hook.'

The present Duke's great great grandfather, the 6th Duke, fished Alten for the first time on 16 July 1859, when he caught his first salmon there, weighing 25lb. One hundred and twenty years later, not quite to the day, the 10th Duke caught his 51-pounder. In 1886, the 6th Duke enjoyed a record year and on 23 July caught thirty-one salmon and two grilse. These details were obtained from his own diary (courtesy of the present Duke) and are reprinted from page 44 of Flury and Dalenson's *Alten: The Story of a Salmon River*.

MORTON SEAMAN'S 51lb AND 52lb ALTEN SALMON
No. 46

For most fishermen, the landing of a 50lb plus salmon is the fulfilment of a lifetime's dream. Landing two fish of that calibre must be an intoxicating experience. Morton Seaman, from the USA, took a fish weighing 51lb from Nedre Sierra pool on a Green Highlander fly, on 11 July 1992. His second big fish, weighing 52lb, fell to a Black and Silver tube fly at Langstilla on 9 July 1994. This information comes from the Alten Records.

The Duke of Roxburghe's 51lb Alten salmon caught on an 8/0 Silver Rat on a single hook

COLONEL W. HOME'S
51½lb TWEED SALMON
No. 50

S ir Herbert Maxwell was a prolific author who wrote good books on many aspects of country life. He even wrote up the *Chronicles of the Houghton Fishing Club* (1908), using the club's diaries – an important historical document on the history of fly fishing on the world's most famous chalk stream.

On page 234 of his *British Freshwater Fishes* (1904), he gives us a short list of four salmon caught on fly, all of which exceeded a weight of 50lb. One of these was a 51½-pounder caught by Colonel the Hon. W. Home in 1892. Interestingly, Maxwell uses the catching of these four fish between 1873 and 1892 to pinpoint a period when very big salmon were coming back – implying that before this period, i.e. in William Scrope's time, the big fish had disappeared.

Birgham Dub on the Tweed, where Colonel W. Home caught one of his 50-pounders in 1892 and the other in 1902 – both on a Jock Scott. Although this stretch of the Tweed looks dull and featureless, the reverse is in fact the case. Skilled boatmen take you down a line that varies with the height of the river, indicating that the character of the water is ever changing but readable.

The problem of a very high bank at Birgham Dub at this point has been overcome by the building of a fine staircase, staked into a natural hollow in the bank, with a series of suitably curved stylish platforms. The last rod and boatman to use the steps can be seen working down the left bank. I daresay that little has changed since General Home caught his second big fish in 1902 – save the fact that nobody catches 50-pounders any more

Depend upon it, had Scrope heard of fish of such as these he would have gossiped about them in his own delightful way, and he could not have failed to hear of them, had they been taken, for nowhere is rumour more fleet than by a riverside among anglers.

Sir Herbert Maxwell included a 53½lb salmon killed on the fly in 1873 on his list of four Tweed 50-pounders, but I have not made an entry for this fish because we do not know the name of the fortunate angler, nor do we know where it was caught on the river.

Another reference to Colonel Home's fish is made on page 263 of *Rod & Gun*, published on 26 November 1892:

> A fine Tweed salmon has been received as a present to the Sergeants' Mess 1st Battalion Grenadier Guards, now stationed at Windsor, from Colonel the Hon. W. S. D. Home, late Commandant of the battalion, and now of the regiment. The weight of the fish was 51½lbs.; the length 51 inches and the girth 28 inches. The head has been sent for preservation to Mr. Bainbridge, of Eton, and will be another addition to the many objects of interest belonging to the Sergeants' Mess.

On page 271 in the same magazine we are told that the fish took a Jock Scott fly of medium size in the Birgham Dub.

GENERAL HOME'S
51½lb TWEED SALMON
——— No. 51 ———

Ten years after catching his first 51½lb Tweed salmon, Colonel Home had been promoted to the rank of General and caught another. The General's fish was recorded in *Where to Fish* (1937) and on page 141 of John Ashley-Cooper's *The Great Salmon Rivers of Scotland*.

Those lucky enough to fish famous beats where portmanteaux salmon have been caught often like to know the exact location, i.e. the name of the pool, because awareness of such a detail greatly adds to the pleasure of fishing. In this instance, the fish was killed on a Jock Scott fly in Birgham Dub in 1902 (also mentioned by John Ashley-Cooper in his *A Line on Salmon*).

DR E. FISON'S
51½lb TWEED SALMON
No. 52

We know from *Game Fish Records* (1936) and *Where to Fish* (1937) that Dr Fison killed a 51½lb salmon on the River Tweed at Norham in October 1922. The length was 50½in and the girth 27in. I discovered a photograph of the fish in *The Illustrated London News* of 11 November 1922 but have been unable to verify that it was caught on a fly. Although I have known many medical men who are salmon fishers, I can't recall one who was a bait fisherman, so I have given him the benefit of the doubt.

The Norham beat fishes best in low or lowish water. Bridge pool, shown here, is being fished from a boat whereas immediately above the bridge wading is normal

Although Dr Fison's fish was caught in October, it seems to be a fresh-run silver cock salmon

MR BAINBRIDGE JUNIOR'S
51½lb NAMSEN SALMON
—— No. 53 ——

When Malcolm Greenhalgh sent me a batch of transparencies, included among them was a a 57½lb Namsen salmon caught on fly by G.B. Bainbridge (No. 143). He also included a very fine photograph he had taken of a half-carving of a 51½lb salmon that had been caught by Mr Bainbridge's son at Grong, also on the River Namsen, some weeks before his father caught the monster fish on 29 June 1937. If it is a case of 'like father like son', then it is likely, but not certain, that Bainbridge's son caught his fish on the fly.

L. FERGUSON'S
52lb CUMBERLAND DERWENT SALMON
—— No. 59 ——

In *Game Fish Records* (1936), on page 15, Jock Scott tells us that the largest salmon caught on rod and line in the Cumberland Derwent was a 52lb fish taken on fly by Mr L. Ferguson in 1885.

Arthur Ransome, the famous author of children's books, was devoted to salmon fishing on the Derwent, on which river – late in life – he learnt to Spey cast. Among other beats, he fished the Ribton stream on the Petworth Castle Estate. I have also fished on this stream, as a guest of the syndicate that included the late Hugh Falkus, that great advocate of Spey casting.

COLONEL JAMES THORPE'S
52lb AWE SALMON
—— No. 60 ——

Augustus Grimble records on page 88 of his fine book *The Salmon Rivers of Scotland* (1913) that Thorpe had a fish of 52lb out of Inverawe Cruive, probably in the 1880s, and that he had had several fish from the same pool between 36lb and 39lb, but tantalisingly never quite 40lb. The fish must have been caught on fly because fly was the only method permitted in Breadalbane's Syndicated Water.

The famous Cruive pool on the River Awe, where Colonel James Thorpe caught his big fish

EDMOND W. DAVIS'
52lb GRAND CASCAPEDIA SALMON
—— No. 61 ——

In his book *Salmon Fishing on the Grand Cascapedia*, which was privately published in 1904, Edmond Davis provides a clear appraisal of the quality of Canada's finest salmon river:

> The salmon of the Grand Cascapedia average more in weight than those of
> any other river in Canada. Although the majority of the fish taken run from

20 to 33lb, many are killed that weigh from 33 to 38lb, and even as high as 43 to 45lb is not unusual; but when one overtops the 45lb mark, congratulations are extended along the line to the lucky angler. Every year there are one or two 47 or 48lb fish landed, and some seasons I have known as many as four or five of these enormous fish to be brought to the gaff. The 50lb salmon are quite rare, although I was most fortunate, in the season of 1900, in taking one of 51lb, and the following year another of 52.

As is apparent from the narrative, Davis was a fly fisher rather than a bait fisher.

Of the many large fish I have taken of 40lb or more, I remember only three which seemed disinclined to give a bit of sport. The rest were wild, raving terrors. One of 44lb sprang clear out of the water, and, seizing the fly, in three successive leaps got halfway across the pool, with 40 or 50 yards of line cutting the water like a knife. Suddenly he turned, and, with a tremendous bound, sped away for freedom; but the delicate little fly held fast, and, with the rod bending like a bow and the reel singing its merry tune, we found ourselves flying along the current, chasing something which seemed almost uncanny. After a while we got close enough for the gaff, and by a quick stroke of the paddle the canoe shot forward, when James, sending the gaff deep into the shoulder, lifted the grand old salmon into the canoe. As most of my large salmon have given me some thrilling experiences, I prefer the killing of large fish. I remember hooking a 35lb salmon in the tail, and another of 42lb in the side. Had I lost these fish without seeing them, I should have thought something mighty had seized the fly. The one of 42lb took me half a mile down the river before I could land him, the fish was so large, and being hooked in the side it made it impossible to bring him to the canoe without losing a lot of time. So after wearing him out we paddled toward the middle of the river and gaffed him in the swift water; he was the hardest fighting salmon I ever killed.

An angler on the Cascapedia once played a salmon three and a half hours, and finally lost the fish by breaking the leader. I heard that another angler, after playing a salmon three hours, lost his fish in the same way. Both of these salmon were seen before they broke the casts, and were supposed to have been of extraordinary size. I knew the men of one of the canoes, and they told me that their fish would weigh 70lb.

They were both experienced canoemen, and no doubt believed the salmon to have been prodigious; but I think they were excited and over judged the weight of the fish, for I have never seen a salmon in the

Pool '4-24' at Middle Camp – so named because someone once caught four 24lb fish there in the same day – is essentially Cascapedian in character. Davis caught his fish on a Silver Grey fly in 'Big Curly' Pool

Cascapedia which I thought would weigh over 60lb, and I have looked in every pool at low water from lazy Bogan down. It is very uncertain judging the weight of a salmon in the water, especially if he is very long, for the longest are often the thinnest, which is always the case with the males. When salmon enter the river and are in good condition, they weigh nearly as many pounds as they are inches in length; of course there are exceptions.

I daresay that owning a private beat on the Grand Cascapedia when the river was in its prime must have been a real joy, and one senses from Davis' writing that he was a determined, clear-headed man, who deservedly landed two salmon, each weighing over 50lb (see entry No. 33 for details of his 51-pounder).

HENRY C. PHIPPS'
52lb GRAND CASCAPEDIA SALMON
—— No. 62 ——

One of a family who owned camps on Canada's Grand Cascapedia River, Henry Phipps caught his huge fish there, taking it from the Swallow's Nest pool in July, circa 1920. In *Grand Cascapedia Giants* (2005), Ronald Swanson has thoroughly investigated the big fish caught on that river, and since he documents Phipps' fish as 52lb, I shall do likewise. According to Swanson, Phipps caught another big fish, a 51-pounder, from the same pool (No. 36).

COLONEL N. DALRYMPLE HAMILTON'S
52lb ALTEN SALMON
—— No. 63 ——

Colonel Hamilton made a habit of catching huge salmon – four over 50lb on fly. This one – a beautifully proportioned fresh-run fish that would be every salmon angler's dream to catch – was taken on a 3/0 Red Jock fly at Vina Gore on the Alten River on 7 July 1926, and weighed 52lb.

Strangely, the Colonel does not look very happy in his photograph. Indeed, he looked decidedly unhappy every time he was photographed with a heavy fish. Roy Flury, who provided both the photograph and the details of the Colonel's catch, reckoned that in those days (the 1920s), it was considered bad form to smile at the camera – at least, it was for men. Perhaps Colonel Hamilton was peeved because he had caught eight fish and a grilse when, fishing a mile or two upstream that same night, the Duke of Westminster caught thirty-three salmon, averaging 24lb. Nevertheless, Hamilton was rarely outfished – the Duke's best fish weighed just 45lb! All the fish were caught on fly.

Perhaps Colonel Hamilton looks so peeved because he had caught eight fish and a grilse when, fishing a mile or two upstream that same night, the Duke of Westminster caught thirty-three salmon, averaging 24lb. Nevertheless, Hamilton was rarely outfished – the Duke's best fish weighed just 45lb! All the fish were caught on fly

CECIL McKENZIE'S
52½lb MARGAREE SALMON
── No. 68 ──

The *Fishing Gazette* of 1 October 1927 published an interesting account of the capture of the largest fish ever taken from the Margaree River in Canada:

52½LB. SALMON CAUGHT IN THE MARGAREE RIVER, NOVA SCOTIA

DEAR SIR – I think this item in enclosed paper might interest you. It refers to the 52lb salmon that was taken this week in the Margaree River, which is in Victoria Country, Cape Breton, N.S. The river has given some very fine fishing this season, both salmon and trout. It is 20 or more miles in length, and there are no leased pools on the river. Free for *all* fishermen. Fish are only allowed to be taken with fly. – Yours truly. GEO H. CHISLETT

North Sydney, N.S. September 7, 1927

Much obliged to Mr. Chislett for kindly sending this cutting from the *Sydney Post*, September 7, 1927. Our readers will remember an article about the Margaree river published in The *Fishing Gazette* of June 4, 1927:-

Record Salmon Taken at Margaree: Fish Weighing 52½lb, Killed.
According to a report given to A. G. McLeod, Inspector of Fisheries for Cape Breton, a salmon weighing 52½lb., length 42 in., girth 30in. was hooked and brought to gaff by Cecil McKenzie, of Saint John, N.B. The salmon rose to a Silver Grey fly in one of the Big Intervale pools and as might be expected, gave the angler desperate battle. This is the heaviest salmon ever taken with rod and line from the Margaree. The previous record for big fish taken in the vale stream, and that a rather hazy one, was a 48½-pounder killed in one of the pools more than a quarter of a century ago. Some two years ago Duncan McKenzie landed a 40-pounder from Plaster Rock Pool. The recent storm partly destroyed nets at the mouth of the stream, with the result there are many salmon in the pools.

(The weight of this fish does not seem in proportion to the measurements. By Sturdy's scale the weight of a salmon 42in. in length is 31.759lb. Again, the condition factor, according to the weight and length mentioned in the report, is the extraordinary figure of 70, whereas the average condition factor in European waters is in the neighbourhood of 49, and on certain rivers, i.e. the Shannon, as high as 46. We think that a mistake must have been made in the measurements. – EDS.)

VISCOUNT DUNGARVAN'S
53lb NAMSEN SALMON
—— No. 74 ——

ere is another example of a big salmon caught by a Briton in Norway. This fish was caught near Grong on the Namsen River on 29 June 1888. I assume that it was caught on fly, that being the method in common use in the last half of the 19th century. A woodcarving of this fish was probably made by J.B. Russell. Russell's carvings can be identified by the fact that some details are often painted on.

A wood carving of the Hon. D. Leigh's fish, probably by J.B. Russell, made soon after its capture. Details of the head and gill were painted on, as was one of the pectoral fins.

HON. D. LEIGH'S
53lb NAMSEN SALMON
—— No. 75 ——

n 30 June 1888, the Hon. D. Leigh caught his fish near Grong on the Namsen River. Although the method of capture is not forthcoming, it could have been caught on fly. Fishermen were unable to cast Devons or similar baits any distance in a big river, whereas wading with an 18ft fly rod gave access to most fish-holding pools. Roy Flury believes that Leigh's fish was caught harling, which raises a serious question. When details of a big-fish catch are published and we learn that such and such a salmon was caught on fly, we have no means of telling whether the fly was cast in the usual way or whether it was harled. Although the problem does not arise on narrow or medium-sized rivers, harling has long been part of a boatman's repertoire on big rivers, such as the Shannon, Tay and Tweed.

Lord Blythswood's 53lb cock salmon, together with the rod used to catch it, from P.D. Malloch's Life-History and Habits of the Salmon Sea-Trout, Trout, and other Freshwater Fish.

LORD BLYTHSWOOD'S
53lb TAY SALMON
No. 76

On page 296 of *The Salmon Rivers of Scotland* (1913), Augustus Grimble gives details of a 53lb salmon caught on a Black Dog fly:

Black Dog

> In 1899, Lord Blythswood, who has a long experience of the Tay, had the Islamouth beat of Stobhall, with one on Taymount as well, so that he had fishing every day in the week. In twenty-three days he got 130 fish to his own rod, the largest of which was one of 53lb., hooked in the lower end of Sandyford Pool by a moderate-sized Black Dog. In the same period, Lord Blythswood's guests had ninety-eight others, Mr. Herbert Praed getting a day of twenty-two fish headed by one of 43lb. The whole of these fish were caught by the fly and casting; and on all the well-stocked autumn reaches. harling is now only resorted to on those pools which cannot be fished in any other way.
>
> Lord Blythswood is strongly of the opinion that the Tay angling has been slowly but surely deteriorating ever since the netting time was extended in 1862 from the 21st to the 26th of August. To the uninitiated a week more or less may not seem of much account: but in one week there are often several thousands of fish netted, which if spared would give a splendid stock of spawners to the upper waters.

Grimble's reference to Lord Blythswood having 'the Islamouth beat of Stobhall with one on Taymount as well' is a bit confusing. Taymount (left bank) and Stobhall are two sides of the same river. Islamouth is immediately above these but includes both banks. Technically, Sandyford pool is now on the Islamouth beat.

River Tay at Taymount, opposite Stobhall where Lord Blythswood's 53-pounder was caught in 1899. Blythswood and his guests had 228 fish in twenty-three days.

W.G. CRAVEN'S RECORD
53lb SPEY SALMON
No. 77

The lower Spey has produced many large rod-caught salmon and Gordon Castle water is pre-eminent in this respect. Mr Craven caught his record fish on this beat in 1897. The *Daily Mail* mentioned it on 7 September 1904 but a description had already been published. A.E. Gathorne-Hardy wrote *The Salmon* in 1898, including a vivid account of the proceedings, which lasted only fifteen minutes – amazing, given the size of the fish.

Although he fought gallantly [the fish] was killed in a quarter of an hour.

Mr Craven, who was fishing at the Dallachy Pool, not more than a mile from the sea, with a small No. 4 Carron fly, with lemon body, silver twist and black hackle wing, tied on a double hook, on a double gut cast with four feet of single, observed the fish rising behind a sunken stone and beyond the rapid stream from which he was casting, the rise, as is frequently the case with very large fish, being only indicated by the swirl of the water. From this position he could only reach him by casting his fly into the comparatively slack water beyond the stream, and allowing it to be dragged past his nose in a manner quite contrary to the rules of casting. Three times this was done without success, but on the fourth occasion there was a wave on the water and a hard pull, and in a second away went 40 yards of line downstream. Mr Craven was beginning to think of the boat 200 yards below, when the fish suddenly stopped and gave two or three unpleasant tugs; but being very firmly hooked, he allowed himself to be reeled slowly up, and enabled his captor to get ashore. He then made for his old resting place and began to sulk, but not for long, as he quickly went upstream as fast as he had come down it, and it became a labour of difficulty to keep above him.

At this point a disagreeable grating feeling indicated that the line was rubbing against the edge of the shingle between the rod and the deep water and it was necessary to take to the water again and get the line perpendicularly over him as he again stopped. At this point Mr Craven first realised what a monster he had hooked, for although the rod was apparently pointing directly over the fish, the line suddenly ran out at full speed. This was because having drowned the line under the heavy stream, the salmon was trying to ascend a small 'draw' on the far side of the river and there he showed himself struggling in about eight inches of water. The strong tackle bore the strain well; the sunken part of the line was successfully reeled up, and but for the bend of the rod, the line was once more horizontal between fish and angler. Now a slow, steady pull not only checked his career, but drew him back with a splash into the deep and the line was reeled up short, so that when he had been carried a little way down he came into the slack water, where fisherman and gaffer were waiting for him, but just out of reach.

This was repeated twice, but the third time, with two or three more feet reeled up, he came well within reach, and the steel went into him just above the dorsal fin, the left hand came to the rescue of the overtaxed right, and W. Davidson, who had not uttered a syllable during the fifteen minutes contest, broke the silence with the exclamation: 'The biggest fish I have ever taken out of the Spey...' His length was four feet one and a half inches, and his girth two feet five; a male fish, rather coloured but perfect in shape and condition. The subsequent examination of the tackle showed that the risk of losing him had been considerable as the reel line was cut a quarter through where it had grated against the shingle, and had to be removed as untrustworthy, and one strand of the double gut eye of the fly was severed and standing out at right angles.

J.M. OLDHAM'S
53lb NORTH ESK SALMON
No. 78

Jock Scott mentioned this big salmon caught on fly on page 168 of his *Game Fishing Records* (1936). He had received details from a correspondent who contributed to the *Fishing Gazette* under the pseudonym 'Greek Nymph':

> Apparently the largest rod-caught salmon for the North Esk – at all events within the last 40 years – was one of 53lb., caught by Mr. J. M. Oldham on the Middle Morphie Waters with a fly. This occurred in either 1901 or 1902.

CHARLES B. BARNES'
53lb GRAND CASCAPEDIA SALMON
No. 79

On 23 June 1911 Charles Barnes was the winner of a competition organised by *Field and Stream* with his 53-pounder, a model of which adorns Lorne Cottage. According to Ronald Swanson in *Grand Cascapedia Giants* (2005), the fish fought for forty-five minutes before succumbing after a dramatic chase in a canoe. Barnes was eighty-two years old at the time. He is credited with another fish that weighed over 50lb, which he caught five years earlier (No. 34).

SIR STUART COATES'
53lb TAY SALMON
No. 81

Although the above fish was reported in *Where to Fish* (1926), it wasn't until I read Arthur Oglesby's *The Big Fish* (1992) that it became clear Sir Stuart caught his fish on a fly. Oglesby reproduced a report dated 23 October 1923, which I presumed came from either the *Fishing Gazette* or *The Field*.

> The record salmon taken on the Tay this season measured 49in. in length and 29in. in girth. It was hooked with a 'Dusty Miller' 6/0 on the last day of the season in the 'Pot Shot', Cargill water of the Tay, by that ardent and skilful fisher Sir Stuart Coates, Bart, of Ballathie and was landed after a fight of thirty-five minutes duration. It was a very shapely male fish and in exceptionally fine condition for the time of year. The salmon is half an inch greater in girth than the 64lb record salmon caught by Miss Ballantine at Caputh on the Tay in October last year. This is the second fish of over 50lbs that Sir Stuart Coates has caught, a feat seldom equalled by any fisher.

Eventually I found the original report in the *Fishing Gazette* dated 1 December 1923 in the form of a caption:

THE HEAVIEST TAY SALMON FOR 1923 SEASON

Weight, 53lb.; length, 49in.; girth, 29in. Caught by Sir Stuart Coates, Bart., on October 15, 1923.

(Mr. Gilbert Malloch, of Perth, who kindly sends the photograph reproduced above, points out that this is the second time Sir Stuart Coates has caught a salmon over 50lb. This fish was taken on Dusty Miller Fly 6/0 in Pot Shot, Cargill, River Tay, and landed in 35 minutes. The girth is ½in. greater than that of Miss Ballantine's 64lb salmon – ED)

The Pot Shot pool on Cargill water, River Tay where Sir Stuart Coates caught a 53lb cock fish on a 6/0 Dusty Miller on 15 October 1923, the last day of the season. The fish had a girth 1/2" larger than the 64lb salmon caught by Miss Ballantine the year before

MAJOR B.D. CORBET'S 53lb ALTEN SALMON
No. 82

This was the first of Bertie Corbet's two big salmon caught on fly, both taken from the Alten River. It weighed 53lb and he killed it on 24 July 1923 on the Joraholmen beat at Alta. His second big fish, caught in 1928, weighed 50lb (No. 14). Both fish appear in the Alten and Roxburghe records.

O.M. PRITCHARD'S
53lb TAY SALMON
—— No. 83 ——

M r Pritchard caught his fish in the Lower Scone beat on 15 October 1924. Apart from the measurements, i.e. length 51½in, girth 29in, we know little else about the capture. It is odds on that the fish was caught on or near Bleachings pool (where the cotton pieces from Stanley Mill used to be washed and then sun bleached on the stones along the bank on Lower Scone).

THE 8TH DUKE OF ROXBURGHE'S
53lb ALTEN SALMON
—— No. 84 ——

W hen Roy Flury was invited by the present Duke to visit Floors Castle, the family home near Kelso, to inspect the Roxburghe Records, he was able to glean the following information:

> The 8th Duke was an exceptional fisherman and was devoted to the Alten. He had taken over the lease of the river from the Corbet family in 1909 and apart from the World War 1 years he visited the river most years including the year he died, 1932. His father had fished Alten as a young man with *his* father but as he became older he became disinterested and the lease was allowed to lapse. It was taken over in 1890 by H. R. Corbet followed by Reginald Corbet.
>
> The Duke and his party travelled by boat from Newcastle to Norway at the end of June and usually fished throughout July.
>
> On the 23rd July 1928 he caught his largest salmon, a fish of 53 lbs from the Gönges pool. Strangely his good friend Bertie Corbet caught a 50 lb fish the same night. Both fish were caught on a 1/0 Red Dusty Miller. A model of the Duke's fish was carved and hangs at Floors Castle, Kelso.

The 8th Duke made 16 visits to Alten each lasting about a month. He caught 1091 salmon including one of 53 lbs and seven others over 40 lbs. All on fly.

The boat in which Clare de Burgh and two ghillies descended the Svartfoss rapids on 9 July 1968 in pursuit of a 53lb fish

CLARE DE BURGH'S 53lb ALTEN SALMON
No. 86

In his bright little book *Salmon Stories*, Jack Chance tells us that a 53lb salmon was caught on the Alten (or Alta) River by an Englishwoman, but for reasons unknown to us, he fails to identify her.

On 9 July, 1968, when fishing the River Alta in Northern Norway as the guest of an American friend, an English lady hooked a fish at 3 am by the light of the midnight sun. She was using a yellow "Bucktail" tube fly and a 12-ft split-cane rod. The river was high, at 2ft on the gauge, and the struggle which followed is worthy, in my view, of a detailed description.

Svartfossnakken pool lies just above the Svartfoss rapids, where boats must be hauled overland. Salmon lie at the head of the rapids where they are clearly seen as they rise to the fly. The boat is allowed to drift down the pool to the head of the rapids, a perilous operation in water rapidly gaining in speed and force. If a hooked fish chooses to descend the rapids, its chances of survival are almost certain, since, except in high water, a boat cannot follow.

Although of poor quality, this photograph shows the main actors in the dramatic capture of Clare de Burgh's 53lb fish from the Alten: the 'two young virile ghillies' – Tormod Mosesen (seated) and Helge Jakobsen, holding a fish – and Clare de Burgh, who is standing beside the big fish with a glass of whisky in her hand

On this momentous night the lady angler had two young, virile ghillies as oarsmen, both able to speak a little English.

After an hour's play in the pool, the fish moved into the main current and down the Svartfoss rapids it rushed. None of the older ghillies would have faced the boisterous descent which followed. Indeed, in living memory, the ordeal had only once been achieved. Instructed to lie down, the brave lady did so as the boat accelerated backwards down the white water with the outboard motor flat out and the oarsmen pulling as hard as they could against the current. She clearly recalls that her fear was alleviated slightly by her efforts to recover the backing on to her reel.

After 2¼ hours the fish was seen for the first time and came within reach of the gaff. At the first attempt the gaff broke and off went the salmon again.

Happily, because the return of the party to the lodge was by now several hours overdue, other ghillies were on the alert. A larger gaff was soon forthcoming and the prize was brought ashore at 6 am, 4½ miles downstream from the point at which it had been hooked.

It could not be weighed until the following afternoon because the lodge scales did not exceed 50 lbs. Luckily, the late Duke of Roxburghe, staying at the next Lodge downstream, was able to record a weight of 53 lbs. It was a cock fish. 52" long and 29" in girth. Scale tests showed it to be nine years old, four of which had been spent in the river and five at sea.

Its captor modestly attributes her success to her two young Norwegian ghillies, but for whose courage and skill this story might have ended in disaster.

Roy Flury came to the rescue with the following note, dated 7 June 2005.

Clare de Burgh on 9/7/1968 was fishing with boatmen Tormod Mosesen and Helge Jakobsen, using a 12ft cane rod, Yellow Bucktail tube fly, when she hooked her fish. After two and a half hours and a four-mile journey downstream, the fish was finally landed. It was not weighed until the following day – 53lbs. When it was taken down to the Sandia Camp and the Duke of Roxburghe heard the story, he was very displeased with the boatmen.

The legend reads: 'Salmon Male 54lbs, Caught with Fly on Finford Stream Taymount Water by Lord Ruthven Oct. 4th 1883. Length 4ft 2in, Girth 2ft 4in'

LORD RUTHVEN'S
54lb TAY SALMON
No. 94

The *Fishing Gazette* of 14 November 1903 reported Lord Ruthven's big fish as having been caught in *circa* 1880. According to Jock Scott on page 199 of *Game Fish Records* (1936), Lord Ruthven caught his fish in Finford stream on Taymount water in 1884, and the fish was set up and presented to the Perth Museum. Augustus Grimble was more forthcoming in his extraordinarily detailed book *The Salmon Rivers of Scotland* (1913) page 297, and it turns out that Jock Scott got the date wrong:

> On the 4th of October 1883, Lord Ruthven took a very heavy fish from the Finford Pool of Stobhall, a little below Taymount – a cock fish fifty inches long and thirty in girth. His captor writes:-

> "We had nothing heavy enough to weigh him with at the riverside, so he was taken into Perth Railway Station, and weighed next day a trifle over 54lb., so he must have weighed considerably more when first taken out of the water. He was a very dull fish, and never showed after he was hooked. The fly was a No. 2 Jock Scott, and we landed him in about half an hour."

Fortunately for the purposes of research, collecting cased fish and carved fish, which have no personal connection with the collector, is a pastime that has developed considerably during the last thirty years, becoming a passion for some. Ron Swanson from Key Biscayne in Florida is one of the most prominent and knowledgeable collectors. In Britain, Richard Pratley of Worcester had an incredible collection of cased fish when I last went to see him. In pursuit of Lord Ruthven's fish, no longer in the Perth Museum, I went to Taymount House, which is owned by William Lindsey. The estate, including the house and the fishings, was a gift from Lord Murray to William's great great grandmother. The current tenant, Robert Walker, showed me the cased fish and kindly allowed me to photograph it.

Finford Stream is one of the most productive pieces of fly water on the lower Tay. It can be waded from the left bank for some sixty yards or fished right down to the end of the pool from a boat. Lord Ruthven fished it when the river was apt to produce very big fish

*Robert Dun with his 54lb fish caught in Dun's Pool on the Grand
Cascapedia on 29 June 1886 using a No.1 Silver Grey fly*

ROBERT DUN'S
54lb SALMON FROM
THE GRAND CASCAPEDIA
No. 95

Robert Dun, co-founder of Dun & Bradstreet, international assessors of financial
standing, caught his salmon in Dun's pool on the Grand Cascapedia on 29 June
1886, using a No. 1 Silver Grey fly. I first came across it in *Game Fish Records* (1936) but
Ron Swanson in his *Grand Cascapedia Giants* (2005) gives a lot more detail, as he does on
other of Dun's big salmon.

The angler seen wading is fishing the Cruive pool (the name comes from the Gælic for trap) on Argyllshire's River Awe. From Grimble's account we know that the 54lb fish took the schoolmaster through every pool before it was finally landed on the very lowest pool of the river

THE SCHOOLMASTER'S
54lb AWE SALMON
No. 96

In *The Salmon Rivers of Scotland* (1913), on page 88, Augustus Grimble tells how in 1887 he was fishing on the River Awe when he walked up to and passed a fisherman who was playing a fish:

> The schoolmaster at Taynuilt had one of 54 lb out of Cassan Dhu, the top pool of the hotel water, and fully a mile from the sea. I was out that day and met him at the Clay Pool on my way up stream; the fish was still going very

strongly. "Foul hokit!" cried he as we passed, and little thinking he was fighting such a giant, and incited to fresh exertions by the sight of my straight rod and his bent one, I, unluckily, did not turn back to see the end of the fight, which eventually finished at Crubeg, the lowest pool on the water, and out of which it is impossible to follow a fish making for the sea.

This was a right good performance, of which anyone might fairly be proud; only a tall active man could have carried it through, as in following from the Otter Pool into the Stepping Stones the water was up to the school-master's chin, and at this part of the fight a man five inches shorter would probably have been beaten. Those of my readers who know the Taynuilt Hotel water will recognize I have not said one word too much about this remarkable feat. I also had the luck one day to get a splendid June fish of 38 lb. out of the Long Pool, and as I was alone and had to gaff it for myself in deep water, I went home with my tail cocked!

We must assume that the schoolmaster's fish was caught on a fly, because it was caught on fly-only water. John Ashley-Cooper in *A Line on Salmon* confirms it and names the pattern as the Childers.

FRED MILBURN'S
54lb SHANNON SALMON
No. 97

A comprehensive list of big salmon caught on the fly was published in the *Fishing Gazette* on 14 November 1903. The largest known Irish rod-caught salmon taken on the fly came from the River Shannon in 1903. Frustratingly, the author of the piece was unable to supply the name of the captor but luckily I discovered the angler's name in an article published by the *Daily Mail* of 4 September 1904. In the article, written by the Duke of Richmond and Gordon commemorating epic struggles with salmon, we read that a salmon weighing 54lb was killed by Mr Fred Milburn on the River Shannon and a carving of the fish, carried out at Fochabers and painted by Miss Russell, also of Fochabers, was shown at the Cork Exhibition in 1903. No location on the Shannon was indicated but as like as not it was caught at Castleconnell or thereabouts.

HENRY NADEAU'S
54lb GRAND CASCAPEDIA SALMON
No. 98

enry Nadeau, who lived in the village of Cascapedia, caught his fish in the Judge's pool on the Grand Cascapedia River in 1920. Although a number of different weights, including 53lb and 54lb, have been recorded for this fish, one fact is not disputed – it was a hen fish. Hen fish exceeding a weight of 50lb are exceedingly rare. One authority states that, according to the Lorne Cottage log, the salmon was caught by a guide.

Henry Nadeau and his daughter Norma pose with Nadeau's mighty 54lb fish caught on the Cascapedia in 1920. Very unusually for a salmon of this size it was a hen.

A.J. Hall, a taxidermist from Romford, possesses a very old cast of a 54¹/₂lb River Tay salmon of unknown provenance. He thinks it could be two hundred years old. Does it take too big a stretch of the imagination to believe that it could be the cast of Mackintosh's fish?

ALEXANDER MACKINTOSH'S 54½lb TAY SALMON
No. 106

In 1765, when Alexander Mackintosh caught a huge fish in the River Tay, it was probably the first time that a salmon weighing over 50lb had been landed on rod and line – certainly the first time such a feat was recorded in print. It pre-dates Captain Cotter's 59-pounder, caught in 1840, by at least seventy-five years.

The fish is mentioned by John Buckland in his introduction to a reprint of Kelson's *The Salmon Fly*, published by the Flyfisher's Classic Library in 1995. Buckland is discussing what tackle was like when Kelson was young:

> There is no doubt that in his youth tackle was crude and heavy, long casting was precluded by the style of the line and the friction in the rod rings. The choice of flies for salmon was small, stylized and supported by dubious logic. Reels were probably too small and were certainly too poorly engineered to give good control of a strong and determined fish. Mackintosh's 54½-pounder from Castle-Menzies, which he relates in 'The Driffield Angler' in 1821, and caught in 1765, must have been a Homeric struggle attended by more than a fair share of luck. Equally the Scots fishers with their wooden pirn attached to their waist belt (and not the rod) must have had interesting moments trying to subdue any fish, let alone big fish.

In the first edition of *The Driffield Angler* (1806), Mackintosh mentions on page 2:

> ...in the sixth year when they have attained their growth, are thought worthy of the name Salmon: their greatest magnitude is much the same in all parts of Europe, the largest weighing from thirty to sixty pounds. I caught one when angling with the fly at Castle-Menzies in the year 1765, that weighed fifty-four pounds and a half.

In the 1808 edition, Mackintosh elucidates a little more – as detailed by Jack Chance in *Salmon Stories* (1983) – mentioning that he caught the huge fish on a Black Dog fly. John Ashley-Cooper, having noticed the dressing, made an interesting comment on it in the chapter he wrote for Douglas Sutherland and Jack Chance's book *Trout and Salmon Flies* (1982):

> *Wings:* Bluish feather from a heron wing, with spotted reddish turkey tail feather.
> *Body:* Lead coloured pig's wool.
> *Throat and hackle:* Large black cock's hackle.
> *Head:* Dark green mohair.

Would such a dressing, in spite of its longevity, not be perfectly effective for killing salmon in these modern days? Incidentally, Macintosh [sic] mentions that he caught a salmon of fifty-four-and-a-half pounds at Castle Menzies (on the Tay near Aberfeldy) on a fly in 1765. It is the large weight of this fish rather than the fact that it was caught on fly which is brought into prominence in his story. This would seem to indicate that fly fishing in Scotland at that date was a common enough practice.

Castle Menzies, where Prince Charles Edward Stuart (Bonnie Prince Charlie) stayed for two nights in 1746 – the same year he was defeated at Culloden. Could Alexander Mackintosh, who caught his giant fish on the Castle water have been alive at the time?

SIR JOHN BENNETT LAWES'
54½lb AWE SALMON
—— No. 107 ——

On page 88 of Augustus Grimble's *The Salmon Rivers of Scotland* (1913), we read that Sir John took a 54½lb salmon out of Pol Verie pool on the River Awe. This beat, owned by Lord Breadalblane, was a strictly fly-only water, so although he does not specifically say so, I must conclude this fish was taken on the fly.

ALEXANDER GRANT'S
55lb GARRY SALMON
—— No. 108 ——

In *Game Fish Records* (1936), Jock Scott refers to a 55lb salmon that Alexander Grant caught in the River Garry in September 1887, at the outlet of Loch Quoich, using a Thunder and Lightning fly.

The rocky and swift River Garry, now with a hydro electric dam taking much of its water, at the top near the outflow from Loch Quoich where in September 1887, Alexander Grant caught a 55lb fish

Alexander Grant was undoubtedly the best salmon distance fly caster of his day. His name is associated with the Grant Vibration rod, in which the timbers that made up the joints, put together with patent splice, were tuned in much the same way as a musical instrument. Grant was a controversial figure and arguments he pursued in the press developed into rancour during the last decade of the nineteenth century. Nevertheless, despite his small build (the previous record holder, John Enright, was a giant in comparison), he beat all his challengers. When asked to what he attributed his great manual dexterity in handling an 18ft or 20ft fly rod, he answered, 'When I was young I went into forestry. Swinging a 7lb axe is the finest training you can have.'

Grant was different from most in that his long-distance casting and fish-catching ability were successfully married. He was able not only to reach fish that others could not but catch them too. Moreover, he was able to demonstrate this skill in front of an audience at times. His greatest achievement was, of course, catching his 55-pounder from the Garry.

MR BRERETON'S
55lb TWEED SALMON
No. 109

On page 234 in *British Freshwater Fishes*, Sir Herbert Maxwell gives a list of four large salmon that were caught on fly in the River Tweed. Included in the list is a fish of 55lb caught by Mr Brereton in the Willowbush run at Mertoun (a favourite cast of Scrope's) in 1889. Brereton caught his fish on a small Wilkinson fly. The catch was reported in the *Fishing Gazette* of 14 November 1903.

Willowbush Run, now known as Willow Pool, on the Tweed below Mertoun House, the home of the Duke and Duchess of Sutherland

HON. VICTOR STANLEY'S
55lb GRAND CASCAPEDIA SALMON
—— No. 110 ——

The Hon. Victor Stanley, son of Lord Derby, the Governor General of Canada, caught his fish in the Big Camp pool on 13 June 1892.

In 1878, when the Marquess of Lorne was Governor General of Canada, he acquired all forty-five miles of the Grand Cascapedia River through his wife, who was a daughter of Queen Victoria. When that great sporting figure the Marquess of Lansdowne succeeded Lorne in 1883, he leased practically all the river and built a lodge at a place he called New Derreen, after his estate in the west of Ireland. Due to his sporting background in Ireland and Scotland, Lansdowne made fly fishing the only option and the rule still applies to this day. Lord Derby was the last governor allowed to rent the fishing rights for a paltry sum.

Stanley's big salmon has been recorded at different weights but the true weight is given in his own account – *A Memoir 1880–1893*. This memoir is one of three pieces, produced in pencil and not yet fully edited, thought to have been written in 1930. I have to thank Hoagy Carmichael (son of the musician) for providing me with a copy and Richard Pooley and Ian Cadell, relations of Stanley's Canadian wife Annie Pooley, for generously making Stanley's writings available. The following is an extract from the memoir:

> I was fishing the middle camp water without much success. Fish were fewer in the river that year (1892) and they were not taking very freely. It was a very hot morning [23 June] and I had fished down all the water that I was entitled to without even the satisfaction of a rise and was just about to give it up when, after the fly having been missed once, I was into a very big fish. He took me a mile and a half down the river and when (after many vicissitudes and anxiety untold – logs were being floated down the river from a lumber camp and whenever one came near him he tried to rub the line under it which necessitated, on no fewer than four occasions, the whole rod, reel and all, being held under the water till the log had floated by) he was finally gaffed, 2 hours and 20 minutes after being hooked, I saw that I had indeed got a big one. He proved to be 55 lbs. And I believe still remains a record for the river, at least he did only a few years ago.

In his third piece, Stanley elaborated on the above with a very well-written description of the battle with his biggest ever fish. These are the last paragraphs, which embellish the original account:

A little distance below us was another rapid with rocks in it that made our case next to hopeless: should he once take us down there. Nearer and nearer did he come in and Pat for the first time laid down his paddle and took up the gaff. But our salmon was still game and fought hard for his life. The clearness of the water enabled us at last to see what a size he was and more and more careful did I become, having learned from bitter experience that the proverb 'there's many a slip...' is applicable no less to fishing than to any other activity. Each time I got him close and began to think that victory was mine, a slight movement of the mighty tail sent him half way across the river again.

At last the supreme moment arrived. Slowly but surely he came within reach and this time the tail did not move. He was game to the last and had died fighting. When the gaff went in there was not a move. I had to lay down my rod to help lift him into the canoe, and then we saw indeed that we had a mighty prize. Luck had been on our side for, as we lifted him out of the water, the fly came away with the barb broken. It is before me now as I write, set in the lid of a silver matchbox, a souvenir of a great triumph.

I stepped out of the canoe onto the bank and got out my scales but they could only show that he was over 50 lbs. It was not until a couple of days later when we returned to civilization that he was properly weighed on a steel-yard and proved to be fifty-five pounds.

Colonel Sandeman, on whose splendid stretch of the Tay the Marquess of Zetland's big fish was killed

THE MARQUIS OF ZETLAND'S
55lb TAY SALMON
No. 111

The Marquis of Zetland caught this fish on a Claret Major fly when he was fishing the Mill stream at Stanley Mill on Tayside. This information has been culled from P.D. Malloch's *Life-History and Habits of the Salmon Sea-Trout, Trout, and Other Freshwater Fish.* Stanley Mill is situated on the right bank about half a mile below one of the most famous pools on the river – Pitlochry pool on Upper Scone, traditionally fished on 15 January to celebrate (with bagpipes) the opening day of the season.

Keith Elliot, editor of *Classic Angling*, has sent me a cutting from the *Fishing Gazette* of 19 October 1895. It should be noted that names of pools on rivers sometimes change over the years.

A 55LB SALMON KILLED WITH THE FLY ON THE TAY

We have received the following very interesting note from Mr. James Temple:
DEAR MARSTON – Herewith a copy of a letter I have just received from Col. Sandeman, which may probably be useful for *Fishing Gazette.*

DEAR TEMPLE – The fish I wired you about was one of three, and a splendid specimen, the heaviest ever caught with fly as far as record goes 50in. in length; 30in. in girth; 55lb.; tail 14½in. broad. Caught by Lord Zetland in

The famous Stanley Cotton Mill showing the Mill stream and the Wash House pool, where the Marquis caught his big fish

the Dungeon Pool below Pitlochry Head, with a Claret Body. He made a rush to the land. The Marquis got out, when away he bolted, taking nearly all the line out. He was followed in the boat, and continued this for twenty-five minutes, when he was safely landed. He was cast in plaster, and photographed and sketched by Mr. Millais, for the *Field*. F. SANDEMAN

A week later, on 26 October, the *Fishing Gazette* published a full account of the capture of this fish together with some photographs:

The following particulars are from the *Dundee Evening Telegraph:* The record fish mentioned in the *Telegraph* as having been caught in Colonel Sandeman's Stanley waters by the Marquis of Zetland deserves more than a passing notice. A cast of him has been taken for his lordship by Mr. Malloch, of Perth. He has been sketched by Mr. Millais, son of the great artist, for the *Field*, while photos have been taken by Mr. Henderson, of Perth, to whose garden round the studio he was conveyed after being liberated from his plaster mould. The lordly monarch of the Tay was visited by many gentlemen

The Marquis of Zetland

and ladies at Mr. Malloch's establishment... He took a Claret Body fly in the Dungeon below Pitlochry Head, rendered famous by Leech's 'Briggs' in *Punch*, 1857, and allowed the Marquis to lead him for a time and to land, when away he rushed into the heavy stream, taking nearly 100yds. of line out. He then had to be followed by the boat, and was played back to near the bank when again the sportsman landed. The monster however made another run for freedom, taking away the line as before, but this time, just as the boat was being landed he turned up stream, and the remainder of the fight was from the shore, where the gaffing was safely performed by the head fisherman, after as gallant run and as good an exhibition of fisherman's skill as ever-lasted for thirty minutes in the wild and rapid Tay Hell's Hole. It is rather a strange coincidence that last year a gentleman killed a 50lb. fish on the same part of the river on the last day of the previous season.

W.A. KIDSON'S
55lb TWEED SALMON
No. 112

John Ashley-Cooper in *A Line on Salmon* (1983) lists a 55lb fish taken from the River Tweed in November 1913. He concludes that it must have been caught on a fly, since that is the only lure allowed on the Tweed in the autumn, and since I have been unable to find any other reference to this fish, I must defer to the maestro.

SIR W. BROMLEY-DAVENPORT'S
55lb RAUMA SALMON
No. 113

Bare details for this fish were gleaned from an entry in the *Fishing Gazette* on 26 June 1926:

FINE SALMON CATCHES IN NORWAY

> News has been received in Brogyntyn, their Shropshire seat, that Lord and Lady Harlech are enjoying good sport in Norway, where they travelled for three weeks' fishing. Lady Harlech has landed three salmon, weighing 93lb in the aggregate. Sir W. Bromley Davenport, their host, has landed a salmon weighing 55lb.

Doubtless the full story of Davenport's huge salmon will surface sometime in the future. Much earlier in his life he caught a 43-pounder on a fly, so I can hardly conceive that he would have caught his biggest fish on anything else. A piece he wrote about this fish, which was published in *Sport* 1885, came to my notice when it was reprinted in Arthur Oglesby and Lucy Money-Coutts' *The Big Fish* (1992). Davenport took ten pages to describe the battle he had with his second biggest salmon in the turbulent Rauma River and it is the best description of man versus salmon that I have ever read. Oglesby and Money-Coutts were equally impressed, saying: 'No description of fishing on a Norwegian salmon river can rival this epic account by W. Bromley-Davenport of Fiva on the Rauma.'

*Sir William Bromley-Davenport
weighing a fish*

MAJOR H.H.R. WHITE'S
55lb FUSTA SALMON
—— No. 115 ——

Major White was an outstanding killer of big fish. He caught his 55-pounder on the Fusta River in Norway on 23 June 1932 on a size 3/0 Silver Doctor fly. In 1925 he caught fifty-seven salmon on fly on the same river. Between 13 June and 7 July that same year he caught fish weighing 48lb, 47lb, 43lb and 40lb. I would dearly love to visit a member of his family and ask to look through their grandfather's or great grandfather's photograph album. If photographs of these fish still exist, what an eye-opener they would be – perhaps he caught them all on fly.

Silver Doctor

A LAPP'S
55lb TANA SALMON
No. 116

John Hunter-Gray, in a piece that he wrote for the *Flyfishers Journal* (Summer 1970, page 58), told an unusual but convincing story about the owner of a *fyellstue* (roadside inn) who was more interested in fishing than he was in inn-keeping.

> He regaled us during the long evenings with fascinating tales of Lapp life and fishing exploits. He himself had caught a mighty salmon of 72 lbs. He was fishing from the bank outside the inn – 'I hooked him, and he tore up the river, so I jumped into my boat, started the outboard engine and followed him upstream. After playing him for about 40 minutes I had him by the boat. I was alone and he was too big to gaff, so I tipped the boat and managed to float him into it. There was a lot of water in the boat and he thrashed about, so I sat on him and brought him home that way.'

Hunter-Gray then recounted a story about a big salmon that he had actually seen in the bottom of a boat.

> We stayed for about a month but did not fish every day, and during that time caught nineteen fish, and an occasional sea trout. More interesting were the fish we saw. The part of the river we fished was popular with the Lapps, and in passing we would always enquire of each other whether there had been any success. The international sign of thumbs up or down provided the answer. One day (or night for all I know) we passed an ancient Lapp who was playing a fish. On our return journey we shouted to him and he gave the thumbs up sign, but did not follow the usual practice of holding up his fish. We rowed over to him and discovered the reason. In the bottom of the boat lay the largest salmon I have ever seen. We later heard that it weighed over 25 kilos. Another time when fishing alongside a major in the Finnish army we watched him battle with a great fish for some 40 minutes, and then had the vicarious satisfaction of seeing him gaff a salmon which looked to be well over 50 lbs.

It is not possible to include the 72lb fish that was mentioned in a conversation, or the fish 'which looked to be well over 50lb', but the 55lb fish that lay in the bottom of the Lapp's boat and was seen by Hunter-Gray reeks of authenticity. Note that Hunter-Gray pointed out earlier in his article that 'the only feasible method of fishing the Tana is to harl' and 'although all manner of lures are used, the Lapps prefer to fish the fly, and the really big fish which we saw were practically all taken on the fly' – and therefore by harling.

ANTTI PARKKINEN'S 55lb ALTEN SALMON
No. 117

This fish appears in Tormod Leinan's list of salmon of 50lb plus caught on fly after the Second World War. Parkkinen, who is a Finn living in Helsinki, caught his fish on 26 July 1985 in the Ovre Sorrisniva pool on a Brooks' Sunray Shadow (tube) fly.

Antti Parkkinen with his big fish caught on a Brooks' Sunray Shadow tube on the Alten River on 26 July 1985

ESMOND BRADLEY MARTIN'S 55½lb or 53lb GRAND CASCAPEDIA SALMON

No. 123

Esmond Bradley Martin caught his 55½lb hen salmon on 27 June 1939 from Canada's classic salmon river, the Grand Cascapedia, on a size 8/0 Lady Amherst fly in New Derreen's Upper Jam Pool. Even though the fish was weighed at 53lb the day after it was landed and the outline carving describes it as 55lb, its weight is now considered to be 55½lb.

A Mr and Mrs Willett were photographed with Esmond Martin's fish

Lady Amherst

EINAR SUHR'S
55lb 9oz ALTEN SALMON
No. 124

This fish was recorded in *Í Storlaksens Rike*, which translates as *A Big Fish Empire*, by Eikeset Heitmann and Neilson, published by the Alta Association in 2001. The salmon was caught on fly in the Mikkeli pool on the River Alten on 1 August 1985.

Einar Suhr with his big salmon from the Mikkeli Pool on the Alten, 1 August 1985

Looking towards the Warwick Hall beat on the River Eden, where George Mackenzie's salmon of 56lbs was caught on a Jock Scott on 2nd November 1892

GEORGE MACKENZIE'S
56lb EDEN SALMON
No. 127

Initially, the only reference to George Mackenzie's big fish that I could find – apart from on a list of big salmon caught on fly, compiled by Henry Fennel and published in the *Fishing Gazette* on 14 November 1903 – was a note in the *Carlisle Patriot* of 25 October 1895:

> On Wednesday Mr. Fennel had a letter in the *Times* on the subject of big salmon. One of the three or four largest ever taken in this country was one of 56lb, caught in 1892, by Mr. G. Mackenzie with a small 'Jock Scott' fly, in the Eden.

Jock Scott

I do not know for certain but this may be the largest salmon ever caught in Britain on that most famous of all flies, the Jock Scott. Eventually I found another reference to Mackenzie's fish in *The Salmon Rivers of Scotland* (second edition, 1913), although Augustus Grimble spells Mackenzie differently.

> The record fish for the Eden was caught in Warwick Hall water at Holm gate Rocks by George McKenzie, a keeper in the employ of Mr. J. Carter Wood, the then lessee; it was caught with a fly on 2 November 1892, and scaled 56lb.; this fish was preserved and is still in Mr. Carter Wood's possession.

John Waller Hills' father rented the Warwick Hall beat at Corby on the River Eden from sometime in the 1880s until 1920, and it was during his tenancy that George Mackenzie, one of the Warwick Hall keepers, caught the 56lb salmon.

John Waller Hills, author of several angling classics, served his salmon-fishing apprenticeship on the river and wrote about his experiences in *My Sporting Life* (1904). To my mind, he found the right words to record the satisfaction achievable by those who have tried all methods but ultimately chose to fly fish, better than anyone else has ever done.

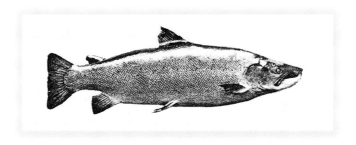

COLONEL A.E. SCOTT'S 56lb DEVERON SALMON
—— No. 128 ——

In the Notable Fish list published in *Where to Fish* (1937), a 56lb salmon is included, caught by Colonel A.E. Scott on 31 October 1920 on a 1in fly, in the River Deveron in Scotland. *The Illustrated London News* published a photograph of Scott's fish on 11 November 1922. Colonel Scott's salmon was 50in long with a girth of 29in. John Ashley-Cooper in *A Line on Salmon* (1983) tells us that it was caught on a size 1/0 Britannia fly. This makes sense since a 1/0 fly would give the rod a much better chance of landing the fish of this size.

MAJOR A.W. HUNTINGTON'S
56lb AWE SALMON
No. 129

There are many kinds of records in fishing but I suppose one of the unlikeliest is when a husband and wife each catch a salmon exceeding a weight of 50lb. The Huntingtons bought a beat on the River Awe in 1918 and in July 1921 the Major caught a 56lb fish on a size 3/0 Mar Lodge fly. It was 52½ in long and had a girth of 27½ In 1930, on the same river, he caught an exceptionally large female fish, weighing 52lb, also on fly (No. 39).

Gladys Huntington, according to Wilma Paterson and Peter Behan in *Salmon and Women* (1990), was a greatly experienced and successful salmon fisher, who could throw a long line Spey casting with a greenheart rod. She hooked a 55-pounder in the Errochd pool on the River Awe and landed it four hours later. Sadly, it proved to be foul-hooked. Her next best fish weighed 49lb, which she caught on the Brander pool on the Awe in 1933.

Mar Lodge

The Errochd pool, once owned by Gladys and Major A.W. Huntington, on the River Awe, where Major Huntington caught a 56lb fish on 8 July 1921 on a size 3/0 Mar Lodge

56lb salmon caught in the River Awe on June 12, 1923 by Mr H.G. Thornton

THORNTON'S BRACE OF 50-POUNDERS FROM THE AWE
No. 130

One angling achievement that has a genuine claim for inclusion in a book about the largest salmon caught on fly is the feat of one person catching a brace of 50-pounders on a fly. Thornton shared this achievement with only a handful of others: Major R.W. Huntington – also on the Awe, Henry C. Phipps, Edmund W. Davis and Charles B. Barnes on the Grand Cascapedia, Professor Merton on the Wye (although it is not certain that Merton's fish were caught on fly), Major Corbet and Colonel Hamilton (who caught four on the Alten).

Thornton's larger salmon was reported in the *Fishing Gazette* on 23 June 1923:

FINE 56 LB SALMON CAUGHT IN THE RIVER AWE.

Just as we are going to press I have received the following letter from Mr. G. D. Malloch, of Perth: -

DEAR MR MARSTON – Thinking it might be of interest I send you a photo of a beautifully-shaped and newly-run 56lb, River Awe salmon caught with fly on June 12 by H. G. Thornton, Esq., of Warmore, Dulverton, Somerset. On June 6 Mr. Thornton landed another beauty of 42lb., both of which we are setting up. – Yours faithfully,

GILBERT D. MALLOCH.

The *Fishing Gazette* report duly followed on 28 July 1923:

THE 56LB AWE SALMON.

As promised in THE FISHING GAZETTE of June 23, I have now much pleasure in giving a reproduction of the fine 56lb. salmon caught in the River Awe by Mr. H. G. Thornton, of Warmore, Dulverton, Somerset. Mr. Thornton had a 42-pounder to his credit six days before he landed the 56lb. fish on June 12. The latter was caught on a 5/0 Green Highlander with an 18ft - Grant rod. It was hooked in Pol Verie in heavy water at 1 p.m., and after a very strenuous fight through the roughest part of the Awe, was gaffed by Sam McIntyre at 3.30 p.m. Mr. J. D. Malloch, who kindly sent the photograph and particulars, also sent the following report on the scales from Mr. J. Arthur Hutton: -

DEAR MR. MALLOCH – Many thanks for the scales: 42lb., 46in. length, 27in. girth, hatched in 1918, two years in river and $3\frac{1}{4}$ years feeding in the sea. There are a few wider rings on the outside of the scales which I think indicate summer feeding in the sea just before the fish returned to the river. This is an especially well-shaped fish and heavy for its length. The "condition-factor" works out at $43\frac{1}{2}$ or $8\frac{3}{4}$ per cent. over Mr. Corbett's standard of 40. I understand that the Awe salmon are usually fairly heavy for their length, 55lb., and 52in. length, 29in. girth, hatched in 1917, two years in river and four years feeding in the sea. I cannot see any trace of feeding in the sea this year. The "condition-factor" works out at $39\frac{1}{2}$ or $1\frac{1}{4}$ per cent. below the standard. I shall be grateful for a photo of the big fish to add to my collection, – Yours sincerely, (Signed) J. A. HUTTON

In April 1940 *Game and Gun and Anglers' Monthly* published Thornton's own account of the capture of both of these huge salmon:

I have been the fortunate captor of two large salmon, weighing 56 and 51 pounds respectively, and had an experience with another. Two fifty-pounders caught in the British Isles by one rod is, I believe, a record shared by myself, Professor Merton and the late Major A. W. Huntington.

Major Huntington and I both caught our fish in the River Awe, Argyll, and Professor Merton his in the River Wye. I shall now tell the tale of my first 56 pound fish.

The River Awe is a short river running out of Loch Awe and flowing into Loch Etive; it is a very strongly flowing river, more than a very long cast across in many places; it is very rocky, and when in spate, tears along with a lot of white water showing. Its banks are rough going in many places, and when a good fish tries to go out of a pool, there is no stopping him, he uses

A cast of Thornton's 56lb fish made by Malloch's of Perth

all his might in the strong water and fights downwards all the time. In 1923 I began fishing on June 1st in good water conditions, and on the 4th had five salmon, 16 to 19 pounds, which is a very notable catch in the Awe.

On the 6th a 42 pound fish took a 3/0 "Bulldog", a perfectly shaped fish which was safely gaffed by Sam MacIntyre. I sent it off to Malloch to be set up, and it now adorns my bungalow on the Awe.

Better still was to come. On June 12th , after a rise in the water, I was fishing Pol Verie with a large "Green Highlander" in a drizzling rain, and near the tail of the pool I had a heavy dead pull, and nothing moved for a second or two; but when I lifted my rod (an 18ft spliced Grant) and put some strain on, the fish moved out into the waves, and after a turn upwards he went off downstream, boring right out of the pool into the Little Verie. Out of that he ran down the rapids which were in spate, which meant a run at top speed with my rod held right up, as high as possible to clear the rocks in that part. I had my line out beyond the backing, and the silk backing cutting into my fingers.

Green Highlander

I had not yet seen the fish, he was dropping behind the rocks as he went down, but I steadied him in the Stone Pool, drawing him as much to my side of the river as possible. Presently he took up a position behind a big rock which had the main current running on the far side of it. It would have been "goodbye" if he went that way, so I held him very hard and worried him for an hour. As the strain increased he moved out and I pulled him back again, always keeping upstream above him, and his head pointed to the cur-

Pol Verie on the River Awe, where on 23 June 1923 H.G. Thornton hooked the first of his two 50-pounders in the tail of the pool. Thornton was fishing with an 18ft spliced Grant rod and the fish took a 5/0 Green Highlander. Now tamed by a hydro-electric dam at its head, the Awe in spate must have been an awesome sight. The fish took Thornton 500 yards downstream, over a waterfall, and was landed after 2¹/₂ hours. It weighed 56lbs.

Grimble described the Awe in its heyday as 'the perfection of angling'. Only 3 miles long, it was 'From start to finish...nearly all quick, strong-running water, in which there is hardly fifty yards that is not broken with patches of white spray and foam, formed by the stream as it rushes over and round rocks and boulders'.

rent; side-strain moved him away, so had to be immediately corrected to a straight pull. The fish came nearer me and, but for a rock jutting out, Sam might have gaffed him. Once his head came up.

Things were looking better and, drawing him to my side, I let him down some series of falls not far from me, but I had a cliff above me and some bad scrambling under trees, but I was pretty confident now I should get him in the Bothy Pool. I had been letting him drop from fall to fall with a light strain on, so when he came to the Bothy he was still strong, and went right out into the heavy stream and out of the pool.

This had been difficult going for some time, but now I came to a grass track with no need to hurry, so I started swinging him to the side and going through the Three Ash Pools. I pulled him to my side, still upright in the water and, in a small quiet bay, drew him inwards. Sam, leaning over a rock, had a good chance to gaff him square, as his head rested between two small rocks. I caught Sam (aged nearly seventy) by the coat, so that he shouldn't fall in, and out he lifted the best fish of my life! A great fight lasting two and a half hours, and ending five hundred yards from where he was hooked. I took him into Taynuilt to be weighed roughly, and sent him off to Malloch of Perth to be set up, who made him 56 pounds the next day; the measurements were 52 inches long, 29 girth. Mr. Hutton said 2 years in the river and 4 years feeding in the sea.

Two ladies, who were looking on from the opposite bank all this time and had brought me luck, drove me to Taynuilt, and I took back a bottle of Giesler to celebrate!

Next day I lent my beat to a friend because I was so stiff in the shoulders. I recommend a long gaff on the Awe; here had been the chance for its use that might have ended the fight half an hour sooner. The power of a heavy salmon with the Awe in spate has to be experienced to be believed. It is a notorious river for the fighting powers of its fish; two out of three hooked and out on the bank is good going. Awe fish are short, thick, and small headed, and this one was fresh run from the sea about three miles away.

The *Fishing Gazette* of 5 May 1934 records the second and smaller fish caught by Mr Thornton in April 1934:

ANGLER'S SECOND 50 LB SALMON: IS IT A RECORD?

We have just heard from Mr. H. G. Thornton that he killed a magnificent salmon of 51 lb. on the River Awe on April 26. He has kindly sent a photograph which we hope to reproduce next week with further details. This is the second fifty-pounder caught by Mr. Thornton, as he had a salmon of 56 lb. from the Awe in 1923. We do not know of any other angler who has equaled this record of two fifty-pounders.

Thornton's personal account of the capture of his 56lb salmon continued with his account of the capture of the smaller fish. How nice it must be to be able to describe a 51-pounder as a smaller fish!

After renting the Breadalbane water on the Awe for nine years, the proprietor wanted more rent, so I gave it up and fished at Soval, Isle of Lewis, which is my property. But always I was thinking of the big fish in the Awe, and of my long rods which had lain idle for three years. I heard my Awe beat was for sale, so, after quick negotiations I secured it, with a very little land and the keeper's house. This was very thrilling for me!

I started on April 24th, 1934, earlier than was my usual custom, and got out my rod. Johnny MacIntyre, the Bonawe keeper, had an 18 pound fish, the first of the season in the Disputed, and next day I got one in the same pool on a Silver Devon, a proper beauty of 32 pounds. This was a nice start for my new ownership.

A day or two later I was fishing a prawn with my 18ft Castle Connel; the water was very heavy and I got nothing, but fancied I had a light touch in the Seal Pool. Next morning I tried Pol Verie, which proved a blank, and then moved up to the Seal about 150 yards above. Coming near the tail of it I had a hard pull at the spot exactly where I had an indication on the previous day.

There was no mistake this time, I was into a heavy fish, and I moved to the good going on the bank above, worked him to the head of the pool, and then to the tail again, and so on for some twenty minutes, everything going excellently and some heavy strain put in; but presently he had enough of that, and bolted out into the centre of the river, making for Pol Nugan rocks. However my ideas were different, and I swung him across to my side where, with a long gaff, John Jack my ghillie, might have had a chance; but the going there was bad, and Jack nearly took a bath. I called him out and let my fish down the falls, I going all out, full speed down the bank beside the long Verie falls, up a steep path onto the road above and holding up now quite easily above him, I steered him down the falls and then stood fast: with a heavy strain on, I brought him to my side in quieter water, plunging and splashing. Here I towed him towards the gaff which Jack got well home, and my fish was on the bank. I knew I had a whopper, but he was heavier than I thought, as he bumped down my 50lb scales; and when I took him to the village and station, I found he weighed 51 pounds.

This was beyond what I ever expected to do with big fish. It was eleven years since I had had the 56 pounder. I have a photograph of him, but no more setting up in a glass case! He measured 50 inches long and 27½ girth – hooked at 11.30 and killed at 12.10, quite quick time for a big fish.

Thornton's account of the capture of his 51-pounder indicates that it was caught on a prawn, albeit using a fly rod.

When I visited Argyllshire, in order to take photographs with which to illustrate the stories of a number of very large salmon caught in the River Awe, I was fortunate to meet Robert Campbell-Preston of Taynuilt, who is familiar with the river, its salmon pools and the salmon fishing. He told me where to locate the cast that Thornton had had made of his 56lb fish by Malloch's of Perth, and some hours later I found myself looking at the salmon at the Taychreggan Hotel, by Taynuilt.

The Stone pool on the River Awe. Thornton wrote of his 56lb-er: 'I had not yet seen the fish, he was dropping behind the rocks as he went down, but I steadied him in the Stone Pool, drawing him as much to my side of the river as possible. Presently he took up a position behind a big rock which had the main current running on the far side of it. It would have been "goodbye" if he went that way, so I held him very hard and worried him for an hour'

MAHER'S 57lb SUIR FISH
—— No. 134 ——

M r Maher took the Irish record rod-caught fish from the River Suir on one of his own home-made flies. Maher was a gillie on the Longfield water, which enjoyed good runs of salmon in 1874, when his fish was caught. The Suir is Ireland's most famous dry-fly trout river and, in the upper reaches, is not too dissimilar in character to England's River Test. Sir Herbert Maxwell gave a full and exceptionally well-written account of the capture of Maher's salmon in his *Fishing at Home and Abroad* starting on page 43. So impressed was I when I read of Maher's ingenious preparations prior to catching this huge salmon that I read the account three times over:

The hero of this adventure and author of the fly in question was one Michael Maher, fisherman on Longfield water of the Suir, who started from home one spring morning in 1874, leaving his fly-book behind and taking only the Devon minnow as bait, for he had heard that the water was thick. He found it, on the contrary, very clear and, seeing a very large fish rise near a certain big stone – a grand taking place – he determined to avoid the risk of alarming him with a sunk bait, and to try a fly over him first. But never a fly he had on him – only a big hook or two for loach-fishing – and the day would be far spent before he could return home for his book and get back to the river.

There was a farmhouse at hand, however, and therein a maiden with whom Michael was on terms of friendship. Repairing thither he begged a bit of silk and some feathers from which to tie a fly on the spot.

The Mystery

"For feathers, sure there's lashin's of them." Replied the nymph, "for I'm after plucking a poultry this very morning; but for silk, Michael, you're after coming to the wrong shop. For sorra a bit of it is there in the house."

Now the fringe of pretty Phoebe's shawl was of pink worsted, and, in default of silk, she willingly allowed Michael to pull out a few strands of the same. Then she showed him where the spoils of the slaughtered cockerel were lying.

"Musha! But them's poor stuff." quoth Michael. "Wasn't there an iligant yulla feather in the hat ye wore at the Chapel on Sunday? And yulla's the colour to fetch a salmon with the could weather we do be having."

Phoebe was too good-natured to refuse the appeal; a pinch of yellow-dyed swan fibres would never be missed from the ample splendour of the Sunday hat. In half-an-hour Michael had rigged up such a fly as had never been displayed on the Suir or any other water – pink worsted body, a yellow swan wing and a hackle from the deceased "poulthry" wound under the same; and off he hurried to the river again. The big fish seized the strange fly at the first offer, and within half-an-hour Michael was on his way back to Cashel, carrying his noble quarry with him. It constituted a record in weight for rod-fishing on the Suir, famous as that river is for big fish, for it weighed just 57 lb. Of course the first question asked by everybody who came to view the great fish was – "What fly did you get him with, Michael?" and to every one the answer was the same – "Ah, that's a mysthery."

When at last the secret did come out, "the Mystery," with suitable refinement of material and garnishing, was received with enthusiasm on many a river side, and was found to do quite as well as any other fly – *and no better.*

Viewed in the cold light of reason, such an incident as this ought surely to enable one to declare that it matters not one spin of a farthing whether the prevailing hue of a fly be red or blue, yellow or black, or an equal combination of many hues; and the only important consideration is that the lure be of suitable size and be given life-like motion. Well, that is the conclusion to which I have been driven, *malgré moi*; but such is the weakness of the human intelligence that I have found it beyond my strength to act upon it. There is such a mute fascination in daintily dressed salmon-flies, their outline is so graceful, their tints so delicately blended or so cunningly contrasted,

The River Suir, looking downstream from Knocklofty Bridge

that no nature sensible of beauty can contemplate them with indifference. Consequently, I suppose I spend as much time as anybody else at the outset of a day's fishing in hesitating between the modest luster of a "Silver Grey," the sombre dignity of a "Black Dog," and the freakish gaiety of a "Popham," deaf the while to the monition of intelligence that the result must be exactly the same whichever is chosen. Truly it hath been said that salmon-flies are designed for the delectation of fishers than for the deception of fishes.

There is a more elaborate account of the taking of Maher's fish in Sir Herbert Maxwell's *Memories of the Months* indicating that Maher had been fishing all morning (without success) with a 'collie', a famous and peculiarly Irish bait consisting of a dead stone-loach fitted to a spinning mount. At a later date, artificial stone-loach baits were manufactured. The collie was used for salmon during the spring months when the water was cold. According to Maxwell, Maher's home at Cashel was six Irish miles (whatever that meant) from the Longfield water. Interestingly, Maxwell tells us that the Mystery fly, suitably refined, became the 'deadliest of all [salmon] flies on the Redbridge and Broadlands waters of the Hampshire Test'. One last nugget of information is revealed when Maher told the farm maid that he had seen the fish – 'the biggest fish that ever swam in the Suir in Dawson's Cradle'.

MISS WHEEN'S
57lb NAMSEN SALMON
No. 135

A note about a big fish caught by Miss Wheen on fly from the Namsen River at Veiumvaldet in 1899 appears on page 69 of *Laksefisket í Namsen och de andere Elvene í Namdalen* ('Salmon Fishing in the Namsen and Other Rivers in the Nam Valley'). The text was translated for me by Jan Eggers.

Miss Wheen is standing behind in the middle at the back behind her parents (third and fifth from right), while her brother Richard (second from right) modestly looks away from the camera. Richard, also an angler, caught two large salmon, one in 1895 and another in 1896, but we have no note of their weight

A 57lb RIVER AWE SALMON
—— No. 136 ——

In the third edition of Augustus Grimble's *Salmon and Trout Waters of Scotland*, the author mentions the capture of a 57lb salmon on the Awe. It was caught on 8 October 1909. Grimble notes that it was caught on the Syndicated water and the two chief rules of this water are that 'fly is the only lure allowed, and no fishing for sea trout after midnight'. I have therefore included it in my fly-caught list. No captor's name was given.

Silver Grey fly as used by Colonel Hamilton to catch his 57lb fish on the Alten. Fly tied by John Wildermuth of Atlanta

COLONEL N. DALRYMPLE HAMILTON'S 57lb ALTEN SALMON
—— No. 137 ——

As I have observed before (No. 63), Colonel Hamilton caught four fish weighing over 50lb on fly. Doubtless taking such a number of these leviathans must be some sort of record, especially since they were all caught on fly. He took this one on 10 July 1923 on a Silver Grey fly on the Nedre Sierra pool.

By the time a reader has worked his way through this book, I am certain that he is likely to remember the name of Colonel Dalrymple Hamilton. Hamilton placed himself in the 'thick of it' as regards salmon fishing and he did so during the golden years when there were good runs of big fish. In his book *Alten Reflections*, Roy Flury paints a picture of a lifestyle that has gone forever:

> Colonel Dalrymple Hamilton was known as Cis to his friends. He enjoyed fourteen visits to Alten between 1913 and 1936 with his good friend the 8th Duke of Roxburghe. After the Duke's death in 1932 he returned with the 9th Duke and the Duke of Westminster.
>
> He caught 1100 salmon, all on fly with an average weight of 24 lbs. This does not include grilse. Of these fish one weighed 60 lbs, three weighed more than 50 lbs and 25 more than 40 lbs.
>
> This was a golden era for Alten fishing. Fish were aplenty as was time – there was no hurry in those days. The outboard motor had not arrived and the canoes were poled up river a journey of 7-8 hours to the top. It was a camp life which he adored and in his later years was to abhor the arrival of the Cutty Sark and a more social scene with the Duke of Westminster.
>
> His rod was a 16 or 18 foot greenheart, the reel a 6 inch weighty Corbet, developed by Farlow and Slater of Newark especially for fishing Alten He invariably used single gut and the flies were traditional and feathered – not a sign of hairwings or tubes of course. (Dalrymple Hamilton invariably fished with single gut. Twisted gut was available which had been developed by Reginald Corbet in the early 1900s for fishing on Alten. It was sold by Farlow for many years but Hamilton preferred single.)

MAJOR H.H.R. WHITE'S 57lb FUSTA SALMON
—— No. 138 ——

I first noticed Major White's fish on the Notable Fish list in *Where to Fish* (1937), on page 391. We are told that it was killed in 1925, was 48½in long and had a girth of 33¾in. Although the river was unnamed, we know from an entry in the 1952 edition of *Where to Fish* that White killed another giant salmon on 23 June 1932, weighing 55lb, and this was on the Fusta River in Norway (number 115).

Agnar Johansen at the helm of his boat at 5a.m. in the 1980s.
The size and power of the Alten River when it narrows is clear

AGNAR JOHANSEN'S
57lb ALTEN SALMON
No. 139

I have two reports on this fish, caught at Bollo, although the spelling of the captor's name is different in each one (the other name was Johnsen). Luckily, Roy Flury knew Agnar and has kindly written a piece about a man for whom he has the greatest respect:

Sadly, Agnar speaks little English and I speak no Norwegian. He has now retired as a boatman but in the early 1990s one evening I enjoyed a drink with Agnar and his fellow boatman Victor Ström at the Sandia camp. Victor speaks good English and I learned that at Bollo on 30 July 1982 Agnar caught a fish of 57lb on fly. He had tied the fly himself but I could not understand its name! This fish is his pride and joy of all the fish he has caught and he has a wooden 'cut out' of it at his home. It is a well-documented fish in the Alten Records. However, he spoke also of two other fish that are not so well documented. He said that the largest fish he landed was at Ovre Stengelsen on 28 July 1951 (when he was a very young man). He was 'hand lining' at the time and the fish weighed 70lb. I stress that we had still only had one drink when he went on to say the following year he caught another fish of the same weight in Detsika on a spoon.

Agnar was a brilliant boatman and had lived on the river most of his life. Like many of the boatmen on Alta, his father had lived on the river for sixty years and he used to take Agnar with him as a lad, showing him the important rocks and lies.

He also trained as a pilot and was a bush pilot for over twenty years. He knew the area known as Finnmark like the back of his hand.

I regret never having fished with Agnar but have always enjoyed our efforts at conversation. He is a 'thinking fisherman' and, talking to others who have been in his boat, there is nothing he likes better than to fish the small holes and lies that other fishermen do not fish. When the fish pulls, he likes to wait and wait. There must be no hurry to raise the rod.

I have absolutely no reason to doubt what Agnar says. He is a great guy.

In later years, Agnar Johansen's boat was always painted yellow and known as the yellow banana. Although he caught a 57lb salmon on a fly at Bollo, and other big fish, his English is limited and he is reluctant to speak of his own fishing.

Agnar Johansen with his 57lb Alten fish caught on 30 July 1982

Harling at Vibstad on the Namsen River

HANNAH COVINGTON'S
57½lb NAMSEN SALMON
No. 141

In the *Fishing Gazette* of 7 January 1911, the following splendid account appeared, entitled 'A Lady's Good Fight with a 57½lb Salmon'. It had been extracted from a piece that originally appeared in *The Field* on 31 December 1910.

The capture took place one evening in August 1885. The lady was fishing from a boat just below the Foss, and Iver Ursted, the big Norwegian boatman, had taken her too near it for her entire comfort. Presently the rod, a light lady's salmon rod, was nearly wrenched out of her hands, and she felt she had "hooked something."

"There was a furious tugging and commotion in the water, and away we raced down stream. The sleeves of my dress and jacket were torn out, my hair was down, and I must have been a fit subject for a post-impressionist! Nothing seemed to matter except the fish. Iver said gruffly, 'Big fish. Keep rod up.' No other words were spoken, no sounds heard but the waters of the Foss, the play of the reel, and the occasional splash of the angry fish. When we neared the shallow water of the rapids the fish turned and headed for the Foss and the deep pools. In our mad race we once or twice caught sight of the fish, and saw that he was very big. He never again went for the rapids.

"For nearly two hours I played him. Being big and heavy, he had been exhausted by his furious rush, and he once or twice lay quite still and quiet.

If it had not been for those quiet moments I could not have held out, for I was growing exhausted too. Suddenly, after a final struggle, there was a dead calm: the fish sank to the bottom behind a rock near the shore. We got the boat as near to the shore as we could. By degrees I gently drew him nearer and nearer in. At last, with a great effort, Iver bent over the side of the boat and firmly gaffed him. We slipped the net under him, and soon had him lying full length on the green grass. He was a male fish, with a tremendous hooked jaw, a mighty tail, a fine head, and weighed 57½lb. He measured over 4ft. from nose to the tip of his tail, and his thickest girth was about 2ft. 2in. He looked enormous as he lay there, and very noble. We admired the beauty of the blackish spots on his silver sides and the fine lines of his shape. I was filled with great wonder at my capture, but when I remembered his fierce and gallant struggle for life I wished him back again - a king - in the Namsen river.

"We made a drawing of him on the wooden dado of the fishing-house, and then we laid him on some sheets of newspaper joined together and cut out his size and shape. I still have this rough memento and the hook [the fly] with which he was caught. In the end we gave him to the fishermen to cut up for 'lax,' and the last I saw of our huge friend he was in a sack tied round a fisherman's neck, and was thus ignominiously trailed through the long grass to his bitter end.

"When our time came for leaving 'Arcadie,' as we drove down to the coast the river men in the little villages turned out to shake hands with the Englishwoman who had caught the big fish. In remembering these dear, delightful days of long ago, this, I think, pleases me most of all.

"Thus ended the capture of the big fish. Many men, pipe in mouth, have bent over the paper slip and talked to me of my luck, but most fishers in Norwegian waters will probably agree with me in thinking that an active salmon of, say, 16lb. gives more real sport and needs greater skill than the capture of the big fish I have described. This simple account may interest those who care for the 'pleasant curiosity of fish and fishing.' In these noisy days of motors and politics, can anyone do better than 'be quiet and go a-angling'?"

ARTHUR PRYOR'S RECORD
FLY-CAUGHT TWEED SALMON
No. 142

This fish was first mentioned in the *Fishing Gazette* on 6 November 1886 but the following note appeared in the edition of 11 November 1903:

THE 57½LB. TWEED SALMON KILLED ON FLY

"Observer." Writing in the *Scotsman*, says: –

"The largest Tweed salmon taken with the rod and fly of which there is authentic record was caught in the Floors Castle water on Oct. 27, 1886. It was 'a well-conditioned and beautifully built male fish,' and weighed 57½lb.
"It is remarkable that almost all extra large salmon are male fish."

I had forgotten that grand Tweed fish, but on turning to the *Fishing Gazette* of Nov. 6, 1886, I found I had a record of it as being killed on the Floors water by Mr. Pryor, Haylands, Chelmsford. It was a very handsome fish, and was killed on a 1½in. double hook Silver Grey. The length was 53in., girth at back fin 28½in. It was set up for the Duke of Roxburghe by Mr. Brotherstone, taxidermist, Kelso.

On page 305 of *The Salmon Rivers of Scotland* (second edition, 1913), Augustus Grimble describes the Floors Water on the River Tay and follows with an account of Mr Pryor's fish:

Next comes the far-famed Floors Water, belonging to the Duke of Roxburghe, with its numerous pools spread over more than four miles of both banks. From the top one of The Slates to the lowest of Maxwheel – from which the late Duke once took in a day six salmon and twenty grilse – one cast is nearly as good as another, and while there is always ample room for three rods, in suitable water and windy weather there is plenty of space for four. It was on this water that Mr. Arthur Pryor, in November 1886, took with a Wilkinson the heaviest fish ever killed by the rod on Tweedside. Unluckily, it was not weighed on the bank, but was carted up to Floors Castle along with fourteen other victims of Mr. Pryor's Forrest rod of eighteen and a half feet. It was then weighed in the presence of the Duke and the Duchess, Lord Hardwicke, Lord Kensington and Lord Lovat, and declared to be just over 60lb. The next morning at ten o'clock the shepherd, bringing in mutton, re-weighed it and made it but 57½lb. There can, however, be no doubt it was 60lb when first caught and first weighed.

The Maxwheel pool at Kelso where Pryor caught his fish in October 1886 is better known these days as the Bridge pool. It is part of the Junction beat, which was sold off in the late 1960s to help pay death duties on the Roxburghe Estate

Bainbridge's beauty – 57¹/₂lb with date of catch confirmed as 29 June 1937. Dr Malcolm Greenhalgh sent me this photograph amongst a batch taken in Norway. Greenhalgh confirmed that Bainbridge's salmon was caught (probably harling) on a fly pattern that was once a popular choice of British fisherman, the Silver Wilkinson

'BAINBRIDGE'S BEAUTY' A 57½lb NAMSEN SALMON
No. 143

Silver Wilkinson

G.B. Bainbridge's salmon, originally noticed in *Namdelens Folkeblad* (21 August 1953), was for six months on my list of fish caught by an unknown method. Eventually, I received a note from Jan Eggers with information gleaned from *Salmon Fishing in the Namsen and other Rivers in the Nam Valley*. Referring to page 119, he wrote, 'On that page there is one more big *fly-caught* [author's italics] salmon mentioned; it is the one that Mr G.B. Bainbridge caught in 1937 in the Moum part of the Namsen, near the village of Grong.'

A woodcarving of the Colonel's fish was made by John Tully and now hangs in a collection in the USA. On the carved model the legend reads '58lbs Ovre Sierra/River Alten/July 27th 1913'

COLONEL N. DALRYMPLE HAMILTON'S 58lb ALTEN SALMON
No. 145

On 27 July 1913, on his first visit to the Alten River, Colonel North Dalrymple Hamilton caught a 58-pounder from the Ovre Sierra pool. Many extraordinary nights of fishing were to follow and he kept a diary of special days. Since this gives the flavour of Norwegian fishing so well, the relevant entries, dated 27 July 1913, are reproduced here:

> A day of days or rather night of nights, though in the Northern regions of Scandinavia it's hard to tell night from day – the land of the midnight sun.

He was fishing with Mervyn Buller, Dolly Dalhousie and Tom Coke, the Duke of Roxburghe being unable to go.

> I alone in my glory was at Vina, my wants being attended to by the faithful 'Anna' a regular demon for ruining food in the cooking. My two boatmen were 'August and Anton' better I never wish to meet. On this day of days things did not promise well, the river was dead low, the water very hot and my last 3 days had produced 3 lax. Also just by way of a treat it was a real mosquito night, necessitating veil and gauntlets, and rendering a pipe a penance instead of a pleasure.

He started fishing at Bollo and caught a fish of 15lb on a size 4 Wilkinson, using a medium single gut cast. Moving on to Vina Gor, he caught three grilse on a small Jock Scott. Then it was on to Ovre Sierra, a pool that he reckoned offered their best chance. By this time the wind had risen and the air was cooler. He fished for a considerable time, catching a 15lb and 14lb fish – and then:

> I turned to August and told him we would just for luck fish the rest of the pool down and then go home. Little did I know what was in store for us.

He was using a single gut cast and a 2/0 single hook Jock Scott, which had already caught two fish.

> I remember the cast well. I had pulled out some extra line and I threw the fly right across the river into the deep slack water. I then put my rod point into the little stream there was, so as to allow it to catch the line and to draw the fly across the still part quicker than it would ordinarily have done. Just as the line was straightening out came a thing like a submarine with a tremendous wallop. I nearly fell into the river I was so astonished. Anton who was half asleep in the stern woke up with a bang thinking a rock had fallen into the river; Old August said 'Stor Lax I <u>tink</u>' [sic] and I said nothing. I was thinking of 40-pounders, single hooks, single gut and what not. He kept quiet for a bit and realising we were in a bad strategical position, I made them take the canoe across to the other side and so get between the fish and a big sunken

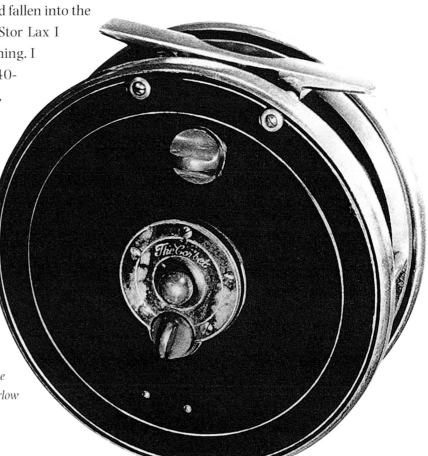

The 6in Corbet reel developed by the Corbet family with Farlow

boulder. Our going across upset the fish and he went off like an express train, the reel fairly screaming and the line cutting the water into showers of spray. August kept saying 'must no let leave pool', all jolly well but how to stop him. Over 200 yards of line out and going all we knew. Mercifully at the tail of the pool the fish stopped and I was very gentle with him and began to lead him upstream bit by bit getting back a certain amount of line. Suddenly he made up his mind to pay a visit to the head of the pool in one agonising rush. Luckily my big Corbet reel holds the best part of 300 yards of line and away we went after him.

It should be stressed at this point that Ovre Sierra is a big pool, about 400 yards in length, with nasty rapids at the bottom as the water rushes down into the next pool, Nedre Sierra. The canoes are very narrow and in those days there was no outboard motor, just two boatmen, each with a long pole and two oars. When Hamilton says the fish tore back to the top of the pool, they followed by poling against the current, not by pressing the throttle. The sport was not for the faint-hearted. Several more rushes are described before:

> ...the next move was a rush down to the tail where he played the big fish trick of crossing over, drowning the line and coming upstream at ten thousand miles an hour – this an anxious moment as I had an enormous amount of slack and I was terrified it would all come away with a bang. I went down-stream after the bag in the line and kept the rod point down. Things held.

Several other events are described as Hamilton insists on keeping the canoe in deep still water and resists August's suggestion of going ashore until the fish is completely beaten.

> By degrees he began coming up and we began to get very excited as the cast began to show and then the fish – he looked enormous and I told Anton to gaff him as near the tail as he could. He was splendid and as cool as a cucumber. Anton put the clip in and we had him. We went ashore and by putting the ring of my weighing machine through the canoe pole and hoist-ing it on to the men's shoulders we got him weighed a shade over 58 lbs. Pandemonium broke loose and we behaved like children.

On the way home they caught another two fish of 15lb and 19lb, making nine for the night. On Alten, fishing takes place from 7 or 8p.m. to 3 or 4a.m. In the land of the midnight sun it does not get dark and the glare of the sun is avoided. Colonel Hamilton finishes the story of this evening with:

> When I returned to England I didn't half thank Mr. Hunter of Farlow for that cast when I saw him. He took it he said as a memento but I imagine as an advertisement! It was not a bad cast either as it looked as good as new when I gave it to him and it had landed about 400 lbs of fish.

Colonel Hamilton had used a single gut cast and caught a 58lb salmon. Today on the Alten, 25lb breaking strain nylon is used and is often changed two or three times during an evening. He fished with 16ft or 18ft greenheart rods and his reel was a 6in. Corbet, developed by the Corbet family in conjunction with Farlow. This was similar to the Slater combination reel. These reels were also used by the Roxburghes until 1927 when Hardy made the 6in. Alta reel, based on the Hardy Perfect, especially for the 8th Duke.

This appealing photograph of three men in a boat on the Alten tells a story. There are always two boatmen. One in the bow rows gently to control the speed of a drift. One in the stern watches intently. The fisherman stands in the middle of the canoe to cast

THE ADMIRAL'S LEVIATHAN
──── No. 147 ────

On 9 July 1962, Admiral W.A. Read from the U.S.A. caught a 58lb salmon at Steinfossnakken on the Alten River on a size 3/0 Red Abbey fly. Admiral Read caught several portmanteaux salmon, including one of 50lb (No. 16). Read was fishing with Ole Andreas Mosesen senior, as always, and with his younger son Tormod. This may be the largest Atlantic salmon caught anywhere by an American on fly at the time.

Ole Andreas Mosesen senior (left) and Admiral W.A. Read

Steinfoss pool on the Alten River, looking down towards the rapids, where Admiral W.A. Read caught a 58lb fish on 9 July 1962 on a 3/O Red Abbey

J. ARTHUR HUTTON'S
CONTROVERSIAL 58½lb VOSSO FISH
—— No. 149 ——

This fine salmon was caught on the Vosso River on 9 July 1922. A photograph published in *The Illustrated London News* on 11 November 1922 shows the captor holding a fly rod with a reel attached at the extreme end of the butt, i.e. where fly reels are attached and so I have surmised that it was caught on fly. There has always been an argument about the method used to catch this fish and that it may indeed have been caught on a Wadham's gudgeon, which certainly sounds more like a spinning bait than a fly, although I have decided to leave it in the fly section. The salmon, a well-shaped summer cock fish, 52in long with a girth of 29in, was caught in the Krok pool at Evanger.

J. Arthur Hutton was an experienced salmon angler, whose home river was the Wye, and an outstanding authority on the fish. He contributed to all the fishing magazines with a constant flow of reports on big fish for them to publish. Hutton was also acknowledged as the master of telling the age of salmon from reading their scales and working out how long they had spent at sea. Before he put his mark on the reading of salmon scales, there were some pretty wild readings. Even that acclaimed expert Frank Buckland, who made such a great contribution to the study of fishes and fisheries – his book *Natural History of British Fishes* was published in 1880 – greatly overestimated the age of individual salmon.

Hutton fished in Norway and made many friends there. He was able to act as a go-between among such interested parties as the fishermen, a high percentage of whom came from Britain, and the Norwegian Government Fisheries Authority.

J. Arthur Hutton with his big salmon of 58¹/₂lbs which, despite the fact that Hutton is clearly holding a fly rod in the photograph may have been caught on a spinning bait

A 58½lb SALMON
CAUGHT BY AN UNKNOWN FISHERMAN
No. 151

One of the most rewarding aspects of researching angling history is sometimes being able to add more detail to what had hitherto been an incomplete report or account of the capture of a large fish.

Many years ago my esteemed friend the late Charles Browne introduced me to his sporting associate Jack Chance, an experienced game shot and fisherman, who was at one time President of the Flyfishers' Club. Chance wrote an entertaining little book called *Salmon Stories*, which was published by Debrett in 1983. On page 62, there is a photograph of a 58½lb salmon caught on the River Eira in 1931. Malcolm Greenhalgh gave the same bare facts about this fish in his book *The Complete Salmon Fisher* (1996). Sadly, neither author provided the name of the successful angler.

The only clue to the identity of the captor is to be found in the 1937 edition of *Where to Fish*, which includes an entry for a large salmon that was also caught in the Eira River in 1931. This fish was 51in long with a girth of 29¼in and was caught by Mr Percy Tarbutt in the month of August. However, it weighed 55¼lb. Judging by the leaves on the trees, the 58½lb salmon in the photograph in Chance's book is also a summer fish. Are we looking at some mis-reporting here or were two monster salmon caught from the same river in the summer of 1931? The first alternative is more appealing in the knowledge that a handwritten 5 and a handwritten 8 are frequently miscopied.

Although we are not told of the method used to capture the fish, we can deduce from the photograph that the pipe-smoking captor of this splendid salmon was using a fly rod – because of the position of the reel – but we cannot tell whether he was harling or casting a fly in the ordinary way when the salmon took.

The photograph of the 58¹/₂lb salmon, with its unknown captor, that appeared in Jack Chance's book Salmon Stories *and was caught on the River Eira in 1931*

THE IRISH FLY-CAUGHT RECORD –
COTTER'S 59lb SHANNON SALMON
No. 153

In one of the finest angling books ever written – and probably my favourite – *The Practice of Angling* (1845), James O'Gorman describes how in 1840 he hooked and landed a 48lb salmon, his largest. He also mentions that the following May, his boat companion, Captain Cotter, killed a salmon weighing 59lb on fly, on the Doonass stream on the lower Shannon.

The late John Rennie, some time President of the Flyfishers' Club and a widely travelled and experienced game fisherman, fished a lot in Ireland. In his very entertaining book, *I Have Been Fishing* (1949), he described the decline of one of these big-fish salmon beats on the lower reaches of the River Shannon (the main beats were Hermitage, Prospect, Doonass, Newgarden and Woodlands):

> At the south end of Lough Derg we find Killaloe. Before 1930 the river commenced again at this point and had an uninterrupted journey to the sea. Now, owing to the Shannon Power Scheme, Lough Derg has been extended for some four miles until you come to a great Dam and head works at Porteen Villa, which is about a mile above O'Brien's Bridge. Six miles below this is Castleconnell.
>
> The total length of the river and lakes is about 250 miles. In spite of the huge length of this river, the only really good salmon water was at Killaloe and Castleconnell, a matter of only a few miles. As Killaloe is now a lake, the only water left is from Castleconnell down.

To give some idea of what the Shannon used to produce, you have to read O'Gorman's book. Twelve years after his death on 30 May 1855, the records reveal that in one year, 671 salmon and grilse were caught on the Doonass beat. It would be a sensation if 71 were killed on any beat in 2005.

The Shannon at Castleconnell today

The Upper Doonass Fishery as it was before the 1930 Shannon Power Scheme ruined the main beats

KRISTIAN STIEMSTRÖM'S
59¼lb INDALSÄLVEN SALMON
—— No. 154 ——

Jan Eggers noted a reference to this fish on page 8 of the journal *F.J. Fiskearet* (January 2000). The 59¼lb salmon was taken on fly by Kristian Stiemström on 19 August 1999 from the Indalsälven River in Sweden, at Sörberge.

Sir Hyde Parker of Melford Hall in Suffolk. Born in 1785, Parker was probably the first Englishman to fish in Norway, owned a house near the River Laugen and used a yacht as the base for his fishing forays. His 60-lber was caught on the Namsen sometime in the 1830s

THE FATHER OF THE NORWAY SALMON FISHERS' 60lb NAMSEN SALMON
No. 155

I found my first reference to the above fish in William Yarrell's *A History of British Fishes* (1841):

> The largest fish ever caught by Sir Hyde Parker weighed 60 pounds. Probably caught in the 1830's, it was recorded in Captain L. Lloyd's *Scandinavian Adventures*. Although it measured only 48 inches long it had a girth of 31ins.

In *Where to Fish* (1937), the Editor, H.D. Turing, tell us that Hyde Parker's fish was recorded in Lloyd's *Field Sports of the North of Europe* (1885). Hyde Parker wrote to Lloyd about numerous Norwegian rivers.

Roy Flury sent me a note with more information about this important fish, which was caught in the early days of English exploitation of Norwegian salmon rivers. Besides having his own house in Norway close to the River Laugen, Sir Hyde owned a yacht that he used as a base for his fishing forays. The most significant fact about Sir Hyde Parker, and a few others, is that they were the pathfinders for subsequent generations who fished for salmon in Norway. The following paragraphs, from Roy Flury's book *Alten: The Story of a Salmon River* (1991), describe Sir Hyde Parker's sporting credentials:

> Sir Henry Pottinger declared in his book 'Flood, Fell and Forest' which was published in 1905, "I regard it as certain that the piscatorial raid of Englishmen on Norwegian rivers did not begin until 1830. It would be deeply interesting to know beyond all doubt who was the first man to cast a line on those waters. In the absence of evidence to the contrary I believe it to have been Sir Hyde Parker". He was, of course, referring to the first man to cast a line on any Norwegian water, not necessarily on the Alten. Sir Henry was no mean fisherman himself and although this book was not published until 1905, he had led an expedition to the Tana in 1857 with Merthyr Guest, a name which was to become illustrious on the Namsen in later years.
>
> Sir Hyde Parker was born in 1785 and lived at Melford Hall in Suffolk. He was a keen sportsman and loved both shooting and fishing. A man of artistic tastes, he brought home many fine works from Italy and redesigned the North wing of Melford Hall. He succeeded to his baronetcy in 1830 and served

This watercolour was painted on 24 August 1849 by J.F. Campbell on one of his expeditions to the Alten. The pool is today called Upper Kista and lies just below the Battagoski rapids.

The Baronet fly described in the classic Jones's Guide to Norway *and tied by John Wildermuth*

as Liberal Member of Parliament from 1832 until 1834, when he retired.

Our final garland to Sir Hyde Parker comes from no less a man than Frederic Tolfrey in his book of 1848. His 'Guide to Norway' is dedicated to him with the words "To your skill in the use of the Rod I am no stranger, and the honourable title of 'Father of the Norway Salmon Fishers' which by universal consent has been conferred upon you is proof, if any were wanting, of the perfection you have attained in the highest branch of the Angler's Art". Some eyebrows may be raised at the inference in 'the highest branch of the Angler's art' but that is another matter. There are no records of his fishing on the Alten other than he enjoyed good sport. His best day was on the Namsen where, in one day, he caught his largest fish of any kind, a salmon of 60lbs, together with eight others, which also included one of 40lbs and another of 30lbs.

Sir Hyde Parker caught his 60-pounder on a Baronet fly, which was the first to be illustrated in Frederic Tolfrey's *Jones's Guide to Norway* (1848), accompanied by the following note:

> Precedence is justly accorded to Sir Hyde Parker for with it, not many years since, he killed a magnificent salmon weighing upwards of 60 lbs.

David Hatfield brought to my notice an article published in the *Flyfisher's Journal* (Winter 1971). Its author, Philip Crowe, sometime American Ambassador to Norway, had considerable experience of fishing on the Namsen River. His piece, *Harling on the Namsen*, contained much interesting material on the early history of Namsen salmon fishing, and included details of the dressing of Sir Hyde Parker's successful fly:

> In 1864 the Reverend M.R. Barnard published *Sport in Norway* and gave a vivid description of that distinguished angler Sir Hyde Parker, who killed a sixty-pounder after a battle of more than an hour. He caught it on a number six hook to which he tied so elaborate a fly that I must quote the good preacher in full: 'The wings consisted of two golden tippets, dyed crimson, sprigged with mallard, teal, golden pheasant, and Argus pheasant. The horns were made of blue macaw. The head was black and the body claret pigs wool, while the tag was made of red mohair with ribbed gold twist.'

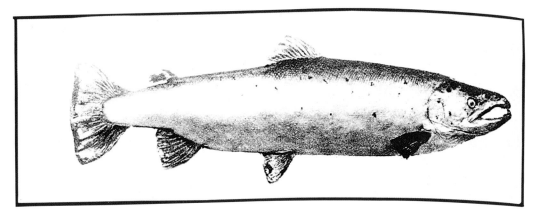

THE LARGEST SALMON
CAUGHT IN ENGLAND ON A FLY
—— No. 156 ——

This fish was caught on the River Eden in Cumberland in 1888. It was 54in long and had a girth of 27in and weighed 60lb.. It is the largest salmon ever to be caught on a fly in England, as mentioned on page 217 of John Ashley-Cooper's *A Line on Salmon* (1983). The photograph of Lowther Bridger's salmon was published on page 764 of *The Illustrated London News*, 11 November 1922.

Lowther Bridger, the captor, wrote a letter to the editor of the *Fishing Gazette* commenting on the weight of the salmon, and the relationship between the weight and the salmon's length and girth. His letter was published on 2 December 1922, together with the editor's comments and a table listing the recorded lengths and girths of salmon weighing between 57lb and 71lb set against the weight predicted by Sturdy's Scale, used when only the length is known.

RECORD SALMON. – WEIGHTS COMPARED WITH STURDY'S SCALE

DEAR MR. MARSTON – Perhaps you have seen the prints of Record Fish in last week's *Illustrated London News*. How do the dimensions there given and weight in each case tally with your FISHING GAZETTE scale?
Taking my Eden fish as a test, viz., 54 in. L. by 27 in. G. = 60 lb., the variation of dimensions in each of the other fish seem to me to agree very fairly with the weight booked in each case. – Yours sincerely
    Lyndhurst. LOWTHER BRIDGER
I feel sure Mr. Lowther Bridger's 60-lb. Eden fish must be the record salmon

killed on small fly on single gut and fishing from the bank, and the Eden is an English salmon river and a very lovely one, too. I think Mr. B. must have got hold of some other scales.

My son has made out the following interesting table (see below).

It shows what a difference "girth" may make, as is only natural. – ED.

Particulars	Length	Girth	Actual Weight in lbs.	Weight in lbs. by Sturdy's Scale
Caught in the Tweed by Mr. Howard St. George, in Feb 1921	54	24½	51	67.500 *
Caught in the Tweed by Dr. E. T. Fison, in Oct 1922	50¾	27	51½	55.294
Caught in the Deveron by Colonel Scott in 1920	50	29	56	53.584
Caught in the Awe by Mr. A. W. Huntington in July 1921	52½	27½	56	62.046
Caught in the Evanger by Mr. J. Arthur Hutton in July 1922	52	29	58½	60.274
Caught in the South Esk by Mr. Somerville in Oct 1922	53	28	59	63.819
Caught in the Eden by Mr. Lowther Bridger in 1888	54	27	60	67.500
Caught in the Tay by Miss J. M. Ballantine in Oct 1922	54	28½	64	67.500
Caught in the Evanger By Jens Grimestad In Aug 1922	56¾	——	69½	78.005
Caught by nets in the Tay June 1870	52	32	71	60.274

*This fish was undoubtedly a kelt. See page 91.

COLONEL N. DALRYMPLE HAMILTON'S 60lb ALTEN SALMON
No. 157

Colonel Hamilton's three other big salmon are included at Nos. 63, 137 and 145. This one, his largest fish, was featured in Flury and Dalenson's *Alten Reflections* (1993), on page 78:

> This fish was to be Hamilton's largest salmon on the Alten. On returning home to Scotland, Hamilton, with the aid of his drawings, photographs and measurements had a wood model carved of the fish. This was probably done at the studio of John Tully on Speyside, for the carving has that master craftsman's hallmark. Although he retired that year, he continued to put his hand to the odd masterpiece. The painting of the fish too has the appearance of the work of his wife, Dhuie Tully (née Russell). Hamilton had had several of his Alten fish carved by Tully, including the 58lb fish caught in 1913 and it is more than likely that Tully would have attended to this carving. The fish was 53 inches in length. The carving was mounted on a board, which was inscribed at the bottom left corner:

60 lbs.
Sandiagoski
11th July, 1929
N. D. H.

Roy Flury gave me details of a few notes that the Colonel made at the time:

That was the end of a gallant fish scaling a shadow over 60 lbs. Exhausted I shook hands all round and the men all laughed and were delighted. Well, well, of all the lucky devils on this river I am undoubtedly the luckiest. I can leave it at that; the fly size 2 double hook; Black Dose single gut very well hooked. I took Peder Larsen and John Sivertsen up to the hut and we all had a drink.

Next morning we had breakfast at twelve midday and I then drew out and photographed the monster. We planted a Rowan tree opposite where I had hooked the big one. It had been a memorable fish.

He mentions that he returned to water the rowan tree before leaving Alten but he found the leaves wilting. The little tree did not survive, but Ulrik Wislotts' father kindly planted a spruce tree in its place. This survived for many years and grew to a considerable size. Sadly, one year it was damaged and had to be cut down. However, the stump of the tree can be seen to this day, high up on the left bank of Sandiagoski, exactly in the place that Hamilton described.

ABOVE   *According to Hamilton's records, the fish was caught on a size 2 Double Black Dose*

OPPOSITE   *This photograph of Colonel Hamilton with his 60-pounder was taken the day after it was caught: the telltale damage of splits in the caudal fin and the ribbing of the body skin – due to its being bent after it has dried out – show positive evidence of delay.*

EARL OF DUDLEY'S
60lb ALTEN SALMON
No. 159

At the time of capture, 24 June 1949, Dudley was a member of the Duke of
Westminster's party and he caught his salmon on fly on the Sandiagoski beat.
Dudley's fish was reported in the *Alten Post* and the landing of this fish is remembered by
several of the Alten boatmen.

OLE ANDREAS MOSESEN'S
60½lb ALTEN SALMON
No. 160

Famous Alten boatman Ole Andreas Mosesen caught this fish at Forbygningen on a
4/0 Thunder and Lightning fly in June 1948. His son, also called Ole, told the
story to Roy Flury on a warm July day in 1992 while sitting on the bank of
the Alten, close to where the fish was caught.

Ole said that his family has been involved with the fishing
on Alten for over five generations. His great,
great grandfather, called Moses Pedersen, disputed the fishing rights with Captain S. H.
Thomas, Director of the Copper Mines at Kaafyord
way back in 1846. He had also fished with the 6th
Duke of Roxburghe on his first visit to Alten in 1859.
Amazingly the following week Ole was to be taking the
10th Duke in his boat, five generations later.

Ole was just twelve years old when the big fish was
caught. His father had taken him in his boat at an early age
when he was five or six. He found it scary as the fish were so much bigger
than he was. On that day in 1948 he stayed on the bank. Isaac Holton was
in the boat with Ole Andreas and it was just before Midsummer day in June.
Ole remembers hearing a shout when the fish took but then he can only

Thunder and Lightning

remember it all took a long long time and he was getting more and more hungry. All he wanted was his dinner.

Ole Andreas became the grand old man of fishing on Alten. Born in 1886 he worked on the river for most of his life, and he lived to be ninety-seven. He caught his last salmon when he was eighty-eight. Alone in the boat, if you please, he never used an outboard and while playing the fish he lost an oar overboard. The boat was taken some 600 yards downriver where a small crowd had gathered. Amidst great cheering he landed a fresh run 22lb fish. His oar was retrieved for him and he was asked if he needed any help in getting home. "No, no" he said "I'm off for my tea now." Off he went rowing to his home a good half-mile up river on the other side.

Ole the son has now retired as a boatman but the family tradition is continued by his younger brother, Tormod. He is well known to many over-seas fishermen and has been involved in many dramas, not least, Admiral Read's and Clare de Burgh's big fish in the 1960s.

Ole Andreas Mosesen with his 60lb salmon caught in June 1948. The Mosesen family have been associated with fishing on the Alten since the 1840s and still fish and work on the river today

Mrs Morison and her keeper Sim with her three fish plus Sim's fish

This photograph was taken from the tail end of Lower Shaw pool, looking upstream. The footbridge was not there when Mrs Morison caught her fish

SALMON 61 LBS, CAUGHT BY MRS CLEMENTINA 'TINY' MORISON IN LOWER SHAWS, RIVER DEVERON, ON 21ST OCTOBER 1924

LENGTH 52¼"
GIRTH 32"

GICLÉE PRINT BY ARMSTRONG ARTWORK

ARTIST © MICHAEL KITCHEN

SIGNED LIMITED EDITION PRINT

Michael Kitchen's painting of Mrs Morison's fish

THE HEAVIEST FISH CAUGHT ON A FLY BY A WOMAN
No. 162

W. Keith Rollo, a noted salmon and angling author, sent a copy of a letter that he had received from Mrs Clementine (Tiny) Morison to R.B. Marston, editor of the *Fishing Gazette*. On 1 November 1924, Marston published the letter, which contained an account of the capture of a 61lb salmon on Scotland's River Deveron, together with Rollo's comments and a photograph of the fish:

Well, I had a day out with the fish on Tuesday last. I had two others of 16lb, each before I got him!! One of them fought like a tiger, and took nearly as long as the big one. You remember the fence in the 'Low Shaw Pool' below the bushes where you lost yours in? I was fishing there and Sim (keeper) behind me (he got one also). I had just said, 'It's dashed funny, Sim, none of us can get a fish out of this pool,' when I saw a huge tail come up a bit and a boil and the line tighten close into the bank.

He then showed for a little, and remained absolutely still, till Sim came to me and said, 'Is he big?' I said, 'I think he is fairly large.' He behaved beautifully, and twice slowly went straight across the pool, and once a little way down, taking me across the fence and then when out again turned over, when Sim said, 'He is a big chap, I think.' By this time Alick was fishing opposite, and seeing me with a fish on came down. He then attempted a little run up. I was afraid he was off, but he caved in very quickly. I held on and he went up and down the side once or twice and Sim took him the first chance he got. Then we realized how big he was. I saw that Sim couldn't get him up the bank (he never moved on the gaff. Luckily), so I rushed down and put my hand in his gills, and together we dragged him up the bank. He looked enormous lying on the grass. Sim said. 'My goodness, he is over 50lb. I believe.' A huge male fish, well hooked, but a beautiful shape, of course, coloured. I was truly thankful, I had no idea what a prize he was or I should have been nervous, and he would have got off; also a mercy he was so peaceful. I don't suppose I could have ever held him had he been otherwise.

Alick says, and so does Sim, he could never have realized he was held at all, and was asleep!

Sim and I dragged him to the hut. Sim went down for the forester and his pony cart.

He did not take half an hour to get out, and I had on a thin cast. A 1¼in. 'Brown wing killer' fly with which I had the other two.

When the cart got up with the four at 6.30 (he was on the bank at 3.20) he weighed 61lb. Next morning I had him photographed by Sim's son. They are A1, and when I get them printed I will send you one or two. We sent him into Aberdeen by the first train to get a plaster cast made. He was there met by the fishing-tackle maker, Mr. Harper, of Brown & Co. He weighed him 61 lb. then, 24 hours after, so he wrote me and said, "Your fish must have been 63lb. when grassed, as these specially large fish soon lose a pound or two.'

He is now being kippered. I am very proud as you can imagine.

He is the biggest ever caught on Deveron, I think either Dee, Don or Spey, by rod and line. We sent scales to the *Field*, also to Mr. Wood, as I am awfully curious to know his age, and if he has ever been up river before. I believe that they can tell. We averaged three fish a day for the last fortnight, but the river though large is still clear, many more will be got, close on ninety, I think; average, I think, about 18 or 19lb.

* * * * *

The landing of this enormous salmon is a magnificent achievement, especially as Mrs. Morison is slimly built, and even to hold a fish of this size would be a great physical strain. I think this must be about the second heaviest salmon ever landed by a woman on rod and line.

Yours very truly

W. KEITH ROLLO (Lt.-Colonel).

I asked Colonel Rollo if he could secure a photograph, and he has kindly sent the excellent one reproduced herewith. The length of the 61 lb. fish was 53in. and girth 33in. Congratulations to Mrs. Morison on her fine achievement.

In October 2005, wanting to photograph the pool where Tiny Morison caught her magnificent salmon, I visited Wood of Shaws to meet Major Michael Kitchen, who looks after a beat on the Deveron that includes Lower Shaw pool. Apart from river keeping, Michael Kitchen is a wildlife artist and he has a studio close to the river. A few years ago he was commissioned to paint a picture of Tiny Morison's fish from the original plaster cast and kindly gave me permission to reproduce his painting, taken from a limited edition print.

The stone at Lower Shaw pool that commemorates Mrs Morison's splendid performance with the rod

GENERAL JOSEPH LAYCOCK'S
61lb ALTEN SALMON
No. 163

On 24 June 1934 General Sir Joseph Laycock caught this fish on fly on his first night of fishing on the Alten. He was a member of the Duke of Westminster's party fishing on the Jora beat. This information comes from the Alten Records and the Duke of Roxburghe's Records. At one time, a painting of this fish (probably painted by Dhuie Russell) was kept at Floors Castle, near Kelso on Tweed.

This fine action shot of the 9th Duke of Roxburghe shows him casting on the Alten with a cane rod and a 6in Alta reel, probably in the 1940s

THOMAS ALLEN'S RECORD ROD-CAUGHT RIVER SEVERN SALMON
No. 165

The indisputable facts concerning this fish are that it was caught on fly by Thomas Allen in 1912, taken to a local taxidermist, mounted in a case, and placed on the wall in a farmhouse at Atcham, near Shrewsbury. The farm, and the fish, eventually came to Richard Adney, a great nephew of the captor, who died in 1923. Since then, more changes in ownership have occurred and the cased fish is now on view at nearby Attingham Hall, an estate administered by The National Trust.

Various weights have been claimed but, as Richard Adney pointed out on page 11 of *The Times* on 29 October 1997, 'We do not know the true weight of this fish, as it was never accurately measured at the time.'

In February 2006, having been alerted to the fish's existence by Brian Clarke, angling correspondent of *The Times*, I visited Attingham Hall, courtesy of The National Trust, and was allowed to inspect and measure the salmon. In the event I found that the taxidermist had not done a very good job and the fish was in very poor shape. (If a taxidermist has to work on a fish that is not fresh, he may find it impossible to make it look like a freshly killed fish.) Nevertheless, it is impressively big, measuring 53in long. This length means that it could have weighed 64lb, which is one of the claimed weights.

Mark Walsingham, deputy head of rural surveying for The National Trust, has interviewed a witness to the capture of the fish, which must be the record rod-caught Severn salmon. The witness, a centenerian, was able to give a definitive account of the event, which was published in *Trout and Salmon* magazine in April 2006.

ANTON PEDERSEN'S
64lb ALTEN SALMON
—— No. 166 ——

The basic details of Pedersen's catch were culled from Flury and Dalensen's *Alten Reflections* but in September 2005, Roy Flury sent me an interesting note about the catch, which I quote in full:

> Ole Mosesen, a well-known Alta boatman and a son of another Ole mentioned before, told me about this fish. His uncle Anton went up river to camp and fish for a week during the 'free season' with his son Alf. This was between 1918 and 1922. They would have poled themselves up river (a journey of 7-8 hours from bottom to top). On their way up they stopped to fish at Ovre Sierra and hooked a very big fish. This was safely landed and caught *on fly*. They then went up river to Kista where Ole's father (also called 'Ole' and one of Alta's most well-known boatmen) joined them. They caught a 24lb fish, which they said looked like a grilse compared to the big fish. They cooked the smaller fish, and the big one was packed in ice and buried. They then went on to Sandia. After 6 days fishing they returned down river, picking up the big fish on the way home. When weighed, after 7 days, it was 64lb. Ole's father, a very experienced fisherman, estimated it would have been over 70lb when caught.

'The portage at Gabo' depicts the hauling of fish (on a good day) down an un-navigable part of the Alten River

HENRY WILLES'
LOST 64lb AWE SALMON
—— No. 167 ——

H enry Willes, a venerable (he was over seventy years old when he wrote this piece) member of the Flyfishers' Club, gave an account in the *Flyfishers Journal* (Autumn 1946), of how, in 1897, he caught a 63lb salmon in the Olden River in Norway. In the same piece he wrote about a huge salmon that he lost while fishing on the river Awe in Scotland.

Another incident is perhaps worth recording, but this time it happened in Scotland. I forget the year, but this could be obtained from the "Field" or the "Fishing Gazette," both of which recorded the incident.

I had booked a room at Dalmally, with a view to fishing the Orchy, and had motored down. On my way I had stopped at Oban to get some Silver Grey flies of a size I hadn't got, and was only able to obtain some with red sealing wax heads. On my arrival at Dalmally I found that so far as the Orchy was concerned there was nothing doing, so I applied to the manager of the Loch Awe Hotel to give me a day's fishing on the Awe. This was granted, but conditions were by no means ideal. I fished down the whole of the beat without seeing a sign of a fish. Feeling very tired and inclined to give it up, I asked my ghillie, Angus McColl, whether it was any use going any further, to which he replied there was just one place a fish might lie but it was a difficult one owing to a shelving rock on which one's line could very easily be cut, and it was agreed he should fish it. On arrival at the spot we put up a silver grey, and at Angus' third cast up came a big red head. Angus came ashore from his perch on a rock "all of a tremble" and said "Did you see him?" to which I replied "Yes, and we will give him five minutes' rest." To fill in the time he filled his pockets with stones, and out he went again with the same fly.

The fish took it at the very first cast, and I relieved him of the rod, leaving him free to pitch in the stones to keep the fish away from the sunken rock. I found I could do nothing with him, and after several pockets of stones my line came back to me severed above the cast. This was bad luck. But it wasn't until much later that I knew what we had lost.

Passing by in my car the following year I happened to see a man fishing, with his ghillie sitting on the stones. I naturally had to stop, and went down to inquire what luck.

It was Angus all right, and directly he saw me he said "You are the man I have been wanting to see. Do you remember the fish we lost last year? Well! It was washed up three weeks later with a cast and line wound round his gills and the fly had a red sealing wax head." It then weighed 64 lbs., and has been mentioned more than once in the "Field."

I now realise the full significance of the loss of this fish – had it been landed and not struggled (for between one and twenty-one days before it died), it would presumably have weighed more than Miss Ballantine's record rod-caught fish.

EARL OF HOME'S
69¾lb ROD-CAUGHT SALMON
—— No. 168 ——

Although the 8th Earl of Home's salmon was taken a long time ago – 1730 – from the Tweed and tends to be dismissed in favour of Miss Ballantine's 64lb fish, I'm of the same mind as R.B. Marston and do not think that old records should necessarily be disregarded unless there is positive evidence of falsehood. In the *Fishing Gazette* of 3 May 1913, writing in response to a letter from G.J. Cook, the renowned editor mentions two large salmon and includes the following definitive statement about the famous fish: 'Earl Home's 69¾lb Tweed salmon, *taken on a fly* [my italics] is the record rod-killed fish.' In 1837, the captor's nephew wrote:

The fish [the largest he had ever killed], which weighed 45lb. killed also in the month of July, 1795, was a fresh-run fish, with what are called tide-lice on it, and the finest I ever tasted.

My uncle, my father's elder brother, caught a salmon with a rod which weighed 69¾lb.

Some eighty-six years later, another correspondent pondered the injustice of no longer recognising Lord Home's huge salmon as the record, with a letter published in the *Fishing Gazette* of 26 May 1923:

THE EARL OF HOME'S RECORD 69³/₄LBS. SALMON

DEAR SIR – This is the second time lately you have referred in The Fishing Gazette to the late Earl of Home's record salmon as too legendary to be classed as a record.

My brother has seen the cast of the record salmon at the Berwickshire seat of the Earl of Home with a plate attached to same, stating date when caught, weight,etc.

When such is the case, where does the "too legendary" come in, when by a few lines from you, Sir, the Earl of Home will give you authentic information regarding the record salmon. – Yours respectfully,

DAVID PROVAN
164, New City Road,
Glasgow

(Acting on Mr. Provan's suggestion, I wrote to the Earl of Home, who has very kindly replied as follows. – ED)

The Hirsel,
Coldstream.

May 18, 1923

Dear Sir

In answer to your letter of 14th, I fear the only record of the big salmon is from a letter of my great grandfather written in 1837 in which he says: "My uncle (my father's elder brother) caught a salmon with the rod which weighed 69¾lb."

There is no cast of the salmon here or any other particulars as to its capture.

Yours sincerely,

HOME

The 8th Earl's nephew allowed William Yarrell to reprint the letter that he had sent to the Earl of Montague on 10 January 1837 about Tweed salmon and his uncle's record fish, in the second edition of his book *A History of British Fishes* (1841):

> Mr Yarrell is correct as to the time of the spawning of the salmon in the Tweed. I must, however, be allowed to make a remark on this subject, that in the Tweed a very great change has taken place within these twenty or thirty years, a considerable portion of the breeding-fish not coming into breeding condition till long after the time they had formerly been in the habit of doing so. On Nov. 2, 1835, I killed, with fly, fourteen salmon, from 10lb. to 20lb. weight, every one of which was in as fine condition as fish caught in the end of July.
>
> It is singular enough that in the early part of the season, when the first show of young salmon comes up the Tweed, however small they may be, they are all denominated salmon. I have killed them under 3lb.; yet that fish was called a salmon, and the fishermen – I mean those above Berwick of Norham - all allege that no grilse ascend the river till the second great shoal come up about the beginning of June. The Berwick people are, however, now convinced that the grilse is neither more nor less than a young salmon, and accordingly call it so.
>
> I have always considered the salmon as a sea fish, leaving it for the river for the sole purpose of spawning. That during the period they remain in the fresh water they are not only nearly stationary as to growth, but lose, and rapidly too, their fine condition, and their flesh its fine and delicate flavour. This I consider chiefly occasioned by their not being able to obtain the more nutritious food of various kinds which they find in the sea. The salmon is, no doubt, a very voracious feeder at times.
>
> The first salmon I ever caught was with the minnow, in the month of June, 1783, when I was a boy of thirteen, fishing for trout. That fish weighed 18lb.; and since that time I have frequently killed ten or twelve salmon in one day with a minnow; the worm also is a very deadly bait, when the river gets low in summer, and in the upper parts of the river the worm is the principal bait used during the whole of the spring fishing season. In the summer, too, numbers of salmon are caught with the parr-tail. I have often known a salmon kelt take away a set of minnow-tackle, consisting of three large hooks at least, and caught with another set as soon as it could be put on; but the instances of clean salmon being so caught are very rare.
>
> During the latter part of last season, 1836, there were more salmon

in the river than I ever remember to have seen, with the exception of one season, about twenty years ago, and certainly a much greater proportion of very large fish by far than I can remember.

I observed many oversetting (the term used when salmon jump out of the water for their own amusement) which must have weighed from 30lb. to 40lb., and one, which I am sure, must have exceeded 50lb. at least. I never saw so large a fish in our streams. It is a curious fact that on both these occasions, when there were such multitudes of fish, they would not take any fly or bait that could be offered to them; some few were caught, no doubt, but only here and there one; and this was more or less the case the whole way from the foot of Gala Water down to my fishing-ground, where I may say the rod-fishing ends. I may here mention that I have killed, and all with the fly, many hundreds of salmon weighing 25lb. and upwards. The two largest I ever killed weighed, one 45lb., in July 1795, the other 40lb. The latter fish was sent to the late Duke of Buccleuch at Bowhill. When his old cook saw the fish he declared it was absolutely impossible that any man could kill such a fish with the rod, and to this moment does not believe that I caught it. The fish, which weighed 45lb. killed also in the month of July, 1795, was a fresh-run fish, with what are called tide-lice on it, and the finest I ever tasted.

My uncle, my father's elder brother, caught a salmon with a rod which weighed 69¾lb.

For a number of years, however, there has been a great scarcity of large fish in the river, few exceeding 18lb. having been caught, and my present fisherman told me he had never seen a clean salmon above 20lb. The reason for this scarcity of large fish was, first, the river down at Berwick was over-fished; and secondly, all the large spawning fish were killed during close time by poachers in the upper parts of the river, particularly in the small streams to which the fish resort in such numbers to deposit their spawn. Of course, very few were allowed to return to the sea, and consequently few of the old or large fish could return to the river the next season.

I may here be permitted to mention that in the month of April, 1795, I killed thirty-six salmon in one day rod-fishing, one of which, 18lb., I took home. Mr Yarrell may form some idea of the size and quality of the fish when I tell him that the fisherman received twenty-five guineas for that day's work, not including the fish I took home. The day after I caught twenty-six.

In the month of June of that year, 1795, I killed in one week, between the Monday morning and Saturday night, eighty-two clean salmon, all in the finest condition, and many of them large fish, which averages near fourteen per day, all but two salmon.

But, alas! those halcyon days in Tweed are ended: rod-fishing is all but entirely over, and is now reduced to a few days in spring and a few days in autumn, when the net-fishing ends on Oct. 15. This change has been brought about by draining the sheep farms on the hills, the effect produced being that a little summer flood which took a fortnight or three weeks to run off previous to 1795 is now completely run out in eight hours. The rain which formerly filled the bogs or sides of the hills, and which then kept giving a constant and regular supply to the river, is now carried off at once by these drains to the different feeders, causing sudden and violent floods, and short as they are sudden, so that the flood is all run off before the river has had time to clear itself, too low for a salmon to rise, and not clear enough to see a hook, even were there salmon to take one. But the worst effects produced by these drains, and consequent diminution in the volume of water, is the advantage it gives to the fishermen below, near the mouth of the river, who now hardly allow a fish to escape, and, indeed, in summer the river becomes so low that it cannot clear itself, as a quantity of filth and sludge is constantly floating backwards and forwards with the flood and ebb tides, which prevent the salmon taking the river at all. Sir Humphrey Davy, in his 'Salmonia' compares the Tweed as it was formerly to what it is now, to two houses, the one covered with thatch and the other with slate; the one dripping for hours after the rain has fallen, and the other ceasing when the rain ceases. In short, salmon-fishing in the Tweed is quite at an end, except in some particular years when there is rain enough to ruin the crops and create almost a famine in our harvest time, September, but that is all. What I regret also, almost as much as the loss of salmon-fishing, is our trout-fishing; that, too, is at an end.

Last year, 1836, we had not one single opportunity, and in 1835 it was much the same; for, of course, the draining has affected the smaller streams as well as the Tweed itself.

My uncle, the same who caught the 70lb. salmon, had a Newfoundland dog which was celebrated for catching salmon. He knew the Monday mornings as well as the fishermen themselves, and used to go to the cauld or mill-dam at Fireburn Mill on those mornings. He there took his station at the cauld slap, or opening in the dam, to allow the salmon to pass, and has been known to kill from twelve to twenty salmon in a morning. The fish he took to the side. The then Lord Tankerville instituted a process against the dog. I had a copy of the proceedings, but I regret to say it was lost when the old library was altered. This case was brought before the Court of Session, and the process was entitled 'The Earl of Tankerville *versus* a Dog, the property of the Earl of Home'. Judgment was given in favour of the dog.

This letter, although rather long, gives an excellent account of a deteriorated river in the 1830s. The twentieth century brought an improvement followed by the most serious decline ever, although the situation is improving again now.

MAJOR IVAR HAUGE'S
70lb TANA RIVER SALMON
No. 169

This fish, caught in 1952, is well-known and documented in Philip Kingsland Crowe's book *Out of the Mainstream*, published in New York in 1970 (page 89). Philip Crowe was US Ambassador to Norway, a great fisherman and traveller and the

This photograph shows the huge size of the Tana River

author of several books. In July 1969, Crowe says he partly followed in Henry Pottinger's footsteps and travelled to Levajok Fjellstue, the fishing camp of Major Ivar Hauge. This was some fifty miles upstream from where the River Tana empties into the great Tana fjord.

> Major Hauge, who looks like Ernest Hemingway, and his nice wife fed us delicious meals spiced with exotic dishes as reindeer steak, reindeer tongue, whole ptarmigan, salmon, trout and grayling.

Later Crowe describes being escorted to the river and, with Major Hauge, they 'trolled' – what Europeans call harling most Americans call trolling – with flies for salmon.

> One of the pools of the river lies in front of the Major's camp and by observing it carefully he saw there were three great salmon. He named them Otto, Oscar and Lazurus. One usually takes the estimate of a salmon's size with many grains of salt but since the Major himself had killed a 70 lb salmon in this very pool in 1952, I gave him full credit for honesty. He used a Jock Scott to take this monster and it was a Jock Scott he had tied himself that he fastened to the end of my leader.

The Major estimated the weight of Otto as 50lb but, sadly, Otto was not interested in the Jock Scott. The 70lb fish is often reported as having been caught on a Jock Scott fly tied by the Major himself. It may have been but that is not what Crowe wrote. The 70lb fish was caught on a Jock Scott fly but was the Major casting the fly or was he harling as he did with Crowe? We will probably never know.

ATHOLE'S RECORD 72lb TAY SALMON
—— No. 170 ——

A letter from R. Anderson of 67 Prince's Street, Edinburgh, was published on page 176 of the *Fishing Gazette* on 8 March 1902:

MONSTER TAY SALMON

DEAR SIR – I note in your last issue of the *Fishing Gazette* that a correspondent asks if there is any record of a 70lb. salmon ever having been killed in the Tay. Perhaps the following may interest him.

A member of the Athole family some time in the early years of the 1800's was fishing on the Tay at a pool called the Fernyhaugh, about three miles above Dunkeld. He there hooked a fish on the fly, and after playing it from the boat for several hours, landed it at the Cottar Park Pool, fully a mile below the town.

My father was present and saw the fish landed, and also saw it weighed in the town, when it turned the scale at over 72lb. There was a rough wooden model made of it at the time, but since 1862 all trace of it has been lost. I have often heard my father and the late Mr. Charles Crerar, who was head gamekeeper to the Duke of Buccleuch, talk about the fish. Mr. Crerar's father was the fisherman who gaffed it.

The above account of the 72lb salmon has all the hallmarks of a true story. The only real problem some readers may have is that the incident happened a long time ago. My view is that distance in time is irrelevant – only the facts are worthy of consideration, and I thought that further research on this fish could pay dividends. Perhaps the Athole or Buccleuch family records would hold details of the catch.

Accordingly, I wrote to his Grace the Duke of Atholl at Blair Castle in February 2006, being somewhat mystified by the spelling of Athole. My letter elicited a reply from Jane Anderson, the estate's archivist. 'Dear Mr Buller,' she wrote, 'I can confirm hat Athole is the Atholl family. The 6th Duke

Illustration of a clamp-foot reel from T. F. Salter's The Anglers Guide *London, (1808)*

The family portrait painted in 1767 by Johan Zoffany, shows the 3rd Duke of Atholl holding what appears to be a 20ft salmon fly rod – together with a reel of the clamp-foot type. The Duke chose as a backdrop the river-side walks of the River Tay at Dunkeld. Any of the three boys pictured could have been the member of the 'Athole' family who caught the seventy-two pound salmon in the early 1800s.

Blair Castle, ancient seat of the Dukes and Earls of Atholl

Landseer's The Death of a Stag in Glen Tilt *features the grey-headed 4th Duke; John Crerar holding a tele-scope; one of the Duke's sons, the Marquis of Tullibardine, pointing towards the hill; and John's son Charles, holding a gralloching knife. The faint images of a pony, the pony man and two hounds complete the picture*

The head of Fernyhaugh pool, where a member of the 4th Duke's family hooked the 72lb salmon. The fish swam four miles downstream before it was killed

A lone fisher at Cottar pool at Newtyle, where John Crerar gaffed the fish

changed the spelling for some reason and the 7th Duke reverted to just the l and no e.'

What was really exciting about this information was the realisation that if authentication of the fish could be found in the Atholl archives, it would go down on record as the largest Atlantic salmon ever taken on fly.

After further correspondence, I was invited to Blair Castle to inspect the records, particularly the letters written to the 4th Duke by his gillie, John Crerar – the gillie who had gaffed the fish for one of the Duke's family. This was probably one of his sons, but which one? Quite a puzzle considering that after John Murray became the 4th Duke in 1774 (he died in 1830) he had nine children with his first wife and two with his second.

Crerar sent regular reports on sporting matters to the Duke when the Duke was away in London, so I had to read summaries of all his letters to see if he had mentioned the capture of the big fish, but alas I could find no reference to it. I assumed that the fish had been taken when the Duke was 'at home'. The main difficulty was not knowing the year of capture. Since the Duke was a prolific letter writer all his life, the vast amount of correspondence to be gone through is a huge undertaking, without any guarantee of success.

John Crerar, I soon discovered, was a remarkable man. Born in Dunkeld in 1750, he lived at nearby Fernyhaugh ('haugh' means meadow beside a river) and looked after the Duke's fishings together with his substantial deer forests. The Dukes of Atholl owned a massive amount of land and let out sporting rights to many interested parties, including the Duke of Buccleuch. The Atholl estate included extensive fishings on the River Tay as far down as the Mill at Stanley, and on other rivers including the Tilt, Tummel and Gary. Edwin Landseer, the artist, was a frequent visitor to Blair Atholl (in 1824, 1825 and 1826) as was William Scrope, who came to study deer. Indeed, during one of those visits, Landseer painted *The Death of a Stag in Glen Tilt*, which the estate has very kindly allowed me to reproduce. John Crerar and his son Charles are featured in the painting. Charles was a stalker at Forest Lodge during its tenancy by the Duke of Buccleuch.

A final thought: was Mr Anderson's father – the man who was present when the fish was played, landed and later weighed in Pitlochry – the same man as James Anderson, falconer for the Atholl estate at the time? If he was, it would explain why Mr R. Anderson of Edinburgh was so knowledgeable about what went on at Blair Atholl.

The two photographs of the River Tay, one taken at Fernyhaugh and the other at Cottar pool on the Newtyle beat, illustrate where the fish was hooked and where it was finally beaten, a distance of at least four miles. This momentous fight, lasting for more than three hours, with what turned out to be a record fish, must have been talked about for years, at least locally, and I firmly believe that somewhere an account of this extraordinary battle will have been recorded. It is my hope that the publicity resulting from these observations will eventually lead to the discovery of a fully documented account of the taking of this staggeringly large salmon.

Landseer's painting John Crerar the Keeper with his Pony *was executed in 1824. John (1750–1840) was head forester, head keeper and fisherman to the 4th Duke of Atholl. Perhaps surprisingly, for a man who spent most of his working life outdoors, Crerar was an accomplished musician and composer*

The prolific Cabin Pool on the Careysville beat of the River Blackwater in Ireland

SALMON BETWEEN 50 AND 60lb METHOD UNCERTAIN

DR ALEXANDER LINDSAY'S
50lb TOWY SALMON
—— No. 172 ——

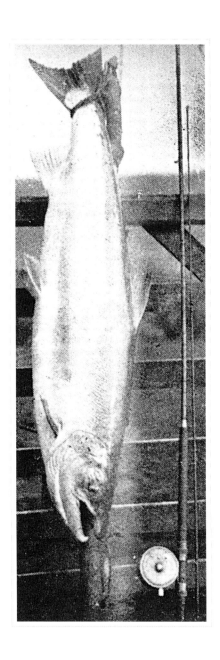

I have not as yet uncovered full details of Dr Lindsay's salmon. What little information I do have has been culled from Jack Hughes-Parry's book, *A Salmon Fisher's Notebook, A Fishing Fantasy* (1949), in which he says that the fish was regarded as the record rod-caught salmon for the Towy, and notes that it shows the condition of a spring fish. The photograph of the fish above this entry is reproduced from between pages 38 and 39 of that book. The fish may have been caught on bait. The reel in the photograph, which may look like a fly reel to the modern eye, in facts shows a small white lever at the back, suggesting that it was in fact a bait reel. Jack Hughes-Parry was a very highly skilled Welsh salmon fisherman whose creed was to get a fish out of the water and on to the bank, rather than advocate any particular method of fishing. He was famous enough in the 1930s and post-war Britain to have spinning rods marketed (by Allcocks) in his name.

DR CYRIL MARSON'S
50lb WYE SALMON
No. 179

The existence of this fish was brought to my attention by Ted Andrews. Dr Cyril Darby Marson was a friend of some noted salmon anglers of the period, including J. Arthur Hutton, the fish-scale reading wizard, and Captain Hughes-Parry. On page 19 of his book *Fishing for Salmon* (1929), Marson reproduced a photograph of nine salmon that had fallen to his rod, two of which had numerous spots on their gills. He maintained this was a clear indication that those two fish had spawned previously.

Another photograph, this time of one very large salmon, is captioned 'The author with a 50lb Wye salmon', but he fails to tell us how it was caught, or indeed if he himself was the fortunate captor. The following note, found on page 9 in a chapter entitled 'Life History of a Salmon', is the only description of the fish:

The male Wye salmon shown with the author (facing p. 28) was caught in April 1915. Its length was 51in. and its girth 27in. It had spent two years in the river as a parr and four years feeding in the sea, and had returned to the river to spawn for the first time. No reliable means were available, when it was caught, of ascertaining its actual weight; but according to the formula in the Appendix, it would be a little over 50lb. and exactly the weight on the Corbett indicator.* The bulk of these very large fish are males generally, and enter the river for the first time of spawning, or, in other words, are 'maiden' fish.

*According to Sturdy's Table, a 51in fish would weigh nearly 57lb.

Dr Marson with the 50lb Wye salmon

D.J.W.'S
50lb RIVER ANNAN SALMON
No. 181

avid Hatwell, who is ever-observant and unendingly searches for items of special interest among piscatorial memorabilia, especially in lists printed in salesroom catalogues, noticed an item that he knew would interest me – the framed head of a salmon auctioned by Neil Freeman on 23 March 1999. The 50lb fish was caught in November 1919 from the River Annan and Lot No. 315 was described as 'An extremely rare MacCleary, Inverness, plaster salmon head, naturalistically painted, and mounted in oak-framed picture showcase, back board with applied ivorine plaque.'

When I approached Freeman early in 2005 he promised to write to the purchaser, who lives in the USA, and the latter very kindly offered to have the fish head photographed for me. The legend on the case verifies the weight at 50lb and tells us that the salmon was caught by D.J.W. I have not been able to trace the identity of D.J.W., nor do I know the mode of capture. So far as I am aware, this big fish has not been noted by those authors who have commented and/or made lists of big salmon. Likewise, it seems to have gone unnoticed by the fishing journals.

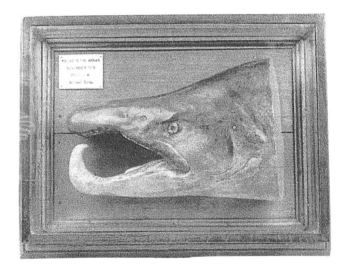

PHYLLIS OR EVELYN SCHWABE'S
50lb LEARDAL SALMON
—— No. 182 ——

Where to Fish (1926) briefly states that Miss Phyllis Schwabe caught this huge salmon in the Leardal in 1921 but a report in the *Daily Sketch* (13 March 1929) reprinted in the *Fishing Gazette* (23 March 1929) revealed that it was her sister Evelyn who actually caught the fish.

ANGLING SISTERS

> Miss Evelyn Schwabe, just engaged to Mr. M. Lawrence, is a mighty wielder of the salmon rod. Some years ago she caught in the Leardal, in Norway, a 50 pounder, and her younger sister, Phyllis, as a girl of eighteen, caught a 30lb salmon on a light cast and a small Jock Scott – probably a record for a woman with a fly. They are daughters of the K. C., Sir Walter Schwabe.

On closer scrutiny, the report in the *Daily Sketch* does not make sense because there are many instances of bigger fish being caught on fly by a woman but very few instances of salmon over 50lb being caught by a woman, using any method. Perhaps the fish *was* caught by Phyllis as reported in *Where to Fish* and, who knows, it may have been caught on fly.

Islamouth, where the River Isla joins the Tay. The Isla is a very productive river in its own right, but when it is churned up by flooding the fishing can be ruined on the beats immediately below the junction. The beats above on the Tay rarely get too dirty to fish

MAJOR F. PULLAR'S 50lb TAY SALMON
No. 185

On 10 July 1928 Major F. Pullar caught his biggest salmon at Islamouth. The beat at Islamouth (where the River Isla runs into the Tay) is the most famous fly-fishing beat on the Tay. Although I have not yet discovered the method used by Pullar, I suspect that he caught his fish on a fly.

PROFESSOR MERTON'S
PAIR OF 50-POUNDERS
No. 192

Professor T.R. Merton belongs to that very small club of British salmon fishers who have caught two salmon, both weighing over 50lb. His heavier fish, 54lb, was caught in the River Wye in 1939. It was 52in long, girth 28in. His other big fish weighed 50lb, length 49in, girth 27in, and was taken at Castleton on the River Wye on 17 April 1930.

J. Arthur Hutton, in *Wye Salmon and Other Fish* (1949), provides an interesting sidelight on big fish when he notes that three hundred and thirty-four salmon exceeding a weight of 40lb were caught on the Wye between 1910 and 1946. As only eleven of these weighed 50lb and over, we can conclude that Professor Merton caught nearly 20 per cent of these so-called portmanteaux fish.

RAYMOND J. MOONENS' BRACE OF 50lb VOSSO SALMON
No. 196

Sometimes the catching of huge salmon is poorly documented and so it would seem with a brace of 50-pounders caught by Belgian angler Raymond Moonens. What we cannot argue about is the evidence – a photograph used in a fishing holiday brochure produced by Norwegian firm Haraldsen Tours of Oslo. We do not know the method or date of capture, but we do know that the fish were caught in the River Vosso.

A photocopy from a holiday brochure -- all that remains of Raymond Moonens' brace of big salmon

DR MARSHALL'S 50½lb TAY SALMON
No. 198

On 21 October 1893 the *Fishing Gazette* published a report on the season's fishing, which included the following:

> The largest fish of the season was taken by Dr. Marshall of Stanley, on Friday last on the Scone Palace water at Horsey Shot and weighed 50½lb.

Scone Palace water is noted for the capture of very big fish. The uppermost pool on the beat, Pitlochrie pool, is where the season's opening ceremony used to be held – resplendent with Scottish pipers. Sadly, the tradition has now lapsed because of the poor runs of spring salmon.

J. LATHAM'S
50½lb BLACKWATER SALMON
No. 201

The Blackwater is not only a prolific river for salmon, it is also a big-fish river. The well-kept records on one beat, only two miles long, reveal that since 1926 Careysville has recorded catches of over 1200 fish in a season three times, and that in 1929 the average weight reached a stunning 19lb.

Looking upstream from Ballyduff Bridge, the Blackwater is sluggish, more suited to bait fishing than fly fishing

In February 1930, Mr J. Latham caught a 50½lb salmon. We do not know what method was used to catch the fish since spinning and prawn fishing is allowed on most beats but not usually on all the pools.

Just before the manuscript of this book went to the printer, I found (with the help of Keith Elliot) a contemporary report on this fish in the *Fishing Gazette* (21 February 1930):

> DEAR SIRS – I am enclosing scales from the shoulder of a 50lb. cock salmon which I caught yesterday. Could you kindly get your expert to tell me the life history. The fish was 48in. in length and 12in. deep: nearly 30in. in circumference: tail 12in. broad. – With compliments, Faithfully yours, JAMES LATHAM.
>
> We congratulate Mr. Latham on his fine fish. Mr. J. Arthur Hutton has examined the scales and sends this report:
>
> "I am not quite sure about the river life. I think it is only one year. Four years in the sea without spawning – a very large spring fish. Fifty pounds is a remarkable weight for a 48in. salmon. This gives a condition factor of over 55 - J. A. H."

That March, the *Fishing Gazette* published another letter from the captor:

MR. LATHAM'S BLACKWATER SALMON WEIGHED 50½lb.

> DEAR MR. MARSTON – I know you would not like unwittingly to be guilty of perpetrating "another injustice to Ireland," but I should like you to note that the fish which I caught was 50½lb. when it was scaled two hours after being landed according to our Salters balance, and it actually bumped the scales at 50lb. when it reached London two days later. I think therefore that we can claim for our fish an equal record for the season so far with that reported in this week's FISHING GAZETTE as being taken on the Wye. – Faithfully yours JAMES LATHAM.

KARL JØRGEN BJØRGE'S
50¾lb VOSSO RIVER SALMON
No. 206

Karl Jørgen Bjørge took a beautifully shaped 50¾lb salmon from the Vosso River while visiting the Oddsbu fishing lodge at Bolstad. His host, Odd Haraldsen, who ran the fishing lodge, seems to have caught a 46½-pounder, but no more information is to hand.

A 51lb RIVER DERWENT SALMON
No. 208

The Cumberland Derwent has produced two salmon exceeding 50lb, which is remarkable for such a small river. The first of these big fish was caught, according to Arthur Oglesby and Lucy Money-Coutts in *Big Fish* (1992), by an unknown angler in 1872. The second, weighing 52lb, was caught on fly by a Mr L. Ferguson in 1885 (No. 59).

Perhaps this river became a favourite for generations of anglers because so much of it is fast-flowing and excellent fly water. It was certainly Hugh Falkus' favourite salmon river and he fished it with his friends Anthony Desbruslais and Bill Arnold until his last illness.

Karl Jørgen Bjørge (right) and Odd Haraldsen, with their big catches of the day – but which day?

BRIGADIER GENERAL E.C. WALTHALL'S 51lb BLACKWATER SALMON
No. 218

Initially, my information on this fish came from page 87 of *Game Fish Records* (1936) – it was caught in March 1930 and weighed 52lb. Later, I found an account of its hooking and landing in Bill Hammond's *An Irish Salmon Gillie* (1984), subtitled *Fun with the Nobility, the Rich and the Famous*. This book is mainly about the gillie Billy Flynn's experiences with the royals and notables who fished at Careysville on the Duke of Devonshire's two-mile beat on the River Blackwater. The photograph above the heading appeared in a newspaper or magazine of the time, together with the following long caption, under the heading :

A RECORD CATCH

Brig General E. C. Walthall DSO, who is one of the Duke of Devonshire's party at Careysville, near Fermoy, Co. Cork, landed a record salmon for this water. The salmon seen in the photograph weighs 52lbs, is 4ft. 2ins. long and 2ft. 2ins. girth. It took 1½ hours to land and in that time, covered one mile of the river. The bait used was a Silver Reflex Devon, and the fish was gaffed by T. O'Neill, the Careysville gillie. General Walthall, who comes from Derby, has a distinguished Military career.

The more detailed story is that on Saturday, 29 April 1930, Billy Flynn was gillieing and fishing for General Wattall in the Top Flat pool (notice the difference in the spelling of the General's surname) when he saw a big fish jump. 'I fired everything at him,' he said, 'hooking him in the tail.' The account that follows is plausible in so far as it describes the playing of a 'giant' salmon, but the denouement leaves us wondering whether the way the story is told is meant to bring out Flynn's readiness to play havoc with facts in order to amuse the Duke's guests, as he was perhaps expected to do.

Well he nearly dried the river, and a mad rush he made towards the weir. When he quietened down a bit, I handed the rod to the General, who played him for half an hour. Then the fish started downstream and near the Sand Hole he continued his battle for freedom. On and on, down the river he went until we were now in the Lane Stream with the fish as full of fury as ever.

We took turns on the rod, playing him for all we were worth until Tom returned from Cork and joined in the battle. Now the fish was heading for the broad water and we took to a boat to chase him, and he kept on this course for another quarter of a mile down the river. Then I turned him back. As we came near the bank, Tom left the boat and running ahead gaffed the fish as he came near the bank. When we lifted the monster didn't the hook fall out of his tail.

The Top Flat pool below Clondulane weir on the Blackwater, where the General and Billy Flynn hooked the 51-pounder

I have no doubt that such a fish was caught by the General but I would have thought that a 52lb fish hooked in the tail would have been unstoppable (Flynn claims a slightly heavier weight – 53lb). Moreover, Flynn only saw the fish jump. He does not claim to have seen the fish in the water – a situation that would lend itself to foul-hooking – and fails to fill in the details. Was he fishing with a fly at the time or was he bait-fishing? I have determined to include the General's fish in the hope that we may yet discover how the River Blackwater's record fish was actually caught. Meantime, I am grateful for Hammond's account and urge my readers to seek out a copy of his hilarious little book. *The Irish Times* said of the author, 'Hammond has the ear for dialogue and the wait-till-you-hear this gusto of the born storyteller.'

In July 2005, through the kindness of Michael Penruddock, the Duke of Devonshire's factor at Lismore Castle and the Careysville fishings in County Cork, I was able to study the Careysville Fishery Record Books dating from 1926 up to the present time. Sitting in the library of Careysville House, also known as the Big House, I was aware that I was at the nerve centre of one of the most famous of all salmon-fishing lodges. I quickly found the entry I most wanted to look up i.e. that for Saturday, 29 April 1930:

> *Gen E. C. Walthall caught on Saturday 29th 1 fish 51 lbs.*
>
> *Water Height 3'10" dirty – southerly gale*
>
> *Temperature 42°. Hooked on Top Flat landed top of Paddy.*

I unhesitatingly settled on the 51lb weight given in the Record Book, rather than the 52lb of *Game Fish Records* (1936) or Billy Flynn's 53lb, knowing that the law of re-reporting or re-recording the weight of a big fish demands a slight weight increase rather than a decrease.

The recording of the weight of every fish taken at Careysville for seventy-nine years has been done so carefully (together with notes on the weather conditions and the height and temperature of the water) that it is obvious the Record Books are of the greatest historical importance. Such catastrophes as the discovery and subsequent exploitation of the Greenland feeding grounds and the fish disease U.D.N. show up quite clearly. Although there has been a recent recovery in the number of fish caught at Careysville, the inability of most large salmon to run the gauntlet of countless miles of gill nets off Ireland's west coast is reflected in the very much lower average weight of the fish – smaller fish have a better chance of getting around or through the nets although many carry net scars. Interestingly, the General caught a 31-pounder on Monday, 24 April, a few days before catching his big fish. From these weights, it is clear what a fantastic fishery Careysville once was. Indeed, the average weight of the fish taken in 1929 was 19lb!

Peter Bielski, who manages the fishery, introduced me to head gillie Paddy Egan and to his assistant Albert Clancy. Albert took me on a conducted tour of all the famous pools on the two-mile beat so that I could take photographs. Starting at Clondulane weir we photographed the Top Flat, the Cabin, the Sand Hole, the Castle, the Lane Stream, O'Donnell's Flat, Joyce's Flat and the Lisineen Bank, and saw others that I didn't photograph. I was also permitted to photograph the picture of General Walthall, his salmon and the head gillie that hangs in Careysville House.

The last word should probably go to the late Duke of Devonshire, writing about his favourite gillie in the foreword of Jack Chance's *Salmon Stories* (1983). He had this to say about his employee:

> ...many of the happiest days of my life have been spent salmon fishing in the River Blackwater in County Cork in the Republic of Ireland, and many of these happy times I spent in the company of Billie Flynn. It is difficult to describe him, but the best I can do is to call him a 'stage' Irishman. Like many of his countrymen, he preferred good manners to the truth. This had the advantage of making him the most delightful company: at the same time one realized that it would be unwise to believe a word he was saying.

The Lane Stream on the Blackwater. The General and Billy Flynn passed through in their battle with the big fish. 'On and on, down the river he went until we were now in the Lane Stream with the fish as full of fury as ever.'

Mr and Mrs Harold de Pass with his 51lb salmon

HAROLD de PASS'
51lb AWE SALMON
No. 220

here is a very good chance that this fish was caught on fly but so far I have not found any record describing the method of capture. Arthur Oglesby and Lucy Money-Coutts mention Harold de Pass's portmanteau salmon in their book *The Big Fish* (1992), in the chapter entitled 'Big Fish River', and feature a photograph of the fish together with the captor and his wife. They tell us that de Pass caught his fish in Little Verie pool in 1936 but fail to mention the date of capture. The heavy mottling on the gill covers, however, indicates that it was an autumn fish. Oglesby and Coutts aver that 'The hooking and playing of every one of them [50-pounders] whether lost or landed, would have provided a drama unsurpassed on any other river in Britain, such was the turbulence and irregular nature of the Awe's headlong descent.'

51½lb RIVER THAMES SALMON
—— No. 224 ——

Prior to the reintroduction of Thames salmon, John Piper, a popular contributor to angling journals in the 1960s, wrote an article for the June 1962 edition of *Trout and Salmon*. Although entitled 'The Last Thames Salmon', it was about a parliamentary debate on the pollution of the River Thames and its chances of recovery. Sir Tufton Beamish reported – presumably after some serious research – that the heaviest fish recorded for the species weighed 51½lb.

> On March 31st 1961 the House of Commons unanimously approved the Rivers (Prevention of Pollution) Bill. In the course of a most interesting debate the council member of The Trout and Salmon Association, Sir Tufton Beamish, reminded the House that from the 13th to the 18th Centuries the Thames was a famous salmon river. The last definite information he had of a fish taken from these waters related to 1823 or 24 and to the best of his knowledge the heaviest fish recorded scaled 51½lb.
>
> 'I should like to make an offer of 100 guineas,' said the member for Lewes, 'for the first man or woman who, with rod and line, above the tidal waters of the Thames, catches a salmon in this century or during my life-time, whichever is the longer.'

We all know that the Thames enjoyed a clean-up to the extent that has enabled salmon to return to the streams where they were released as parr, but so far the population has not become self-sustaining. Sadly, Tufton Beamish did not give us any details about the big fish – not even the year of capture – but I am sure that sooner or later I shall discover his source and be able to remedy the situation.

O'MAHONY'S
51½lb BLACKWATER SALMON
No. 226

The *Fishing Gazette* reported this fish in their issue dated 13 April 1929. They in turn had picked it up from the *Cork Examiner* of 8 April 1929.

A Grand Irish Salmon

Fishing on the free part of the River Blackwater at Fermoy, Mr. O'Mahony, a local fisherman, hooked a monster salmon, which was landed after a fight lasting an hour. The salmon weighed 51½lb., and is the heaviest fish caught on rod this season in the British Isles. We are able to give a good photograph of this fine specimen, taken by Mr. Frank O'Brien, photographer, Fermoy.

THE RECORD
51½lb ANNAN SALMON
No. 227

The heaviest salmon to be taken from Scotland's River Annan was caught by John James Varrie in Geordie's Hole on 14 November 1929. Geordie's Hole is located in the Royal Four Towns section of the river. Six and a half years old, the fish had spent two and a half of those years as a parr.

John Varrie, who lived in Lockerbie's high street, decided to present his fish to the burgh. The salmon was set up and once adorned the Public Reading Room in Lockerbie. In April 2005, I telephoned the library to see if the cased fish was still extant but, to my dismay, I was told that it was no longer on display and its whereabouts was unknown. A month later, having in the meantime met the Annan gillie, Russell Frank, I received a welcome letter from him – 'Enclosed is a photograph of the fish from Lockerbie Town Hall. The pool called Geordie's pool today is marked on the Ordnance Survey 1:25,000 as George's pool, behind Hightae village.'

John Varrie's salmon which used to adorn the Public Reading Room in Lockerbie. It appears to be leaking at the gills. This happens when some of the fish's body fat has not been completely removed by the taxidermist

Geordie's pool on the River Annan, looking downstream from the right bank, where John Varrie caught the record fish for the Annan on 14 November 1929

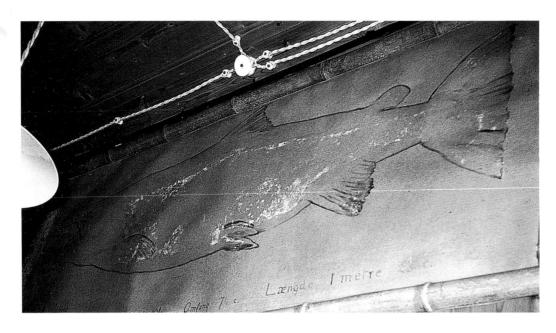

MISS ANNIE OLDFIELD'S
51¾lb NAMSEN SALMON
No. 229

I first came across reference to Annie's salmon in *Where to Fish* (1952), where it was listed as weighing 52lb. No date was given but the location of the catch was included – the Moum beat on the Namsen River.

No more information on Annie's fish came my way for a year until I received a batch of transparencies from Malcolm Greenhalgh. When I had these printed, I found the outline of a large salmon that Malcolm had himself photographed in a Norwegian lodge. An outline of Annie's salmon was painted on canvas, appropriately framed with Tonkin cane. The undulating surface of the fish is due to the canvas billowing like a slack sail. Close scrutiny with a magnifying glass revealed a legend that read:

> *Miss A. Oldfield, Moum 3/9/21, weight 23¹/₂ kilos, girth 74cms,*
> *length 1 metre 28cms.*

So Annie Oldfield caught her 51¾lb salmon (girth 29in, length 50½in) in 1921. One important piece of information is still missing – how was the fish caught? Doubtless in time this will be forthcoming and my guess is that it was caught on fly. Annie was quite young when she caught the fish and was most likely to have been harling with fly.

Harling on the Moum beat on the River Namsen, showing the enormous size of the river where Annie Oldfield caught her fish in September 1921

E.P. BATES'
52lb ERNE SALMON
No. 230

The Reverend Newland's book *The Erne, Its Legends and its Fly-Fishing* (1851) is one of the gems of angling literature. It is quite impossible, if you have read the book, not to feel the magic of the little town of Ballyshannon in County Sligo that crouches over the River Erne where it exits to the sea. It was in this town and on this beat that most of the incidents described by Newland took place.

Sadly, the spectacular quality of the salmon fishing that Newland and the characters in his book enjoyed has gone forever. The development of hydro-electricity during the late 1940s, despite many protests, succeeded in ruining the best stretch of salmon-fly water in Ireland. During my last visit in the spring of 2005, a senior local salmon fisherman confided, 'The appeal to prevent the scheme foundered when a pro-hydro scheme speaker said to a meeting, "Do you want your children to have jobs when they grow up or do you want them to emigrate?" ' My confidant, not without some rancour

The River Erne at Ballyshannon as it is today, looking upstream from Mill Quay towards what were, prior to the hydro-electric scheme, the Great Falls and the Great Pool of Ballyshannon. According to the Reverend Newland, 'The pool between the bridge and the Great Falls is by the far the most killing station on the river.'

added, 'They once employed over a hundred people locally, now it's down to twenty.'

Although I have yet to discover an account of the capture of E.P. Bates' fish, the short length of the best fly-fishing from Belleek to Ballyshannon pretty well ensures that it was caught somewhere between those places.

Visitors to Ireland, regardless of their interest, inevitably discover evidence of the terrible plight of the people during the great famine that plagued Ireland in the 1840s. If you stand on Mill Quay just above the island in the tidal section of the River Erne in Ballyshannon and read the placard, it tells you the story of how hundreds of the starving populace left Ireland for America. Even getting beyond the sandbar at the river mouth was dangerous – so dangerous that after many sailing ships were wrecked, Ballyshannon's days as a shipping port came to an end.

The last surviving bollard (left foreground) from the days of the Great Hunger still stands at Mill Quay, Ballyshannon

The photograph found in the 'The Bulman' inn at Kinsale in Ireland. A note on the back gives the weight of the four fish as 51lb, 33lb, 14lb and 13lb. The catching of four salmon of this size must have been quite an event

THE 52lb RIVER BANDON SALMON
—— No. 242 ——

A boat builder in Ballinrobe in County Mayo told me that many years ago he had delivered a new boat to a client in County Cork and while he was there he had seen a cast of a very large salmon on the wall of an inn in Kinsale. He could not remember the name of the inn but it was to be found at the top of a very steep hill. I enquired at a number of licensed premises in Kinsale without success until I found The Spaniards Inn at the top of Heartbreak Hill (the boat builder should never have forgotten that name!).

Although the salmon was of dream-like proportions to a modern Irish salmon angler, at 35lb it did not qualify for my list. However, the helpful Irish landlord cautioned me not to give up because he said there was another hostelry barely half a mile down the road, The Bulman, where I might find the cast of a bigger fish.

I arrived at The Bulman before it had opened but with the help of the postman penetrated the establishment and found myself conversing with the owner, Conor Ryan. Mr Ryan knew nothing about the cast of a big salmon – all he could offer was a photograph of several fish, including one big one. The fact that the photograph was framed and screwed to the wall eight feet up from the floor was no problem. Steps, an electric screwdriver and a knife to break the seal cocooning the framer's masterpiece soon enabled Mr Ryan to put the photograph into my hands. A legend on the back gave the weight of the four fish as 51lb, 33lb, 14lb and 13lb. Presumably the fish were Bandon salmon and I daresay the best fish was the biggest ever to have been taken from that fine salmon river – or at its mouth, for the fish may well have been netted in the estuary where traditionally eight draft nets operate.

Egil Larsen with a fish as big as his son. Odd Haraldsen used this photograph in his brochure Giant Salmon in Norway, *to advertising angling holidays*

EGIL LARSEN'S 52lb VOSSO SALMON
—— No. 243 ——

Although the angling brochure in which this very appealing father-son-big-fish photograph appeared does not give the method or date of capture, it looks as if son is carrying father's spinning rod, while father is taking the strain of holding up the big fish for the cameraman. However, we do not know the method of capture for certain. Nevertheless, because it is such a marvellous photograph, it is included.

SALMON 52½ lbs.
Caught By R.G. DEVEREUX, april 14ᵗʰ 1888 TheNyth, WYE.

R.G. DEVEREUX'S
52½lb WYE SALMON
No. 246

A photograph of Devereux's salmon featured in an article written by Ron Swanson for *Classic Angling* No. 10, February 2001. Ron Swanson is not only a collector of cased, carved and cast fish, he is a world authority on the master craftsmen who made them, be they carvers, taxidermists, casters or painters. I suspect that he gets more excited about fish modelled in wood than anything else because he is able to appreciate the distinctive styles of the carvers' art. Devereux's fish was modelled by John Forrest, tackle dealer. John Forrest produced a few of what carvers call 'three quarter models' in which the fins are part of the body wood. In this instance, the fish is fitted with a glass eye of the kind used by taxidermists.

According to Jock Scott in *Game Fish Records* (1936), Robert Devereux caught his salmon on the Nyth water on 14 April 1928. It weighed 52½lb, length 52½in and girth 28½in. Although the method of taking the fish is not given, John Ashley-Cooper, one of the greatest authorities on such matters, has suggested that most salmon caught during the Victorian period were taken on fly. The lettering on the case says 1888 but I daresay that Scott's date is the correct one because, as Ron Swanson says:

> Besides the Tullys and Hardy, several other first-rate model makers were represented in London during the 1920s. The John Forrest tackle shop produced a few very fine three-quarter models, in which all the fins were made from the body wood like Malloch and the late Hardys.

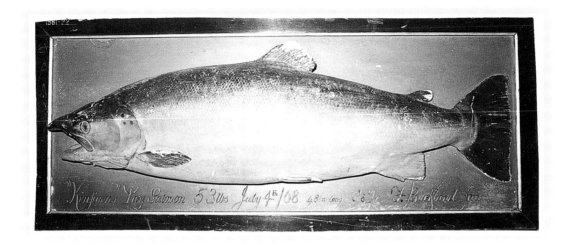

A 53lb TAY SALMON
No. 249

A cast of this salmon is in store at the Scottish Fisheries Museum at Anstruther in Fifeshire. It is not on show because it is damaged – the lower jaw is broken – and like other items that once belonged to that great Victorian ichthyologist Frank Buckland, it awaits funding for restorative work. We know from the legend inscribed on the case that it weighed 53lb, was caught on 4 July 1868 and was 48in long, and that Frank Buckland made the cast.

No captor's name is revealed, but the inscription shows that the fish was caught at Kinfauns, probably in a net, about three miles downstream of Perth.

LORD VANE-TEMPEST-STEWART'S 53lb NAMSEN SALMON
No. 250

Lord Vane-Tempest-Stewart caught his 53lb salmon on 22 June 1898 on the Namsen River near Grong. The fish was brought back to Scotland so that a wood-carving could be made, although the Vane-Tempest-Stewarts, marquises of Londonderry, had an Irish seat. Incidentally, in 1952 Lady Margaret Vane-Tempest-Stewart, a descendant of the successful angler, married one of the most famous of all salmon fishers, (the late) Hugh Falkus.

J.T. NESS' 54lb TAY SALMON
No. 265

W e know little about Mr Ness's big salmon other than that it was originally reported in *Where to Fish* (1951–2) and mentioned in John Ashley-Cooper's *The Great Salmon Rivers of Scotland* (1980). Nigel Houldsworth in his *Fisherman's Map of Salmon Pools on the River Tay* (2001) adds one extra detail – Ness's first name, John. All the aforesaid authors recorded that the fish was caught at Almondmouth, i.e. at the mouth of the River Almond where it enters the River Tay, approximately three miles above Perth.

The beat where the River Almond joins the Tay is known as Almondmouth. This photograph shows High Bank pool on the opposite side (Lower Scone) and the Middle Shot, where seine netting was once practised, immediately below the exit of the Almond on the right bank. A lot of salmon run up the Almond to spawn but they rarely move into the river until the autumn

V. IANETTA'S 54lb TAY SALMON
No. 268

There is some confusion regarding this fish's captor because Malcolm Greenhalgh spells his name as above, whereas Nigel Houldsworth who created the *Fisherman's Map of Salmon Pools on the River Tay* (2001) spells it Ianetti.

Nigel Houldsworth notices that the fish was caught in September 1965 in the Cradle pool at Ballathie whereas Malcolm Greenhalgh gives the year of capture as 1969, as does John Ashley-Cooper in *The Great Salmon Rivers of Scotland.*

This is the Cradle pool on the Tay, where V. Ianetta caught his big fish in the 1960s. The photograph was taken from the right bank at Ballathie, looking towards Collin's Croy

55lb SALMON FROM THE SAND RIVER
No. 274

Two splendid photographs from Jack Chance's *Salmon Stories* (1983), give us all the clues we have about this fish. The fish weighs 55lb but no other details are provided.

ODD HEIA'S 55lb NAMSEN SALMON
No. 275

The best fish taken from the Namsen River in 1984, which was otherwise a very poor year, weighed 55lb. Odd Heia caught it on 17 June.

ODD HARALDSEN'S 55lb 2oz VOSSO SALMON
No. 277

The late Arthur Oglesby thought that the Norwegian Odd Haraldsen 'probably catches more salmon than anyone else in the world' and, with his vast experience, was well worth listening to on the matter of feeding or not feeding line to a taking fish. Oglesby's chapter 'Hooking, Playing and Landing [salmon]' in his book *Fly Fishing for Salmon and Sea Trout* (1986), some of which is based on Haraldsen's experiences, is in my estimation definitive on this very important aspect of fly fishing for salmon.

PIRKKO SEPPONEN'S 55lb 2oz TANA SALMON
No. 278

In the March 1985 edition of *Urheilu Kalastus* magazine, a particularly impressive photograph shows Risto and Pirkko Sepponen with Pirkko's magnificent fish, which looks like a springer. The method of capture was not given in the article.

TOP LEFT: *Two little girls, possibly Norwegian, help to hold the Sand River salmon off the ground.*

TOP RIGHT: *Odd Heia's 55lb-er*

BOTTOM LEFT: *Odd Haraldsen caught his 55lb 2oz salmon on the Vosso River at Bolstadoyri in June 1981*

BOTTOM RIGHT: *Risto and Pirkko Sepponen with the portmanteau salmon*

A 56lb OR 57lb DEE SALMON
— No. 286 —

M r C. Gordon, a gillie on the River Dee's Ardoe water, a beat that is known to be better for bait fishing than fly fishing, nevertheless is said to have caught a 57lb fish there on a fly. The date of the catch was reported by the *Fishing Gazette* (14 November 1903) to be 1884, but is challenged by John Ashley-Cooper. In *The Great Salmon Rivers of Scotland* (1980), he tells us that it was caught in October 1886. Moreover, he says the weight is also uncertain because another report points to a weight of 56lb. More information is needed before this fish can be properly documented.

MAJOR GREEN'S BRACE OF
NAMSEN SALMON, 52lb AND 57lb
— No. 288 —

I n Audun Koren's forty-page illustrated booklet *Norwegian Fishing Rights and Shooting* (1929), written principally to attract North American sportsmen to Norway, the following entry for Major Green's fish appeared on page 7:

McAlpin's photographer must have taken great care to place the fish and the people so as to make them all clearly visible. This photograph reveals how easy it is to make fish look a good deal larger than they are in real life!

BEAT 1. SELLÆG-RISTAD. Extent abt. 3 miles. This is the bottom beat for sports fishing on the Namsen, as the tidal water goes right up to its beginning. In 1921 the Sellæg part of the beat was fished by Major Green who caught 52 salmon weighing 1086 lbs., two of which, caught the 8th & 13th of June, weighed respectively 52 and 57 lbs. For the two last seasons the beat has been fished by an American, Mr. Brewster, whose records have not been available. When the Ristad water is included, the beat should be an excellent one for at least two boats. Accommodation in comfortable house, where 5 rooms, bath, electric light & heating.

In the same booklet, there is a particularly well-arranged photograph of three large cock salmon caught by Colonel B.B. McAlpin in 1928 from the Vibstead beat. Five salmon weighing between 40 and 53lb were caught on the same beat in 1927, but sadly no specific weights or any catch data are given.

A 57lb RIVER TAY SALMON
No. 291

In November 2005 Malcolm Greenhalgh sent me a note on several large salmon, including details of a cast of a 57lb Tay salmon caught in 1957. He had obtained this information from a retired tackle dealer, who had operated from premises in Bloxwich near Walsall. Luckily, I managed to contact the dealer and it turned out to be Alan Barker, whom I had met several times in the 1980s.

Alan no longer has the fish but he kept notes regarding its provenance. The cast fish was mounted on a board with a simple legend:

Caught D.O.H. 1957, River Tay. Weight 57lbs.

Alan had purchased the cast from Bill Smith, a local taxidermist, who had in turn purchased it from another taxidermist in Carlisle about ten years ago.

J. GRAHAM PARSONS'
57lb VOSSO SALMON
No. 292

A photograph of Ambassador J. Graham Parsons' 57lb Vosso River salmon appears on an American website, edited by Louis Bignami, under the heading *Fine Saltwater Fishing*. The photograph depicts an incredibly beautiful salmon.

Many months after coming across this photograph, I received a note from Roy Flury drawing my attention to a statement in Philip Crowe's book *Out of the Mainstream*. On pages 73 and 74, he says the reason that he went to fish the Vosso was that his friend and diplomatic colleague, J. Graham Parsons, American Ambassador to Sweden, landed a 57-pounder there in June 1965. As a result, Crowe rented the Bolstad fishing the following year. He goes on to say that very few salmon are caught there on fly in June and early July, the time when the fishing is at its best.

A carving of Morch's fish was probably made by the most famous of all fish carvers, John Tully

PER MØRCH'S
57lb 6oz OTRA SALMON
— No. 294 —

The carved salmon that is pictured on page 318 of Arne Krogstad's book *Vigeland í Vennesla* (1999) looks like the work of the famous fish carver John Tully. The salmon weighed 57lb 6oz and was caught in Vigeland Foss pool by Per Mørch in July 1899. Henry Peter Alexander Mørch arrived in Norway from Liverpool with his family in 1895, and became a manager for Mr Hawkshaw, an industrialist who owned substantial properties in Vigeland. It is not surprising that Per found time for fishing, living and working as he did so close to the Otra at a time when big fish were running in numbers.

GIJSBERT STRUIK'S
57lb 6oz DUTCH SALMON
—— No. 295 ——

A lthough Holland is not now readily associated with big salmon, or any salmon for that matter, before industrialisation the situation was quite different. In 1910, for instance, Gijsbert Struik from the village of Woudrichem caught a salmon weighing 57lb in the Bergsche Maas River. Piet Hartman mentions it on page 204 of his book *Zalm Vernomen* (1995), but does not specify the method of capture.

This angler fishing the Bergsche Maas River at Woudrichem in Holland may be hoping for a salmon to match Gijsbert Struik's portmanteau fish

57½lb TAY SALMON
No. 298

In P.D. Malloch's *Life-History and Habits of the Salmon Sea-Trout, Trout and Other Freshwater Fish* (second edition, 1912) an excellent photograph of a 57½lb cock salmon adorns page 122. The fish was 53½in long with a girth of 28½in. It was caught on the River Tay on 24 May 1907. Other than illustrating a scale from the body of the fish, from which he was able to read its age, i.e. six years one month, Malloch supplied no other details of its capture.

58lb RIVER SHANNON SALMON
No. 301

A very brief entry for a 58lb salmon caught in 1872 appears on the list of notable fish in *Where to Fish* (1937). Since I have not, as yet, seen any other reference to this fish, it is impossible to elaborate on the entry, other than to say that if it was a rod-caught fish, the most likely spot is somewhere on the Castleconnell beats.

G.C. WAUD'S 58lb VOSSO SALMON
No. 304

A letter from J.A. Hutton published in the *Fishing Gazette* (16 July 1921) reported Waud's fish:

I am sending you a photo which I think is well worth reproducing. It is of a magnificent salmon caught by Mr. G.C. Waud in the Evanger River [part of the Vosso River] in Norway last year. Weight 58lb., length 51ins, girth 30 ins. It was a cock-fish and as will be seen from the photo, it was really a beautiful specimen. I am sending you a photo of one of the scales of this monster which shows that it was a six-year-old maiden fish which had not spawned before – two years in the river and four years in the sea.

The Evanger was always noted for its heavy salmon, which were particularly well-shaped fish. Mr. Sturdy's scale was based on Evanger fish, and this probably explains why his scale is rather above the average of most rivers. I have before me the scales of three monsters caught in this river last year.

July 19th 53lb., length 49in, girth 27¾in.
June 15th 58lb., length 51in, girth 30 in.
June 9th 65lb., length 55in, girth 34½in.

The reference to Mr Sturdy's scale is interesting because it is not widely known that the scale was based on data obtained from Evanger salmon.

Mr Waud and his fish, caught on 15 June 1921

*C.M. Wells with the two large Vosso salmon that he caught on
26 June 1926. They weighed 42lb and 54lb*

C.M. WELLS' 58lb VOSSO SALMON
—— No. 307 ——

C.M. Wells had some spectacular catches of Norwegian salmon. A practical man, he always used the method that he thought was most likely to get the best results in varying conditions and, as a result, caught a prodigious number of salmon – 1,486 all told. That figure included twelve over 50lb, a record. They weighed between 50lb and 58lb, were listed by Jack Chance in *Salmon Stories* (1983) and are included in List 1. Alas, no methods or dates of capture were given by Chance for individual fish, although he wrote on page 54:

> Rather more than half of Wells' salmon were killed on prawn, just over a third on fly and the remainder by spinning with spoon and sprat.

Mathias Bolstad, a famous Norwegian gillie, looked after Wells until fishing ceased in 1940, so far as foreigners were concerned, due to the war.

HALVOR UGLAND'S
58lb 6oz TORRIDAL SALMON
No. 309

The only reference to this fish that I have been able to find is in Arne Krogstad's *Vigeland i Vennesla* where, on page 319, there is a photograph of Halvor Ugland with two fine summer fish.

The larger of Halvor Ugland's fish weighed 58lb 6oz and was caught on the Torridal

E.M. CORBETT'S
58lb 6oz VOSSO SALMON
—— No. 311 ——

E.M. Corbett caught his great fish in July 1902 on the Evanger beat of the Vosso River. Unlike the Alten River, where most fish are caught on the fly, this is not the case with the Vosso River. The rod that Corbett is holding has its reel fitted high on the rod handle, which would seem to indicate that a spinning or a bait-fishing reel was attached.

Twelve months or so after I wrote the above, I found a reference to Corbett's big salmon in the *Fishing Gazette* of 15 November 1902, confirming that the fish was not taken on fly. It was caught in Mr Sturdy's stretch of the Vosso River at Evanger. Sturdy was the man who invented the famous scale from which the weight of a salmon can be read if its length was known. Also, perhaps more importantly, when the fish's weight is known, the scale can provide a condition factor:

> By the couresy of its captor I am able to give a picture of the 58½lb salmon caught in July in Vos Elv (or river Vos) on Mr Sturdy's water near Evanger. Pictures of the pool were given in the Christmas Number of the *Fishing Gazette* last year. It was taken with prawn on single gut trace supplied by Mr John Forrest of Thomas-street, Oxford-street, on an eleven-foot Hardy spinning rod, and on a large size Coxon "Ariel" slightly altered from the usual pattern, having German-silver rim and two small castors to relieve the strain on the centre pin. The extreme length was forty-nine and a half inches girth, just forward of dorsal fin thirty and a quarter inches.
>
> I think it is a great feather in Mr. Coxon's cap that his delicate "Ariel" reel should have stood the strain of a fight with such a grand salmon.

It was typical of Victorian and, as in this case, Edwardian salmon fishermen to look pretty unhappy if they landed a monster fish. E.M. Corbett (right) portrays a grimness that would have been considered exemplary.

D.K. SOMERVILLE'S
59lb SOUTH ESK SALMON
—— No. 314 ——

ood photographs of portmanteaux salmon that were caught in the nineteeth or early twentieth century are very difficult to track down, so I decided that Somerville's salmon deserved a place. Not much is known about it, other than the bare details published in *Where to Fish* (1937): '59lb Caught on the South Esk by Mr Somerville in October 1888. Length 53in., girth 28in.' However, in the *Illustrated London News* (11 November 1922) the caption reads: 'Caught in the South Esk by Mr Somerville in October 1922: a 59-lb salmon (4 ft. 5 in. by 28 in.)'. I thought that perhaps the typesetter working for the magazine had automatically picked up the figures for the current year, or alternatively, the typesetter working on *Where to Fish* made the mistake.

In *A Salmon Fisher's Odyssey* (1982) John Ashley-Cooper mentions the fish on page 168. Talking about the South Esk he says:

> The record fish for this river attained the astonishing weight of 59lb. It was caught by Mr. J.K. Somerville in October 1922. I wish I knew the story of its capture and could relate it here. It must have been highly dramatic. What can have induced such a monster to run up this comparatively small river? And it must have looked like a veritable porpoise in such restricted surroundings.

Although the date of capture agrees with the date given by *The London Illustrated News*, it could be that Ashley-Cooper gleaned his information from this very same news magazine. On the other hand, that may not be the case because he gives Somerville two initials, J.K., that were not included in the other references.

There the matter stood until my friend William Daniel mentioned that he had seen

None of the references to Somerville's capture of an amazingly large salmon in the South Esk mention the pool, or the mode of capture. From the bridge at Brechin, the river is especially beautiful in the autumn and shows the smallness of the river. Ashley Cooper wrote, 'I wish I knew the story of its capture and could relate it here. It must have been highly dramatic. What can have induced such a monster to run up this comparatively small river?'

Somerville's fine cased fish when he was one of the Earl of Southesk's shooting guests. It was mounted on the wall in the shooting lodge. The legend under the case revealed that the salmon was preserved by P.B. Malloch of Perth and presented to J. Milne by D.K. Somerville. I wrote to the Earl in March 2006 and in due course received a reply, part of which is reproduced below, clearing up the problem of the date and the captor's initials.

Kinnaird Castle
Brechin
Angus
DD9 6TZ   *21st April 2006*

Dear Mr. Buller

GIANT SALMON

Unfortunately I have not been able to discover a great deal. We do not seem to have any relevant records going back to 1922 which is frustrating so I have looked through the local libraries to see if there might be anything there. I did find a very brief mention in the Brechin Advertiser but it did not add much, other than the fact that Somerville was staying in the Crown Hotel at the time. Consequently, all I know is contained in the caption to the enclosed photograph [unfortunately the photograph mentioned is of such poor quality as to be unpublishable] which confirms that it was 1922 not 1888 and that Somerville's initials were D.K. (not J.K. per Ashley-Cooper). I'm sorry that I cannot help you further, I would be as interested as you to know the story of the fish's landing.

The enclosed photograph is one that I have taken at a quite high resolution, the problem being that the original is out of focus at either end of the fish, presumably its size made it difficult to capture.

Yours sincerely

Earl of Southesk

ODD HARALDSEN'S
59½lb VOSSO SALMON
No. 317

Haraldsen's fishing holiday brochure *Giant Salmon in Norway* includes a photograph of a 59½lb salmon that Odd Haraldsen caught on the Vosso River in 1965.

Odd Haraldsen's big fish from the Vosso

The snow visible on the hills, even on a summer night, gives some idea of the latitude of the Alten River. Snowmelt keeps up summer levels and helps the flow of rivers within the Arctic Circle

SALMON OVER 60lb CAUGHT BY ANY METHOD

MISS D. DAVEY'S
59½lb RECORD SPRING SALMON
No. 318

Miss Davey's fish is the only bait-caught fish listed that is under 60lb in weight and is included for three reasons. First of all it would be ungallant to leave out a lady's fish that is so close to qualifying. Secondly, it is the biggest spring fish ever caught on rod and line in Britain, and thirdly, it is the record rod-caught Wye salmon.

J. Arthur Hutton contributed a chapter about the salmon catches on the River Wye to Jock Scott's *Game Fish Records* (1936), and on page 46 he notes:

Then on March 13th, 1923, Miss Davey beat all previous records by landing a fish weighing 59½lb.; length 52in., girth 29in., condition-factor 41;

two years' river-life and four years in the sea. It was caught at Winforton by spinning, and after a very long struggle was landed in the dark with the aid of bonfires. This is, I believe, the heaviest *spring fish* ever caught by rod in the British Isles.

Doreen Davey, daughter of Major G. Davey of Kinnersley Castle who owned the Lower Winforton beat, hooked her fish in the Cow Pond pool. Here she is seen with her gillie, John Jellis, and the record fish.

This view from the Boat Inn at Whitney is just upstream of Winforton, where Doreen Davey caught the record Wye salmon. This stretch of river at Whitney was also the scene of the tragic loss of an even bigger salmon. The fish was subsequently found dead and eventually recovered from the river in a rotting state at Even Pitts Bridge, below Hereford

THE REVEREND A. COOK'S 60lb ANNAN SALMON
No. 319

In *Game Fish Records* (1936), on pages 150–1, Jock Scott mentions Cook's huge salmon:

> A correspondent living in the district writes that his late father frequently told the story of a 60lb salmon having been landed in the Sand Pool, Mount Annan, by the Reverend A. (?) Cook, of St John's Episcopal Church, Annan, some 85 years ago. No details are forthcoming; but to this day the name "Cook's rock" is applied to a certain stone in Sand Pool. The mere survival of the name indicates that Mr. Cook achieved celebrity in some way, and the story is worth repeating I think. Possibly some reader of these lines may be able to give us the true facts.

Whether or not Jock Scott subsequently received any help from a reader I do not know, but when I told this story to the keeper of the Newbie beat on the Annan, he was able to show me Cook's rock.

Cook's rock, almost under water in a spate, in the Sand pool on the River Annan, where many a salmon has received its last rites, but mostly at the hands of laymen

According to the inscription the fish was 4ft 5in long, with a girth of 2ft 5in and was 'taken in the net' at Upper Bulwark

A RIVER SPEY 60lb SALMON
No. 320

Sadly, the River Spey's largest salmon was not caught on rod and line. It was netted at the mouth of the river on 21 August 1894. A carving of this fish was made at Fochabers probably by John Tully and hung for many years in the smoking-room at Gordon Castle, along with carvings of other fish of forty pounds or more that were caught on the Gordon Castle water. Today the carving hangs in the Tugnet Museum at the mouth of the Spey. When I visited the museum at Tugnet, I found that the carvings of large salmon have been removed because of funding problems and are now with the Fisheries Department.

THREE GIANT TAY SALMON IN ONE WEEK
No. 321

In July 1902, while Sir Herbert Maxwell was working on the manuscript of his book *British Freshwater Fishes* (1904), he received a letter from P.D. Malloch of Perth. Malloch later wrote a classic book on the natural history of salmon, *Life-History and Habits of the Salmon, Sea-Trout, Trout and Other Freshwater Fish*, but that July he wrote: 'We got two salmon (in the nets) over 60lb last week, and one yesterday 50lb, only 4ft. 1in. long – a great beauty.'

I have not heard or read reports on these huge fish from any other source and it leads me to conclude, as many have before me, that rod fishermen have never been privy to the facts and figures regarding the destruction of large salmon by those who have netting interests. Even Malloch, who was privy to the netsmen's secrets, chose to reveal the details only to his scientist friend and not to his customers, the rod anglers. Since Malloch does not provide specific weights for the two largest fish, I have recorded both at 60lb.

A 60lb NAMSEN SALMON
—— No. 322 ——

Woodcarvings of big salmon were much in vogue during the later part of the nineteenth and early twentieth century, and have been, spasmodically, ever since. One was made of this 60lb salmon, caught at Hollandsoi on the Namsen River in 1903. The model, by Rowland Ward, hangs in a house close to where the fish was caught. This exquisite detail of the carving suggests that it may have been done by John Tully.

A 60lb RIVER TWEED SALMON
—— No. 323 ——

In one of the frequent exchanges of letters between the *Fishing Gazette*'s editor and Mr W.L. Calderwood, Chief Inspector of Scottish Salmon Fisheries, Calderwood refers to a 60lb Tweed salmon that managed to get itself caught out of season. In his letter to R.B. Marston published on 14 January 1908, he offers no explanation but he does give an excellent account of the previous life of the fish that was hatched in 1900 and grew to its final weight by 1907:

> In connection with the 60lb. Tweed fish, it will, I am sure, be of interest to many of your readers to see the note which Mr. H. W. Johnston kindly sent me after reading the scales so as to show the history of the fish:

Year	Spring/Summer	Autumn/Winter
1900	Hatched	River
1901	River	River
1902	Smolt (late) sea	Sea
1903	Sea	Spawned as grilse
1904	Sea	Sea
1905	Sea	Spawned
1906	Sea	Sea
1907	Sea	Captured in December when partly spawned (?) and nearly eight years old

> I am much obliged to Mr. Calderwood for kindly sending the photograph and the information contained in his letter. I expect it is not possible to measure the fish very accurately, and it was probably more than 4ft. 6in. in the flesh. The history of the Tweed fish as told by its scales is very interesting.

Since there is no record of a hen fish ever reaching a weight of 60lb, we must assume that it was a cock fish, but this assumption is questionable because there is no known example of a cock fish spawning three times. A year later, in *The Salmon Rivers of Scotland* (1909), Calderwood tells us that the fish was not captured as previously reported but found dead at Mertoun on the River Tweed in 1907:

> While referring to big fish, I may mention that in Mertoun Water in December, 1907, a fish was found dead which weighed 60lb. It is possible that some lucky man may yet beat Mr. Prior's monster? From an examination of its scales made by Mr. H. W. Johnston, it appears that the fish was nearly eight years old, and had spawned twice in its lifetime, once as a grilse in 1903, and again in 1905.

The 60lb fish was found in December 1907 at Mertoun (pronounced Merton). One of the most famous fly-fishing beats on the Tweed, the prolific Upper Cauld pool is shown here

ONE OF MAJOR W.H.S. ALSTON'S
60-POUNDERS FROM THE VOSSO
No. 324

In his most entertaining little book *Salmon Stories* (1983) Jack Chance tell us on page 53 that Major W.H.S. Alston killed salmon of 60lb, 61lb and 63lb on the Bolstad beat of the Vosso River. The 63-pounder is No. 370 on this list. A photograph of Alston with a very impressive salmon appeared on page 119 of the *Flyfishers Journal* (September 1962). I had seen it before and thought the fish to be one of his 60-pounders but, according to the caption, it weighed 55lb, which is still a pretty big fish by anyone's standards.

Major Alston with a big Vosso salmon. Judging by the length of the rod that he is holding, together with the position of the reel, he may have caught this fish on the fly

A SECOND MONSTER WYE SALMON
—— No. 325 ——

On 10 January 1914, under the heading 'A Monster Wye Salmon' the *Fishing Gazette* reported that a huge Wye salmon that had been found dead. J.A. Hutton, who sent the details to the editor wrote, 'I should think this monster was nearer 65lb as our *Fishing Gazette* scale of weight for length gives 67½lb for a 54-inch salmon.'

Some six years later the *Fishing Gazette* reported the finding of an even bigger corpse, weighing approximately 60lb. Allowing for a loss of one-fifth of its weight due to spawning, this fish must have weighed well over 70lb in its prime. Interestingly, apart from the 75½lb salmon netted from the Drummen River in 1881, this fish measuring 57in. is the longest salmon ever recorded. A full report of the discovery of this dead fish appeared in the *Fishing Gazette* dated 10 July 1920:

THE MONSTER WYE SALMON

I have to thank Mr. Hutton for this photo of the great Wye salmon which was found dead. The portrait of Mills, the head Wye bailiff, gives a good comparison for size. As our readers will remember, this fish was found at Even Pits Bridge, about eight miles below Hereford. It was 57in. long, 26in. in girth, and weighed approximately 60lb. R.B.M.

A 60lb RIVER USK SALMON
No. 326

Jock Scott records on page 39 of *Game Fish Records* (1936) that the biggest River Usk salmon – a 60-pounder – was caught in 1924 in a trammel net. Sadly, he also reports that the second largest Usk salmon was also caught in a net. This one weighed 56lb and was taken in the Porton nets in 1913. The biggest rod-caught fish was killed by Colonel Hegan in 1931 and weighed 48lb.

It's not known where the 60-pounder was caught but it may have been in tidal water. Towards the end of the nineteenth century the Usk was a prolific salmon river. In the fifth edition of his *Book on Angling* (1880), Francis Francis wrote: '...perhaps more salmon yearly fall to the rod there than in nearly all the other English rivers put together.' In 1891 some 4,931 salmon were killed on rod and line.

BJARNE MANNSVERK'S 60lb ALTEN RIVER SALMON
No. 327

In his list of big Alten River salmon caught after the Second World War, Tormod Leinan mentions Bjarne Mannsverk's 60-pounder, which was taken from the Bollo beat in 1960. Tormod explains that, up until the early nineties, spinning was allowed on the whole of the Alten in the month of August.

Bjarne Mannsverk and two colleagues with his big fish

LORD DAVENPORT'S
60½lb RAUMA SALMON
No. 332

We have only the barest details on this fish, i.e. its weight, the name of its captor, the name of the river where it was caught – the Rauma – and the year of its capture – 1926. This sparse information is to be found in *Where to Fish* (1937) and, since the fish was documented in such a reliable publication, I have included it in my list. However, there is some confusion because 1926 was the year in which Sir W. Bromley-Davenport caught a Rauma River salmon, weighing 55lb, as reported in the *Fishing Gazette* of 26 June 1926.

I believe that Lord Davenport obtained a lease on the Rauma River and I *know* that W. Bromley-Davenport was the author of *Sport*, a famous book published in 1885. Just how these two successful fishermen are related, if at all, I do not know.

60½lb BALTIC SEA SALMON
No. 333

In their book *Atlantic Salmon* (2005), R. Sutterby and Malcolm Greenhalgh record this huge salmon as having been caught in the Bay of Pukavik in the Baltic Sea on 9 May 1995. They also mention that another fish, weighing 58lb, was taken from the same bay on 10 April 1992. No indication of the mode of capture is given in either case. Then in December 2005 I received a copy of a cutting taken from *Sportfishing In Sweden* (1995), documenting the bigger fish. It was the biggest salmon taken in 1995 and it was caught trolling. That year turned out to be a good one for giant salmon – twenty-seven rod-caught fish weighing from 45lb to 60½lb were landed in Swedish waters.

On the subject of big Baltic salmon, Sutterby and Greenhalgh make an interesting comment, 'Currently, one of the best areas for catching salmon is the Baltic, where the populations of prey species such as herring and sprat have exploded in recent years.'

HIS FIRST FISH – 60lb 10oz
No. 334

You have to read through a letter published by the *Fishing Gazette* on 3 November 1923 to appreciate fully that sometimes – too often for comfort – the largest fish are caught by undeserving anglers. Details of a huge rod-caught salmon from the River Vefsen were given in a report by R.H. Venables Kyrke.

EXTRAORDINARY CAPTURE OF A 55LB SALMON

DEAR SIR – On July 23 last two young boys, aged respectively eight and twelve, sons of one of my boatmen, were paddling about in a deep pool on the Fosgrid beat of the Vipen (Vefsen), pretending to be fishing. The pool was known to hold big fish, which hung about it indefinitely, but none had ever been taken there! The lads had procured about 20 yards of twine, and to this had attached one of their father's three-inch spoons, *upside down*, and trailed this a few yards behind the boat. A fish took it, then ran a yard, but lay on its side flapping. A man saw that the boys had a fish on, and putting off from the bank gaffed it! The spoon was so deep down in its gullet that the salmon could not use its gills, and so was helpless! Had it only run a yard or two it would have broken the thin twine for a certainty. It was 25 kilos or 55lb. when weighed by the water bailiff and 133cm in length by 73cm in girth.

Another fish was taken in one of my favourite pools a week after I had left in 1921, when I had given the boatmen and farmers permission to fish. A man who had never fished before, borrowed a rod, line and spoon and immediately got hold of a large fish, which, after a long struggle, he killed. It weighed 27.5 kilos, or over 60lb.

In 1917 another man, equally inexperienced, got one of 57lb. on my lower water, on a shallow reach of gravel considered useless, as the ice flood had carried away all the big stones and there was no holding.

Yet another big fish was taken by a lady fishing from my lowest lodge, which I had placed at the disposal of her husband when I moved up to my top beats. A few days after their arrival he asked her if she would like to try for a fish, and she said she would, so he rigged up some tackle and went up the river. When he returned he asked her if she had had any luck? Yes! I got one she replied. Was it a good one? Yes! I think so! He went out to the ice house to find a 50 pounder! This was her first, and I believe her last, fish.

But what made the capture more extraordinary was the fact that the rod and line had been discarded by her husband's father some 25 years before and given to him as more or less worthless, and it had not been used for a quarter of a century!

Yours faithfully,

R.H. VENABLES KYRKE.
The Châlet, Symonds Yat, Ross-on-Wye

KENNETH OLSSON'S
60lb 10oz BALTIC SALMON
No. 335

In 1995 Kenneth Olsson from Sweden won the Laxfestivalen salmon angling competition with the above portmanteau fish. It was a tournament record and it was caught trolling a spinning lure.

Presumably the 60-pounder is being held by the angler on the right but the other fish also looks a corker

The plaque reads: 'Salmon, Male. Caught at Holandso, Namsen River, Norway. 30th June 1910. Length 54ins, Girth 31ins, Weight 61lbs

A 61lb NAMSEN SALMON
No. 337

On July 2005, Roy Flury sent me details of this salmon caught on 30 June 1910 from the Namsen River in Norway. A carving of the fish hangs in a house close to where it was caught. Although the salmon was caught in Norway, Roy Flury attributes the carving of this fish to Hardy Brothers of Alnwick. He also points out that Hardy used a rectangular plaque whereas Rowland Ward invariably used an irregular oval plaque.

Harling is probably the most popular method of fishing very large pools on the lower beats of big Norwegian rivers, including the Namsen as shown here. The method is also popular on big rivers in Scotland, such as the Tay, but the Norwegian fishermen, unlike their Scottish counterparts, harl with a fly as well as with bait. Harling with a fly rod is sometimes practised with a fly spoon – a large fly to which a small Mepps-like spoon is attached

H.C. CHARRINGTON'S
61lb VOSSO SALMON
No. 338

The only reference I had for H.C. Charrington's big salmon was on page 222 of Jock Scott's *Game Fish Records* (1936). However, Jock Scott noted that J. Arthur Hutton had received scales from this fish, so presumably somewhere in Hutton's records there will be catch data relating to this huge salmon. The fish was caught on 8 July 1924 from the Bolstad beat on the Vosso River in Norway. Although I am much too old to learn about computers, I am aware of the unique benefits of email and the internet, particularly when there is someone around who is able to use them skilfully. Such a person is

H.C. Charrington with his perfectly shaped salmon caught 8 July 1924. Charrington owned a beat at Bolstad on the Vosso River

my friend David Hatwell, who found the same data as I had found on Charrington's salmon in an article written by Skot McColl for the Norwegian fishing magazine *Netfishno*, 14 July 2003.

Seven months later I received a letter from Karl Magne, whose father used to assist Henry Charrington. Charrington owned a farm in Bolstad, which he eventually sold to Karl's father, and Karl was kind enough to take copies of the framed photographs that still adorn the walls of the farmhouse. Included among those of 60lb-plus salmon is one of Charrington's 61-pounder.

After protracted correspondence I was fortunate enough to find out more about the Charringtons. Isabelle Charrington, daughter of Henry, was an extremely successful salmon fisher and I am privileged, through the kindness of her daughter Mrs Sonia Hunterston, to reproduce some of her notes about the fishing at Bolstad on the Vosso River during the golden age of Norwegian salmon fishing:

My father always kept up his association with Norway, and being a keen fisherman, owned a share of a river in southern Norway and eventually bought Bolstad, the lower half of the Evanger River [all part of the Vosso River in fact]. The top half was owned by his friends, the Barlow family, who are still there nearly a hundred years afterwards. I inherited my share of the river on my father's death in 1928 and continued to fish, sharing the river and the house with C.M. Wells, a very well-known Eton master who rejoiced in being a Double First and a Double Blue. When he died in August 1963 I gave up the river, and it has now been taken by a fishing broker, Stohl, an American brewer, who rents it commercially.

Since the War, they do not get the big fish my father and I caught. I am proud to say, I caught eight fish over 40lbs, including five over 50lbs, and my father had the record for the river – a 61-pounder. These fish were caught with prawn spinners, or metal bait, as you could not really land such heavy fish on a fly. Unfortunately, all my father's records are lost, owing to my many moves in the War, and I think they were lent to somebody. A number of photographs still exist.

PAUL AAS'
61lb ALTEN SALMON
—— No. 339 ——

aul Aas caught his 61lb salmon in Bolvero in 1956 on a spoon. The length of the salmon is prodigious – no less than 61in. In fact, it is so long that a weight of at least 70lb would have been expected. After wondering about the fish's weight, all was revealed when I received a note from Roy Flury, reporting what Tormod Leinan had told him:

> At Bolvero in 1956 Paul Aas caught on a spoon a huge fish 61 inches in length. He did not have any scales. The fish was gutted and when weighed at home *two days* later the weight was over 61 lbs. Experienced fishermen reckon this fish would have been around 70 lbs when caught.

From this rather poor quality photograph, it appears that the salmon's girth measures more than the captor's waistline. The fish weighed 61lbs two days after it had been caught and after it had been gutted. It would probably have weighed 70lbs or more when it was caught

Unusually, the original fish appears to have been set up by a taxidermist, whereas it is customary with salmon (unlike pike, for example) to make a plaster cast of the original.

RICHARD VOYSEY'S
61¼lb RIVER EXE SALMON
No. 340

The clerk of the Exe Board of Conservators suggested that this fish was a record for all West Country rivers. It was not, but the claim warranted a comment from the editor of the *Fishing Gazette* (29 March 1924) and that put me on the track of another big salmon – a 61¼-pounder from the River Taw (No. 344):

THE 61¼LB. EXE SALMON

A fine salmon weighing 61¼lb. was taken in the nets from the River Exe last week. A correspondent kindly sent some scales which I forwarded to Mr. Hutton, but I have not yet received his report. I asked Mr. H. Ford, Clerk to the Exe Board of Conservators, if he would kindly send full particulars. Here is his reply: -

The Exe Board of Conservators
25 Southernhay, Exeter,
March 21, 1924

DEAR SIR – The following are the particulars of the salmon recently taken in the Exe by net:

Voysey caught his salmon on 18 March 1924 at Counterfeit Sands, Starcross, at the mouth of the River Exe near Topsham, which is just three miles downstream from Exeter. Although the photograph shows a team of three fishermen, there were actually four involved, namely Dick Voysey (in the flat cap), 'Urchard' Voysey, 'Noll' Voysey and Alf Tancock. The nets can be seen behind the man in the trilby hat

Cock Fish

Length, 54in. Head, 12in.

Girth, 29ins. Weight, 61¼lb.

Width of tail, 14in.

It is not only a record for the Exe, but I think I am right in saying for all West Country rivers, except possibly The Severn, but as to this I cannot speak authoritatively.

I am enclosing a cutting from a local newspaper which will give you an idea of the fish which has been sent to Messrs. C. Farlow and Co., 10, Charles Street, St. James's Square, from whom no doubt you will be able to obtain some scales. I am writing to them that you will be calling upon them. I may say that I have sent scales to Mr. J. Arthur Hutton, and I shall be very pleased when I receive his report to communicate with you. Yours truly,

H. FORD

According to the "List of Notable Fish" in *Where to Fish – The Anglers' Diary*, a 61½lb. salmon, netted from the River Taw on July 15, 1890, is probably the record for the West Country.

R.B. MARSTON

Every salmon fisherman dreams of catching a portmanteau salmon. The fish of dreams would be a silvery, fresh-run perfectly shaped fish with undamaged fins, and it would weigh in excess of 60lb. It goes without saying that the possession of a clear photograph of the fish, demonstrating all these features, would be most acceptable. Well, it's all here but there is a snag – the lucky captor caught his dream fish in a net.

Although it was the *Fishing Gazette* that alerted me to the existence of this monster salmon, it was David Hatwell who brought the photograph of it to my attention. The picture had been used as the frontispiece in a little known but excellent book, *Guardians of the Salmon* (2001), by Gordon Bielby. I wrote to Bielby, sometime employee of the Devon Board, an organisation born out of the earlier Exe Board of Conservators, and he was able to show me a copy of the original report for 1924 by the Clerk to the Board. The report delineated this extraordinary fish, which was twice as big as you could reasonably expect from a medium-sized river:

A fine specimen was caught by Richard Voysey of Topsham on 18th March, 1924. It was a cock fish and weight 61¼lbs. Its length was 4ft. 6ins., girth

2ft. 5ins., width of tail, 1ft 2ins., and head, 12ins. Examination of the scales showed that it had spent two years in the river and five at sea.

The fish was purchased by Captain Crisford, of MacFisheries, Ltd., and generously presented by him to the Board, who have had it mounted and handed over to the Royal Albert Memorial Museum, Exeter, where its graceful lines can be seen and studied to advantage.

Appropriately, Exeter Museum has returned the cased fish to Topsham – specifically Topsham Museum, where it is currently on view to the public, the centrepiece of a large display on the life cycle of the Atlantic salmon. I am greatly indebted to David Hatwell for taking the photographs and to Catriana Batty, the archivist at Topsham Museum, and Peter Davies, the Honorary Secretary, for granting permission to use the pictures on behalf of the Topsham Museum Society.

PER WALLE'S
61¼lb TANA SALMON
No. 341

According to the *Fiske Journalen Yearbook*, Per Walle caught this huge salmon in the Tana River in 1983 on an ABu Wobbler plug. ABu also made the reel, which is readily identifiable from the photograph.

J. HAGGART'S 61½lb TAY SALMON
No. 342

On 28 January 1939 the *Angler's News* published a letter sent to them by Mr F.J. Buchanan of Sheffield:

Dear Sir – Whilst going through some of my grandfather's letters and papers, I came across the enclosed, and I wondered if the item mentioned respecting the salmon 61½lb, would be of any interest to you and your readers. I, of course, have no other authority than the letter itself, but to me, it would appear a most amazing weight. What is the record salmon weight? Your views will be very much appreciated. – I am Sir, yours faithfully,

F. J. BUCHANAN
Sheffield 3. Jan. 20th

The editor explained:

The enclosure Mr. Buchanan mentions is a letter dated 6th January 1881, from Mr. J. Haggart of Stanley in Perthshire in reply to one from his old friend, Mr. Francis Buchanan of Sheffield. The friends had not met for many years and among personal details Mr. Haggart's letter states as follows:-

"I am still killing the noble salmon in the proud rolling Tay. Killed one of 62½lb a few years ago with the rod – a trophy – I am fond of angling still."

This was indeed a noble fish. The last salmon reaching 60lb recorded in our annual list of *Notable Freshwater Fish of the British Isles* was the 61lb fish killed by Mrs. Morison on the Deveron on 21st Oct. 1924.

    Where to Fish records Mr. Haggart's fish as "61lb killed on the Tay in 1870." The 1937-38 edition of *Where to Fish* also records four others of this weight and larger: 61½lb, Tay, Mr. T. Stewart, 1907; 64lb, Tay, Miss Ballantine, 1922; 67lb, Nith, Jock Wallace (a poacher), 1812; 6943lb, Tweed, the Earl of Home, about 1730. Previous editions of *Where to Fish* described this 1730 capture as "somewhat legendary" but in the 1937-38 edition the Editor, Mr. H.D. Turing, states that he received in 1935 particulars from "the present Earl Home" which justified him in stating that it was

The tail end of the Wash House pool by Stanley Mill, looking down to Cornpaw and towards Horsey pool – the last is probably the best pool on the upper Stanley beat

"the record rod-caught salmon for the British Isles".

We are much indebted to Mr. Buchanan for the loan of Mr. Haggart's very interesting letter. Bigger fish than those mentioned above have been caught by anglers in Norway and America but not (authentic) very much bigger. The biggest salmon (caught otherwise, probably in net) on record "a fish of 103lb, caught in 1901 or 1902 in the Forth district at the mouth of the Devon" (*Where to Fish*). – Ed.

On page 269 in *The Salmon Rivers and Lochs of Scotland* (1909), Augustus Grimble discusses prime beats on the lower River Tay, including Stobhall, Benchil and Burnmouth, and you know somehow that what he tells you is factual. Interestingly, he identifies the bait used by John Haggart:

There are between thirty and forty-nine casts, the whole of which were formerly rented by the late Mr. Barclay Field. Here he and his two well-known fishermen – Joseph Panton and John Haggart – made many great scores; to the latter belongs the honour of killing with a Phantom perhaps the heaviest fish ever landed by the rod in the United Kingdom, which weighed 62lb.

The earliest reference I can find for Haggart's fish appeared in the correspondence column of the *Fishing Gazette* on 2 November 1895. A letter from Frank Sanderson verbally assaulted Mr Henry Ffennell – a noted authority on the catch data of big salmon.

> ... The 1870 fish, killed by Mr. Haggart, draper, Stanley, 61½lb., was an unspawned repulsive spring rawner. Mr. Haggart refused to show it and it was cut up for the pigs, I hope immediately ...

Later, Ffennell mentioned Haggart's fish in a piece published by the *Fishing Gazette* on 14 November 1903: 'In 1870 Mr. Haggard (sic) landed on the Stanley water of the Tay a fish of 61lb. I believe it was in very poor condition.'

A 61½lb MYSTERY SALMON
No. 343

In 1879 Frank Buckland received a 61½lb salmon from Messrs. Grove of Bond Street, fishmongers, but failed to give us any more details other than it was netted. Buckland wrote:

> During the last few weeks of the net fishery season of 1879, there was an unusually large number of big salmon on the market: namely, one of 61½lbs., from Mr. Dennis of Messrs. Grove, Bond Street, and also four others weighing respectively 53lbs., 51lbs., 49lbs., and 46lbs.; this makes a total of 325½lbs. for six salmon, viz.: no less than the weight of four sheep and a half (averaged sized sheep) as dressed for the butcher's shop.

Note that Buckland omitted to mention a 65lb salmon – that is if his figures are to make sense.

THE 61½lb
RIVER TAW SALMON
No. 344

The first clue I had of this salmon was in a note published by the *Fishing Gazette* on 24 March 1924, repudiating a claim from the River Exe Board of Conservators that a 60¼lb Exe salmon was the record for the West Country (No. 301).

> According to the "List of Notable Fish" in *Where to Fish – The Anglers' Diary*, a 61½lb salmon, netted from the River Taw on July 15th , 1890, is probably the record for the West Country.
>
> R.B. MARSTON

In Grant and Waters fine little book *Salmon Netting in North Devon* (1998), we learn:

> Setting aside a newspaper report of 1890, that a 61½lb salmon, presumably taken locally, was on sale in a Barnstaple fishmonger's, the local record appears to be held by a fifty-seven pounder netted at Fremington in 1925.

I have not been able to locate a photograph of the 61½lb fish but in order to establish the possibility of the River Taw producing big fish, I can at least show a photograph of the 57lb salmon.

Mr Stephens and Jimmy Hill with the 57lb salmon netted at Fremington in the Taw Estuary in September 1925. A 61^1/$_2$lb fish was seen on sale in a Barnstaple fishmonger nearby in 1890

THE LARGEST BRITISH FISH ON A WORM
A 61½lb TAY SALMON
—— No. 345 ——

C.J.H. Cassel's fine piece on large salmon published by the *Fishing Gazette* on 9 November 1907, includes a note on Thomas Stewart's catch of a 61½lb Tay salmon:

Then on October 15th – the last day of the Tay season – an even heavier salmon than the last noticed Awe one, and indeed a fish that would rank as phenomenal anywhere, was caught in the former river at Lymire Heuke, near the end of the Willowgate, one and a half miles below Perth. Its captor was Mr. Thomas Stewart of that city, and its weight was 61½lb. This leviathan, length 4ft. 6in. and depth 13½in., was taken at eight o'clock in the morning, just an hour before high water, by means of the somewhat ignominious lure known in Scotland as the "Minister's Garden Fly" otherwise the worm. It did not give very much sport considering its great weight, but it took exactly an hour to land. It is the largest fish caught with rod on the Tay for at least thirty-five years, and its head (a photograph of which is given) has been set up by Mr. Malloch for preservation in the Perth Natural Science Museum.

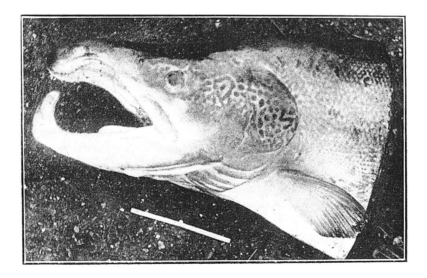

Malloch's photograph of the head of monster that fell to the 'Minister's Garden Fly' 1¹/₂ miles below Perth on the Tay on the last day of the season in 1907. Cock salmon prior to spawning have a peculiar colouring, described by Charles Dickens as 'a mottled purple complexion that was to be found only on boiled beef and on the faces of mail coach drivers'

John Ashley-Cooper, in his *A Line on Salmon* (1983), tells us that Stewart's salmon is the largest ever to be caught on a worm in Britain, and W.L. Calderwood observed in his *Salmon Rivers and Lochs of Scotland* (1909):

> Below the Bridge of Perth, in the tidal water, the public are allowed to fish by rod. This is only taken advantage of in the autumn when the nets are off. The banks are in places rather muddy and sedge grown, and wading or bank work is quite necessary. Some heavy fish are taken at times. It was here that in the back end of 1907 a citizen of Perth took, by what method I have never heard, a salmon of 61½lb. The head of this immense fish is now in the Perth Museum.

KILLED BY AN OTTER
A 61½lb LYON SALMON
—— No. 346 ——

On 2 December 1922 the *Fishing Gazette* reported the finding of a huge dead salmon on the banks of the River Lyon in Scotland:

> Mr. Gilbert D. Malloch, of Perth, kindly sends the following cutting from the *Dundee Courier* of November 21, 1922. As Mr. Malloch remarks in his letter to me, "This has indeed been a wonderful year for 'big' fish."
>
> "Peter M'Callum, keeper, while walking along the bank of the River Lyon at the Duneaves Water, near Fortingall, found a dead salmon weighing 61½lb. The fish was lying in the Colonel's Stone Pool, and had evidently been killed by an otter, as a piece had been bitten out of the shoulder.
>
> "The fish was the biggest ever seen in the Lyon, a tributary of the Tay. It was 51 inches in length and had a girth of 24¾ inches."

The *Fishing Gazette* of 20 January 1923 followed up their original report with another after receiving a letter from a reader:

THE 61½LB. LYON SALMON

DEAR SIR – There must be something wrong with the measurements of the

61½lb. Lyon salmon. According to your note page 504 a length of 51in. and a girth of 24¾in. would give a weight of 50lb. or less. But perhaps the piece removed by the otter would account for the difference.

Yours faithfully

S

[The measurements given certainly do not seem to accord with the weight, a mistake may have been made in measuring the length – an inch or two makes all the difference. The weight for length of a fish of 51in. is nearly 57lb. according to Stanley's scale. – ED.]

I have to agree that with closer scrutiny the measurements given for the River Lyon fish do not square up. A glance at the chart for fish weighing from 60lb to 62lb indicates that one of the measurements, be it either length or girth, must be incorrect.

The Colonel's Stone Pool at the Duneaves Water on the Lyon, where a 61½lb fish was found dead in 1922

KILLED IN A DRIFT NET
A 61½lb SALMON
No. 347

We can only guess at how many huge salmon have been killed in drift nets but at least one catch has been properly documented. The information appeared in the *Fishing Gazette* of 16 June 1934. Nowadays, fish of this weight no longer seem to exist in British waters.

61 ½LB SALMON NETTED OFF THE NORTHUMBRIAN COAST

Here is a record of a fine salmon netted recently: -

> Catering Department
> Northumberland Street
> Newcastle-on-Tyne, 1.

> DEAR SIR – We are enclosing at the request of our catering manager, Mr. Graham, the scales of a large cock salmon caught in the North Sea and landed at North Shields [which is at the mouth of the River Tyne]. This fish, which is the largest landed at this port for twenty years, weighed 61½lb., length 51 in., girth 31½in.
>   We used this fish in our restaurant, and found the quality good.
> It would be of interest if you could let us know the approximate age.

> Yours faithfully

> *for* FENWICK, LTD., F. W.

Mr. J. Arthur Hutton has examined the scales and reports:

? North Sea. May. 61½lb., male, length 51 in., girth 31½in. Two years river life and four years feeding in sea. A very large spring fish which has not spawned before. It must have been a fine fish, for its C.F. is 46½. I wonder where and how it was caught; probably in a drift-net off the Northumbrian Coast.

J. A. HUTTON

Despite the fact that during the nineteenth century the River Tyne was considered to be one of the big three rivers in terms of the size of its salmon and sea-trout runs, the river died. For years, the devastation caused by industrialisation in the catchment area seemed to be permanent but now rehabilitation work has improved the river beyond recognition.

Seemingly to avoid criticism, Messrs Fenwick, or their advisors, warded off the possibility that the big salmon was caught at the mouth of the river Tyne. I bet it was, or at least it was almost certainly a Tyne fish. The Tyne is England's best salmon river because it has a huge catchment area with a veritable network of spawning streams – not unlike Scotland's River Tweed.

62lb TAY SALMON
No. 353

Each January Mr Henry Ffennell used to write for *The Times* a summary of all the big salmon caught in British and Irish waters during the previous season. *Rod & Gun* (30 January 1892) reprinted Ffennell's list of big fish for the 1891 season. In his report on the River Tay, Ffennell documented the capture in the nets of a 62-pounder: 'One of 62lbs. I had the opportunity of measuring when it reached London. The dimensions were: Length, 55½in. girth, 29in.'

Mr Ffennell had a great reputation for getting his facts right – indeed he was often the final arbiter when disputes occurred – so it was no wonder that the editor of another journal, *Game & Gun*, wrote: 'Mr. Ffennell's facts are always reliable as he takes, to our knowledge, the greatest care in personally getting all the details. '

A 62lb RIVER STINCHAR SALMON
No. 354

The River Stinchar in south-west Scotland surprisingly provides quite big salmon for a small river (27 miles long), and fish of up to 42lb have been caught on rod and line. Bag nets are traditionally placed beyond the gravel bar in the river estuary and along the immediate coastline. In *Salmon Rivers and Lochs of Scotland* (1909), W.L. Calderwood tells us that in 1897 one of those sea nets took a fish of 62lb. He also describes the river and makes it sound very attractive: 'Throughout its course this beautiful little river has a most agreeable gravelly bed; pools and stream often alternate most pleasantly; from time to time, and more especially in the lower reaches, it is pretty closely wooded, but there is a fine running character in the stream which adds greatly to the enjoyment of angling.'

John Ashley-Cooper in *A Salmon Fisher's Odyssey* (1982) spoke highly of the Stinchar, where he had often had 'magnificent sport'. His observation that 'there is no small river where I would rather fish' gives us a good measure of the quality of this salmon and sea-trout stream, which is mostly fly only. Ashley-Cooper repeated Augustus Grimble's assessment of the Stinchar – 'For its size, this river yields larger fish than any other in Scotland' – but then says, 'This was in days long past; and this statement would, I fear, no longer hold good in our times.' There is a long high gravel bar on both sides of the river mouth, which changes its exit from time to time. Beyond the mouth, spasmodic netting takes place and doubtless this is where, over a hundred years ago, the 62-pounder was netted.

The River Stinchar from Ballantrae Bridge, with the sea in the distance According to Ashley-Cooper at one time it was possible to count as many as 500 fish and more off the old road bridge.

HENRY WILLES' 62lb SALMON
No. 355

On 9 November 1907, C.J.H. Cassel wrote a fine piece for the *Fishing Gazette*, sum-marising the details of all the big salmon caught in 1907, mostly in Scotland. Included in Cassel's round-up was a note on a 61½lb Scottish salmon followed by a note on an even larger Norwegian salmon:

> The latter fish is beaten by the way, in weight by only ½lb., by one of 62lb. killed on the Olden river, Nordfjord, Norway, this year. This Norwegian salmon was landed by Mr. Henry Willis in what is probably a record for time, considering its heaviness. It was gaffed within fifteen minutes after being hooked, and it is probably the weightiest rod-killed fish captured in Norway for many seasons past.

W.D. Turing features this salmon in his list of Notable Norwegian Salmon in *Where to Fish* (1937). It was caught in the Olden River on 12 August 1907. Turing noted that Hardy Bros of Alnwick had a model of the fish in their Manchester shop. Hardy's closed this branch in the 1960s but I daresay the cast of the fish survives despite the closure.

Turing spells the captor's name Willes, whereas Cassel spells it Willis. I suspect that Turing will have visited Hardy's shop in Manchester and carefully made a note of the spelling whereas Cassel merely read a report.

This was all I knew about Henry Willes, or Willis, until August 2005, when David Hatwell sent me a copy of an article by 'H.W.', which was published in the *Flyfishers' Journal* Autumn (1946):

> For many years I contented myself with the wet fly as I considered the dry fly quite beyond my capacity, and my brother and I spent many happy holi-days in Norway in quest of trout, sea trout and salmon in the numberless lakes and rivers.
>
> Beyond a sea trout of 9¼lbs. we had not accounted for anything really big, but in 1897, feeling I had to expand a bit, I rented the Olden River

which lies at the top of the Nord Fjord for the months of August and September. This river is only about 2½ miles long, and had a delightful house midway between the falls from the Olden lake and the Fjord, and had been in the possession of an Englishman for at least 40 years.

On my arrival in early August I found the river extremely low and realized that until we had some rain the fly was out of the question, but I couldn't sit down and wait, so determined to try a prawn in one or two of the possible lies in mid-stream.

In those days my salmon rod consisted of an 18-ft. greenheart with a very heavy reel, and it was at least a week before one's back was properly able to cope with it, and having mounted a prawn I decided to start on what looked like a fairly deep run just in front of the house. Leaving my ghillie on dry land, I waded out a convenient distance and made my first cast up stream to the head of the run. When my line was about opposite me it stopped, and I naturally thought I was hung up, so I lifted my rod fairly sharply and found I was into a fish. After a short while he made a move, and a tremendous tail lashed the water right on to the bank, on seeing which my ghillie rushed out and clasped me around the waist.

The fish then started to move up and down the run, which was little more than a longish lie, but after repeating this movement four or five times he decided it was probably more healthy below, so off he went, and I had to agree with the idea as I couldn't do anything else, but down below he found only broken water with no possible resting place, so back he came to the run. How often he repeated this manoeuvre I cannot now remember, but I eventually persuaded him to try a new route into a pool of still water at the side of the river, and there we were able to put a gaff into him and get him on dry land, where my ghillie threw himself full length on him while I gave him his quietus. He proved to be a cock fish, slightly red, with a terrific beak on him, and the next thing was to weigh him. My spring balance went up to 40 lbs, but this didn't even lift him off the ground, so we had to take him to the hotel at Olden, where he registered 63 lbs., the biggest fish ever taken on rod on the Olden River.

Since two weights are given for this fish – 62lb and 63lb – I have adopted the lighter weight.

Samuel Bough's unfinished, life-size painting of the salmon caught in a bag net in Largo Bay, Fife

A 62lb FORTH ESTUARY SALMON
No. 356

The editor of the *Fishing Gazette* and Mr W.L. Calderwood for the Fishery Board of Scotland frequently exchanged letters on matters relating to large salmon. Mr Calderwood's letter of 14 January 1908 referred to a 62lb salmon that was netted in the Forth estuary.

DEAR MR. MARSTON – I have no objection to your reproducing the photo of the 62lb. fish which I sent you to see in connection with length measurement of salmon of this size. The picture from which I took the photo was unfinished and in this connection has a melancholy interest, since the painter, Sam. Bough, R.S.A., met his untimely death when he had the work in hand. The fish was painted life size, and the length is 4ft. 6in., as near as I could estimate by running a tape along the canvas. It was captured in a bag-net in Largo Bay, on the Fife coast, when the late Mr. Anderson, Edinburgh, owned the fishings. The picture is now the property of his widow.

'The frame of the lave net is shaped like a large Y having a flowing bag-net suspended between the arms (or rimes). The fisherman sees the mark or loom of the salmon as it rushes upstream through the shallows and running to intercept it, he lowers the net into the water just as the salmon approaches; once the fish is over the head-line he raises the net from the water, grounding the handstaff, and dispatches his catch with a priest.' – Fishing on the Lower Severn

This case, reproduced from the 6th Duke of Portland's memoirs, is still kept at Langwell House, Berriedale less than a mile from where the fish was caught. The legend reads 'Salmon taken in Berriedale Nets, 27 June 1894. Weight 62lbs, length 43 ins, girth 29ins, depth 12ins, thickness 6ins'. In fact, the length is more likely to have been 53ins.

DUKE OF PORTLAND'S 62LB SALMON
No. 357

In the *Fishing Gazette* dated 1 May 1920, the editor published a letter from J.H. Scott on the subject of large salmon. Scott had seen a 62lb salmon in a fishmonger's shop in Inverness.

The fish was netted in salt water (the estuary of the River Berriedale?) belonging to the Duke of Portland. The Berriedale River runs into the sea approximately ten miles north of that much-favoured river (especially by fly fishermen) the Helmsdale. It may well have been a wandering Helmsdale fish or a Brora fish.

DEAR SIR – I read Mr. John W. Macpherson's letter in your issue of March 27 with some interest, as I saw the 62lb. salmon to which he refers. I was in Inverness at the time it was received by Messrs. Macleay, and on visiting their shop I had the privilege of inspecting the fish. It was the largest salmon I have seen, and it weighed 62lb. in Inverness, probably more than twenty-four hours after being taken out of the water. But, actually, it was some pounds heavier than what appears, as fish lose considerably in weight when kept for any length of time. It was caught by net in a sea fishing belonging to the Duke of Portland at Berriedale, Caithnesshire.

One hundred and twelve years after the 6th Duke of Portland's men caught the 62-pounder at Berriedale, I wrote to the present Duke enquiring about the fish. To my surprise, I received a note from Mr Robert Howden on behalf of the Portland Estate (the Duke had died), advising me that a cast of the fish in question had been made and was kept in nearby Langwell House. Subsequently, after an exchange of letters, I was given a photocopy of a chapter taken from the 6th Duke's book *Fifty Years and More of Sport in Scotland*, Faber & Faber (1933), which included a photograph of the big salmon. As a result, there was no need for me to make the long journey to Caithness, which I had contemplated. The material in the Duke's memoirs is astonishing. The Duke describes the fishing and the catches made in the Berriedale, the Helmsdale, the Beauly, the Ness, the Garry and the Tay when these rivers were at their best (the account begins in 1882).

A 62lb SHANNON FISH
No. 358

This is probably the best-documented of Ireland's largest salmon. A report appeared in the *Fishing Gazette* of 13 August 1921:

MOST EXTRAORDINARY GROWTH OF A 62LB SALMON

Mr. Reginald Beddington sent me recently the two large photographs of a 62lb. salmon referred to in the following letter:

DEAR MARSTON – On June 7 I found a 62lb fish in Messrs. Gow's shop, Connaught Street, W.2. The fish was bought at Billingsgate, and I understand that it came from the Shannon nets. I got a local photographer to take its portrait and I enclose two photos, which kindly return when you have done with them. The measurements of the fish were 48in. by 29½in. I expected his age to be six or seven, but on looking at his scales I was not at all sure that he was not considerably younger. I, accordingly, sent the scales to Hutton, who writes as follows: -

"Some of the scales have imperfect centres, but others are quite clear and show two years river life and only three and a half years in the sea. This is the most extraordinary growth I have ever heard of and I can hardly believe it, but there seems to be no doubt about my reading of the scales, as those that are clear are, all alike."

Yours sincerely,

Reginald Beddington

It was certainly a magnificent fish and very deep for its length. The late Mr. Edward Sturdy's *Fishing Gazette* scale of weight of salmon from their length was based mainly on the salmon of Norwegian rivers and is considered to be rather too high for salmon from our British and Irish rivers, but this great Irish fish, 48in. in length and weighing 62lb., is no less than some 12lb. above the weight of a 48in. fish according to Mr. Sturdy's scale, which gives 47.407lb. for a 48in. fish.

ANOTHER 62lb SHANNON SALMON
No. 360

The 1930 edition of *The Angler's Guide to the Irish Free State* includes a note to the effect that a 62lb salmon was netted by the Abbey fishermen on 27 March 1925 at Carbally Mill Dam. Looking upstream from Thomond bridge, which carries the N7 road over the River Shannon at Limerick, you can see the remains of the old lax weir. Lax means salmon in Norwegian and Swedish – perhaps the name comes from the times of the Vikings, like the names thwaite, beck and tarn in Cumbria. The weir, which is still in tidal water, is situated just below the dam where the fish was killed by the netsmen. King John's Castle lies immediately below the bridge on the left bank – a reminder of the turbulent history of these parts – and Limerick cathedral is sited downstream on the same bank.

The view upstream from Thomond Bridge on the Shannon. Parts of the old salmon weir are visible

SIR HENRY GORE BOOTH'S
62½lb PASVIK SALMON
No. 361

According to the *Fishing Gazette* of 18 December 1920, Sir Henry caught a 62½lb salmon on rod and line in Norway's Pasvik River in 1876 Sir Henry had some sort of lease to fish on the Pasvik from 1860 to 1876. Sir Henry would have been living locally at the time by arrangement with Magnus Klerck (No. 454), possibly at his house at Elvenes.

The painting was found in Derby and bears the inscription: 'Portrait of a Salmon caught at Llantrifsent near Uske AD 1782. Wt 68¹/₂lbs.' The weight is in pounds Dutch

REECE AND LEWIS'S
62¾lb USK SALMON
—— No. 363 ——

A painting of a large salmon, caught at 'Llantrifsent, near Uske', is featured in Arthur Oglesby and Lucy Money-Coutts' book *The Big Fish*. The caption below the painting indicates that the fish weighed 68½lb but at the time, or indeed at any time before about 1825, it was customary in Britain to use pounds Dutch. Since one pound (*avoir dupois*) equals 1.0892 pounds Dutch, the salmon actually weighed approximately 62lb 12oz.

Llantrifsent or Llantrissent or Llantrisant, as modern maps would have it, is about three miles south of Usk. (It was once much more important in the nation's history. Men from Llantrisant fought in the Black Army at Crécy – so called after a bold black diagonal stripe in the arms of Hugh Despenser, the Lord of Glamorgan, who raised three hundred archers and spearman locally.)

In the correspondence column of the *Fishing Gazette* of 5 March 1932, there is a short letter from Edward Coulman of Chesterholme, Newport, Monmouthshire which reads, 'I had occasion recently to refer to the *Usk Gleaner* of September 1875, in which I noticed a rather curious record, viz "A salmon weighing 69½lb was caught in the River Usk near the town in 1783".' This puts the fish at a slightly heavier weight which is not borne out by the last but most important data on the taking of the Usk monster salmon which appeared in a letter published in *The Times* of 26 November 1996:

RECORD CATCH
From Sir Richard Hanbury Tenison

Sir, Your report (November 21) of Mr. Bond's record catfish mentions the 'next biggest freshwater fish ever caught in Britain, a 64lb salmon taken by Georgina Ballantine in 1922'. That was certainly the largest salmon taken in British waters by rod and line but in June 1782 a 68½lb salmon was taken by net trawled by a coracle on the River Usk. The Usk fish was considered so remarkable that it was toured round the local towns by its captors until it fell to pieces.

Yours faithfully

R. Hanbury Tenison
Clytha Park,
Nr. Abergavenny, Gwent

Further enquiry revealed that the salmon was taken in a net trawled between two coracles on the Crown Fishery water, which stretched twelve miles from Clytha Park to Caerleon, and that the successful netsmen were named as the leaseholder Richard Reece of Usk and his fisherman, James Lewis. It is likely that Lewis was manning one of the coracles. The salmon would not have been hauled into the coracles which were solely used to sweep the pool with the net.

A 63lb WYE HEN SALMON
No. 368

The *Fishing Gazette* of 8 June 1895 recorded the capture of a 63lb salmon from the River Wye:

A splendid salmon has been taken by Mr. T. Miller, the lessee of the fisheries in the Tintern district. The fish (a hen) was taken with a net, and measured 55½in., girth 28in., width of tail fin 15in., and turned the scale at 63lb. This is supposed to be the largest fish ever taken in the Wye.

W. STEWART'S 63lb TAY SALMON
—— No. 369 ——

I nformation about big fish comes to me from many sources and in many different ways. The strangest so far is notice of the capture of a 63lb salmon that is engraved on a disc set in a salmon priest made of laburnum wood. The inscription reads:

Cock Salmon 63lbs killed at Perth Oct' 1903 by W. Stewart.
Presented by Peter Malloch

Peter Malloch was Perth's famous tackle dealer. The 12in priest figured in Bonham's sale at 65 George Street, Edinburgh on 24 August 2005 and thanks are due to Bonham's for allowing me to reproduce their photograph and David Hatwell for sending me the details.

Curiously, because such a big fish usually causes quite a stir, no hint of its capture appears in other sources, such as newspapers or magazines. A Mr T. Stewart caught a 61½lb fish on the River Tay (No. 345) but the date and initial indicate that this must be another successful Mr Stewart. Surely the fish must have been caught on rod and line because a fancy priest would be an inappropriate gift to a commercial fisherman?

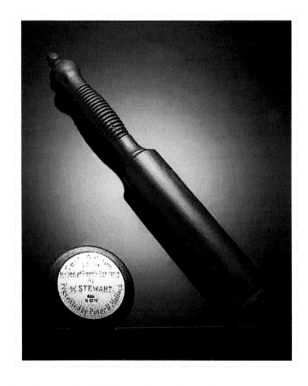

The priest inscribed: Cock Salmon 63lbs killed at Perth Oct' 1903 by W. Stewart. Presented by Peter Malloch

MAJOR W.H.S. ALSTON'S
63lb NORWEGIAN SALMON
—— No. 370 ——

A letter sent by C.M. Wells to the editor of the *Fishing Gazette* was published on 18 November 1950.

BIG NORWEGIAN SALMON

DEAR SIR – Some of the older anglers who have fished in Norway have caught many fish of exceptional size which have never been recorded. It may, therefore, interest some of your readers to know that Major W. H. S. Alston, who died recently, during his various visits to Norway landed eight fish over 50lb., the best being 63lb., 60lb and 60lb.

Yours faithfully
C. M. WELLS.

(Few anglers can have equalled this remarkable record. – ED)

Unfortunately, Wells failed to provide any of the essential data, such as the name of the rivers, the dates of capture, and the method or methods used to capture the fish. To make matters worse, the editor has left out the correspondent's address and so we have not the faintest idea of where Major Alston lived or C.M.Wells lived.

C.M. Wells was a remarkable man – an outstanding scholar, sportsman and angler. If I have to pick a cherry from all his outstanding achievements, it would be to recall that Wells, who taught classics at Eton, had the distinction of twice bowling out W.G. Grace.

As a tenant, Wells fished all three miles of the Bolstad beat of the Vosso for a total of twenty-five years (1920–39 and 1946–50). He used fly, prawn and spinner to catch twelve salmon weighing between 50lb and 58lb (featured in the list as Nos. 188, 189, 190, 191, 222, 240, 241, 259, 267, 271, 290, 307). When he fly fished, his favourite flies were Thunder and Lightning, Mar Lodge and Dusty Miller, tied to double gut-eyed hooks.

Chance suggests that the absence of any fish over 60lb on the list of Wells' catches was due to his policy, as the host, of always offering the most promising pools to his

Major Alston's best fish was a 6 3lb salmon caught at Bolstad. The gillie, Karl Magne's neighbour, is standing beside the fish

C.M. Wells, an extraordinarily successful angler, stands by his favourite lie for 'great fish' on the Bolstad beat of the Vosso

guests. This is where we come back to the feats of Major Alston because Alston was one of Wells' regular guests. He caught eleven fish (rather than eight as Wells stated in his letter to the *Fishing Gazette*) weighing 50lb or more, including two of 60lb and one of 63lb. (One features as No. 324 on this list). Surely no salmon angler has ever achieved such stunning success. Perhaps as a result of this book being published, a correspondent will emerge to provide the facts and figures for what must be the most remarkable record of an individual's capture of portmanteaux salmon.

* * * * *

As a postscript to this story, in September 2005 David Hatwell received a letter from Karl Magne, of Norway, enclosing three photographs of salmon all of which exceeded 60lb. The originals adorned the walls of his farmhouse, which had previously been owned by an English fisherman, H.C. Charrington (No. 338) Karl 'first learned to speak English with the help of old Mr Wells', sometime housemaster at Eton, and he mentioned that Wells caught some nine hundred and thirty-five fish during his tenancy.

Erik (left) and Svein Moum with their splendid salmon. It is clear how big the salmon's dorsal fin is when compared to the fisherman's hand.

THE MOUMS' 63lb NAMSEN SALMON
No. 371

Two brothers, Erik and Svein Moum, regularly fished together and on 19 June 1946, when they were harling on the Namsen at Moum, they hooked, played and killed a salmon weighing 63lb.

CHARLES BERGESEN'S
63lb SAND RIVER SALMON
No. 372

On page 118 of his book *Angler's Cavalcade* (1966), Eric Horsfall Turner describes the recovery of the Sand after the netting rights in the river were purchased in 1956:

I say there was nothing very remarkable about the early morning catch for a simple reason: the fosse pool was full of big salmon. On the evening of the day after my morning excursion, a fish of 41½lb was taken from it. A glance over the fishing records in the anglers' hut showed that several fish of that weight had been taken during the season. On the second afternoon I sat on the rocks near the fosse and photographed the frequent runners against the foaming white background. At least three, in my judgement, were fish of 40lb or more. If the big fish are there, and the angler has reasonable competence, there is nothing remarkable in his catching one or two. Exceptional though the stock of the river was for modern times, and in comparison with other rivers I had fished in Norway, it was more the history of the river and its recovery to earlier standards that interested me. This history can start, for our purposes, about 1884 when two remarkably adroit Englishmen, one of whom spoke Norwegian like a native, persuaded the farmers of the Sand bank to lease them the fishing. From that year until 1924 they retained the fishing rights, and salmon were caught by angling only. Then the farmers regained control. Heavy netting and trapping started at once. Within a few years the salmon stock of the river dropped to the trifling. There were still occasional good fish to be taken. Charles Bergesen, the present controller of the fishing rights, took one of 63lb from the fosse pool in 1953. The cast of this fish adorns the wall of the lounge in the superb lodge he had built on the estuary shore where the river joins the fjord. But, in general terms, the fishing had dropped to the level of most other Norwegian rivers which were under the control of farm communities. In 1956 Bergesen managed to reach an agreement with the farmers which ended the netting and trapping of salmon on the river (but not in the fjord) for a term of twenty years. The cost of this agreement was quite fantastic, even by modern standards. In two or three years, after considerable and intelligent restocking, results began to show. Then, seven or eight years later, the quality of Sand stock, and therefore the quality of its fishing, has reached something near that of the halcyon years from 1884 to 1924.

THE LARGEST ROD-CAUGHT
BALTIC SEA SALMON – 63lb
No. 373

Using modern deep-water trolling methods, some very large salmon have been caught in recent years in the Baltic Sea. I received the following information on 25 September 2005 courtesy of Jan Olsson IGFA:

> Laxfestivalen is the most famous of all European Trolling Tournaments. The event takes place in the Baltic Sea (Bay of Hanö) in the province of Blekinge. The Baltic strain of the salmon is a powerful, fast growing, large-sized salmon with a maximum weight of 95lb. The heaviest one rod-caught so far set the record at 63lb (28.82kg).
>
> Details of the biggest fish caught by this method can be found on the Internet (www.outdoor.se/sportfishnews/articles/laxfestival/).

In December 2005 David Hatwell sent me this photograph together with a cutting from Sportfishing in Sweden (1995), which confirmed that the fish was caught in the Bay or Sound of Hanö in the province of Blekinge and is now recognised as Sweden's record rod-caught salmon Although a fish caught by Vwikko Haleinen in 1991 appears to be larger at 63lb 6oz (No. 378).

THE WYE'S LARGEST SALMON
63½lb
No. 379

J. Arthur Hutton, who documented the rod-caught salmon catches on the River Wye for a twenty-five year period (1910–35), mentions this fish in a chapter he wrote for Jock Scott's *Game Fish Records* (1936), page 46, 'The largest Wye salmon of which we have any authentic record was caught in a net at Llandogo in 1905, and weighed 63½lb.'

H.A. Gilbert also mentions this salmon in *The Tale of a Wye Fisherman* having noticed details of the fish in Hutton's report on scale reading for 1921. He mentions the name of the captor, Miller, who was presumably the leader of the netting team. Curiously, Gilbert tells us that the fish was caught in 1895.

The exploitation of the fish resources of the River Wye has been an important aspect in its history. Huge runs of elvers are, or rather were, a feature of the river. Roger Brown, proprietor of the grocery store at Llandogo, remembers being told that in the spring his grandfather used to catch, wash and cook elvers. He would press them into a solid shape like big double-Gloucester cheeses and carry them on foot to Monmouth market to sell.

Twaites, or twaite shad, were also caught, usually in May when they ascended the river in large numbers but, as his grandfather put it, 'Twaites had more bones than the devil in hell.' Salmon, of course, would have been the most important visitors and netting was carried out all along the lower reaches. Philip John, also of Llandogo, has in his possession a map of all the salmon netting stations of the lower Wye and it is about seven yards long.

A fourth cash-crop activity would have been the trapping of lampreys. The Wye enjoys a good run of sea lampreys and these would have been of the greatest importance at one time. In 1066, the usurping Norman knights brought to England all things Norman, including their preference for the dietary delicacies of their homeland. Thus it was that lamprey dishes, traditionally made with lampreys caught at the mouth of the Seine, made their appearance.

Marti Remes from Rovaniemi in Finland caught his salmon on the Tana River on 3 July 1984. A glance at this photograph shows that the salmon was not a long fish for its weight but had an incredibly large girth. It was 50¹/₂in long with a girth of 31¹/₂in

MARTI REMES'
63lb 9oz TANA SALMON
—— No. 381 ——

arti Remes from Rovaniemi in Finland caught his salmon on the Tana River on 3 July 1984. Its length was measured at 50½in and girth 31½in. At first no details of how the fish was caught were forthcoming, but in August 2006 I received a batch of data on big Finnish salmon from Matti Kettunen, which included a cutting about the catch taken from the fishing magazine *Urheilu Kalastus*, March 1985. The story goes that Marti Remes and his wife Hilkka were fishing with a favourite Finnish wobbler bait called a Nils Master on a cool but sunny day on the Tana. Hilkka was attending to the rod and Marti was rowing. This information tells us that Remes and his wife were trailing the bait behind the boat, i.e. they were harling. The weighing of the fish was witnessed by Pentti and Inga Lansman.

OLA SEEM'S
63lb 14oz NAMSEN SALMON
—— No. 382 ——

n October 2005 Jan Eggers wrote to tell me about some big fish that I had not previously come across, and included in his list was Ola Seem's Namsen salmon:

> In 1914 Mr Ola Seem caught a salmon of 29 kilos in the part of the Namsen River called Seemsvaldet and it is a part of the Moumvaldet area of the river. It was the record salmon until Svend Kjolstad caught in 1923 his record salmon of 31.65 kilos in the Jorumvaldet area. Information on page 52 of the book *Laksefisket í Namsen och de andre Elvene í Namdalen* (*Salmon Fishing in the Namsen and other Rivers in the Namvalley*).

A MONSTER KELT FROM NAMSEN – 63lb 14¾oz
No. 383

This fish had just spawned when it was found dead in the Namsen River. As noted in the correspondence published in the *Fishing Gazette* on 4 January 1936, it could have weighed 80lb when it entered the river, perhaps in the spring of 1935:

We have received the following interesting letter from Mr. A. Johansen, of Namsen, Norway:

Namsos den 3/12, 1935

DEAR SIR – As an old subscriber of your paper I thought that you and your readers might be interested in knowing about a capital salmon found dead in the Namsen lately. I am sending you a photo of the fish, which was found by the chauffeur Magnus Anjön on November 15, at Gjetabekhöla on the Fossland beat. The fish was a cock-fish, had spawned, weight 29 kg. (63.93 lb), length 1.46 meter (57½ in.). I think it will not be far from a record. I have read about fishes, which have been supposed to have been so and so big if in condition. But has there been caught or found a larger fish? The record fish caught on rod on the Namsen weighed 31.5 kg. (69.4 lb) and had a length of 1.38 meter. If the found fish had been in the same fine condition it would have weighed 80 lb.

The found fish had been hurt in the left under-jaw – as will be seen on the photo. The jaw was corroded quite through. Otherwise the fish was in fine condition taking into consideration that it had just spawned.

The finder, Mr. Anzjön, telephoned me as soon as he had found the fish. I asked him to send it to Trondhjem Natural Museum, where I have asked about details, which I, however, have not got yet. I got some scales of the fish and enclose the only one, which, perhaps, can do for examination.

Yours truly

ALLEN JOHANSEN

Kelt salmon weighing 63lb 14³/₄oz, found dead in the Namsen River, Norway in November 1935. The fish was 57¹/₂in long and is thought to have weighed 80lb when it entered the river.

Mr. Hutton kindly examined the scale and sent this report and particulars of other large salmon:

DEAR MARSTON – I have heard about this big fish from the Namsen last Tuesday. A fish of 1.46 meter (57½in.) would certainly weigh 80 lb. if it was in decent "Namsen-condition." A condition-factor of 42 for this length would be almost exactly 80 lb., and usually the Namsen salmon have a rather high condition-factor, say 43 or 44.

Unfortunately, the one scale sent is of no use. It is one of those "regenerated" scales which has been formed in the place of one which is lost.

The four heaviest fish I have in my collection are as follows (all cock-fish):

DATE		RIVER	WEIGHT	LENGTH	LIFE	C. F.
			lb.	in.	Years.	
1920	June 9	Voss	65	55	4	39
1921	July 31	Aaro	68¼	53¾	5	44
1924	June 13	Namsen	69½	54	4	44
1923	May 14	Lillebergen (nets)	74	56	4+	42

In the Annual Norwegian Report for 1932 Herr Aagaard gives particulars of several heavy male salmon caught in Norway. (See *Fishing Gazette*, August 5, 1933.)

DATE		WHERE CAUGHT	WEIGHT LB.	
1922	August	Evanger	69.7	Rod
1919	November	Voss	70.5	Net
1927	Summer	Aaro	70.5	Rod*
1878 or 1879		Tana	73.9	Rod
1923	June	Sulen	73.9	Net
1925	July	Drammen	75.0	Trap
1928	July	Tana	79.4	Rod

Yours sincerely J. A. HUTTON

A few days later Mr Hutton wrote:

I have received another scale from that big Namsen fish. It is very much eroded but as far as I can make out it was about 7½ years old, two years in the river and about 5½ years in the sea. And had not spawned before.

J. A. HUTTON

* Roy Flury questions the existence of this fish.

Ten months later, the *Fishing Gazette* (31 October 1936) published a follow-up to the story of the huge Namsen kelt:

THE MONSTER KELT FROM NAMSEN

We have received this interesting letter from Professor Dr. Knut Dahl, Oslo. It is dated February 19, 1936, and in a covering note Professor Dahl explains that for some reason or other, possibly his absence on field work, the letter was not posted at the time.

DEAR MR. MARSTON – Referring to the article "A Huge Salmon" in THE FISHING GAZETTE for January 4, 1936, I may add that certain details about this remarkable fish have also reached my laboratory. The fish was measured and weighed for me by Mr. Bernhard Hansson, of the Trondhjem Biological Station, and a fair sample of scales was forwarded to me for examination.

As for the probable size of the fish when in prime condition, I have little to add to what Mr. Allen Johansen and my friend Mr. Hutton say. In my opinion, the fish must have weighed between 35 and 36 kilos, that is very near 80 lb. and consequently touches the Tana record fish, caught in July 1928. Whether it breaks this record cannot, of course, be decided. In one way, however, it holds the record: As far as I can see *it is absolutely the largest salmon whose scales have ever been read.*

As to the reading, I am afraid the bad sample is responsible for Hutton's reading (only one scale).

I have been able to pick out half a dozen fair scales and I think there can be no doubt about the following result: -

Three winters in river (possibly four).
Four winters in sea.
Maiden fish.

Yours sincerely
KNUT DAHL

Putchers set in place on the Severn

A 64lb SALMON FROM THE SEVERN
—— No. 384 ——

In Augustus Grimble's *The Salmon Rivers of England and Wales* (1913), a chapter is devoted to the net catches on the Severn. Grimble writes:

> The navigation weirs, of which there were five constructed in 1842, had done much to ruin the river, as none of them were provided with efficient passes, while above and below Shrewsbury there were also eel weirs, which were illegally fished in the spring, solely for the capture of salmon smelts. The estuary was fished by "putts" and "putchers," each shore being thickly studded with these engines, which were easily erected and self-acting, also unlicenced and worked with total disregard of all close times; enormous was the damage they did, while so long as the exertions of the upper proprietors protected the spawners and increased the number of salmon, so *pa passu* did these fixed engines multiply, and at this period it was estimated that between 8000 and 9000 "putts and putchers" were at work! By 1863 they had increased to 11,200!!
>
> Then an Act of Parliament provided against any further increase, titles were closely scrutinized, and they were limited strictly to those that were lawfully exercised at the time of the passing of the Act of 1861, and all those that could not produce charters or show usage from time immemorial were abolished; until by 1867 the putts had been reduced to 238, each working with a 2s. 6d. licence while the putchers fell to 4680, with a

licence of 20s. for each fifty. These putts and putchers are of great antiquity and, when once set, will continue to catch by day and by night.

In 1873, 10,400 salmon were netted, including one of 64lb that was caught in a putcher – a conical-shaped wicker basket about 24in in diameter at the mouth. "Their mouths are turned upstream so as to catch fish dropping back to sea on the ebb tide." While others are set with mouths set "down stream so as to catch fish coming up with the flood tide".

A 64lb TAY SALMON
No. 385

The first notice I had of this salmon was in a letter published in the *Fishing Gazette* on 4 June 1921:

LARGE SALMON

DEAR MR. MARSTON – Frank Buckland's *Natural History of British Fishes* (1891 edition), pages 291-2, gives a list of monster salmon, headed in 1870 by a Tay fish of 70lb., 4ft. 5in. in length, 2ft. 7in. in girth, and head 12in. from Charles, of Lower Grosvenor-street, he also, on page 300, mentions a 64lb. salmon from the Tay, sold at 3s. a lb. The fish your inquiry refers to would hardly be between 1868-1880, or Buckland would have mentioned it, as Messrs. Grove, of Bond-street, used to notify him of special fish. I have a recollection of a very large Rhine salmon of more recent date.

Yours truly

C. 3.

Sure enough, there is a note on page 300 of my earlier edition of Buckland's book (1881) about a 64lb Tay salmon: 'This big 64lb salmon from the Tay was sold at three shillings a pound. The total value therefore of the 'beast' was £9 12s, or about the cost of three ordinary sheep.' This short statement seems to imply that he has mentioned the fish elsewhere in the book, but I can find no trace of it.

MERTHYR GUEST'S
64lb NAMSEN SALMON
—— No. 386 ——

Merthyr Guest caught his salmon on 20 July 1889 from the Gartland beat on the Namsen River. In a photograph taken to commemorate the event, the rod appears to be a four-joint 17–18ft greenheart fly rod. Traditionally, it is said that Guest caught the fish harling with a spoon, but because he is pictured with a fly rod and the reel is positioned for fly fishing and not bait casting, it may be that Guest was harling with a fly. There is nothing to stop a fisherman attaching a spoon and fishing with a long soft-actioned fly rod, except that the chances of getting a good hook-hold on a fish are greatly reduced.

Merthyr Guest with his 64lb cock salmon. This classic photograph of a huge fish and its captor recaptures an era of Victorian salmon fishing in Norway that is now distanced by more than a century. The Norfolk jacket, tweed shooting knickerbockers, tweed cap, waterproofed leather or gutta-percha boots and a gralloching knife in a sheath, all help to make up the fashionable but practical outfit that was stereotypical of a Victorian gentleman of means

A 64lb RIVER TAY SALMON
No. 387

On 14 November 1903, Henry Ffennell, in his attempt to expose false claims about huge salmon supposedly taken from Scottish waters, had a letter published by the *Fishing Gazette* and in so doing documented the capture of a 64lb salmon that seemingly had not previously been reported to the angling press.

LARGE SALMON

MR. HENRY FFENNELL very kindly replies to my query about large salmon as follows.

MY DEAR MARSTON – You ask me if I can tell you the weight of the heaviest salmon taken on the fly. With much pleasure I send you a list of some of the more remarkable fish landed by anglers, the weights of which were verified at the time of capture. I have not got all my notes at hand, so I cannot give you a complete return; but doubtless the following will be sufficient for your purposes. You mention a fish over 69lb., supposed to have been taken by a former Earl of Home. In 1870 Mr. Haggard landed on Stanley water on the Tay a fish of 61lb. I believe it was in very poor condition, but the weight at any rate is correct. In 1874 a fish of 57lb was landed on the river Suir (co. Tipperary) by a poor fisherman. In the same year one of 55½lb. was taken on the Cumberland Derwent. In 1877 Mr. J. B. Lawes landed a salmon of 54lb. on the Awe. In 1884 the keeper on the Ardoe water on the Dee took a fish of 57lb. In 1886 Mr. Pryor on the Floors water of the Tweed one of 57½lb., and in 1889 Mr. Brereton took one of 55lb. on Lord Polwarth's water at Mertoun. In 1892 Mr. G. Mackenzie caught a salmon of 56lb. at Warwick Hall on the Derwent. In 1895 Lord Zetland on the Stanley water of the Tay took a salmon of 55lb. Lord Ruthven many years previously took one of 54lb., also on the Tay. In 1888 Mr. Edwin Francis, of Liverpool, captured a salmon of 55½lb. in the Corby water of the Eden. The Shannon this year (1903) yielded one of 54lb. The vague and startling statements based on no solid foundation, which appear from time to time regarding the capture of exceptionally large salmon said to have been taken a hundred, fifty, forty, twenty etc. etc., years ago, are to my mind most misleading, if not utterly worthless. For some years past I have taken considerable trouble to verify the weights of heavy salmon at the time of capture, and I believe unless this work is done promptly and thoroughly dire mistakes are bound to occur, leading eventually to the placing on record the capture of what are nothing more or less than bogus or mythical salmon. I could give many cases where false reports as to the capture of monster salmon have gained a considerable currency throughout the country. Here is one. Some few years ago it was reported that two mighty monsters had been captured in the river Tay. One was said to have weighed 87½lb. and the other 80lb. A fishmonger in an obscure part of London had indeed the temerity to exhibit in his shop window a very poor specimen of *Salmo salar*, which was labeled 'Tay salmon, 80lb. weight.' With the kind assistance of the then editor of the *Scotsman*, Mr. Malloch, Mr. Speedie, of Perth, and other tacksmen throughout Scotland, I promptly ran this falsehood to earth. All the people most likely to know had indeed heard of this great capture, but no one had seen the monster. Messrs. Anderson and Son of Edinburgh, wrote me: 'We beg to say that the fish mentioned was taken notice of by some of the London papers, and was said to have weighed 87½lb., but we ascertained that the fish weighed only 57½lb., and was caught on Lord Zetland's fishings below Newburgh on the Tay. We may say the heaviest taken on the Tay this season was one of 64lb. weight.' Many other salmon, than those mentioned above, of 50lb. and upwards have been taken by anglers during recent years. I cannot enumerate them all as I have not my notebooks by me, but I think I have mentioned most of the heaviest fish.

HENRY FFENNELL

Miss Ballantine's mighty fish was presented to the patients and staff of Perth Hospital, but not before it was sent off to Malloch's of Perth to have a plaster cast made. Later a limited edition of the cast was made, one of which is reproduced here

GEORGINA BALLANTINE'S 64lb BRITISH RECORD ROD-CAUGHT SALMON
No. 388

On 7 October 1922 Georgina Ballantine was harling with her father – she fished while he handled the boat – on the Glendelvine beat of the River Tay when she hooked a huge salmon. There has always been some mystery about what bait they were using. It is usually reported that she was using a dace but since this species is not indigenous to Scotland, it seems unlikely However it is clear from a letter she wrote to the magazine *Angling* in April 1954, in which she refers to a 'spinning lure' that the dace in question was artificial and not natural.

I also thought the choice of dace may well have reflected the general disinterest in almost any fish species other than salmon in Scotland. I remember being told by my mentor Harry Britton when I asked him about the availability of pike baits when I was about to fish Loch Lomond for the first time, over fifty years ago, he replied, 'No bother, you can get the local boys to catch you some "brae" in the River Leven – what you Sassenachs call bream.' His bream were, in fact, roach. Moreover, the local laddies couldn't catch them.

Then I noticed in a copy of *The Field* (October 1992) that auctioneer Neil Freeman, who has long specialised in angling books and angling memorabilia and obviously knows a great deal about vintage tackle items, said that Miss Ballantine caught her salmon on a Malloch dace bait, which implies the existence of a proprietary artificial bait of that name – problem solved.

In 1978 I visited Miss Ballantine's home at Caputh to photograph her house and the place where she caught her fish. The kind owners of the estate, and the original owners of Georgina's cased salmon, kindly allowed me to photograph her fish at their home, and even allowed me to set up my camera tripod on their billiard table. I expect the two fishermen who were walking along the footpath in front of her home pondered their chances of catching a fish as big as Georgina's. Doubtless such thoughts have been in the mind of every fisherman who has walked along that path since 1922.

Miss Ballantine's mighty fish was presented to the patients and staff of Perth Hospital but not before it was sent off to Malloch's of Perth to have a plaster cast made. Later a limited edition of the cast was commissioned and one of these sold for £4,200 at auction.

Georgina Ballantine and her father, James Ballantine, who was a fisherman for the Gelndelvine estate, photographed with her great fish the next day

Glendelvine beat on the River Tay seen from Caputh bridge – it was along this stretch of the river that Georgina played out her fish

This is the house where Georgina and her father lived. The bridge, which can just be seen on the right-hand side of the photograph, was not in existence when Georgina caught her fish on 7 October 1922

GEORG STROMME'S
64lb VOSSO SALMON
No. 391

Georg Stromme caught his 64lb salmon on the Liland beat of the Vosso River on 30 June 1954. A report of it appears on page 2 of Arthur Oglesby and Money-Coutts' *The Big Fish*.

As well as a 64 pounder, Stromme caught a 55-pounder on the same day

A 64¼lb THAMES SALMON
No. 392

On page 292 in H. Cholmondeley-Pennell's *The Angler Naturalist* (1863), there is a reference to a large salmon that was netted from the River Thames:

> Salter, in one of his works on Angling refers to the capture of a Salmon of 70 lbs. in the Thames near Laleham in the year 1789, which was subsequently sold to Mr. Howel, a fishmonger in the Minories, for a shilling a pound. The fact of the taking of this fish is confirmed by Mr. Wright, who says that he went off in a boat to see it, and found it "enveloped in nets between two punts which were kept apart by short spars lashed head and stern."

In those days Britain used the Dutch pound. After conversion, the 70lb Laleham salmon would have weighed, in the current scale, approximately 64¼lb.

Laleham features again in the history of the Thames as a salmon river. A. Courtney Williams in *Angling Diversions* (1945), talking about the late eighteenth century, said:

The Thames at Laleham where salmon were netted in the eighteenth century

...at that date the River at Laleham narrowed and had a swift current known locally as the 'Salmon Pass' from which a great number of fish were taken.

He also noted that prior to 1866, John Harris told Frank Buckland (Her Majesty's Inspector of Fishes) that his grandfather once took a 47-pounder in his nets between Chertsey and Laleham. It appears that Laleham and its salmon were inseparable because, on page 209, Williams says:

> It is perhaps not generally realized that there was a time when salmon were plentiful in the Thames, that they provided good sport for London anglers, and that the river supported a fishery of some magnitude and value. Nevertheless it is on record that Roman soldiers, set to guard the fort at Laleham, near Staines, saw many big salmon leaping the ford on their way up to the spawning beds higher up the river and that for more than 1,500 years afterwards, salmon still frequented the Thames, which they ascended as far up as Lechlade in Gloucestershire.

Old London Bridge, completed in 1209, was demolished in 1832. Note the old starlings (barge-shaped piles that protected the bridge pillars) and the powerful stream created by the reduced waterway. In their day, these runs must have been the finest salmon holding water on the lower Thames. Remember what Thomas Best said in A Concise Treatise on the Art of Angling (1787) – 'the best places for Thames angling is from London Bridge to Chelsea.'

John Hampton in two editions of *Angling*, Summer 1942 and Winter 1943, gave us some information on specific captures of Thames salmon, as well as the prices they fetched. Although the Thames declined as a salmon river as weirs, locks and mills multiplied – the last wild salmon was caught in 1833 – there were periods when the fish made some sort of recovery. For instance, in 1580 the Churchwarden's Book for Wandsworth recorded:

> In the somer, the fysshers of Wandsworth took between Monday and Saturday seven score salmon in the same fishings to the great honour of god. As to the price, in 1486 – the year of the first printing of the *Book of St. Albans* – the Brotherhood of Corpus Christi at Maidstone paid 6s. 8d. for a salmon that was obtained from Shene (Richmond on Thames).

Undoubtedly, the best fishing on the Thames, though, was to be had at London Bridge. *The London Chronicle* of 14 April 1764 reported:

> Yesterday a salmon which weighed near 30lb. was taken off one of the starlings of London Bridge by the watermen, who saw it leap out of the water at low-water mark, and immediately put off with their boats.

The starlings consisted of a series of barge-shaped piles that protected the bridge pillars from damage. At low tide these were revealed and, because they were planked on top, served as stands, albeit dangerous ones, for fishermen.

Before leaving the subject of Thames salmon, it is interesting to note that their flesh has always been highly regarded, not least by Izaak Walton, who wrote:

> It is observed by Gesner and others that there is no better Salmon than in England: and that though some of our Northern countries have as fat and as larfge as the River Thames, yet none are of so excellent a taste.

A 65lb RIVER TAY SALMON
No. 394

In 1879, Mr Towell, who had a fishmonger's shop in the Strand, asked Frank Buckland to measure a huge salmon he had been sent. Buckland recorded it on page 295 of *The Natural History of British Fishes* (1881):

> In August, 1879, Mr. Towell of the Strand sent for me to examine a very large salmon from the Tay; it weighed 65lbs., and measured from the tip of the nose to the end of the tail along the curve of the body, 4ft. 5¾in.; the girth, 2ft. 1¾in.

It is fortunate that Buckland specifies the way that he measured the fish – from the tip of the nose to the end of the tail (not to the fork) along the curve of the body – because it indicates to me that all measurements given for historical catches are open to interpretation, which is another way of saying that it is one big muddle. I have been criticised for trying to take account of this muddle in my book *The Domesday Book of Mammoth Pike* (1979) but anyone involved in recording measurements of fish from historical accounts should realise from the above that it is fraught with uncertainty.

Nowadays, we measure a fish from nose to fork, not along the curve but with the fish lying flat on the table. For big fish, that probably makes at least an inch or more difference in 'real' length.

FINN ISDAHL'S 65lb SALMON
No. 395

The *Fishing Gazette* of 17 December 1921 recorded that Mr Finn Isdahl caught a 65lb salmon on the Vosso River in June 1920. In *Game Fish Records*, page 223, Jock Scott brought to light a second fish that Finn, a Norwegian, caught on the same day:

> One of the most extraordinary angling feats on record is that of Herr Finn Isdahl. His two salmon weighing 65lb and 47lb in one day – reported in the *Fishing Gazette* – must surely be the world's record brace of salmon. They were, I believe, caught on fly; and were taken from the Vosso River. The date June, 1920.

Further discussion with Roy Flury about Isdahl's fish led to the discovery (via personal communication with Per Gulbrandsen) that it was killed on 8 June on the Range pool at Bolstad. Its length was 54in and girth 30in. Although Jock Scott believed that this well-documented fish was caught on a fly, he provides no evidence of this, and Roy Flury is not convinced. He comments that, 'The Bolstad is the part of the Vosso before entering the fjord. It is not fly water and in early June it would be enormous.' In support, Philip Crowe in *Out of the Mainstream* (1970, USA) notes:

> According to the records kept by Haraldsen, only a few of the 106 salmon taken during June of 1965 and the 126 taken during June of 1966 were caught on flies.

THE 65lb 'ROYAL ASCOT' SALMON
—— No. 396 ——

The *Fishing Gazette* of 24 June 1922 published some correspondence about this fish.

A ROYAL "ASCOT" SALMON

June 13, 1922

DEAR SIR – On my way to work early this morning I discovered a remarkably fine salmon on the slab of a most enterprising fishmonger, Mr. J. H. Humphreys, of 7 Strutton Ground, Westminster, S. W. 1., weighing 65lb. This is by far the largest "spring" salmon I have ever heard of in this country, and can only be compared with the uncouth monsters of Campbell river, British Columbia.

It was a male fish, and the following are the dimensions which I took most carefully, with Mr. Humphreys' assistance: weight, 65lb (good); length 53½ inches; girth, (at widest), 30 inches; width of tail (tip to tip), 12½ inches. River – Tweed. Sex, male. One of a consignment of which the largest was a 25 pounder – a mere baby!

I happened on a newspaper friend on my way to the City, and mentioned this big fish to him. Before you could say "Jack Robinson" as the saying goes, Mr. Humphreys' shop was besieged by the camera men, and the fish photographed end on and sideways.

Comments from the crowd were entertaining, so I heard later: "That

The Daily Mail's photograph of the fine 65lb fish that was put on show by Humphreys, the Westminster fish-monger, and became known as the 'Royal Ascot' salmon. Another photograph of the same 65lb salmon can be seen in Oglesby and Money-Coutts' book The Big Fish *(1992) which came from Miss Georgina Ballantine's scrapbook in which she kept letters, cuttings and photographs from her fellow anglers. The cutting reports that this fish is the third largest salmon to be caught in Britain (by any method).*

salmon is 300 years old," says one; "takes 'em that time to grow" says another.

Meanwhile I beg to enclose a series of scales which I took bright and early, and which may help to trace the history of this really very fine salmon.

Mr. Humphreys tells me that he never can resist the purchase of a fish of abnormal attractions, and certainly his big "Ascot" salmon of 1922 will draw attention to his enterprising stall in Strutton Ground, S. W. 1.

Yours very truly.

J.H.W

On 8 July, the *Fishing Gazette* continued to discuss the large salmon:

REPORT ON SCALES FROM THE 65LB SALMON

The *Field* of July 1 has the following note about the 65lb salmon.

A BIG TWEED SALMON

The *Fishing Gazette*, in its last issue, gives a good photograph and description of a fine salmon from the Tweed recently exposed for sale by a Westminster fishmonger (Mr. J. H. Humphreys, 7, Strutton-ground). It weighed 65lb., and was 53½in. long. The correspondent who reported it was able to send some scales to Mr. Marston, so its life-history will no doubt be available in due course. The Tweed maintains its old reputation for big fish, and might some day yield a 100-pounder. We remember that some fifteen years ago a dead one was found in the river late in the autumn which weighed 60lb or more, and was estimated to have been a great deal heavier when alive. It may have met with a fate similar to that of the monster, 59½in. long, which was found dead in the Wye in 1920, and which had been hooked and lost by some unfortunate angler. The Wye fish was not weighed, but was esti-mated at about 85lb.

Mr. Hutton has very kindly reported as follows on the age of this great fish:-

"I am not quite sure about the river life and I think it is three years. This monster (65lb., length 53½in., girth 30in., male) spent four years in the sea without spawning, so it would now be over seven years old.

"For comparison I give the measurements of all the salmon over 60lb of which I have had scales."

DATE			LENGTH	GIRTH		
		lbs.	ins.	ins.	River	Sea
1921 June	Shannon	62	48½	39½	2 yrs	3½
1920 June 9	Voss River	65	55	34½	3 yrs	4
1921 July 31	Aarp [Aaro]	68⅓	53¾	30⅓	3 yrs	5

On 12 August the *Fishing Gazette* followed up with a letter from J.A. Hutton, correcting the reported facts and figures:

A CORRECTION RE SALMON OVER 60LBS.

DEAR MARSTON –I have only just returned from Norway, which will explain the delay in answering your various letters. Let me first correct a mistake, to which my attention was drawn by Mr. A. L. Allen, in the figures you published in the *F.G.* of July 8, of the weights and measurements of some large-salmon. The Shannon fish of 62lb. was 29½in. girth, not 39½in. The length of 48½. seems very short for the weight, but this is what was sent me with the scales. I can't guarantee that it was correct. As regards the Aaro (not Aarp) salmon of 65⅓lb, the particulars given me by the Bergen Museum were as follows:- Weight, 31 kilos. length 136.5 cms., girth 77 cms. These figures in English equivalents are approximately as follows:- Weight 65⅓lb., length 53.74in., girth 30.31in. When I was passing through Bergen the other day I saw a cast of this salmon and it was certainly a most magnificent specimen.

Yours sincerely
J.A. Hutton

A 65lb NORWEGIAN SALMON
—— No. 397 ——

In Arne Krogstad's *Vigeland i Vennesla* (1999) a fine photograph of a very large salmon appears on page 308. On the same page there is a photograph of a six-strong salmon netting party, which may be significant, but no specific details regarding the fish's capture seem to be given. It was killed in the Sødal River in 1938.

Judging by the little girl's sleeveless dress and her father's rolled-up sleeves, this perfectly shaped cock salmon was probably caught in the summer months

MURRAY SOWERBY'S
65lb VOSSO SALMON
—— No. 398 ——

In *Salmon Stories* (1983) Jack Chance recalls a conversation he had in the Flyfishers' Club with C.M. Wells, the rather shy and reticent one-time leaseholder of the fishings on a three-mile stretch of the Vosso River. Chance asked him how the fishing had been at his beloved Bolstad, the lowest section of the river. Chance was conscious that, had others been present, such a question would have been inappropriate, but on this occasion he got an answer.

'Oh very poor,' Wells murmured from behind *The Times* city page, but then added, 'Sowerby did quite well.'

'Oh really? What did he get?'

'His first fish weighed 65lb and the second 52.'

There we have it – the largest brace of Atlantic salmon ever caught in sequence. Mr Murray Sowerby must have been a very shy and reticent man himself because his deed, as far as I know, has never been broadcast. A few months after the above was written, there was an interesting development when Karl Magne, from Norway, sent David Hatwell a photograph of Sowerby's fish. He wrote: 'I can myself remember the 65lb fish hanging on the wall of our house. I was thirteen years old at the time.' Karl Magne and his family lived in the house that was once owned by H.C. Charrington (No. 338). He added, 'The 65lb fish is the biggest that I have ever seen, although I have heard tales about them being bigger – but only tales.'

*Murray Sowerby with his big fish. From the position of his reel it would appear that he is holding a fly rod –
and so the chances are that he caught this magnificent salmon on fly*

THE BALTIC SEA 66lb SALMON
No. 401

On 7 June 1913 the *Fishing Gazette* published a note from 'Rugde', their correspondent on Scandinavian matters:

> 'The following may interest you: A magnificent specimen of a Baltic salmon was exhibited a few days ago in Munkbrogatan, Stockholm. It weighed 29.5 kilos as nearly as may be 66lb., and measured 140cm [55ins] in length. The owner, Herr Sjödin, said it was the largest he had seen since 1887, when he received one from Ljusdal which weighed 34 kilos, or 76½lb. They would have attracted attention in Bond-street, would they not?' I wish 'Rugde' could have sent some scales from near the shoulder.

The larger fish is included at No. 446 on this list.

The Baltic still produces very large salmon, although the tactics have changed. Nowadays a considerable range of equipment is needed for deep-water trolling, or trailing, as this photograph illustrates. The boat is about to leave for the Baltic Sea, near the mouth of the Mörrum River. An echo sounder is also essential in order to locate the shoals of fodder fish – sprats and herrings – which feed at variable depths.

THE FISHMONGER'S 67lb SALMON
No. 407

The celebrated fishmonger Grove had the distinction of exhibiting three huge salmon weighing 67lb, 70lb and 72lb on his premises. The 70-pounder was Bishop Browne's fish (well nearly), which Grove exhibited in 1871 in his shop in Westminster (No. 425). The other two were displayed together in 1877, by which time he had moved his shop to New Bond Street.

Another fishmonger, Crump of New Bond Street, also exhibited a 70-pounder in 1877 (No. 427). All three fish caught in that year were netted from the River Tay. This information comes from Courtney Williams' *Angling Diversions* (1945), page 144. The author added, 'These three fish came from the Tay nets and the weights in each case were verified.'

A 67lb SWEDISH SALMON
No. 408

The *Fishing Gazette* of 19 September 1914 published a note that was originally sent to the editor of *Country Life* by a correspondent who signed himself 'L'.

'SIR – A few days ago a very fine salmon was captured at Lulea. It weighed 29.5 kilos (about 67lb), and its total length was 142cm. From point of nose to gills the head measured 39cm., and the width of its tail was 39cm.'

It will be seen that this grand fish approximates closely to Mr. Edward Sturdy's *Fishing Gazette* Scale of Weight for Length, which gives 67½lb. for a 54in. fish, and this Swedish monster was between 53in. and 54in. in length. I wish 'L' had given us details as to mode of capture, but doubtless it was by net, as I see from Mr. James Dowell's capital map of Norway and Sweden, in his 'Norwegian Anglings', that Lulea is right at the mouth of the Lulea River, almost at the top of the Gulf of Bothnia.

JOCK WALLACE'S
67½lb NITH SALMON
No. 410

ock Scott in *Game Fish Records* (1936), pages 186–7, tells us about this monster salmon:

> The Nith rises in Ayrshire and runs into the Solway Firth, a distance of approximately 50 miles. As a salmon river it is an autumn stream, the best sport usually being obtained from August until the close of the season in November.
>
> The Nith will always be notable as the river wherein the famous 67lb salmon was caught in 1812. The story has been told in many different books; but in this instance the various accounts seem to agree in the essential details, which is unusual where fishing stories are concerned!
>
> The captor was one Jock Wallace, a noted poacher and extremely expert angler. According to the majority of the accounts, Wallace hooked his fish at 8 a.m. and eventually gaffed it at 6 p.m. The story then runs that Jock found that only two strands of his horsehair line were left, the others having parted under the strain. If this is true, then the fish was a remarkably unlucky one. Of course, horsehair lines, as then used, possessed great elasticity, and to this fact Wallace probably owed his fish. Apart from this, to play a fish for practically an entire day without a break or, more likely, the hold giving way argues great skill on the part of the fisherman, and remarkably good tackle, which one is safe in saying, must almost certainly have been made by Wallace himself. Anglers of his stamp and day usually made everything possible for themselves. Assuming all the details to be correct, the fact is one of the most noteworthy in angling history.

The details of this salmon first appeared in *Galloway News* of 30 June 1922:

THE 'GREAT SALMON' KILLED IN THE NITH

This salmon was killed in the Boat Pool of Barjarg in the river Nith, in September, 1812, and weighed 67½lb. It was killed by an old man named Jock Wallace – a bit of a poacher now and then – and was hooked about half-a-mile further up the river at a pool called the Clog, which does not exist now, the course of the river having changed. Wallace hooked the salmon in the forenoon, and had it on all day. At 6 p. m. when the men came out of Barjarg Limeworks, the clerk of the works, Andrew Paterson, waded into the water and gaffed the fish. It had been stationary for several hours through exhaustion, and Wallace was afraid to disturb it, and he was wise not to do so, for it was found that of the eighteen hairs which formed his casting line – there was no gut in those days – only three held the monster. To carry the fish home Jock put his arms through the gills, threw the fish over his shoulder, and the tail reached his ankles. (June 21, 1872.) [This is not one of the usual big fishing stories, but it was duly authenticated and a witnessed memorandum of the details and weight drawn out. So far as we are aware this monster salmon still holds the record for the Nith. ED.,*Galloway News.*]

The pools at Barjarg have changed since the day of Jock Wallace's 67¹/₂lb leviathan.. The Clog and Boat pools have gone, but other pools have taken their places, including the Trolley, the Caulback and the Sandbed. This is the Sandbed pool from the top of Trolley pool, close to Boatcroft Farm. Perhaps the Boat pool, where Wallace landed his fish, was adjacent to the farm. The photograph was taken in low-water summer conditions

On 4 July, a Mr D. Davidson of Kirkcudbright sent the above cutting to the editor of the *Fishing Gazette* but mentioned that it was taken from the *Kirkcudbright Advertiser* of 30 June 1922. However, the editor of the *Fishing Gazette* saw fit to publish his letter without drawing attention to this contradiction.

A 67 ½LB. NITH SALMON CAUGHT BY AN ANGLER OVER 100 YEARS AGO

DEAR MR. MARSTON – In these days of record capture I thought that the enclosed cutting might interest your readers. It is taken from the *Kirkcudbright Advertiser,* of June 30, 1922, a column of which is devoted each week to reports of 50 years ago. The report says the fish was killed in 1812, so it would appear to have taken nearly 60 years before the paper got hold of it – the story, I mean, not the fish. It certainly gives Count Denissoff's Norwegian fish a close run, and quite puts the lid on the Tweed salmon of 65lb., besides the Tweed fish was netted. I rather like the description of the way Jock carried his kill home.

In those times little inns flourished all along the country roads, and the whisky is said to have been good. Perhaps that might account for – no, perish the thought, and held by three hairs too. But I mustn't pick holes in the story, it wouldn't be sporty, as there's no one now to stick up for it.

Yours faithfully

D. J. Davidson

Kirkcudbright
July 4, 1922

The wood carving of Wilfred Kennedy's 1894 salmon, which was made by Johan Neset (1877–1951), is mounted on the outside wall of a fishing hut beside the Aaro River in Norway

WILFRED KENNEDY'S
68lb AARO SALMON
No. 411

When reporting the result of reading the scales of Count Denissoff's 68lb 4oz Aaro River salmon (No. 415), J. Arthur Hutton noted in the *Fishing Gazette* of 13 August 1921, 'The late Mr. Kennedy caught a 68lb salmon in the same river several years ago.' That was all I knew about Kennedy's big salmon until I found mention of it on page 224 of Sir Herbert Maxwell's *British Freshwater Fishes* (1904): 'Mr. Wilfred Kennedy landed one of 68lb. in the Aora [sic], a Norwegian river, in August 1894.' Subsequently, I was very lucky to notice a photograph of a carving of Kennedy's salmon on page 9 of *The American Fly Fisher*, Summer 1992, Vol. 18, number 3 (*The Journal of the American Museum of Fly Fishing*). The photograph figured in Ronald Swanson's piece entitled 'Fish Models, Plaques, and Effigies'. Swanson is well known for his large collection of mounted fish, be they cased, carved or moulded, and he is probably the foremost authority on the subject of carved fish effigies.

The wood carving of Wilfred Kennedy's salmon, which was made by Johan Neset (1877–1951), is mounted on the outside wall of a fishing hut beside the Aaro River in Norway. From the carving it can be observed that the fish is male, although that could have been deduced without having seen the effigy. The legend mentions (in English) that the fish was caught by Mr Kennedy in 1895, which turns out to be incorrect. Along with Herbert Maxwell, the *Fishing Gazette* put the date at *circa* 1894, and a note published on page 251 of the 30 March 1895 edition seems to indicate that by March 1895 the fish had been preserved, cased and exhibited:

A photograph of Wilfred Kennedy playing his fish appeared in the Fishing Gazette *of 30 June 1906*

> One of the finest sights at the Fisheries is the Norwegian salmon (weighing
> 68lb) taken from the Aaro, a Norwegian stream, by the late Wilfred
> Kennedy, with a 20ft. steel centre rod made by the exhibitor (Mr. J. J. Hardy)
> at Stand No. 1. It is a work of art. I will not say who 'set it up,' or whether
> it is a genuine 'Cooper.' See if for yourselves!

This notice gives the impression that Kennedy's fish had been to the taxidermist but this
was not the case. In an article about the Fisheries Exhibition on page 247 of the same
edition we read:

> The *facsimile* of the fish, which is now on view at Messrs. Hardy's stall, is a
> model by Mr. J. J. Hardy, and painted by Mr. Thomas Gibb of Alnwick. It is
> labelled as 68lb. Not only is the model a perfect one, but the painting
> thereof rivals anything that the great fish painter, the late H. L. Rolfe, ever
> executed. It is life itself, and must be seen to be believed.

The mystery photo sent by Hardy's to the Fishing Gazette *in 1953, which shows Wilfred Kennedy's brother, Myles (seated) and Wilfred's massive salmon*

I had been unable to trace a contemporary photograph of Wilfred Kennedy with his 68-pounder, which is one of the most famous nineteenth-century rod-caught salmon, until in the November 2004 issue of *Classic Angling* I saw a piece headlined 'Mystery of the 72lb Salmon', including a letter and photograph culled from the *Fishing Gazette* of 2 May 1953. Hardy's had sent a photograph of a mystery fish together with a plea for readers' help:

> This photograph of a huge Norwegian salmon was forwarded to us by Mr. Fred Hardy of Messrs Hardy Bros Ltd, Alnwick, Northumberland. It was found among old photographs, including that of the 52lb River Earn record salmon, that had been stored for many years. The only particulars given on the back of the photograph are the caption 'Will and 72½lb salmon with witness.' We cannot find any record of this salmon. Can any reader say who Will is, and when and on what river the fish was caught?

It occurred to me that the reported weight might not be the correct one. As research for this book has shown, the weights of many big fish caught in Europe and weighed in kilograms are distorted when converted to pounds. Further delving brought evidence that Will is in fact Wilfred Kennedy, who caught a 68lb and not a 72lb or a 72½lb salmon on the Aaro River on a prawn. However, the man sitting in the chair is not, as you would expect, the captor of the fish but his brother Myles Kennedy. Proof comes in a letter published by the *Fishing Gazette* on 30 May 1953:

72 ½LB. NORWEGIAN SALMON

DEAR SIR – On page 419 of the May 2 issue of *THE FISHING GAZETTE* – this cock-fish was caught by my uncle, Wilfred Kennedy, in the River Aaro about 1897. It took him twenty minutes to land the fish on a 21 ft. greenheart rod. My father – the late Myles Kennedy – is sitting in the chair. I will look up my records of the other men.

Hardy's had the cast of the fish in his window prior to 1914 – it was bombed out in the last war.

The original fish is now in the Bergen Museum – it weighed 68 lb. four days after it was caught.

It is the heaviest salmon caught on rod and line – artificial prawn bait – although to complete the picture, old John Hardy had in the corner of the mounting a large overdressed fly!

Yours faithfully

M. S. NIGEL KENNEDY (Major)
Ulverston
North Lancs.

MODEL OF 68lb SALMON KILLED ON THE RIVER AORA NORWAY BY THE LATE WILFRED KENNEDY ESQRE AUGUST 1894 with a 20ft. Cane built Steel Centre Rod. MADE BY HARDY BROS ALNWICK.

Although this letter resolves Fred Hardy's problem of identification (despite Nigel Kennedy citing the wrong date) and the confusion over the weight, it creates another but less important dilemma. Was Wilfred Kennedy fishing with a 20ft steel-centred split cane rod or was he fishing with a 21ft Greenheart rod? Incidentally, I think I know why Wilfred Kennedy did not feature in the photograph. I believe that he was holding the camera to avoid a slip-up with such an important fish.

A clue about the rod arrived via Roy Flury, who wrote to me on 8 June 2005, enclosing a photograph that had appeared in the *Fishing Gazette* of 30 June 1906. It had been published in support of a letter from John James Hardy about greenheart and split-cane rods:

> The salmon was caught on prawn in the Sea Pool, (54in length 29½in girth). He was using a 20ft Hardy split cane steel-centred rod.

Finally, the remaining confusion about the date was settled when, in September 2006, through a chain of kind helpers I received a photograph of a plaque that was once attached to a plaster model of Kennedy's fish. The model had been on display in Hardy's Pall Mall shop which was found by Harry Clark in the debris after Hardy's shop was bombed during the war. Clark eventually gave it to Charles Kewley, following his retirement from Hardy's in the early 1980s.

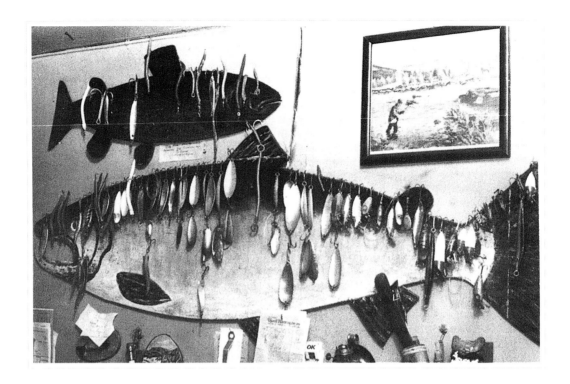

FRIDGEIR SAGMO'S
68lb NAMSEN SALMON
No. 413

I have had three different weights given for this fish, 68lb, 67½lb and 67¼lb. It was weighed at 30 kilos and the problem seems to lie in converting kilos to pounds. The fish was caught on a spoon in the Namsen River by Fridgeir Sagmo when he was gillied by Johan Williksen on a very cold day in May 1931. A model of Sagmo's fish is on view in a sports shop near Grong, where it is suffering the indignity of being used as a display rack for numerous spoons and plugs.

Laks Salmo salar. L. Han. 8aar. 31 Kg. Aarøelv, Sogn. 31.7.21. Gave fra N.Den

The cast of Count Denissoff's fish made by Finn de Lange and on show at the Wild Salmon Centre in Laerdal in Norway

THE MYSTERIOUS TALE OF COUNT DENISSOFF'S 68¼lb NORWEGIAN SALMON
No. 415

O
n 13 August 1921, the *Fishing Gazette* announced the capture of a possible new world-record rod-caught Atlantic salmon:

THE RECORD NORWEGIAN SALMON
CAUGHT BY COUNT DENISSOFF

This has been a great year for big salmon taken on rod and line in Norway. In the *Fishing Gazette* summer number, July 16, we had a picture of Mr. Waud's splendid 58lb. fish, and now comes news of a 68lb. fish caught on the prawn by Count Denissoff; it must be the record for a Norwegian rod-caught fish and nearly the world record for Atlantic salmon (*Salmo salar*), though I believe that is still held by the Earl of Home for his 69lb. 12oz. fish, caught in the Tweed. One of 67lb. was caught on the Nith by T. Wallace in 1872.

PARTICULARS RESPECTING THE BIG FISH

The following copy of a letter by the captor was kindly sent to me by Mr. James Dowell:-

It is not clear from the photograph whether this is a cast of Count Denissoff's 68¹/₄lb Aaro salmon (two casts were made), or a cardboard cut-out that was subsequently destroyed in a fire. On the other hand, it could be the original fish

A 68lb and Other Fine Norwegian Salmon

COPY OF LETTER RECEIVED BY MR. JAMES DOWELL,
34, ST. JAMES'S STREET, S. W. 1,
FROM HERR N. DENISSOFF, AUGUST 8, 1921.

Aaroen, Sogndal I Sogn, Norway,
August 2, 1921.

DEAR SIR – I thought it might interest you to know what sport I have been having on the Aaro river in Sognefjord, Norway.

I have killed the largest salmon since Mr. Kennedy's one in 1895. My salmon weighed 68lb. and girth 30in., length 55¼in. which makes it longer and slightly larger than Mr. Kennedy's salmon, which is also 68lb. I caught it on prawn and played it twenty-five minutes at the end of which time it was cleverly gaffed by my gillie, L. Tenden. It has been sent to the Bergen Museum.

This has been a good season for salmon and on two occasions I personally have caught six in one day and seven another – five salmon on

Count Nicholas Denissoff and his gillie with the 68¹/₄lb salmon caught in the Aaro River on 31 July 1921. This is the photograph that Finn de Lange sent to the Fishing Gazette and, although a poor one, I must say that it shows the most perfectly shaped big salmon that I have ever seen.

one day has, till now, been the record of this river. The total weight of the six salmon caught on July 23 was 157lb; on July 27, the day of the seven salmon, two more were caught by the second rod, making it *nine salmon in one day*, the total weight of which was 267lb.

My largest salmon on July 27 weighed 52lb., girth 28½in.

On three other occasions I have killed salmon weighing 41lb., 41lb and 38lb. All other fish have been large ones, fourteen weighing between 31lb and 35lb. The total bag from July 16 till August 1 was *thirty-nine salmon*!

The second rod having caught nine and I the rest.

Yours truly

(Signed)

DENISSOFF

Age of the Fish

Since the above came from Mr. Dowell I have received the following further information from Mr. J. Arthur Hutton:-

This wonderful photograph of three big fish, weighing 48lb, 40lb and 30lb, was taken on Norway's River Aarø in the 1920s or 30s. The angler wearing a cap is the famous L.R. Hardy of Hardy Brothers fame

DEAR MARSTON – Thanks to the kindness of Herr Grieg, of the Bergen Museum, I have just received the scales from what I believe is the record Atlantic salmon caught with rod and line. The following is translation of Herr Grieg's letter:

'On July 31, Count Denissoff caught a salmon weighing 31 kilos in the Aaro River, Sogn, with a prawn. As they will probably be of interest to you in your scale investigations, I am sending you some of its scales. It was a cock fish, and its measurements were as follows:-

Length 136.5 centimetres = 53.74in
Girth 77.0 " = 30 31 "
Head 31.5 " = 12.40 "
Tail 27.0 " = 8.13 "
Depth (in front of back fin) 31.00 " = 12.20 "
1 kilo equals 2.2046lb., so 31 kilos equal 68.34lb.

The late Mr. Kennedy caught a 68lb. salmon in the same river several years ago, and I have a recollection of a fish of the same weight being caught in the Tay, also some years ago. The scales are a little worn, as is usually the case with a big cock fish during the approach of autumn and when the spawning season is getting nearer. They are, however, quite clear and show three years' river life and five years' sea feeding; so this monster was rather over eight years old. It was a maiden fish, and had not spawned before.
Yours sincerely
J. ARTHUR HUTTON.

It will be seen that there is a slight difference in the length of the fish in the above account due to the measurements taken on capture and perhaps a day or so later at the Museum not being identical. I believe a fish contracts a bit at first, stiffens, and then slackens. In a big fish even an inch makes a lot of difference.

On 8 October 1921, the editor of the *Fishing Gazette* published a letter from Finn de Lange, who ran a sports shop in Bergen, containing more information and a photograph of the fish with its captor and the gillie.

DEAR SIR – I am just back from salmon fishing...I also had the new Norwegian record fish on the Aaro river, of which you have already had a report in your paper, sent to me during first days of August, and I brought personally the fish to the Bergen Museum and got the weight, 68¼lb., length 55in. and girth 30in controlled. A casting is now being made of the fish, and it will be exhibited in the museum. I certify that both these fish are of the exact weight and measures given. You will find enclosed a photo of the happy angler, Mr. Nicholas Denissoff, and his gillie, if you should like to show this very big fish in your paper. Some scales I also enclose, to get to know the age. You might kindly return me the photo after use, as I would like to keep it. Being the only specialist in fishing tackle in this country, I get in touch with most of the anglers for salmon, and will always get to know if a record fish is taken. If you should like to get any information of this kind, I shall be more than pleased to forward the reports I get.

Yours truly
FINN DE LANGE
Bergen den,
August 14, 1921

(I have to thank Herr de Lange for kindly sending these reports and the photograph of Mr. Nicholas Denissoff and his splendid salmon, and am much obliged for his offer to send reports of any record fish that are taken in Norway. – ED]

In the course of investigating Denissoff's 68¼lb salmon, I had to sift through a number of confusing references to bigger fish that supposedly fell to his rod, and it transpired that Roy Flury had come across the same problem. Some of the attributions that caused the difficulty are listed, because, as Roy observed, 'this well illustrates the difficulties involved in maintaining a true record of the facts.' These fish were supposedly caught by Denissoff in the Aaro on 31 July 1921.

Date	Citation	Weight	Length	Method
13/8/1921	Letter from Denissoff to Mr James Dowell published in the *Fishing Gazette*	68lbs	55¼ins	Caught on prawn
13/8/1921	Letter from J. Arthur Hutton published in *Fishing Gazette*	68¾lbs	53¾ins	
1936	Report in *Game Fish Records*	68½lbs		
1953	Listed in Peter Prag's *Salmon Fishing in Norway*	68½lbs		
1955	Letter from Denissoff to Carnes Weeks	74lbs		

Dr Carnes Weeks from the USA met Charles Ritz, of the famous family of hoteliers, and Nicholas Denissoff briefly in Norway and on his return wrote to Denissoff asking for details of his big fish. Denissoff replied confirming that on 31 July 1921 he caught a 74lb salmon that was 1.5 metres (59in) long on a No. 6 Denissoff fly. Carnes Weeks included this information in an article on 'Record Atlantic Salmon' that he contributed to the *Atlantic Salmon Journal* in 1955.

1959   Charles Ritz, in the first English edition of *A Fly Fisher's Life*, states 'I saw a drawing on the dining wall [in Denissoff's house] – 76lbs in weight, 4ft 8ins [56ins], taken on a prawn 31/7/1921'.

1972   In the revised edition of his book, Charles Ritz describes the same fish on page 242 but has changed his mind about the prawn and claims that the Aaro holds the world record for a fish caught on fly. He said that the fish

These are the famous 'Platforms of Despair', specially built to give anglers a chance to hook, play and kill big salmon in the Aaro's fierce waters

had been 'set up' and was on view in the Bergen Museum.

1991   In *Alten, the Story of a Salmon River*, Flury and Dalensen note that the largest salmon caught on fly was taken from the Aaro and weighed 76lb.

1997   Unhappy about the claimed weight of this fish, Roy Flury wrote to the Norges Fiskers Museum in Bergen for confirmation. In their reply, dated 20 February 1997, the museum stated:

The fish that you refer to was caught by R. Denissoff on the River Aaro on 31st July 1921. The salmon was male, 8 years old and weighed 31 kilos (68½lbs).* It measures 136cms long [53½in]. The model of this fish was previously in the Zoological Museum, University of Bergen. It is now lent out to the Centre of Wild Salmon in Leardal. There is also a casting of this fish in a sports shop in Bergen and another in the Ritz Hotel in Paris.

*31 kilos converts to 68lb 6oz and we have chosen to round it down to 68¼lb rather than up to 68½lb.

Having corresponded with Helen Maristuen, the curator or manager of the Norwegian Wild Salmon Centre in Lærdal, I was lucky to find it in possession of the cast of Denissoff's salmon that was originally made by Finn de Lange on behalf of the Bergen Museum. At the time, she was planning an exhibition about 'the English Lords' who came to fish in Lærdal in 1906 – 'I would like to know as much as possible about them i.e. why they came here, who they came with, how long they stayed, why Lærdal, what clothes they had, what food they ate, what did they do when they weren't fishing, how much did it cost them.' It will be interesting to see what information she manages to discover.

The head of the Corrib salmon, from which can be seen the enormous depth of the fish just at the rear of the pectoral fin

IRELAND'S LARGEST SALMON –
THE 69lb CORRIB FISH
No. 416

In Francis Day's *British and Irish Salmonidæ* (1887), a note on some of the largest salmon caught in Ireland includes one of 69lb taken in March 1866 in Galway. This is the first reference I found to what is unquestionably Ireland's largest known salmon. A plaster cast of it was put on exhibition in the Museum of Queens College. The location given does not specify whether Galway refers to city or county. The fish could have been netted downstream of Galway Weir (the most likely), or netted in the Clare River, or been taken by some means from Lough Corrib. Subsequently, I noticed that Frank Buckland, her Majesty's Inspector of Fisheries, in his book *The Natural History of British Fishes* (1881), documented the netting of the same near 70lb Irish salmon.

In April 2005 I visited the Western Regional Fisheries Board office on Nunn's Island in Galway in the hope of discovering the sites of the old netting stations on the River Corrib, so that I could take a photograph that I hoped would enhance the reality of the 69lb salmon that was netted there a very long time ago.

When I spoke to a group of salmon anglers, which included staff man Paddy Glyn, about this incredibly large salmon of yesteryear, I was surprised to learn from one of the

Galway Weir – one of the best-managed and most productive fisheries in Ireland

fishermen that a plaster cast of another huge salmon, weighing more than 50lb, could be viewed somewhere in the buildings that constitute the University College of Galway. Imagine my delight when, having combed the University's campus in search of this fish, I found that it was not a second fish but the original 69-pounder that had been killed over 139 years ago. Barry Dawson, the man in charge of the University's collection of specimens in their natural history section, helped me to measure and photograph the salmon. The legend, painted on the inside back plate of the case, revealed the following information:

> *weight 69lbs, sold in London March 5th, 1866 for the sum of £12.3.0;*
> *presented to the U.C.G. by Thomas Ashworth.*

The length turned out to be 55½in and the depth 14in. The fish itself is a magnificent cock fish. Indeed, it is the most impressive salmon that I have ever seen. It was obviously a fresh-run springer when it was caught since it was still in tidal water at the time.

After my visit to the University I went back to Nunn's Island to talk to Seamus

Hartigan about my delight in finding a plaster cast of the fish that was No. 416 in the big fish list in my manuscript. Seamus, besides managing the fishery, has a deep knowledge of local history, which proved to be very helpful. He knew all about the salmon donor, Thomas Ashworth, who, together with his brother Edmund, once owned the fishery rights – netting, trapping and rod fishing – from the sea up to Lough Corrib, and most of the riverside buildings as well. In 1852 they had paid £5,000 for these rights.

The Ashworths were Quakers with many business interests in England and Ireland but they were progressive and were perhaps the first in the west of Ireland to strip salmon and raise their young in a purpose-built hatchery in Galway. They even employed 120 river keepers and bailiffs to protect salmon on their spawning beds. Perhaps their boldest adventure was to expend £1,700 building a salmon pass and a fish ladder to take Corrib salmon up to Lough Mask. This work took place in 1865, just one year before the 69-pounder was netted, but alas it was a failure. Incidentally, although the Western Regional Fisheries Board now owns the trapping and netting rights, these are no longer exercised.

Before I left, Seamus escorted me to what was historically the most important netting station. On the right bank of the river, immediately above Wolftone Bridge, stands a watchtower. Built in 1850 by the Ashworths, this is now a romantic relic. There are three floors with large windows but close inspection reveals a small cubbyhole by the top right-hand window. At high tide, the fish spotter would sit behind this window looking down over the main holding pool at a time when shoals of salmon were expected to move into the pool. When they arrived, he would shout instructions through the cubbyhole window to the netting team of three men on the slipway. The routine was quite simple. A rope securing one end of the net was tied to a big metal ring on the bank. One man rowed the boat while another played out corked and leaded netting from a big flat board on the stern. They rowed across then down the pool, and then back to the slipway, where the rope tied to the other end of the net was handed to the third man, on the bank. All three men then pulled the net, which had encircled the salmon, across the pool and up the smooth, sloping slipway. Their eyes must have bulged when the 69-pounder flapped as it became grounded. The big fish may, of course, have been caught at the lower netting station but it would have had just the same affect on the netsmen.

There is still one mystery. Was the plaster cast of the fish made in Galway or was it made in London? I suspect it was made in London by Frank Buckland, who had a standing arrangement with London fishmongers to allow him to make a plaster cast of a fish before it was sold. If it was made in London, how did it get back to Galway? (Perhaps, as Seamus Hartigan has pointed out, because the Ashworths and Frank Buckland were friends?)

Readers may wonder what the metal rods (they can be seen clearly in the photograph) are doing inside the case that holds the cast of the mighty salmon. I discussed this matter with Barry Dawson and we came to the following conclusion. When the fish was mounted on its original painted board, i.e. the one on which the legend appears, it was probably screwed to a wall over the fireplace in the Victorian mansion, whereas after it was presented to the University it was put in a contemporary wooden case that needed the rods, due to the great weight of the plaster, to reinforce its structure. It is my ambition to convince Barry Dawson to remove the salmon from its prison and allow me to take a proper photograph of what could be the largest cased Atlantic salmon extant.

On the right bank of the river, immediately above Wolftone Bridge, stands the watchtower built in 1850 by the Ashworths. There are three floors with large windows but close inspection reveals a small cubbyhole by the top right-hand window. At high tide, the fish spotter would sit behind this window looking down over the main holding pool at a time when shoals of salmon were expected to move into the pool. When they arrived, he would shout instructions through the cubbyhole window to the netting team of three men on the slipway.

A 69lb RIVER RHINE SALMON
No. 417

I am quite sure that if the European newspapers and sporting journals prior to industrialisation were thoroughly searched, reports on the River Rhine would produce catch details of a great many of the largest salmon that were ever documented. As it is, we have knowledge of only one, which is described by Frank Buckland in his book *The Natural History of British Fishes* (1881). In the chapter on monster salmon, on pages 291–92, he gives the names of London fishmongers who would allow him to handle exceptionally large salmon so that he could make individual plaster casts of the fish. He lists eleven large salmon of which plaster casts were made and gives useful information regarding their lengths:

MONSTER SALMON

For several years past I have, by the kindness of London fishmongers – especially Mr. Thomas Grove, of Charing Cross; Mr. Charles of Lower Grosvenor Place, Pimlico; Messrs. Gilson and Quelch, Bond Street; Messrs. Grove Bond Street; Messrs. Smithers, London Bridge Railway Station; Mr. Towell, Strand, &c. – been enabled to cast nearly all the monster salmon that have come to the London market. I generally have the fish sent up to Albany Street in the evening, and I can now (having had so much practice) cast a mould and return the fish uninjured in about two hours; the process of casting does not injure the fish in the least, sometimes not a scale is rubbed off.

The following is a catalogue of the largest salmon I have in my museum and I am happy to say the largest is a British fish:-

			WEIGHT	LENGTH
1	Tay	Salmon	70	4ft. 5in.
2	Rhine	"	69	4ft. 8in.
3	Shannon	"	54	——
4	Tay at Kinfauns	"	53	4ft.
5	Rhine	"	51½	4ft. 3in.
6	Tay	"	51	4ft. 3in.
7	Wye	"	50	4ft. 2in.
8	Tay	"	49¾	4ft
9	Shannon	"	46	4ft. 3in.
10	Wye	"	44½	3ft. 10½in.
11	Tay at Kinfauns	"	42	3ft. 8in.

Charles F. Holden, on page 14 of *The Game Fishes of the World* (1913), tell us that the South Kensington Museum had the Rhine 69lb fish on display. On the same page he notes that 'in 1789 a seventy pounder was taken in the Thames near Fulham' but offers no evidence or his source for this statement.

SVEIN KJOLSTAD'S 69lb 7¼oz SALMON
⸺ No. 418 ⸺

On 5 July 1924, the *Fishing Gazette* published a letter from Mr Johansen of Norway. Some scales from the fish described were enclosed and the editor passed these on to their scale-reading expert Arthur Hutton, who in due course reported back.

On Friday, June 13, the record salmon in the Namsen was taken by an old farmer, Svein Kjolstad, at Jörum, [near the village of Grong]. The fish weighed immediately after capture 31.5 kg.; length, 137cm.; girth, 80.6cm. The fish is a cock fish, and was taken on a spoon of local pattern; the fisherman is 75 years old. It took about 20 minutes. I enclose some scales. As far as I can see, the fish has four years in the sea and probably three years in the river. Hope to send photo in a couple of days. Yours truly,

CHR. JOHANSEN

Mr. J. Arthur Hutton has examined the scales and writes:

DEAR MARSTON – Very many thanks for the scales. I am not quite sure about the river life. I think it was three years, but the scales are not very clear, and it is just possible it was only two years. The sea life is quite clear – four years – so it was either six or seven years old, and had not spawned before. It must have been a remarkably fine fish, for the condition factor works out at 44.3, which is above Mr. Sturdy's scale. It is rather curious that the three largest rod-caught salmon of which we have authentic records were all almost exactly the same weight.

A.HUTTON

A BILLINGSGATE 69½lb SALMON
No. 420

The Rev. W.B. Daniel, on page 10 in Part II of Volume II in *Rural Sports* (1801), wrote:

The largest *Salmon* MR. PENNANT ever heard of, weighed *seventy-four* pounds. In September 1795, one measuring upwards of *four feet* from nose to tail, and *three* in circumference, weighing within a few ounces of *seventy* pounds, was sold at *Billingsgate*, and was the largest ever brought there.

JOHANN AARVEN'S 69½lb SALMON
No. 421

Count Denissoff, who caught a 68lb salmon himself (No. 415), employed Johann Aarven as his gillie. Johann caught his even-bigger salmon from the Aaro River in 1921, managing to tail the fish by hand, which is a quite remarkable achievement. H.D. Turing supplied this information in *Where to Fish* (1937).

JENS GRIMESTAD'S
69½lb VOSSO SALMON
No. 422

A huge salmon was taken from the Evanger River in Norway in 1922. It was first reported in the *Fishing Gazette* of 2 September 1922:

A NORWEGIAN ANGLER GETS A NEARLY 70LB SALMON!

I have to thank our correspondent, Mr. H. B. Isachsen, for sending me the following brief particulars of the capture by a Norwegian angler of what is, I think, the third record rod and line-killed salmon – that is, an Atlantic salmon (*Salmo salar*) – which is the best of all the salmons from the angler's point of view.

Here are the particulars of this big Norwegian fish. I see it was caught in the river, which was for so many years fished by our old friend, the late Mr Edward Sturdy:-

En Laks PAA 31.5 kilo
Blev forleden dag Fisket I Vosse-elven av Sportsfiskeren Jens Grimestad Bulken. Fisken var næsten 1.5 meter lang.

Mr Isachsen says: "The above note appeared in one of our papers of August 24, 1922. It reads in translation: 'A salmon of 31.5 kilos, was landed the other day in the Voss River by an angler, Jens Grimestad [from] Bulken. The fish was nearly 1.5 metres long.' The angler is, of course, a Norwegian, the weight (31.5 kilos) is equal to 60.4lbs. If the length of Mr Grimestad's fish was 58½ inches, it ought to have weighed about 75lb if in good condition, by Mr Sturdy's scale, which was based on big Voss River fish. Mr. H.T. Sheringham, in 'Where To Fish' gives a list of notable fish, including the 69¾lb Tweed salmon credited to the Earl of Home about 1750 (were they Scotch pounds or English pounds? I believe it would mean a lot of difference – R.B.M.); then comes the 69½lb salmon caught by John Aarven on the Aaro in 1921; the 68lb fish caught by the late Wm. Kennedy in the same river in 1894. I hope to get Mr. A.J.H. to let me have the portrait of his big fish which he killed in Norway recently – nearly 60lb and landed in about ten minutes, I believe.

A mistake made in Mr Isachsen's letter, which the editor failed to pick up, was noticed in the next issue of the *Fishing Gazette* (9 September 1922) when J. Arthur Hutton, of River Wye fame, wrote:

> Dear Marston,
> In this week's F.G. you have a note about the big salmon caught in the Evanger*[*Evanger, Vosso and Bolstad are all part of one river system. Not surprisingly, many Britons get confused.] River, but there is a mistake about the weight – 31.5 kilos is nearly 69½lbs – 31.5 x 2.2046 = 69.445lbs. The length, as you will see from the accompanying letter from Herr Grieg, of the Bergens Museum, was 144 centimetres, or 56.693in. (144 x 3.937). It is, therefore, probably the heaviest Atlantic salmon caught with rod.
>
> Yours sincerely,
> J. Arthur Hutton.

Grieg's letter to Hutton was translated and also published:

> Bergen, August 29, 1922
>
> Dear Mr Hutton,
> On August 17 a salmon was caught at Bulken in the Evanger River weighing 31.5 kilos. The fish, which was an exceptionally fine one for its size, was 144 centimetres long and it is, as far as I know, the largest salmon caught in this river.
> I wrote immediately to Bulken to get some scales to send you, but the fish had been sent off at once to a fish dealer in Kristiania, so it was impossible to get you any.
>
> Yours sincerely,
> James A. Grieg

R.B. Marston, the editor, added:

A NORWEGIAN ANGLER GETS A NEARLY 70LB SALMON!
THAT BIG NORWEGIAN SALMON

There was an unfortunate mistake in giving the weight of Grimestad's big salmon in F.G. September 2, p.223. Mr Isachsen had written 69¼lb, and I had headed the note, "A Norwegian Angler Gets A Nearly 70lb Salmon!" but in the note it appeared as 60¼lb. It will be seen Mr Hutton makes it 69½lb and every ounce is worth recording when it is a case of records.

Finally, on 23 September 1922, the contrite editor published another letter from Mr H.B. Isachsen:

THE BIG 69½LB NORWEGIAN SALMON

Dear Sir,
Re the 69½lb salmon from the Evanger River, I am in hopes of sending you a photo and further details. I thought you would notice the mistake in the weight without my drawing your attention to it. Mr Hutton is quite correct: 31.5 kilos = 69.44 lbs – *not* 69¼.
This salmon *may* prove to be the heaviest *rod*-caught on record.
I will write you again when I hear further from the lucky fisherman.

Yours truly
H.B. Isachsen

However, in December things hotted up again when the editor published another letter from Isachsen (9 December 1922), who had in turn had received a letter and photograph of the fish from the captor Jens Grimestad from Grimestad, near Bulken:

Dear Sir,
Referring to previous correspondence re above, I give you below, translation of letter from Mr Jens Grimestad, the lucky angler, which may interest you:-
    At last I am able to send you the promised photograph of the big salmon I caught on August 19 last. I have made enquiries re the big salmon you mentioned as having been caught last year in the Aaro River, and am informed that same was caught more than one month earlier than mine, and I therefore believe that my fish would have weighed several kilos more had he been taken so much earlier in the year. As you will notice from the photograph, he has not the depth that he ought to have in proportion to his length. As you will also notice, it was a male salmon. The photograph shows some square stripes across the side, which are due to the fish having been left over the night on some narrow boards. I can also tell you that I

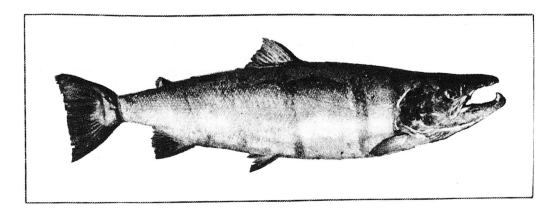

The photograph of the 69$^{1}/_{2}$ lb salmon caught by Jens Grimestad in the Evanger River, Norway on 19 August 1922 and sent by him to H.B. Isachsen who sent it to the Fishing Gazette. *Grimestad added that two days afterwards he had lost 'another salmon that was really much broader'.*

believe I was about breaking my own record two days after catching above fish, inasmuch as I lost another salmon that was really much broader. But I am sorry to say that I was very unlucky, or rather, the gillie was, because in trying to gaff the fish, he broke my line, in spite of the salmon lying absolutely motionless. Is not this too bad? I was in bad spirits several days after, and when I think of it I am still vexed.

With regards
(Signed)

Jens Grimestad
Grimestad
near Bulken
per Bergen

I also enclose the photograph, which shows clearly the length of the fish, when comparing same with the floorings forming the wall of the house. Particularly those of your readers who have been in Norway will be able to make this comparison. The length of this salmon being 1 metre 44cm (or 56.693ins), do you not think that same must be considered the biggest, or at least the longest, known salmon ever caught by rod or by net? The Tay salmon caught by net in June 1870 and weighing 71lbs was 53ins long, but with a tremendous girth, and this is, I presume, really the heaviest salmon known to have been caught in the United Kingdom. In the Pasvik River – or, rather, close to the mouth of this river, – a salmon weighing 33 kilos (72.75lbs) was caught by net in 1886. (Reported by Mr Klerck, bailiff, of Elvenes.) This is, as far as I know, the heaviest Norwegian salmon on record. I remain, dear Sir,

yours truly

H.B.I. Stavanger

I am much obliged to "H.B.I." for kindly sending these particulars and the photograph, which is reproduced. Most anglers would be satisfied if they could boast of having caught a 69½lb salmon; no doubt that is why Mr Grimestad can speak so moderately of the other monster he lost, or rather, of the ghillie who lost it for him. I think "H.B.I." is very likely right in claiming this as the biggest rod-caught or net-caught salmon – that is to say, as far as Atlantic salmon are concerned. Considerably larger specimens of Pacific salmon have been recorded from American waters.

When the gillie learned that he had been blamed for the loss of the second salmon, he sent a marvellous letter to his own local newspaper in Norway in which, according to the *Fishing Gazette* of 16 December 1922, he stated:

> I see that that great sportsman, Jens Grimestad has been telling tales in the papers. It was his own fault that he lost that second fish, because he had himself been the cause of losing the good old gaff, and the gaff I was using afterwards was an old, useless thing, no good at all. I said to Grimestad that I did not think it would end well with that gaff, but G. replied that I was to try it, and this was the reason the salmon was lost, and Grimestad should not put the blame on me.

The *Fishing Gazette* correspondent who brought the above comment to light continued:

> Well sir, I seem to see those two arguing on the riverside about that gaff, and with a 70-pounder waiting patiently to be released, and when the gillie had succeeded in proving how bad the gaff really was, would it not have been priceless to have been able to listen to that conversation following? I know exactly what both of them said! But would rather not try to repeat it.
>
> I also send you a cutting from a Norwegian paper with reference to the "record" salmon.

GIANT GEORGE HÄGGLUND'S
69lb 15oz SALMON
No. 424

George Hägglund from Sweden caught his huge salmon on a plug – Abu's famous Hi-Lo wobbler – and it turned out to be the largest caught in 1992, although from the photograph the fish looks as though it turned the scales at a good deal less than the claimed weight.

Naturally enough, all of us use our critical abilities to make judgements on such matters but I can say emphatically, having spent many years studying big-fish catch data, that although photographs are a valuable aid when making judgements, they can be dangerously unreliable. A classic example of the unreliability of photographic evidence can be found on page 24 of my book *The Domesday Book of Mammoth Pike* (1979) where the famous angler Mumford Smith can be seen beside a 38½lb pike that he caught on Lough Conn in 1928. I daresay that if most pike anglers looked at this photograph in a 'guess the weight' competition, the average guess would put the weight about 15lb. Fortunately, Mumford Smith had the fish cased by the famous Dublin taxidermists Messrs Williams and Sons and the fish is now on show at Newport House Hotel in County Mayo, where 'in the flesh', so to speak, it looks magnificent and every ounce of its 38½lb.

Despite appearances, George Hägglund's salmon weighed a massive 69lb 15oz. The captor is clearly as much of a giant as his fish

Said to be the authentic record at that time for the British Isles, this 70lb salmon (4ft 4in by 32in) was net-
ted in the Tay on 21 June 21 1870. The curious looking wooden frame in the background is a stretcher that
fishermen use to carry nets from the drying shed to the boat. The stretcher is placed across the stern of the boat
so that the net can be pulled off as the boat goes forward and likewise pulled on to the stretcher when the net
is being taken in

BISHOP BROWNE'S
MYTHICAL 70-POUNDER
No. 425

After Miss Ballantine's record salmon, Bishop Browne's is certainly the next most famous salmon – although he never actually landed it.

The full story of hooking, playing and eventually losing this monster salmon has become an angling classic that should be read by all fishermen, young and old, although some small discrepancies in the various reports cannot be resolved satisfactorily. A. Courtney Williams in *Angling Diversions* (1945) gives a fine précis of the basic facts:

Another exceptionally fine fish, which nearly made history, was a seventy-one pounder which was on view at Messrs. Grove's shop (then in Westminster) in the year 1871. This specimen was 52in long, with a girth of 31in. It might well have been the British record rod-caught salmon, as it was hooked one day at noon in the Tay by the Bishop of Bristol (Bishop Browne), who played it for 10½ hours, when the trace broke. Two days later it was taken in the nets, with the Bishop's small Phantom still in its jaws.

On 14 November 1903, the *Fishing Gazette* gave us some information on the above salmon, which had been culled from the 'Observer' column, published in the *Scotsman.*

> The largest Tay salmon, so far as I know, was taken with the net near Perth. It weighed 71lb. A beautiful cast of this splendid fish was made by the late distinguished naturalist, Frank Buckland.

Seventeen years later (26 March 1921) H.L. Eagles wrote to the editor of the *Fishing Gazette* correcting a statement made in the previous week's edition, and then commenting on Bishop Browne's lost salmon.

> I do not think that the fish netted in the Tay in 1870 has ever been exceeded in weight in this country, and its length was very short for its weight, 52in. for 71lb., but the girth of 31in. was unusually great. I saw the fish myself at Groves' shop, then in Westminster, and heard a wondrous tale from Bishop G. Brown, late of Bristol, who hooked this fish at noon in the estuary of the Tay on a small Phantom and lost it at 10p.m. The minnow was in its mouth when taken in the nets two days afterwards. Poor old Bishop! I wonder what he thought when the fish broke away.

> Yours sincerely

> H. L. EAGLES

Frank Buckland had an arrangement with a number of London fishmongers whereby any very large or rare specimens would automatically be brought to his notice so that he could make plaster casts of them. He was building up a collection to exhibit at the British Museum. Sadly, his collection has been broken up and, in the main, destroyed.

A correspondent of the *Fishing Gazette* (17 May 1913) drew readers' attention to the existence of the cast of the bishop's salmon, which had found its way to Brighton long after Buckland's death.

THE HOME OF BIG FISH

DEAR SIR – I notice in the *Fishing Gazette* of May 3 that you mention the 70lb salmon from the Tay as being the largest well-authenticated fish caught in the United Kingdom. It may be of interest to you to know that the cast made of this fish by Frank Buckland is in a glass-case in the entrance hall of the Brighton Aquarium. The dimensions of this fish are given as, length, 4ft 5in.; girth, 2ft 7½in.; weight, 70lb. The fish was netted two miles below Newburgh in June, 1870. There is also in the entrance hall at the Aquarium a collection of stuffed fish caught by our own members, amongst which are pike of 35lb., 32½lb., and several over 20lb., from which you may gather that our Sussex waters are fairly well stocked with fish monsters.

Yours truly,
ALFRED TRAFFORD
Hon. Sec. Sussex Piscatorial Society
The Aquarium, Brighton.

Buckland wrote his account of the fish in the journal *Land and Water* (25 June 1870):

MONSTER SALMON FROM THE TAY

Mr. Charles, of Arabella Row, has kindly sent me word (June, 1870) that he had purchased at Billingsgate a very large salmon, and that he wished me to examine it. I have seen many big salmon, but never saw such a fine "beast" – as the Scotch fishermen call a salmon – as our friend from the Tay. He had been caught in the nets of my friend, Mr. Alexander Speedie, the energetic and well-known tacksman, of Perth. Mr. Speedie writes me that his men caught the fish on the Haggis fishing-bank, about two miles below Newburg [Newburgh], on the Tay. Wishing to be certain of the weight of this Tay fish, Mr. Charles was good enough to put him in the scales in my presence. He was within an ounce or two of *seventy pounds*. And he would have turned the scale at this weight, only from exposure on the slab he had become somewhat dry, and therefore lost a little of his weight. I measured him carefully. His total length from tip of nose to edge of tail was 4ft. 5in.; his girth, 2ft. 7½in.; and length of head, 12in. Reader, chalk or pencil out these measurements, and you will see what a wonderful fish this was, and

Frank Buckland holds the cast of the huge Tay salmon. This photograph was published posthumously in Notes and Jottings on Animal Life in 1882

he was as handsome as he was bulky. The wholesale price was over £9. I took up the fish to Albany Street. I soon had him under the plaster, and before dark I got a very fair mould of this king of fishes. I then took him back again to sleep in the ice in Mr. Charles' shop. I did not injure a scale with the casting process, and he tumbled out of his mould like a great bullock. Mr. Charles gave me his head and his inside; of the head I have made moulds with fins expanded, as it will make a capital "gargoyle." I have filled up his intestines with plaster; their total length is 4ft 3in., his oesophagus and stomach together. His pyloric appendages were covered with fat, and there was also much fat about his intestines – this latter fat alone weighed 3 ounces. There was, of course, nothing in his stomach, as he had all his fat on board for his summer expedition up the river.

Bishop Browne's own account of his struggle with a mighty Tay salmon was published in *A Night with a Salmon* from *Off The Mill: Some Occasional Papers* (1895), but as this book is now hard to find, *The Magic Wheel* by David Profumo and Graham Swift (Heinemann 1986) may be a better source. One of my favourites, this book may be easier to locate in secondhand bookshops. The story is reproduced on pages 317–20. Browne's last paragraph, after describing ten hours of battling, ends on a note of disappointment bordering on distress:

> Time passes on as we drift slowly up the river towards Elcho. Ten o'clock strikes, and we determine to wait till dawn, and then land and try conclusions with the monster that has us fast for ten hours. The tide begins to turn, and Jimmy utters gloomy forebodings of our voyage down to the sea in the dark. The fish feels the change of tide, and becomes more demoniacal than ever. For half an hour he is one incessant flurry, and at last, for the first time, he rises to the surface, and through the dark night we can hear and see the huge splashes he makes as he rolls and beats the water. He must be near done, Jimmy thinks. As he is speaking the line comes slack. He's bolting towards the boat, and we reel up with the utmost rapidity. We reel on; but no sign of resistance. Up comes the minnow, minus the tail hook. Jimmy rows home without a word; neither he nor the fisherman will ever get over it.

The connection between Browne's fish and the fish that was subsequently netted by Mr Speedie becomes somewhat tenuous after Browne added the following note to his account:

> A large fish was taken in the nets at Newburgh the next year, which was popularly recognized as the fish of the above account. It had a mark just where I saw the tail hook of the minnow when the fish shewed itself once in the strong water above Newburgh; and a peculiarity of form of the shoulder, which I then noticed, was seen in the great fish taken in the nets. Correspondence with Mr. Frank Buckland, who took a cast of the fish, appeared to establish the identity of the two. It was the largest salmon ever known to be taken, weighing seventy-four pounds as weighed at Newburgh, and seventy pounds in London the next day.

But Browne's fish, a cock fish, could not have survived as he supposed for another year. Its destiny was to spawn and die.

This photograph of fishermen's moorings at Newburgh also shows the southern shoreline of the Tay estuary, looking eastwards over the Haggis fishing bank. Bishop Browne, who later became bishop of Stepney, received sustenance in the form of food and drink from Newburgh fishermen during the course of his epic struggle with a mighty Tay salmon

A 70lb RIVER SEVERN OR WYE SALMON
No. 426

On pages 141–42 of *British and Irish Salmonidæ* (1887) there are two paragraphs on large salmon. In the first of these, in a section dealing with the rivers Severn and Wye, the author, Francis Day, states that in 1873 a salmon weighing 70lb was taken in June at Littleton. Littleton-on-Severn is mentioned presumably because it is the nearest village to the point of capture, just north of the Severn road bridge. Since the outflow of the River Wye into the Severn estuary is opposite Littleton, the fish could be a Wye fish that was netted or trapped before it had a chance to enter its natal stream.

The Severn estuary is a dangerous place. In 1607, 200 square miles of the surrounding countryside were flooded, resulting in extensive damage and loss of life. An exceptionally violent storm was thought to be the cause but some seismologists now believe that it was due to a home-grown tsunami – an enormous tidal wave that travelled up the Bristol Channel and into the estuary as the result of seismic adjustments to plate boundaries off the coast of south-west Ireland.

If you go to Littleton-on-Severn where the salmon was landed, there is nothing to see other than a two-mile wide sweep of the river and, at low tide, huge mudflats.

At Whale Wharf, near Littleton, the far bank of the Severn is obscured by mist. The flood bank is very high and a drain or gullies at this point afford the shelter that fishermen need when they pull up their boats to safety on a ramp. A handrail assists them with the steep climb when they are laden with fish and the steel rail on the left-hand side allows them to hang up their nets to dry

A 70lb RIVER WYE SALMON
No. 429

Wheddon Cross wrote a comprehensive study of some important historical aspects of fishing in *The Shooting Times* (22 September 1951). At the end of the article, he mentioned an incident that was discussed at the Wye Board of Conservators' Annual General Meeting in1950: 'The second story dated only from the summer of 1950, and was told at the annual meeting of the Wye Board of conservators early this year. An angler fishing the Wye, hooked and played a salmon for some hours, eventually experiencing the wretched sensation that is the lot of all anglers at some time or another – a dead line reeling in without resistance. This fish might well have joined the crowded ranks of the "big ones that got away" had there not been a sequel. Three weeks later, a salmon identified by the remnants of the angler's tackle, was washed up, dead. It measured 5ft and weighed 70lb.'

70½lb ALTEN RIVER SALMON
No. 430

It is likely that this huge specimen was caught on rod and line, probably with a fly, because the two men in the photograph are gillies rather than professional netsmen. Professor P. Nielsen at Tromso University believes the fish was caught in the late 1870s at a time when the Duke of Roxburghe held the lease. The photograph appears on page 94 in Roy Flury's *Alten: The Story of a Salmon River* (1991).

Gillies Jorgen Romsdal and Mathis Kombola with the huge salmon, probably from the late 1870s

JAKOB VASSENDEN'S
70½lb VOSSO SALMON
—— No. 433 ——

Roy Flury, the author of *Alten: The Story of a Salmon River* (1991), received a letter dated 1 September 1997 from Norvald Vik, the librarian of Norges Fiskers Museum in Bergen, in answer to queries about large Norwegian salmon. Included are details of Vassenden's huge fish: 'An old gaffer, named Nils Bolstad, living at Bolstadøyra, near Voss, told me that he knew of a salmon of 32 kilos, taken in the Bolstad River [part of the Vosso River] in 1931 by Jakob Vassenden, on a metal bait (spoon).'

A 70½lb NEIDEN SALMON
—— No. 434 ——

In a round-up for the 1954 season of fish caught in Norway, the *Fishing Gazette* described the taking of a 50½lb fish on rod and line and then the landing of a much larger fish in a net:

> However, an even heavier which scaled 70½lb was caught in a net off
> River Neiden near the North Cape. It came barging into the net just as the
> owner was taking it ashore, and he was lucky to get the monster salmon
> safely into his boat.

NILS VALLE'S
71lb 10oz NORWEGIAN SALMON
—— No. 437 ——

Nils Valle of Polmak caught his huge salmon on the Tana River near Storfoss on 7 July 1951. This information appears on a list of notable Norwegian salmon in Peter Prag's little book entitled *Salmon Fishing in Norway* (pages 13–16). The book was published in 1953 when Prag was working for the Norway Travel Association in Cockspur Street, London. At the time, the association was promoting fishing opportunities in Norway, giving visitors the chance to fish rivers where most of the largest Atlantic salmon have been caught. Prag was conscious of the need for a travel book that would provide salmon anglers with all relevant information before they set out.

THE FISHMONGER'S 72lb SALMON
—— No. 438 ——

Grove, the London fishmonger, went out of his way to buy and exhibit very large salmon. The biggest, weighing 72lb, went on display at his New Bond Street shop in 1877. Like the 67lb fish (No. 407) it was netted in the River Tay. Courtney Williams mentions these details in *Angling Diversions* (1945) on page 104, and notes:

> In 1877 Groves [a fishmonger] had a wonderful brace of salmon on show in the New Bond Street shop. They weighed respectively 67lb and 72lb. In the same year Crump [another fishmonger] of New Bond Street exhibited a seventy-pounder. These three fish all came from the Tay nets and the weights in each case were verified.

Incidentally, this underlines a social change in London life by revealing that in the last quarter of the nineteenth century at least two wet fish shops could trade in that famous thoroughfare New Bond Street, competing both with each other and other businesses.

THE 72lb SHANNON FISH
No. 439

O n 1 January 1880 Thomas Satchell, of *Bibliotheca Piscatoria* fame, published the first of what was to be a monthly notebook, which he called *The Angler's Note-Book and Naturalist's Record*. This turned out to be a very scholarly and extremely interesting publication. Suffice to say that it survived with a struggle for some years and those who are lucky enough to have acquired the bound volumes, published in 1880 and 1888, possess a literary quarry that can be mined for some of the finest gems in the way of angling stories and associated historical matters.

On page 76 in the 'Yellow [second] Series' (1888), some serious plundering of the Shannon estuary is featured:

At Tarbert on the estuary of the Shannon the chief industry seems to be salmon fishing; "and the salmon almost drop into the fishermen's mouths. You drive the stake nets and the fish entangle themselves; you cast the drag nets to drift with the tide, and the fish are taken out to be knocked on the

The few houses on the left constitute the village of Knock. The 'borreen' or lane, on the right, leads to the stake netters' red hut, just visible on the Shannon estuary shoreline

head with the smallest possible trouble. So many as 70 salmon are some-times taken out of the stake nets at a single tide, and I was told by my intelligent car-driver of a haul last year which sounds miraculous if not fab-ulous. I only repeat the story as it was told me. *Last year the owner of one of the stake nets opposite Tarbert landed in a couple of nights £1,000 worth of fish.* By an odd coincidence it was on the nights of Saturday and Sunday, when the stake nets, according to law, should be left open. Threatened with pros-ecution, the fortunate gentleman quietly replied that if the case was proved against him, having realized his £1,000, he should have great pleasure in paying his fines. The case was never proved, and he pocketed the undimin-ished profits. According to the same authority, even gentlemen who retain their fishings in their own hands are exceedingly lax in their observance of the Act. The watch kept up cannot be very strict, since there is but a single boatful of water bailiffs, with their headquarters at Tarbert, to look after eight miles of estuary. When these bailiffs find a net shut that should be open they are supposed to cut it and then proceed to lodge information. Besides that, they are charged with overhauling the boats casting the drift nets to see that each crew is duly provided with a licence. *The Shannon fish are steadily increasing in size, and the largest taken this year weighed 72 lb.*"

In July 2005, when I decided to investigate the landing of one of the heaviest recorded Irish salmon, I had little to work on other than the fact that the fish was taken in 1886 in a stake net opposite Tarbert, a town in County Kerry, thirteen miles west of Limerick on the southern shore of the River Shannon estuary.

When I visited the northern shore of the estuary opposite Tarbert, in County Clare, I found what I thought seemed a likely fishing village, Knock, complete with its own stone-built harbour. I called at the nearest house – the home of Mr and Mrs Claerhoudt – and discovered that it was built on the site of Knock House, which, since 1858, had belonged to Patrick McAuliffe and his descendents. McAuliffe was a mer-chant who marketed the salmon caught in the stake nets, transported loads of locally dug peat and imported lime – all shipped from Knock's little harbour.

Mr Claerhoudt showed me the surviving building, where the curraghs were built, stored and repaired. Curraghs were canvas boats that were waterproofed with hot pitch and used by all the fishermen who worked the stake nets. He also showed me the old ice-house, where the McAuliffes stored the salmon until there were enough to make a shipment.

The main stake net, locally called a weir, was some four hundred yards long and started from a rocky point about two hundred yards west of the harbour. A second weir, some two hundred yards in length, was operated by the same team of fishermen. A small cabin, which can be seen in the photograph, was used as a shelter and store for the men who manned the curraghs. In 2005, octogenarian Brendan Tooney of Knock was the last, or one of the last, still alive. The stake netters' living was jeopardised by the Shannon Hydro Electric Scheme, which effectively reduced the runs of salmon in the Shannon system, and finally brought to an end in the 1960s when miles of nylon gill nets were put in the path of salmon migrating round the western side of Ireland.

Interestingly, in this part of Ireland the word weir has survived since Saxon times with its meaning unchanged. Weirs were fixed sites or fixed engines on a river or shore-line where gebors (serfs) fished for lords of the manor with various types of nets or traps on certain days of the week in lieu of payment for a small parcel of land from which they could eke out a living. Weirs and stake nets were described by Francis Day in *British and Irish Salmonidae* (1887):

> *Stake nets* are formed by driving stakes firmly into the sands and attaching nets to them. The principle is by means of a leader running to about high-water mark to obstruct or divert the natural course of the salmon and guide them into an opening leading to a trap or chamber from whence they cannot get out. Some of these are of great extent and have many chambers, as the Scottish bag-nets, or they even have attached what is termed a fly-net, being anchored and floated by corks with leaders extending a very long distance out.
>
> The old weir or *yair* is on much the same principle, being an enclosure situated within tidal influence and which starts from the shore, and made by driving very strong posts into the ground to form a crescent, and this is made firm with wattlings. The open side of the crescent is up stream on the tide flowing over it, consequently on the ebb the fish are left impounded.

Stake nets at work

A POACHED VOSSO
SALMON OF 72lb 9oz
—— No. 440 ——

The *Fishing Gazette* of 23 January 1926 reported that a 72lb 9oz male salmon was caught in Norway's Vosso River in 1919. It was 55in long and, although the girth is not given, the photograph of the plaster cast of the fish shows that it was huge – possibly 34in or more. Here is the original report:

A BIG NORWEGIAN SALMON

DEAR SIR – Fishery-Assistant Jon Bakke, of Bergen, just called on me in regard to artificial hatcheries in this district, and showed me the enclosed snapshot, which may be of interest to you. The salmon was caught (poaching) in the "Flagehöl", Voss River, on November 7, 1919, and Mr. Bakke, who is on the left, got hold of it to have this snapshot taken. Mr. Bakke is by

A photograph of the life-size cast of the 72lb 9oz salmon poached from the Vosso in Norway in 1919. It is recorded that the man on the left was 5ft 9in tall

the way a well-grown man of 1.75 metres. So one can guess that this was a "goodly" fish. Length was 1.40 m.; weight, 32 kilos.

Mr. Bakke considered it must have weighed about 35 kilos when coming up from the sea. Kindly return photo after perusal.

Yours truly,
H. B. I., Stavanger.

In the following edition (30 January 1926), the *Fishing Gazette* published a follow-up, which is interesting because it adds the girth measurement to the fish's vital statistics:

DEAR SIR – I have duly received the photograph of the big salmon at Kroksund. (A reproduction of this photograph appeared in our issue of January 16 [sic] – ED.)

By the way, the photo was published a few days ago in an Oslo paper under the title "Norway's Biggest Salmon," and I noticed that in the text the girth was given at 0.88 metre [33¼ ins], which information I have not so far given you, I think. The "condition-factor" does not seem to be up to much, but she was, as already mentioned, "old on the river," so must have been a veritable giant when entering the river from the sea. – I am, dear sir,

Yours truly,
H. B. ISACHSEN

A 73lb 13½oz NORWEGIAN SALMON CAUGHT IN A BAG NET
—— No. 441 ——

On 9 June 1923, the editor of the *Fishing Gazette* in his 'Occasional Notes' gave a scale-reading report on a huge Norwegian fish that was sent to him by the high priest of scale-reading, J.A. Hutton:

Herr Grieg, of the Bergen Museum, has just sent me the scales of a very large salmon, weight 33.5 kilos (73.85lb.), length 142 centimetres (55.9in). It was caught in a bag net on May 14, at Lillebergen, which is about 9 miles north of Bergen. The scales show 2 (possibly 3) years of river life, and 4 years feeding in the sea. This is the biggest salmon of which I have seen the scales, but I believe heavier fish have been recorded. Day mentions one of 74lb – 'British and Irish Salmonidæ,' page 141 – and Mr. Calderwood alludes to a fish of 84lb. ('The Life of the Salmon' – page 106). It would be interesting to have full particulars of this last fish. The 'Condition-factor' of the above Norwegian fish works out at just over 42, or 5 per cent above Mr. Corbett's standard of 40. This a little bit below Mr. Sturdey's scales.

When data are passed from one organisation to another, or from one person to another, mistakes sometimes creep in. An original Reuter report from Bergen becomes an *Evening Standard* report and finally a *Fishing Gazette* report on 30 June 1923:

69LB SALMON

What is thought to be a record salmon for Norway has been caught at Sulen, telegraphs Reuter from Bergen. The salmon weighed 33.5 kilogrammes, or nearly 69lb. – the *Evening Standard*.

If indeed the fish weighed 33.5kg then its weight in pounds must have been 73lb 13½oz. Jock Scott got nearest in *Game Fish Records* (1936) with 73lb 3½oz and also noted that the fish was netted.

Reuter's report came under further scrutiny when I discovered that H.T. Sheringham, editor of *Where to Fish* (1926), noted that this fish was netted in May 1923 from the Gulen Nordfjord, which I am inclined to think is more likely to be the case.

It is clear that although the reports would seem to indicate that there were two Norwegian fish caught in 1923, each weighing 73.85lb, there is in fact only one. Duplication of entries has occurred many times and it indicates the problem authors face in attempting to gather big-fish statistics.

A 73lb 14oz ALTEN RIVER SALMON
No. 442

There is no escaping the fact that this is a real monster salmon, despite the photograph being out of focus. It originates from the Alta Museum.

The fish was caught in the nets at the mouth of the Alten River in 1923 and weighed 73lb 14 oz.

PENNANT'S REFERENCE
TO A 74lb SALMON
No. 443

In *British Zoology* (1776) the author, Thomas Pennant, briefly mentions a very large salmon on page 257, but he gives no details of its captor or location, merely noting, 'The largest we ever heard of weighed seventy four pounds.' Since Pennant was a serious and very highly respected naturalist, we can be pretty sure that such a fish existed and that his documentation of this very big salmon is probably the first 'over sixty' salmon recorded. However, William Yarrell mentions a large salmon on page 54 in his *A History of British Fishes*, second edition (1841) – 'In a note to the history of the Salmon in several editions of Walton, one is mentioned that weighed seventy pounds.' Are these authorities discussing the same fish?

A 74lb NORWEGIAN SALMON
AT BILLINGSGATE MARKET
No. 444

In the issue dated 9 May 1937, the *Fishing Gazette* carried a report originally published in *The Times*, after they received some scales taken from a 74lb salmon:

> Mr. G. Scriven writes: – "I am enclosing scales from a salmon on which I gazed this morning with envy and admiration. I have seen some good fish but never one to come up to this standard, in perfect condition, and turned the scale at 74lb. It came all the way from Norway." In *The Times* the measurement of this great salmon was given as length 4ft 6in. and girth 34¼ in. The report adds: – "Mr. W. W. Cupit, manager of the firm of fish salesmen to which the salmon was consigned, said the fish was the largest known in that market for at least fifty-four years. The salmon realized 2s 11d. a lb at auction – £10 15s. 10d. for one fish!"

Having speculated about the age of the fish in a subsequent issue, the *Fishing Gazette* duly published Hutton's report on the scales on 12 June 1937.

74LB NORWEGIAN SALMON –
REPORT ON THE SCALES BY MR. HUTTON

As will be seen by the following report from Mr. Hutton on the scales of the monster Norwegian salmon, we were correct in stating that this fish was six years old but incorrect in concluding that it had spawned in its fifth year.

DEAR MARSTON – Very many thanks for the scales from the Norwegian "monster." The river-life is not quite clear, two (possibly three) years, but four years in the sea. It must have been a beautiful fish for its C.F. is 47. Messrs. Grant and May sent me the scales of a 73½lb. Norwegian salmon, which was shown at Billingsgate in June, 1923, but I have no particulars of the length – three years in river and four years feeding in sea.

Also in May, 1923, I had some scales from a similar fish caught in Norway, 74lb., length 56in. C.F. 42½; two (possibly three) years river-life and four years in sea.

The next largest fish in my collection was caught by rod in June, 1924, in the Namsen, 69½lb., length 54in., girth 31¾in., C.F. 44: three years river and four years sea.

I hope you were able to get a photograph of the "monster."

Yours sincerely

J. A. HUTTON

We were not able to obtain a photograph of this fish.

THE MAGISTRATE'S
74lb 3oz RUSSIAN SALMON
No. 445

Jock Scott records the capture of this fish in *Game Fish Records* (1936), but an earlier account was submitted by 'Rugde', a self-appointed Scandinavian angling correspondent of the *Fishing Gazette*, and published on 16 December 1922. From these accounts we know that the captor's name was Krono Foged and that he was the magistrate of Utsjok. The Tana River, where the fish was caught, was then the official frontier between Russia and Norway.

THE TANA

Through the courtesy of the Editor I have been permitted on some previous occasions to describe personal experiences on the Tana River, which discharges on the North Coast of Norsk Finmarken, and which has been visited from time to time by so many wandering Englishmen. I venture once more to refer to this splendid salmon stream in order to convey some idea of the loss to the angler which the treatment accorded to it inflicts. The natural advantages which the Tana possesses are such as would, were it fairly treated, make it the finest and most prolific salmon river in Europe. For a distance of 50 miles upwards from the fjords it flows with a smooth, even current, from 2 to 300 yards broad, entirely without obstacles of any kind. Then comes the series of heavy rapids some 2 to $2\frac{1}{2}$ miles in length, known throughout Finmarken as the "Stor Foss," and which go to form the most sporting and, under certain water conditions, the best beat on the river. From this point upwards for a distance of some 60 miles a series of pools extends, the like of which does not exist in Norway, while the tracts of spawning ground on the main stream and its confluents are practically unlimited in extent.

The Tana drains an area of some 18,000 square kilometers, and with its tributaries it is accessible to the migratory salmonidæ for a distance of approximately 400 miles.

But the many natural advantages which nature has conferred on this magnificent and stately river are now neutralized more than ever before by man. The mouth and lower reaches are severely netted by the Norwegians, and so are some of the upper tributaries that flow through Norwegian territory. Above the "Stor Foss" the Tana now forms the frontier between Finland (formerly Russia) and Norway for an immense distance, and as soon as the first brunt of the heavy snow flood has run off the inhabitants on both sides set about the erection of "Stengles" (a kind of fixed method of capture) in every pool, and there they remain until the time for fish to run is over. The Lapps and Finns, moreover, spear all fish which by any chance have survived the dangers of the journey up from the sea and reached the spawning beds, and in summer they are always dragging the pools over with spinning baits and flies.

The conditions which prevailed in the seventies, when I first fished the river, were very different. The netting at the mouth was not nearly so severe, "Stengles" were few and far between and one could go for weeks –

sometimes for an entire season – on the river without coming across a Lapp using a rod. From 2,000 to 3,000lb. of salmon was the usual bag per rod, and with a little more luck – for instance, arriving at the spot at the proper time – this might sometimes have been materially increased. The fish averaged about 20-21lb., and in the course of each season one always got a number between 30 and 40lb. Of the latter weight I caught a good many, but never anything heavier, although on several occasions I was broken by or otherwise lost much larger fish. The biggest I ever heard of as being taken with the rod was one of 73lb., said to have been landed by the Russian "Krono Foged" in '79 near Utsjok, about 18 miles above the "Stor Foss."

Although on account of the size of the pools all the fishing was done by harling, there was always plenty of excitement, and one never came home without an incident of some kind – delightful, amusing, disgusting, astonishing, or at any rate unusual. It was never safe to have less than 200 yards of line on each reel, and even with that considerable length I was more than once within an ace of being run out by the first rush of heavy spring fish.

The best Tana bag of which I have authentic record was made by an

Storfossen on the Tana River

English sportsman in 1867, where in 26 days' fishing he killed to his own rod 208 salmon weighing 3,764lb. His best day was August 5, when he landed 22 salmon of 438lb.

In 1886 two rods got 153 fish weighing 3,100lb.; in 1887 one rod got only 51 fish of 1,005lb.; in 1888 two rods had 164 fish weighing 3,650lb.; and in 1890 two rods had 137 fish of 2,990lb. After that angling on the Tana began to deteriorate steadily, until, as is now the case, the river was no longer worth going to.

RUGDE

It is interesting to note that the Chief Inspector of Fisheries in Norway considered Krono Foged's salmon to be the record rod-caught Atlantic salmon, as he explained in the *Fishing Gazette* dated 25 February 1928, although in June that year, Henrik Henriksen caught a bigger fish.

THE RECORD ROD-CAUGHT ATLANTIC SALMON

Mr. J. Arthur Hutton has kindly sent the following letter, which he received from Herr Birger Aagaard, Chief Inspector of Fisheries in Norway:-

Oslo,
February 14, 1928

DEAR SIR - It will possibly be of some interest to you to know that in my description of the Tana, there is a note by Mr. Landmark stating that the "lensmann i Utsjok" in 1879 (or 1878) *on rod* caught a salmon weighing "5 bismerpund og 15 merker" = 33.62 kg. or 74.1 English pounds. I think this salmon is the record rod-caught Atlantic salmon, not the 69½lb salmon taken in the Namsen on June 13, 1924.
The record salmon taken in Norway is from Drammenselven, and taken in a trap on July 13, 1923. The salmon weighed 34 kg. = 74.95lb.

Yours truly,
(Signed)
BIRGER AAGAARD,
Chief Inspector of Fisheries in Norway

THE BALTIC RECORD
75lb SALMON
No. 446

The *Fishing Gazette* of 7 June 1913 published a letter from their Scandinavian correspondent 'Rugde' concerning a 66lb Baltic salmon (number 401). The owner of the fish (or the fishing rights – it is not clear) mentioned in passing a 76½lb salmon:

> The owner, Herr Sjödin, said it was the largest he had ever seen since 1887, when he received one from Ljusdal which weighed 34 kilos, or 76½lb. They would have attracted attention in Bond-street would they not?

I have included this salmon at 75lb rather 76½lb because this is closer to 34 kilos.

AN ENGLISHMAN'S
75lb PASVIK RIVER SALMON
No. 447

Although few details are known about this fish, it is said to have been caught on the Pasvik River in 1905. Magnus Berg mentioned it in *Nordnorske Lakseelver* (1964), and in 1997 the angling author Per Gulbrandsen received a letter from a Mr Aarnes, a Pasvik man, saying that 'Mr Torseth, a local customs officer, watched the fish being landed'. Interestingly, Mr Torseth himself was a keen fisherman who had caught a fish of 44lb. He described the 75-pounder as 'a true monster, not a very pretty sight with large rough scales and a solid kype'.

Perhaps documenting the fish in this book, despite the sparse information, may provide the spark of interest that will lead to the unfolding of the story of how, when and by what means this truly colossal salmon was caught.

THE LONGEST SALMON RECORDED
A 75½lb NORWEGIAN FISH
No. 449

What is believed to be the *longest* salmon ever recorded (no length measurement of the heaviest of all salmon weighing 103lb 2oz was documented) was netted at Hougsund, Eker in Norway in 1925. The fish was 63¼in long. The photograph was first published in the *Fishing Gazette* following an initial report on 15 August 1925:

75½-LB. SALMON NETTED IN NORWAY

DEAR SIR – Last summer – in August, I believe – I mentioned that a remarkably big salmon had been caught by net near Hougsund, Eker (south of Drammen River, in the east of Norway). She weighed 34.4 kilos: length 1.58 metres. The length is, I believe, a record.

I am now able to send you a photo of this fish. She looks thin, so must have weighed several kilos more in the spring. I am sorry to say no scales were taken.

Kindly treat the photo carefully and return after perusal.

Yours truly,
H. B. I.

(Much obliged to our correspondent for sending the excellent photograph of which I am pleased to be able to give a reproduction. The previous reference to this big fish appeared in THE FISHING GAZETTE, August 15, 1925. A mistake was made in the weight, which was given as 64 kilos instead of 34.4 kilos. – ED)

The photograph reappeared in the second edition of *Falkus & Buller's Freshwater Fishing* (1988) page 202. It is easy to see that the fish is a cock fish – as practically all very large salmon are – and not a 'she' as described by H.B.I.

As a matter of interest, in his piece 'Record Norwegian Salmon' published in the *Flyfishers' Journal* (September 1962), S.J. Carr wrote:

Another 76 pounder is known to have been netted in the River Drammen near Oslo, many years ago, and Kjell Aaserud – a journalist on the staff of Alten Posten – reports seeing an old press cutting with a photograph of this monster fish, but Hans Hansen of Hokksund who owns this press cutting does not answer letters so it has not been possible to obtain sight of it. Fortunately as we have already seen H. B. I. sent a photograph of this fish to the *Fishing Gazette.*

The longest salmon recorded – 63¹/₄in – and weighing 75¹/₂ lb, netted in Norway in 1925

IRELAND'S LARGEST SALMON 76lb
—— No. 450 ——

The largest ever salmon caught – presumably netted – in Ireland was reported in *The Field* in 1880 (volume 55, page 244). Their correspondent wrote:

> On the arrival of the Lismore train at Mallow last Monday evening, the railway porters began to take the luggage out of the van for the purpose of transferring it to other trains. Amongst the goods taken out was a deal box, over five feet long, and it was in the act of being removed by two porters, when the cover, which was very insecurely fastened, gave way, and the porters, looking inside, found that it was occupied by a magnificent salmon. The box was weighed, and found to contain 91 lb. The box was computed to weigh 15 lb., so that this would leave the weight of the salmon to be 76 lb.! It had a very small head, and was bright as a new shilling. It measured over four feet in length, and had a tremendous girth. It is supposed to have been captured between Ballyduff and Lismore. It was sent off by the night mail to Mr. Pine, a fish dealer in Dublin. It was seen by several at Mallow station, on the evening of its arrival there, and the gentleman who furnished me with the foregoing particulars says it was the most beautiful and largest salmon that he ever saw, and I believe that it is the weightiest salmon of which there is any record.

The railway line between Lismore and Mallow no longer exists but Ballyduff is approximately seven miles upstream of Lismore on the River Blackwater, which is probably the most productive salmon river, in terms of rod-caught salmon, in Ireland. On re-reading the above account, I sense that the lid of the deal box was not so insecure. It was perhaps the curiosity of the porters, knowing that the box was consigned to a Dublin fishmonger, that caused them to take a peek at the fish, and I for one am pleased that they did so.

The platform at Mallow station, where the deal box containing Ireland's biggest-ever salmon was glimpsed by the ever-watchful porters in 1880

MAGNUS KLERCK'S
79lb 6oz PASVIK RIVER SALMON
No. 454

R oy Flury sent me the facts as he knows them about Magnus Klerck's truly giant salmon. This fish weighed about the same as Henrik Henriksen's well-documented salmon (No. 455).

Caught in 1863 this is an important fish, which has only come to light in recent years and is notable not just for its size but for the likelihood it was caught on fly. Its captor too, Magnus Klerck, will be well known to readers of travel books on Norway published in the 19th century. Details of the fish were sent to me by Per Gulbrandsen, a good friend, lawyer and fishing historian who lived in Oslo, Norway and on his retirement moved to Espedalen. Per gives the story of the fish in his book *Med Karjol og Laksestenger* [which translates as 'With Carriole and Salmon Rod'], published in Norway 1994. The first report did not appear until 1896 and was sent in a letter from 'Mr. B' to the Journal '*Norsk Fiskeritidende*'. Printed on page 214 it describes the

Stor Lax.

J 1863 var jeg i Besøg hos Lensmand Klerk i Sydvaranger og den første Dags Eftermiddag spørger den nu afdøde Lensmand: „Har De Lyst paa Lax tilaften?" Da jeg naturligvis Intet havde imod en saa delikat Aftensmad drog vi op ad Pasvikelven, efterat Lensmanden havde besvoret, at Fiskevand maatte holdes færdigt i Kjøkkenet.

Ved Boris Gleb Kapel begyndte Lensmanden at fiske fra Land, og da vi efter nogle Kast var komne op under den nedre Fos, bed det og yttrede Lensmanden strax: „her har jeg en Storkar" og saa forholdt det sig ogsaa; thi efter at have arbeidet med den i omtrent 1¼ Time, drog han iland en Lax, der strax blev veiet og viste sig at holde 6 Bismerpd. (2 Voger), altsaa 36 Kg.   B.

The letter from Mr. B to the journal Norsk Fiskeritidende *which describes the capture of Magnus Klerck's enormous fish*

catch of an enormous salmon on the River Pasvik. The Journal was of inter-est more to the fishing industry than the sport fisherman. It was spotted however by the editor of the Norwegian Hunter's and Angler's Association magazine (N.J.F.F.) who promptly reprinted the letter on page 148 of his magazine, the same year. He also added his own comment that the fish was caught on fly but gave no explanation of this. Magnus Klerck had died in 1891 and possibly 'Mr. B' felt he needed to record the story of the big fish. Maybe the editor of the N.J.F.F. then, on reading of this, contacted Mr. B. as to whether it was caught on fly.

A rough translation of this letter is as follows:

BIG SALMON

In 1863 I was visiting Lensmann Klerck in Sydvaranger and on the first day towards evening the now deceased Lensmann asked "Would you like salmon for supper?" Naturally as I had no objection to such a delicious sup-per, I followed his instructions to ensure water was ready for boiling in the kitchen and we set off up the Pasvig river.

At Boris Gleb Chapel he started fishing from the bank and when below the lower falls, there was a strike. After a short while he exclaimed "Here, I have a giant." And so it was. He fought it for about 1¼ hours before being able to land it. The salmon was promptly weighed: 36 kilos. B.

We must be grateful to Mr B for this letter, written thirty years after the event, despite its being disappointingly low key. Where is the drama? Had they boiled enough water for cooking the fish? He does state, however, that Klerck was 'casting from the bank'. This confirms he was not harling, always a popular way of fishing the bigger Norwegian rivers, and strongly suggests that in 1863 he was fishing a fly.

Aged forty-six when the fish was caught, Magnus Klerck was born and spent his youth in Bossekop, in those days just a hamlet of a few houses, close to Alten. The

Magnus Klerck 1817–91, captor of the giant fish from the Pasvik River

The Pasvik River and Boris Gleb chapel (on the right). The dam in the distance has replaced the Skoltefossen Falls below which Magnus Klerck caught the 79lb 6oz fish in 1863, probably on a fly

family name is mentioned in numerous books of the time. Even Frederic Tolfrey, who never set foot in Norway, mentions Klerck in his *Jones's Guide to Norway*. In 1843 Klerck became one of the first to lease a stretch of the Alten between Gabo and Sautso for sport fishing, not netting.

In 1856 Magnus Klerck was appointed Lensmann (a sheriff or magistrate) in the district of Sör-Varanger and he moved to Elvenes. Barnard wrote of him in his book *Sketches of life in Norway and Sport* (1871): 'Had he lived in the days of Harald the Fair-haired, his great strength, accomplishments and manly bearing would have handed him down to posterity as having been one of the most remarkable Vikings Scandinavia possessed.'

I see him on that evening in 1863 striding out along the bank, holding a four-piece 24-foot rod, as was used on Alta by the 6th Duke of Roxburghe the following year. Possibly, as he only wanted a fish for supper, he used his small rod, a four-piece 20-foot rod of hickory as used by Henry Pottinger on the Tana in 1857. He was confident, he knew exactly what he was doing and the fly was already tied to the gut, a large single iron size 9 of his own tying.

My reasons for believing he fished with a fly are not only that he was casting but that the great majority of salmon caught on rod and line in the mid-nineteenth century were on fly. Klerck had learned his fishing as a young man on Alten where they used fly.

HENRIK HENRIKSEN'S
79lb 6oz SALMON
No. 455

The *Fishing Gazette* was, as usual, the first to notice Henriksen's salmon in their 14 September 1929 issue. The authority for the facts about this fish came from a translation of the Norwegian Fishery Inspector's Report for 1928:

A 79 ½LB SALMON

In the latter end of July, 1928, Postmaster Henrik Henriksen, of Bodeng in Polmak, when fishing with a bait by the Stor Foss, in the Tana River, caught a salmon weighing 36 kilograme (79.4lbs). This is certainly the record Atlantic salmon (*Salmo salar*) caught with rod and line.

The last statement is untrue, although Henriksen's fish certainly challenges Klerck's, but there is an even bigger one to consider – Pekka Rutuna's 88lb Finnish salmon (No. 467).

According to the website *arcticangler.no* Henriksen was fishing with a lure bought in Finland that he 'had hammered and mended several times to make it move the right way through the water'. We are also told that Henriksen was boat fishing when he hooked the fish and that it took nine hours to land. An illustration of Henriksen's spoon, which looks quite like the modern Salmo spoon, was shown in *Villmarksliv* magazine in January 1983.

AN 80lb SALMON BITTEN BY A SEAL
No. 457

On 24 October 1906, the *Daily Mail* reported that 'an enormous salmon weighing nearly eighty pounds had been captured on Spittal Beach near Berwick, having been severely bitten presumably by seals.'

AN 80lb RIVER TAY SALMON
No. 458

While noting an 83lb rod-caught salmon (No. 459), the *Fishing Gazette* of 15 April 1911 briefly documented a second fish, an 80-pounder, but somewhat strangely omitted the usual particulars, such as the captor's name, date of capture and the sex of the fish. The fish was netted at the mouth of the River Almond where it enters the River Tay, not far above Perth.

RECORD SALMON, ETC.

Dear Sir,

Will you, or any of the readers of the *Fishing Gazette* be kind enough to tell me the weight of the record salmon caught with rod and line; also record salmon caught with net in England or Scotland?

Yours truly,

John Spence

(The largest salmon recorded to have been captured in British waters was a female fish of the weight of 83lbs, in the year 1821. The largest recorded netted salmon was taken from the Tay at Almondmouth, estimated to have weighed over 80lbs. Ed.)

A second account can often be found to amplify original sparse details, as I usually discover when combing through my angling library or the Flyfishers' Library or the British Newspaper Library at Colindale. In this case, David Hatwell found one in H. Cholmondeley-Pennell's book *Fishing* (1895, seventh edition, page 147). After reporting details of a large salmon caught in the River Thames near Fulham, Pennell continues:

> ... and during the present season when fishing for ova on the Tay at Almond Mouth, a fish was netted considered to have weighed over eighty pounds, as it was six and a half inches longer than one of seventy pounds taken in the same river, of which there is a cast in the South Kensington Museum. It was a male fish in splendid condition and measuring in length four feet eleven and a half inches, and in girth two feet five inches. As it was the close season the fish was, of course, returned to the water, and, as Mr. Malloch who reports these particulars, observes, some one may get him with the fly later on. Whoever does will have his work cut out!

Pennell's reference to a 70lb fish netted on the Tay in 1870, a cast of which was made by Frank Buckland (number 425), helps to build a picture of the massiveness of the 80-pounder. The measurements of the 70-pounder are length 53in, girth 32in, and of the 80-pounder length 59½in, girth 29in. Pennell tells us that the fish was netted 'during the present season', meaning the year or at most two years before publication of his book. Since the first edition was published in 1885 we can be pretty certain that the 80-pounder was netted in 1883–84. Moreover, as Pennell reports, it was a cock fish.

AN 82lb SALMON FROM THE MOUTH OF A GERMAN RIVER
No. 459

A report on this huge salmon was published in the *Fishing Gazette* on 25 June 1938. Although the correspondent had some weird ideas about the nature of salmon, he has assisted in documenting the existence of one of the largest specimens of *Salmo salar* ever recorded:

82LB BALTIC SALMON

Dear Mr Marston,

In the issue of the Berlin newspaper *B.Z. am Mittag* of March 3, 1938, there was a short report about a monster salmon catch made near Altbeelitz in the Eastern Brandenburg. Being born in the farther neighbourhood of this region and being therefore somewhat interested in the circumstances of the fish's landing, I wrote for some particulars of the catch and was answered a few days ago as follows:

The salmon in question had indeed the reported weight of 82lb (37 kilos) and a total length of 1½ yards, but for reason of the fact that this species takes as well as no food in the inland waters and that none of the few anglers can hope to get such a shy big fellow with his gear the salmon has been captured in a small stake-nett during the night by two professional fishermen of the said village. They had to endure a very strong fight before landing it in their boat. The river they got it in was an effluent of the Warthe, the Netze, in the effluent of which again, named the Drage, a very quick river, the fish is usually spawning.

Hence it follows that the fish was a Baltic Sea salmon, which often are growing up to a marvellous weight. So I saw when being a grammar school boy, 15 years ago, some splendid specimen of 55lbs (25 kilos) – netted (hélas!) by coast fishermen in a small Pomeranian coast river's mouth and I likewise saw and hooked (but failed) such a monster fish of about 25 kilos on my tackle as I have told in the Fishing Gazette of November 2, 1935.

I think all this will interest both you and the readers of your esteemed paper. Perhaps anyone of these may be able to define my position regarding a conclusion I made from the giant measure of our salmon being almost wild-spawned in comparison with the British specimen having almost been stocked in and showing only the half average weight of the Baltic species. It seems the nature-spawned fish is better and quicker growing up than the hatchery-fish that I believe to be strongly endangered by inbreeding. Or is there no more food for the fish in the Northern Sea respective Atlantic?

Yours very truly,

Fariosus Goslar,

Germany

AN 82lb 14oz SALMON
FROM THE MOUTH OF THE EDEN
—— No. 460 ——

Courtney Williams in *Angling Diversions* (1945), noticed the following reference to a huge salmon:

According to a note in the *Field*, July 16th 1881, the specimen weighed 82lb14oz and was shown in a Manchester fishmonger's shop in that year. It was supposed to have been netted in the River Eden 'district'. Again no measurements or any other details are known.

From my studies of the capture of exceedingly large salmon, it would seem that a high percentage are netted, rather than trapped, in the estuaries or at least in the tidal reaches of salmon rivers. Since the precise location of the 82lb 14oz fish's capture has not been documented, it would be reasonable to assume that it was caught in the tidal reaches of the River Eden, a noted big-fish river and the nearest one to Manchester.

The full account of the letter in *The Field*, signed W.B., is most revealing and convincing:

A MONSTER SALMON

Sir – I am desirous of communicating to you the intelligence of a leviathan salmon having been received by one of the fishmongers here about a fortnight ago, the dimensions and weight of which are so extraordinary, and the evidence of their trustworthiness so unquestionable, that I trust you will consider the subject a fitting one to be recorded in your columns.

The salmon was purchased from the fishmonger by a restaurant keeper in Market-Street, here (an old and most respectable house and worthy landlord). I got the first information about this monster from Mr Ramsbottom, fishing tackle manufacture here, when I called upon him on Saturday last. He told me he had seen the fish and had spanned it with his hands; but had not seen it weighed. Mr Ramsbottom's description of the fish's length and dimensions and reputed enormous weight interested me very much and determined me to obtain every information I could about it. I have therefore seen both the fishmonger and restaurant keeper who sold and bought the fish, and my examination of them separately have given to me details in regard to it which practically correspond with each other.

I have seen the entry in the restaurant keeper's day book, which records the receipt and payment for the fish, which is as follows: 'One salmon, 4ft. 6ins, 82 lb 14 oz, £4 15s.' This corresponds with the information given to me by the fishmonger, with the exception that he says the length was 4ft 7½ins, and the girth at shoulders 34in. The fishmonger likewise told me that he had first asked five guineas for the fish which he thought it was worth as a 'show' one (it was exhibited in the restaurant keeper's window, and it was there Mr Ramsbottom saw it); but eventually he sold it at the weight and price mentioned, allowing at the same time the odd 8d. (£4 15s 8d) to which the above weight and price swung out. The transaction was a ready-money one, so that no account passed between seller and purchaser. As to where the fish came from, the fishmonger could tell me no more than he had got it from Carlisle, and upon my asking whether he could show me an account for it, he told me he never 'bothered' with accounts, as all his transactions, both purchases and sales, were made in ready money. The fishmonger, however, promised to write to his Carlisle correspondent for this information, which I shall be glad to communicate to you hereafter should you think it worthwhile. From what the fishmonger told me abundant further evidence could be produced as to the weight of the fish. He tells me it was a wonder in the market while there with the other fishmongers and the public, and that many shillings and glasses were won and lost about its weight. Mr Ramsbottom tells me the fish was a fresh-run one, in good condition, though in no wise remarkable in that respect, and that it was a male fish. Will you kindly say how the above weight, &c., compares with previously well-authenticated monster salars. What a pity a plaster cast was not got from it.

Manchester, July 17

A tidal stretch of the River Eden, looking upstream to the town of Rockcliffe. Salmon are not indiscriminate in their choice of resting places and tend to return to the same spot. However, the strength of the tide and the rate of river flow affect the choice of resting place, and another factor to be taken into account is that rivers change their course from time to time, especially during very heavy floods. Netsmen become aware of what salmon do in varying conditions and place their nets accordingly. Half nets, stake nets and traps are, on the other hand, placed to catch running fish

AN 83lb BRITISH SALMON
—— No. 461 ——

Responding to a reader's enquiry about the record weights of salmon caught on rod and line or netted in English or Scottish waters, the *Fishing Gazette* (15 April 1911) briefly documented two large salmon, of which, at the time, I could find no other fully supporting evidence. One weighed 80lb (No. 458), and David Hatwell later discovered a reference to it in H. Cholmondeley-Pennell's book *Fishing* (1895). The other weighed 83lb and I eventually found another mention of it in the *Fishing Gazette.* In the issue of 3 May 1913, they published a letter from C.J. Cook that included a few facts about this mysterious fish:

THE 83lb SALMON

Dear Sir,

Re capture of large salmon of which we have been hearing a good deal lately. It may interest your readers to know that apparently odd ones of very large size are still to be captured in English waters. From an old magazine of seventy years ago, in an article 'Salmon and Trout', I cull the following: 'In the comparatively un-fished rivers of Scandinavia large salmon are much more frequent [than in British waters], but the largest we ever heard of was one which came into the possession of Mr Grove, of Bond-street, and which weighed 83lbs. It was an English fish, and a female.'

The writer of the above does not state whether captured by rod or net, nor the name of the locality, or of the lucky captor.

Yours truly,

G.J. Cook

(The fish is mentioned in several works on fish, but no particulars are given. It may have been 83lbs. I am inclined to think our biggest authenticated United Kingdom salmon is the 70lb fish from the Tay, of which Frank Buckland made a beautiful cast. Earl Home's 69¼lb Tweed salmon, taken on a fly, is the record rod-killed fish – Ed.)

Cook's statement that the Bond Street fishmonger Grove handled this big fish is important. Grove was a man who would go out of his way to get hold of huge salmon because of their publicity value, and would not publicly be credited with the possession of a non-existent fish.

Following Cook's acknowledgement that all he knew about the fish was culled from 'an old magazine of seventy years ago', i.e. *circa* 1843, I looked through sporting magazines of 1840–45 but without success. However, I did find an earlier reference to the fish in William Yarrell's *A History of British Fishes* (1841, second edition, page 54):

> ... the largest known, as far as I am aware, came into the possession of Mr Grove, the fishmonger of Bond Street, about the season of 1821. This salmon, a female [?] weighed eighty-three pounds; was a short fish for the weight, but of very unusual thickness and depth. When cut up, the flesh was fine in colour and proved of excellent quality.

Although exceptions do not prove rules, I cannot help thinking that a mistake may have been made on the sexing of this giant salmon, simply because, so far as I am aware, this is the only one over 60lb that has ever been classified as a female. The earliest reference to this fish is to be found in Hofland's *British Anglers Manual* published in 1839, which simply reports that the fish was 'in the possession of Mr Grove' and weighed 83lb.

FINLAND'S 83lb 12oz SALMON
No. 462

In August 2006 I received a letter from Finnish angling author Matti Kettunen with a good deal of data regarding some of the largest salmon ever taken in Finland. The photograph of an 83¾-pounder, netted in the Tana River in 1943 by Yrjö Alaollitervo and his father Ville Alaollitervo, is not a good one but at least it provides a visual record of this great fish.

Väinö Alaollitervo, Yrjö's brother, holds the 83¹/₄lb fish netted in the Tana River in 1943

WULLIE WALKER'S 84lb TAY SALMON
—— No. 463 ——

This is the second largest authenticated salmon ever taken from British waters. It was netted from the River Tay estuary in 1869, as described by John Ashley-Cooper on page 223 of *A Line on Salmon* (1983). Jock Scott reported it in *Game Fish Records* (1936):

> The absolute record Tay fish – caught in a net – is one of 84lbs; it was captured in a sparling net by a local worthy, one 'Wullie' Walker, above Tay Bridge, in 1869. Mr Calderwood, in a letter to me, states that this fish ranks as the second largest salmon ever landed – by any means – in Scotland.

A.Courtney Williams in his admirable *Angling Diversions* (1945), page 143, also wrote about this salmon:

> Nevertheless, a few fish of 70lbs or so have certainly been taken by netsmen from time to time, and at least two of over 80lbs. The larger of these weighed 84lbs and was taken in a net some miles above Tay Bridge in November 1869. The fisherman's name was said to be 'Wullie' Walker, but beyond that nothing further seems to be known about this fish, although it must rank as the heaviest *S. salar* ever to be taken in the British Isles.

In the event, we know more about this fish from a report issued by the Fishery Board of Scotland, which was written by W.L. Calderwood, sometime Chief Inspector of Scottish Salmon Fisheries, and published by the *Fishing Gazette* on 22 August 1908:

THE NEXT HEAVIEST FISH IN SCOTLAND – 84LBS

> So far as I am aware, the record fish for Scotland, previous to the capture of the fish just referred to, was a Tay fish, which I referred to elsewhere some years ago, but which may be briefly mentioned here. It was taken by a man named William Walker, who, so far as I know, is still alive and living at Newburgh. In November or December 1869, Walker was fishing two landside sparling nets – one fixed at Sea Side Dyke, the other fixed at Port Allen Dyke, both on the north side of the Tay estuary some miles above the Tay Bridge. In the Port Allen Dyke net, a salmon of 84lbs was taken.

This is Port Allen Dyke. Before I located the dyke I was intrigued by the use of the word port. I expected to find some sort of stonework to justify such a grand name for such a small tidal watercourse or drain, and I was not disappointed – the right bank has a stone wall for about thirty yards

This photograph of Port Allen Dyke reveals the shortness of the waterway leading out to the Tay estuary. At the point where the two meet, William Walker set the sparling net that caught the 84lb salmon. Newburgh, where Walker lived, is opposite Port Allen, on the south bank of the Tay estuary

At Chanonry Point – where the white lighthouse stands on the distant bank – the Moray Firth narrows down from over four miles to about three quarters of a mile wide. The 84lb salmon was netted in this channel, probably heading for the River Ness or the River Beauly

84lb SALMON FROM
THE MORAY FIRTH
No. 464

In the *Fishing Gazette* of 1 May 1920, J.H. Scott from Glasgow had a letter published in the correspondent's column. He told the *Gazette*'s readers that he was present when a 62lb salmon was delivered to Messrs Macleary, fishmongers, in Inverness (No. 357), and went on to give a few details about an 84lb salmon:

> When in Inverness I heard that a good many years ago a great salmon of 84lb was netted in the Moray Firth at Chanonry Point, Ross-shire, distant about ten miles from Inverness. There seemed to exist a belief that the story is true, and it is strange if no record has been kept of such a notable event, and I wonder if any information can yet be got concerning it. This would be our record salmon if the truth of the occurrence could be established.
>
> Yarrell, in "British Fishes," speaking of big salmon, says: "The largest known, as far as I am aware, came into the possession of Mr. Grove, the fishmonger of Bond-street, about the season of 1821. This salmon, a female, weighed 83lb." It is remarkable that it is not stated where it was caught, or by what means. One would think that the fact of the existence of such an

extraordinary salmon would have led to all particulars being noted. If details are yet available it is important that they should be recorded. Last summer I saw in the shop of Messrs Sawers, Howard-street, Glasgow, a fine salmon that weighed 56lb, and was caught near Montrose.

Yours truly

J. H. Scott

AN 84¾lb IRISH SALMON
No. 465

On page 82 of volume 2 of Francis Day's *The Fishes of Great Britain and Ireland* (1880–84), mention is made of a monster salmon: 'Several instances of 70lb. fish are alluded to by Thompson and in July, 1881, an Irish fish of upwards of 84¾lb. weight was exhibited at a fishmongers in Manchester.'

William Thompson was an Irish naturalist and I have read the chapter on salmon in his book. In fact, he mentions just one 70lb fish, which was caught in the Bush Fishery, near Bushmills in Co. Antrim: 'I have been told [in 1842] that a fish weighing fifty-five pounds was taken here last year and some years ago one of seventy pounds weight.' The only mention of an 80-pounder comes in the following statement:

Ballyshannon, July 15th 1840 – A gentleman whom I met at the hotel here has assured me that he had seen two salmon taken here, one of which weighed forty-five pounds and the other sixty-three pounds; and that a friend of his saw one which weighed upwards of eighty pounds. Colburn, of the hotel, does not credit the weight of the last two.

Francis Day must have found his information about the 84¾lb salmon elsewhere because William Thompson's book was published in 1856, twenty-five years before the 84¾lb salmon was caught.

Thompson made an interesting comment about the market price of salmon: 'The price is up one half since "ice and steam" came into play.' He was referring to the introduction in the early nineteenth century of steamships, which could carry salmon in iceboxes to the markets of Europe. Prior to this development, all fish not for local consumption had to be salted.

Domeſtic Occurrences.

A B E R D E E N.

THE Recruiting Buſineſs goes on very ſuc-
ceſsfully in this Place, ſeveral Officers of
the new Regiments having nearly completed their
Quota.

2. The following deſerves to be mentioned as
an Inſtance of public Spirit: When the Gazette
containing the Account of General Burgoyne's
Surrender reached this Place, a Woolcomber was
ſo affected with the News, that he flung down his
Combs, and ſwore he would never work again till
he was revenged on the American Rebels. He
went immediately to a Recruiting Officer, and declared his Purpoſe of entering: being a ſtout Man
he was offered Five or Six Guineas Bounty-money; but he refuſed it, deſiring him to enliſt another Man with the Money, and would accept of
no more than a few Shillings to drink the King's
Health

3. Laſt Week a Salmon was thrown aſhore at
Spey weighing Ninety One Pounds.

AN 84lb 14oz SPEY SALMON
AND OTHER LARGE 18th-CENTURY
SCOTTISH FISH
No. 466

Although we can hardly expect to find records of eighteenth-century rod-caught 50-pounders, it is I think interesting to hear about any big salmon catches. Dr David Summers, fisheries manager for the Tay District Salmon Fisheries Board, has very kindly given me references to five huge Scottish salmon that were caught by various means and recorded in the *Aberdeen Journal* during the last half of the eighteenth century.

The heaviest four of these weighed 61lb, 66lb, 70lb and 91lb but before these fish could be entered in my list I had to make due allowances for the system of recording weights then in vogue, that is I had to convert Dutch to English pounds, which meant the 61lb fish dropped off the list. The three heaviest fish's weights are, approximately, 60lb 13oz, 64lb 8oz and 84lb 14oz.

Morag Penny, Assistant Librarian of the Local Studies Department of Aberdeen's Central Library, very kindly provided me with copies of the data I needed from various issues of the *Aberdeen Journal*. The issue dated 9 December 1778 held the details of the so-called 91lb salmon – number three in a column of three items. Because of the juxta-position of the news of the salmon with grave news of political matters, I have included a transcription in modern print of the whole column, followed by a photocopy of the original that has been greatly enlarged.

DOMESTIC OCCURRENCES IN ABERDEEN

The recruit business goes on very successfully in this place, several officers of the new regiments having nearly completed their quota.

2. The following deserves to be mentioned as an instance of public spirit: when the gazette containing the account of General Burgoyn's surrender reached this place, a wool comber was so affected with the news, that he flung down his combs, and swore he would never work again till he was revenged on the American rebels. He went immediately to a Recruiting Officer, and declared his purpose of entering: being a stout man he was offered five or six guineas bounty-money; but he refused it, desiring him to enlist another man with the money, and would accept of no more than a few shillings to drink the King's health.

3. Last week a salmon was thrown ashore at Spey weighing Ninety One Pounds.

I found four more news items relating to big salmon in the the *Aberdeen Journal* and these are listed below in chronological order

[4 July 1749]

On Thursday last, there was a salmon catched near the Mouth of the Dee, reckoned the largest ever seen in this Place, which measured 4 Feet, 4 Inches in Length, 2 Feet in Circumference, the Head 10 Inches Long, and weighed full 56lb weight.

[22 July 1755]

On Monday last, there was a Salmon of a most enormous Size, caught on Ythan. The Length of the Fish was four Feet, four Inches; twenty seven Inches round, weighs near 70lb. and is the Property of Mr. Mitchel at Bridgefoot, Newburgh.

[23 March 1764]

On Thursday, there was caught at the Raik fishing on the river Dee, one of the largest and best sized salmon ever seen in this country. She measured four feet six inches in length, two feet four inches in circumference; and weighs sixty six pounds English. This fine fish was put on board Capt. Bull, who sailed on Saturday morning; and it is probable, will make its appearance at Billingsgate-Market, in a few days, as the wind is favourable.

[3 August 1772]

We hear from Banff, that on Monday Night last a young whale got entangled in a salmon net near the Harbour, and was with some difficulty brought to shore alive. – It measured 12 Feet in Length, and about the same Number round, where its body was thickest. They expect to make near two Barrels of Oil from it. About the same time they caught a Salmon weighing 66 pounds, the largest ever seen in that place.

THE WORLD RECORD
88lb ROD-CAUGHT SALMON
No. 467

The *Flyfishers Journal* included an article by S.J. Carr in the September 1962 edition, in which he refers to an 88lb salmon:

> … but the heaviest salmon in the world as far as it has been possible to check is the 88 lb. fish which was caught on a spoon in Finland in 1953 by Pekka Rutuna. This fish was also mentioned in the "Fishing Gazette" on the 26th September 1959.

I eventually found the reference in the *Fishing Gazette* but it was dated 26 September 1953:

ENORMOUS FINNISH SALMON

DEAR SIR – The enclosed newspaper cutting taken from the Finnish paper "Lansi Savo" of August 16, 1953, may be of interest to you and possibly your many readers. In case you do not have an interpreter handy the story I briefly append, very roughly interpreted.

Yours faithfully

Wm C. Bevan   Ross-on-Wye

'Whilst fishing in Lake Liekovedessä, Pekka Rutuna and his pal Antti Prusi caught a 40 kg salmon. They had intended going home, but thought they would have that last cast with a spoon bait, just for luck, and apparently their luck was in, and the fish took an hour to land. Upon reaching home they put it on the scales and found it weighed as stated 39 kg 900 gm. The length was 1½ metres (unfortunately no girth is stated).

(Taking the weight of this fish as 88 lb. and length just under 5 ft. the Condition Factor by Corbett's scale is about 42, which suggests that the weight tallies with the length according to C.F. The words "would have that last cast" imply that this huge salmon was caught on rod and line. Further particulars would be interesting. ED)

THE ALL-TIME RECORD SALMON
WEIGHT 103lb FROM SCOTLAND
No. 469

The *Daily Mail* of 7 August 1908 published the following note regarding what must be the largest Atlantic salmon ever recorded:

RECORD SALMON OF 103LBS

The record British salmon weighing 103lbs was caught in the Forth in 1907, but the announcement is only made public today by the report of the Scottish Fishery Board, whose expert heard of the capture last winter.

He slyly remarks that the matter was kept secret as the 'possession of the fish was fraught with a certain amount of danger to the captors.' But after full inquiry he is satisfied that he records the greatest known weight for any British salmon.

The next heaviest was 84lbs caught in the Tay. In the same river a 61½lbs fish was taken by the rod last year, which was remarkable for the number of heavy salmon.

A note in *The Angler's News*, 28 January 1939, points to where the fish was caught, i.e. at the mouth of the River Devon, where it runs into the north side of the Firth of Forth just three miles below Stirling. The editor of *The Angler's News* culled this information from *Where to Fish*, but did not append a date. In *Game Fish Records* (1936) on pages 148–191, Jock Scott (D.G.F. Rudd) bolstered up the existing data:

The 'absolutely largest ever' salmon for the British Isles is a huge fish of 103lbs, and I think that it may also claim the world's record for Atlantic salmon. This fish was caught by poachers. Mr W.L. Calderwood, at that time Chief Inspector of Scottish Salmon Fisheries, investigated the case, and kindly wrote an account in a letter to me. He said: 'With reference to the 103lb 2oz fish, I would ask you to make it clear that no actual record of the weight or of the length, etc., was available for me. The fish was poached in the month of December at the mouth of the Devon in the tidal waters of the Forth. But I had the whole story from the ex-soldier who was one of the three men involved. I arranged to meet him in Messrs Anderson's fishing-tackle shop in Princes Street, Edinburgh (now gone), for the man made fishing baskets for the Andersons and it was through them that I heard of the fish. I had also asked Mr Roderick Anderson to let the man know that I was not going to use the information against him in any way. My impression was that the man made a very straight statement.

'The fish was netted, and it took the three of them to lift it out of the water. He described it as the ugliest big male fish he had ever seen, and that the head and hooked jaw were immense. They conveyed it to a neighbouring farm because they knew the farmer, and they weighed it with care, fully realizing the exceptional nature of their catch. The weight I have already mentioned was the result.

We do not know anything as to the accuracy of the farmer's weigh-

The confluence of the Devon and Forth at low tide. The largest Atlantic salmon ever caught was netted at the mouth of the River Devon where it cuts through the bank of the Firth of Forth, some half a mile south of Cambus and about three miles west of Stirling

ing machine, but even if it were a pound or so out, the fish would still be a record. On the whole I was inclined to accept the whole story.

'I should have added that after satisfying themselves about the weight, they cut the fish up and distributed the pieces. It is a thousand pities that they did not take an outline of it.

'It seems, therefore, that there are fairly satisfactory reasons for believing in the existence of this truly enormous fish, undoubtedly a world's record.'

A report in the *Fishing Gazette*, 22 August 1908, delineates the story of this huge salmon:

HEAVY SCOTTISH SALMON

In the recently issued report of the Fishery Board of Scotland, Mr W.L. Calderwood has the following notes:

THE RECORD BRITISH SALMON – 103LBS

Early in the past winter I heard from Mr Roderick Anderson and Sons, fishing tackle makers, etc., Princes-street, Edinburgh, that a few years ago a salmon of unusually heavy weight had been taken in the estuary of the Forth. At a later date, I had an opportunity of speaking with the man who, with others, had landed the fish. From him I learned that the capture was made in the winter of 1902, or possibly of 1901, at the mouth of the Devon in the Forth, in the neighbourhood of Cambus, a few miles below Stirling. The fish weighed 103lbs and a few ounces. It was blacker in colour than he or the men with him (who were fishermen of experience) had ever seen. It was a male, the hook of the lower jaw being sufficiently long to penetrate the upper jaw. No measurements of length or girth were taken. Sea lice were very numerous in the region of the pectoral fins.

No visible record of the fish was retained, since the possession of the fish was fraught with a certain amount of danger to the captors. I have, however, no reason to doubt the guarded statement of my informant, who is well known to Messrs Anderson, and personally believe that in reporting the matter I am recording the greatest known weight for any British salmon.

The first weir on the River Devon is close to a whisky distillery (seen in the background). The tide can run up the Devon for about a thousand yards. At low tide and in low water, any salmon below the weir could easily be taken by poachers

The Namsen, Norway below Fiskum Foss

TALES OF LOST FISH

Many of the stories I came across in the course of researching this book concerned huge fish that either got away or were caught after epic struggles only to be cut up and distributed before they could be weighed or any details recorded. Others were found dead. Informative and entertaining as these tales may be, there is another reason for including some of them here and that is they are bound to touch a chord with any salmon fisher.

WILLIE DUFF'S 80lb TAY KELT

reader's letter to the *Fishing Gazette*, asking if there were any existing records of Tay salmon exceeding 70lb in weight, elicited a response from a Mr Anderson of 67 Princes Street, Edinburgh. His letter, published in the 8 March 1902 edition, included two stories of huge Tay salmon. This is the second one:

In the spring of 1872 the late Willie Duff, fisherman to the Athole family, was one morning rowing his boat up to the top of his beat when he saw a large fish hanging in the easy water at the tail of a pool. Dropping his oars he quickly slipped the gaff into it, and after a stiff tussle, aided by some workmen who pulled the boat to the bank, the fish was landed and a 'veritable monster' it was.

Hearing about it in the afternoon I went in search, but could only find the tail half of the fish. This had been cut off close behind the back fin, and when I had it weighed it turned the scale at 35½lb. I offered the party a sovereign if he could procure the other half so I could weigh it and have the fish measured but unfortunately it had been cut up and distributed.

The fish was a spent male slightly diseased about the head. Now what was the weight of this fish when he went up in the autumn to spawn? I should say nearer 90lb than 80lb.

Although this fish was not killed with the fly, it at least proves that veritable monsters do occasionally frequent the river Tay.

Beardie Willie lived to be 90 years old. The photograph gives some idea of what poachers had to face if they dared to practise their art on the Atholl Estate

In April 2006 I visited Blair Castle and was allowed to look through letters, photographs and memorabilia belonging to the Atholl family (Athole is a variant spelling). William Duff, known as Beardie Willie, was 6ft 6in tall and although we shall never know how much the giant salmon weighed, we can easily visualise 'Scotland's tallest gillie' cradling what surely must have been the biggest-ever Tay salmon.

DISASTER ON THE SAND RIVER

J.C. Mottram wrote several fine books about various aspects of fly fishing. In one, *Thoughts On Angling* (*circa* 1945), he describes the loss of a 60lb salmon in chapter xiv headed 'A Triumph and a Disaster'. The word disaster is, to my mind, not over the top when describing the loss of a big salmon, i.e. anything over 50lb in the old days (pre-1930) or for that matter anything over 40lb these days. It could also apply, I suppose, to the loss of a huge pike, but perhaps it is too strong a word to describe the loss of any other kind of fish. Mottram sets the scene on the Sand River where it flows out of a great Norwegian lake 'at once a mighty stream':

> At first a fly was tried, but it is a bad place for a fly, the turbulent water tossing it this way and that, so that it is impossible to present it properly. A prawn was then lowered into the eddy, well weighted, for the water has eaten out a deep hole. Sink and draw, and then let out more line and sink and draw again cast to the left and draw-cast to the right. Ah! What was that? Yes! Strike hard, bringing the rod right back. Olaf doesn't wait to see what will happen, he at once rows up-stream, fit to break the oars: he must get back to the island A in order to cross the river – the water is much too fierce to make a direct crossing and too full of swirls and surges. Whilst Olaf rows up I slack away and try to let the salmon lie quiet in the eddy where it was hooked. I must not pull hard if I can help it, as it would be pulling against Olaf, who has a very hard task.
>
> We reach the island. So far I have hardly felt the fish; I have about 100 yards of line out. Suddenly everything goes slack, I murmur many stout English words which Olaf knows very well, and then a magnificent salmon springs into the air. Olaf shouts, "Twenty-five kilo." He is frighteningly huge, though my eye was in for a big fish, having caught one of 45 lb. the day before. Then the rod was almost jerked out of my hands, the reel began to spin alarmingly; braking as hard as I dare made no difference, the fish easily reached the base of the cliff where enormous boulders lay on the bottom, fallen from above: there he stopped, doubtless trying to burrow and hide. Putting on tremendous strain, I try to hold him off. What is happening under the cliff I cannot tell, sometimes I feel the fish, sometimes he seems dead. Meanwhile Olaf has edged across the stream and we drift down the far side of the island whilst I reel in. Soon the nose of the boat is against the lower island, Olaf helps me out, and I run to the corner of the island

nearest the cliff. I reel in and then pull, the line sings in the current, but no life is felt at its end. I pull and I pump. Suddenly away she comes, the salmon makes off down-stream away from the cliff into the wide pool. Hurrah!

There is plenty of sea-room here. It's true I am anchored on an island, but I can again take to the boat if necessary. A hard fight ensues, long runs down-stream and pumping him back; I grow very tired and shaky as the end nears. I pull him close in, but one wag of his huge tail and he is out in the current again. It takes a long time to tire out a big fish and swing it in, and by the time this is nearly done he has recovered enough to make a few more wags and heads from shore again; I do this time and time again, and then I lose my head. I am trembling with anxiety, for he is a 60-pounder, my knees shake, the rod shivers. I turn him round once more and, instead of swinging him in to Olaf with the gaff, I put on great pressure and pull him straight towards me by walking backwards; he opens his mouth and shakes his head, the prawn hooks fly out and whiz past my head. Olaf stands agape. I seize the gaff from him, dash into the river: the salmon sinks and drifts away out of reach.

A MONSTER WYE SALMON

On 10 January 1914, the *Fishing Gazette* published a letter from J.A. Hutton about a huge Wye cock salmon that had been found dead after spawning. This fish is of interest because it was judged it to be about 65lb prior to spawning, and also because Hutton mentions that such a fish would have spent four or five years at sea without spawning.

Mr J.A. Hutton writes: -

"DEAR MARSTON – I enclose particulars of a very big cock fish which was picked up dead the other day in the Wye just below Hereford: Weight, 46¾lb.; length, 54½in.; girth, 26½in. My informant states that it was quite the largest salmon he ever saw, which I can quite believe. Assuming that the fish had lost one-fifth of its weight in spawning, it must have weighed close on 60lb. when it was in good condition. The scales were too much worn to enable one to decide anything as to its age, but presumably like most of these big cock fish it had spent four or five years in the sea without spawning."

I should think this monster was nearer 65lb., as our *Fishing Gazette* scale of weight for length gives 67½lb. for a 54-inch salmon; but the Wye salmon are, generally speaking, not quite so deep as those of most other big rivers, and probably a 54½in. Wye fish would not exceed 65lb. It is a great pity that it did not live to come back to spawn again as a 70 pounder; but it shows Wye anglers what they may find themselves up against. Also it is to be regretted its scales were so knocked about as to be useless as indicating its age. – ED

A MONSTER KELT
FROM THE BORDER ESK

No weight is recorded for this kelt but it may still be of interest to all those who fish this fine border river for salmon – just to know what the river is capable of producing helps the angler when his spirits are low, following a long unrewarding day of flogging the water. This report appeared in the *Fishing Gazette* of 2 February 1907:

THE LARGEST FISH SEEN IN THE SOUTH OF SCOTLAND FOR YEARS

Dear Sir – A spawned male salmon is reported as having been taken out dead from the English portion of the River Esk, in Netherbie reserved water. It is stated that he was the biggest kelt seen in the south of Scotland for years, and before he ascended to the breeding grounds must have been between seventy and eighty pounds in weight. The weight is the largest seen in the Esk for a long time.

Yours truly,

W.S.B.

In October 2005 I set out to find the relevant stretch of water on the Border Esk, which I could not locate on my maps. I asked a gentleman in Longtown if he could direct me to 'the English portion' of 'Netherbie reserved water' where the fish had been caught in

The Border Esk at Kirk Andrews, Netherby, looking downstream

1907. He directed me to the Netherby Hall Estate (note the different spelling) at Kirk Andrews, despite the name of this church showing that it must be on the northern or Scottish side of the River Esk, whereas we know the angler, or netsman, caught his fish on the English side. The beat still fishes well, although an angler I spoke to said that the really big salmon no longer feature in the runs. His own best fish weighed 27lb.

Sir William Wallace's monument

THE LARGEST TWEED SALMON – 70lb?

In the chapter he wrote for the book *Great Hours in Sport* (1921), Sir Herbert Maxwell tells the story of Colonel Haig, the Laird of Bemersyde, fishing Haly Weil – the chief holding pool on the Bemersyde water of the Tweed.

> The time was an autumn evening, and the Laird had only come down to try a few casts, for the light was already growing dim. At the point known as the Cradle he hooked a fish which, from the strain it put on his rod, seemed to be a heavy one. It never showed itself, but bored away out of the pool into Jock Sure, then through the Woodside, and passed over the Monk's Ford into Dryburgh Water.
>
> At the place called the Tod Holes, Colonel Haig began to master it, for big as it was it was a typical sluggish autumn fish. Still quite uncertain of its size, he managed to pull it in near the shore, and as it was growing late, and time pressed, told a boy who was with him to get it out. The boy had a net and did his best, but he failed to get the fish into it.
>
> "He's that big," he said, "he'll no go in the net."
>
> "Oh, nonsense," said the fisherman: "I can't wait here all night. Get him out somehow."

The boy made another attempt, but the light was bad. He struck the line with the net and broke the cast, and the great fish slipped back into deep water. Colonel Haig had that moment of annoyance which comes to every fisherman who loses anything. But the contest had not strung his expectations high, and after making some remark appropriate to the occasion he turned to go home.

There the story might have ended but for the fortunate presence of two poachers. The poachers of Tweedside are a race by themselves, for poaching there is a kind of hereditary profession, and is accompanied usually by uncommon knowledge and skill. The two who were that night lurking on the river bank were to enlighten the Laird as to what he had lost.

A few days later he was in St. Boswell's station, where the old porter accosted him.

"Yon was a gran' fish ye lost in the Tod Holes yon nicht, sir," he said.

"Oh yes," replied Colonel Haig. "It was a good fish enough, but I never got a fair sight of him."

The porter stared at him solemnly. "It was the biggest saumon that ever cam' oot o' the water o' the Tweed."

"How do you know that?" asked the astonished Laird.

"Fine I ken it," said the porter. "There was twae lads sittin' under the Wallace Monument forenent ye. They had a cairn net wi' them, waiting for the darkenin'. They seen ye loss the fish. And they seen the wave o' him as he cam across the water. So they up and whuppit the net roon' him, and had him oot. He was that big he wadna gang into the sack they had wi' them. So they cuttit him in twae. They brocht the tae half to me to send awa' by the train, and the weight of that was five and thirty puns!"

Because I have fished the River Tweed on and off for over thirty years, Sir Herbert Maxwell's story of a lost monster held a particular fascination for me, so it was no surprise that, when I took time off to make my investigations, I felt quite excited. First of all, I decided that a photograph of Sir William Wallace's monument above Tod Holes would be a novel way of setting the scene – so I took one.

Subsequently I parked my car in the visitor's car park at Bemersyde, where I found a notice inviting me to inspect the grounds and gardens or take the path to 'The Riverside Walk'. I took the second option.

Thirty minutes later, at the end of what seemed like a downhill track without end, I arrived at a turning-round area for privileged car users. Here I could go left or right on a rough path through thick woods. I turned right but soon gave up because only occasional glimpses could be had of the river far below.

Once back at the turning-round area, I decided that, rather than start the long uphill walk to my car, I would try the other track. Although the going was tortuous (for a seventy-nine year old) I soon came to a clearing beside the river. Some fishermen were gathered by a fishing hut and I approached the person who looked as though he might be the host to explain my reasons for being there and to ask permission to photograph the pool. That request was immediately granted. With a degree of temerity, I asked the host if he would be kind enough to give me his name.

'Haig,' he replied, whereupon I rather more boldly asked him if he belonged to the distilling Haigs or the army Haigs and he answered, 'Both.'

It soon transpired that I was talking to the second Earl Haig, or more precisely, George Alexander Eugene Douglas Haig, the eighty-six-year-old son of Field Marshal Douglas Haig, commander of the British Army in France during the last two years of the First World War.

After that, it became obvious to me that it was Field Marshal Douglas Haig who had lost the fish *circa* 1905 at Tod Holes when he was a younger man with the rank of Colonel. The present Earl confirmed my assumptions, and I asked one more question of him – had Bemersyde belonged to the family for a long time? He answered, 'Yes, since the twelfth century.' Soon after, Earl Haig gave me a lift back to my car.

Looking upstream from Earl Haig's fishing hut at Bemersyde

The jawbone from the Loch Awe salmon

A TRAGEDY AT LOCH AWE

Such was the heading given to a piece published in *The Field* on 31 March 1927 about an estimated 70lb to 80lb dead salmon found on the shore of Loch Awe:

In another column that experienced angler, Mr. Wanless, gives an account of the remarkable fish found dead on the shore of Loch Awe. It is another of those tragedies that *will* happen because insufficient details are preserved. If only the dimensions had been taken, one of the useful formulæ prescribed for ascertaining a salmon's weight would have given us enough to go upon for recording purposes. As it is, things are too uncertain, especially with the added difficulty of such unusual teeth. We are tempted to recall the fact that Loch Awe once produced the heaviest brown trout ever recorded in Great Britain, the fish of 30½lb. caught by Mr. W. Muir in 1866. This fish was discussed in the *Field* of November 15th, 1913, by our old contributor "R. Clyde." Unfortunately, though it was set up and exhibited once in London), the case was lost in a fire. Whether such a trout would exhibit dentition like that displayed in the photograph it would be rash to say, but old trout seem to preserve their teeth longer than salmon. Another tragedy worth recalling is that of the Wye monster found dead in 1920 with a fly in its mouth. It was 59½in. long and 33½in. in girth, but it was not weighed when found. A portion of it, much decayed, nine days later weighed 43lb. Before death it must have weighed at least 85lb. Mr. C. Tate Regan, of the Natural History Museum, has very kindly reported on two photographs of the Loch Awe fish's jawbone which we submitted to him. His view supports Mr. Wanless's opinion, as to him "they appear to be præmaxillaries of a salmon." That big trout of 1866 had a hook of some 3in. which almost protruded through the upper jaw, a fact noted by Mr. D. E. Campbell Muir in writing to "R. Clyde."

Here is Alexander Wanless' letter:

A VERY LARGE LOCH AWE SALMON

Particulars have been given to me by an eye witness of what seems to have been one of the largest salmon ever encountered in this country. The fish was found recently lying on the shore of Loch Awe and a Glasgow angler, who was fishing the beach with some friends, cut off part of the upper jaw, (which I have seen and had photographed). It is exceedingly unfortunate that exact measurements and photographs of the fish were not taken as these are the only means by which one's natural scepticism can be removed. But apparently nobody seems to have realised the importance of the occasion. Although the fish was intact when found save for the head which had been picked by crows, and was not decomposed to any extent, nobody seems to have thought of dimensions or weight although all were impressed by the size of the fish which they had never seen approached. Not even scales were taken although it might easily have been done. The boatman estimated the weight of the fish to have been between 70lb. and 80lb.

Apart from the probable weight of the fish the condition of the teeth is, as the photograph shows, sufficiently remarkable. Fortunately the upper jaw has been preserved. The photograph is as near actual size as possible, but it should be kept in mind that the jaw had been some days out of water before this picture was taken and was not agreeable to handle.

The jaw was sent to the Scottish Fishery Board by the angler who procured it, and Mr. Calderwood replied as follows.

"Many thanks for sending me the jaw of the fish with the pronounced dentition. In your letter of 16th inst. You refer to it as a salmon head. It would have been of great assistance if the whole head had been procured and if the mandible and the vomer bone had been available for comparison. As an upper jaw the teeth are certainly remarkable, for in large and old fish one of the characteristics generally is that the teeth have disappeared. They go on the vomer bone and run over the length of the mouth first of all and continue on the jaws. On only one occasion have I taken fish (two) which approach this condition and I was then netting at spawning-time for marking purposes in the West of Ross-shire."

Mr. Calderwood is obviously not prepared, or is unable to say that the jaw was taken from a phenomenally large salmon. Indeed, he seems to throw doubt on the fish being a salmon at all. But there seems to be no doubt about the point in the minds of those who saw the fish, and they were experienced salmon fishers. In any case, the boatman could hardly mistake a salmon for a pike, which is the only other fish it could possibly have been. And, by the way, the discovery of an 80lb. pike or one of 70lb. for that matter, would be still more remarkable than the discovery of such a salmon. [A. Wanless]

(For reproduction the photograph has been somewhat enlarged. The fragment would seem to have been about 4⅝in. long. I take the original as the measurement. – Ed.)

The best illustration that I could find to give credence to Wanless' assertion (and Doctor C. Tate Regan's for that matter,) that what we are looking at are the premaxillary bones of a salmon is on page 298 of Day's *British And Irish Salmonidae* (1887).

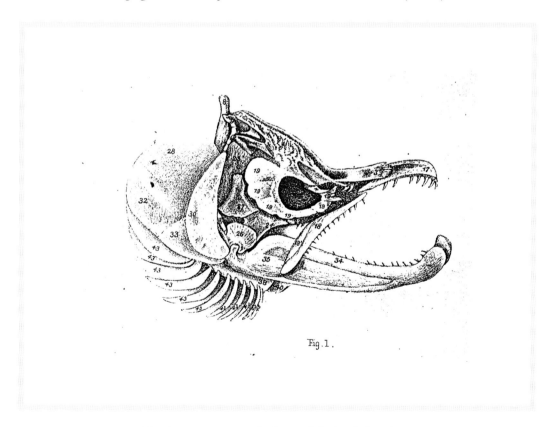

Fig.1.

The vignette represents the bones of the head of a salmon

Looking upstream from the east bank towards The Manse on the River Ewe at Poolewe.

WAS THIS THE LARGEST ROD-CAUGHT SALMON?

The River Ewe may be only two miles long but it has a huge catchment area in Ross-shire because it links Loch Maree, the famous sea-trout loch, to the saltwater Loch Ewe. The River Ewe is famous for big fish. An account of the largest fish ever caught there, written by Kenneth MacKenzie, was published by his brother Stuart of Poolewe. The following is an extract from *The River Ewe Reminiscent Recollections of a Ross-shire River* (2000), a book now sadly out of print, Thanks are due to the MacKenzies for allowing me to reproduce the story of a young man's struggle with an enormous fish.

THE McCORDIE

Apparently one of the many working crofts which were situated along the west bank of the River Ewe was tenanted at that particular time by a certain crofter, who had originally come there from Muir-of-Ord a number of years previously. This man, a popular and respected member of the community, was blessed with a name which was very common in the Poolewe area at that time so, to avoid confusion with others of the same name he became known locally as Ordie. Ordie was of course married and had a large family, and his eldest son, a big strapping young fellow by the name of Iain, was employed as a general estate worker and river ghillie by the local laird of that era. One of the perks of that job was that when there were no fishing guests on the river he was permitted to fish for "one for the pot" during his leisure hours, and that's exactly what Iain was doing at the beginning of the particularly fine summer evening leading up to the episode which later that same evening provided the river pool which is now known as the McCordie with its present name

After having had his supper Iain took the big rod and went down to the west bank of the Manse pool which was not far from his father's croft. He started fishing there and after only a few casts he hooked a fish which, after swimming deep around the pool for several minutes, then sank to the bottom and refused to be moved. Iain tried everything he had ever been taught to do to move a sulking fish but all to no avail. There was absolutely no movement whatsoever and he started to suspect that his fly had become snagged on the bottom and that the fish was no longer there. He eventually eased off the pressure on the line in the hope that the strong current might possibly free the hook but he had no sooner done so than the line began to move slowly upstream!

As he tightened up his line again and set a good curve to the big heavy greenheart rod the fish at the other end of the line suddenly *really* took off. Iain was no weakling and he was equipped with a big powerful rod but he could do absolutely nothing to control this fish, it just went on and on, up to the Hen pool, through that and on through the rough water beyond, not at any great speed nor with the usual surfacing and splashing about, but just as if it was swimming normally upriver and totally oblivious to the young fisherman who was now struggling almost a line's length behind it in a frantic effort to stay in contact! Relentlessly on and ever on it went until eventually it powered through into the actual pool which was destined in the very near future to receive a change of name.

As the fish reached the deeper water of the pool it again sank to the bottom and came to a complete stop, allowing Iain to catch up with it, compose himself after the frantic scramble up from the Manse, and look around for a suitable spot where he would be able to beach it, for by now it must have been more or less played out or so he thought. However, the best, was yet to come, for as Ordie's son and heir stood on the river bank, arm aching, soaking wet, but with the adrenaline continuing to stimulate his circulation and feeling supremely confident that the salmon was as good as "in the bag", that same fish decided to get going again on its seemingly effortless journey up the river! As the line snaked out again Iain stood his ground and applied more pressure on the rod in anticipation of fairly overpowering his quarry in its final few runs before eventually bringing it exhausted in to the bank, but the fish would have none of it and just kept on going up through the headwaters of the pool and then steadily on into the smooth tailrace of the T-Pool.

As the big brass reel reluctantly released more and more line it began to look as if Iain's rod was connected to an unstoppable robot of some sort but, just as the salmon appeared to have effortlessly surmounted the powerful T-Pool current, the cumulative effects of its non-stop power drive up from the Manse pool finally slowed it down enough to allow Iain to haul it back again gradually. Twice more it made a determined run for the T-Pool and twice more it was slowly reeled back in again, and eventually, after it had been "brought to heel" for the third time, it sank to the bottom of the pool as before and refused to be moved. Fearful that the prolonged fight may have loosened the big hook's grip in the salmon's jaw Iain now contented himself with keeping steady pressure on the fish while he rested himself and waited for the next move, and for almost half an hour there was complete stalemate, but then the line started to move again, slowly at first but rapidly gaining speed as the salmon once more made a run for the T-Pool. Iain braced himself and applied more pressure and once again he managed to "put the brakes on it" and slowly hauled it back to the pool where it settled on the bottom once more. After this brief but still powerful breakaway the young ghillie relaxed and settled down for another wait but all of a sudden things *really* started to happen.

The line began to move again, but this time, instead of powering upstream as before, the remarkable fish literally exploded through the surface of the water for the first time, like a modern-day rocket taking off for the moon or wherever. From when he had first hooked it Iain had been left in absolutely no doubt whatsoever that he was into a really big fish, but just how big it was he did not fully realise until that first leap exposed its true dimensions. It was *ABSOLUTELY ENORMOUS!!* and the poor boy started to go weak at the knees. Each great leap and resulting splash on returning to the water caused such a commotion in the still of the summer evening that crofters working on their fields nearby were attracted to the water's edge, and within a remarkably short time there was a considerable audience of people of all ages gathered on the west bank of the river to witness this epic performance.

Iain soon recovered from his temporary shock and astonishment at the sheer size of this huge salmon and eventually, after prolonged and exhausting struggle which gradually weakened it over a total period of almost an hour from when it first broke surface, the great fish finally turned over on its side for the last time at the water's edge and was expertly transferred to the river bank by two willing helpers armed with gaffs.

After having been suitably commented upon and thoroughly examined by the assembled crowd of men, women, and children for some considerable time, the bradan mor (big salmon) was tied into a suitably strong croneangach (sections of rejected sea-fishing net which were used on crofts for securing hay while it dried) and carried along to Ordie's crofthouse where it was, without further ceremony, cut up and distributed among friends and neighbours within a wide surrounding area.

As a matter of general interest to knowledgeable anglers who may happen to read this exclusive account of the impressive and heroic capture of Iain Ordie's great fish, the incredibly large and powerful salmon proved itself throughout the whole long protracted fight to be a particularly determined and single-minded individual which had apparently been specially programmed since entering the river to head in one direction only, and that direction was invariably upriver! Anytime that it had been forcibly persuaded to change direction (apart from dashing about within pools and turning somersaults in the air) it had done so tail first, very reluctantly. That perverse trait in its character was most certainly its undoing, because if at any time during that epic fight it had simply decided to turn around and head for the sea no rod and line that was ever constructed could possibly have stopped it!

The name by which this pool (McCordie) was previously known is, at least to my knowledge, not recorded anywhere, but apparently the final outcome of the great giant-killing demonstration of power-angling by young Iain Ordie so far as the River Ewe is concerned was that the pool where the enormous fish was finally taken from the water became known eventually to all, in Gaelic, as Poll MacOrdie (Ordie's son's pool). This name was abbreviated simply to MacOrdie over the intervening years, and then over a further period of time to McCordie as it remains today.

The great fish which played such a prominent part in the naming of the pool was never actually weighed (the necessary equipment for weighing such a large fish was probably not readily available at the time) but its exact measurements *were* taken and duly recorded before it was finally cut up and distributed. They were as follows – length sixty-three inches, girth thirty-nine inches. Incidentally, when the cruives were in operation on the River Ewe previous to the mid-nineteenth century it appears that fish of over seventy pounds in weight were occasionally netted there and local men who regularly worked at the cruives and saw those very large fish, and who also saw Iain Ordie's leviathan, unanimously agreed that it was considerably larger than anything they had ever before seen coming off the river, either by net or by rod. In addition to that, the men who took turns in carrying the big salmon from the river to Ordie's crofthouse were reported to have been of the opinion that its weight appeared to be very similar to the weight of a bag of potatoes (one hundredweight, or in fish language, one hundred and twelve pounds!)

Anyhow, that is the rather interesting account which I was given of how this excellent River Ewe pool came to be known as The McCordie. Maybe there are other different versions of the story, I do not know, but if this one *is* true and the above measurements are correct, it would appear that not only was Iain Ordie's big salmon a record weight for the River Ewe, it must also qualify, unofficially maybe, as an all-time British record, because the fish which was caught on the River Tay in nineteen twenty-two by Miss G. W. Ballantine and which was officially accepted as the British record for a rod-caught salmon at a total weight of sixty-four pounds, measured only fifty-four inches long with a girth of twenty-eight and a half inches.

Although it is a minor tragedy that the fish was not weighed, it is possible to salvage something from the above account. First of all, the measured length of 63in is the second longest ever recorded for an Atlantic salmon. The photograph on page 388 shows the longest recorded salmon – 63¼in – and that weighed 75½lb, so imagine the size of MacOrdie's fish. However, the 75½lb fish, for which no girth measurement is available, was a slim fish, whereas MacOrdie's had a girth of 39in. That is the largest salmon girth ever recorded – some three inches more than the next largest.

A 60lb SALMON –
DUNCAN CAMPBELL'S TRAGEDY

ock Scott (G.D.F. Rudd) was a popular contributor to the sporting press during the first half of the 20th century. He also wrote some excellent books, *Game Fish Records* (1936), *The Art of Salmon Fishing* (1933) and *Lake Fishing for Salmon, Trout and Pike* (1932) among them. Sometimes he wrote for newspapers, and the following extract comes from the *Blackburn Weekly Telegraph* of 9 November 1901:

> Something like a record has been created by a Loch Awe angler. About five o'clock in the evening he hooked a huge salmon, played it all night, and lost it, the fish effecting its escape the next morning about seven o'clock. The hero was one Duncan Campbell, and Mr Portal has told in the "Field" the story of the great battle with the king of fishes. According to Mr Portal the fish was estimated to be well over 60lb. In spite of all he could do the fish took Campbell to the river and about a mile and a half down it. Several times, the river being very high, he had to wade up to his waist round the rocks. About nightfall they reached a big pool, and there the fish stayed all night, doing nothing but slowly swimming round and round. As day broke it got restless and began to move off down stream again, Campbell being powerless to prevent it; no help came, and at last, about seven o'clock, after a fourteen-hours' struggle, it got round a rock and broke his cast.

THE LONGEST FIGHT
WITH A SALMON

most diverting little book that I have come to love is, unsurprisingly, A. Courtney Williams' *Angling Diversions* (1945). Williams describes the longest ever fight between a salmon fisher and his quarry. This story is particularly interesting to me because I have fished the North Esk many times and have broadcast the unprovable theory that North Esk salmon are the hardest fighting salmon, certainly that I have ever met up with.

> The longest fight with a salmon, which can be authenticated, would appear to have taken place in 1866; it was described in detail in the *Dundee Courier* and the *Warwick Advertiser* in November of that year. The fish was hooked by Mr. Colin Wood, a very experienced fisherman, in the North Esk. He played it for 10½ hours before handing the rod to a friend, Mr. A. Bower, for an hour. Wood then took it over again until midday, when fatigue obliged him to pass it on to another skilful angler, Sergeant Milne, who continued to play the fish. About 1 p.m. the hook came away – just 19¾ hours after the fish had first taken hold. This exceptionally strong salmon was viewed several times by the large number of onlookers which collected during the day, and it was generally agreed that the fish must have weighed at least sixty pounds.

THE ADMIRAL'S 77lb 2oz NORWEGIAN SALMON

his fish is 'lost' in the sense that it is somewhat of a mystery – did it exist or didn't it? The case remains unproven.

H.B. Isachsen from Stavanger wrote to the *Fishing Gazette* about a large Norwegian salmon on 23 July 1920, and his letter was published in the following week's edition (31 July 1920).

> DEAR SIR – I have noticed with great interest the recent discussion in the *Fishing Gazette re* the largest British Salmon. etc.
>
> It might interest your readers to know that the biggest fish on record caught by rod and fly in Norway weighed just above 35 kilos, or about 78½ English lbs. This fish was caught in the Pasvik River, one or two years before the outbreak of the war, by an English gentleman, Admiral Hammond. The above has been reported to me by an absolutely trustworthy person.
>
> You mentioned the Voss River to me some time ago. A few weeks ago a Norwegian angler caught a salmon there weighing 29.5 kilos, or about 66 English lbs. The salmon was considered to be of such interest, owing to its size, that it was handed over to the Bergen Museum to have a cast made of it. – I remain, dear Sir, yours truly,
>
> H.B. ISACHSEN

> Mr. Hutton referred to this fish in the *Fishing Gazette* recently, and also to the admirable way in which the fish in the Bergen Museum are set up. I do not remember that we had any account of the Admiral Hammond's great fish.
>
> R.B. MARSTON

The 65lb (not 66lb) fish that Isachsen refers to is Finn Isdahl's salmon (No. 395). It seems that news of the Admiral's fish stirred things up somewhat because in due course the *Fishing Gazette* (18 December 1920) received a letter of apology from their original correspondent.

BIG NORWEGIAN SALMON

DEAR SIR – A couple of months ago there was a discussion in your paper *re* the biggest British salmon, and I wrote you on July 23 in connection with the said discussion that I happened to have heard from apparently a trustworthy quarter, that the biggest salmon on record, caught in Norway, was taken in the Pasvik River some years ago by Admiral Hamond [sic] the fish weighing 35 kilos or about 78½lb. (English).

This information was repudiated soon afterwards in your paper, and I much regret that my informant had been mistaken.

He is, by the way, a conservator at the Zoological Department of the Stavanger Museum, and he also much regrets that his memory had failed him on this occasion.

In order to obtain, if possible, absolutely trustworthy information *re* the matter in question, I wrote to Mr. Klerck, of Elvenes on the Pasvik River, and he writes me in translation as follows: -

"Your informant is mistaken as regards Admiral Hamond [sic] having caught a salmon of 35 kilos in the Pasvik River. I have lived on the Pasvik all my life, and since 1891 have administered the letting of the salmon fishing. The English anglers having fished here since 1867 have stayed at my father's and my house at Elvenes. I should, therefore, know about this fishing, both as regards quantity and sizes of fish caught. I have not made many notes, but what I know definitely is the following. In 1876, Sir Henry Gore Buth (an Irish gentleman) caught a salmon of 28 kilos (about 62½ English lb.) The skin was taken off, put into spirit and brought along to Ireland. In 1882, Lord Dudley caught a salmon of 25.6 kilos (57.3 English lb.) In 1886, my father's assistant caught in net close to the mouth of the Pasvik River, a salmon of 33 kilos (73.9 English lb.) [actually 72lb 12oz].This is supposed to be the biggest salmon ever caught in or by the Pasvik River.

Mr. Klerck's letter ends here. I have had pleasure in translating this letter to you (adding weights in English lb.) as I thought the contents might interest you, as also to aplogise and try to make good my unfortunate and much regretted mistake as regards Admiral Hammond's record salmon.

I have the honour to be, Sir,

Yours very respectfully,

H.B. ISACHSEN

Stavanger, Nov. 23, 1920.

Mr Klerck's letter, although demolishing an entry previously thought to be *bone fide* in my list, added to it by reference to Sir Henry Gore Buth's (Booth's?) fish of 62½lb (No. 361), and by confirming the story of a 72lb 12oz fish netted in 1886. Another interesting point raised by Klerck's letter indicates the start in 1867 of the English anglers' invasion of one of Norway's great salmon rivers. After reading the above, Roy Flury commented:

I find Arthur Klerck's letter confusing. He dismisses the Admiral's fish but gives no reason. Perhaps the weight was inaccurate but surely the Admiral didn't make it all up. He fails to mention a 34.5-kilo fish caught there in 1905 by an Englishman and witnessed by Mr Torseth, a custom's officer. He also makes no mention of his father's 36-kilo fish caught in 1863, three years before he was born. And he adds, "I have not made many notes".

He also states that the English anglers stayed at his father's, or his, house. Yes some did but many in the early days camped out or visited the fjord by yacht. I do not believe his letter eliminates anything.

In fairness to Arthur Klerck I would emphasise a few points. Firstly, the catching of a big fish in those days was no big deal and did not cause the hullabaloo as in later years. His father, Magnus, had fished all his life, on Alten, Tana and Pasvik. Surely he must have caught several 'giants'. He fished Pasvik from his arrival in 1856 as Lensman, until his death in 1891. There are no records of any of his fish, apart from the one big one written up in a fishing journal after his death.

Secondly, the organisation of the fishing would only have been a part-time job. The season was short and the visiting fishermen relatively few in number. The best fishing was below the Skoltefossen for a distance of only two miles. Most of it was best fished from a boat. His father had not only been Lensman for the district but was also a custom's officer, a ferryman, a forester of the area and a farmer.

Of interest is that Arthur was one of twelve children in the family. The seventh child, a girl, had been named Septima Ultima. Alas to no avail as there were five more to come. I feel his mother's name should certainly be recorded. Her maiden name was Christiane Figenschou.

The Sea Pool on the Morrum River, Sweden where a number of 50-pounders have come from in recent years

NOT STRICTLY SPEAKING...

These fish may not fulfil the specific criteria for inclusion
in this book, but they are nevertheless irresistible.

A 72lb(?) RIVER EARN SALMON

Recently I received the following details in a letter from David james who is a member of the Flyfishers' Club.

'My very good friend, Brian Parker, who is the head keeper at Bossington on the River Test, was telling me about a recent fishing trip on the River Earn in Perthshire. John Young, the gillie that he met there, told Brian that in the early 1960s an enormous fish was recovered dead from the river after the gillie's lad reported that he had found this huge fish on the bank and that he had dug a hole and buried it. Because his description of the size of the fish was so unusual they returned to the spot, dug the fish up, washed it off and then hung it by its tail from the branch of a tree and photographed it.' At David James' behest John Young, while making enquiries on my behalf, talked to David R Cowan who had taken the photograph that depicts John McClorie kneeling down beside the fish and he reported back: 'The fish was weighed on scales that went up to 60lb and the fish pulled the scales to the maximum and was clearly heavier. A conservative estimate of its weight, allowing for the missing part and the dehydration, was 65lb.'

In his second letter to me, which included a photograph of the fish, David James commented:

'Lastly, it is intriguing to speculate on the weight of the fish when it first entered the river. If it was in excess of 60lb in its partly decomposed state, it could have been 72lb or 73lb when fresh run, as first rumoured. Also, as it was found in the early summer, what was the cause of death? I wonder if it had been hooked and lost?'

'Sadly it seems that nobody thought to measure the length of the fish, but judging from the photograph, it was a very long fish.'

The fish in this photograph was probably the largest recorded salmon to run a British river since the last war. It was found dead below Crieff Bridge in June/July 1963. One can imagine what it must have weighed when it first pressed its silver and sea-liced body against the flood of its natal stream – the River Earn.

KEN JAMIESON'S
RESTIGOUCHE RECORD

In Drakstown, New Brunswick in Canada, there is Salmon Conservation Centre (museum really) exhibiting a cast of an Atlantic salmon with the following notice:

'This 72lb salmon is the largest ever caught by using a fly rod, in North America. After playing it for one and a half hours, Ken Jamieson, along with his guide, Charlie Adams of Quebec, landed the 68.5inch salmon on June 23, 1990 near the mouth of the Restigouche River. The salmon was carefully released to continue its journey to the spawning bed after being photographed and measured. Mr Jamieson was using a No. 4 Silver Rat fly.'

In fact, the fish was never weighed, nor was the cast made from the body of the fish.

The detailed information that Hatwell gave me indicated that the weight of 72lb was arrived at by multiplying the length of the fish (68½ in) by the square of its girth (29 in) divided by 800. However, Lee Straight, a respected Canadian authority on such matters recommended the 'tried and true British Sturdy Formula', which is four thirds (1.3333) times the length of the fish, times the square of its girth, divided by 1000. According to Sturdy's formula, Jamieson's salmon would have weighed 76½lb.

Photo by J. Croottucker, Hereford.

J. WYNDHAM SMITH'S RECORD BRACE FOR ONE DAY'S FISHING

So far as I am aware, the finest brace of big salmon caught in one day is Wyndham Smith's pair of Wye salmon, which he caught on 30 March 1914. Smith, from Aramstone, near Hereford, wrote to R.B. Marston on 31 March 1914 and the letter was published in the *Fishing Gazette* on 11 April 1914.

> DEAR SIR – Mr. Hutton has asked me to send you particulars of my two fish of yesterday, both caught in the one day on my own water.
>
> 51-pounder: length, 50 inches; girth, 29 inches; tail expansion, 11½ inches; girth, at tail 10 inches. Took me fifteen minutes to land it.
>
> 42½-pounder: length, 49 inches; girth, 25½ inches; tail expansion, 11 inches; girth at tail, 10 inches. Took just over five minutes to land.

> J. WYNDHAM SMITH

J. Arthur Hutton, of salmon-scale-reading fame, commented on Wyndham Smith's brace on pages 8 and 9 of *Wye Salmon and Other Fish* (1949):

There is no doubt that as a rule fish like cover when they are running, and that is why they often begin to move in the evening when the light is beginning to fade. In the same way they run best in coloured water. But the Lugg cuts both ways, for often when our water was too low for fishing we would hear that they were having excellent sport down below at Holme Lacey, Fownhope and Ballingham. It was in this length that on March 30, 1914, Wyndham Smith caught a very fine fish weighing 51 lb. length 49 in. girth 29 in. Like Miss Davey's Salmon this fish had also spent two years in the river and four years in the sea without returning to spawn. Not content with this exploit he proceeded to catch another monster weighing 44 lb. I have a photograph of these two fish and I often wonder if anybody else has ever caught two Salmon in one single day which weighed together 95 lb.

Nearly twelve years later, the *Fishing Gazette* of 6 December 1926 published Wyndham Smith's own account of the battles he'd had with two big fish:

My other memorable day occurred on March 30, 1914. I had a friend staying with me, and we tossed up who should go to the upper water. He won, and decided to go there. I began on the lower water, at the Quarry pool close to the fishing hut. About five casts and I felt a heavy pull (a 2 1/2 in. Devon). I immediately tightened (this is not an actual strike), and at once the fish moved off to the opposite bank, then back to the centre. Four times he did this, and I could never get him closer than the centre of the river. I knew by the feel he was a lump, and my only chance of dealing with him was to do my best to keep him on the move. So when he meant going to the other side he went, but when he came back to the middle I put all the strain on him that I dared, to upset his rest. This evidently annoyed him, and all of a sudden down-stream he went for quite 60 yards. Then just as suddenly he stopped, turned and came slowly up, close in to my bank. I kept just a feeling strain on the line, and as he came opposite to where my keeper was waiting, he had him out after a little struggle, owing to his weight. I had nothing capable of weighing him, so sent him up to the house to be weighed, and my keeper said, "He just turned the scales at 51lb." After wetting him in the usual way, I went off up the river to see how my friend was getting on, and met him coming down to me. "No good", he said, "but a big fellow came for my minnow close up to the bank, but I could not get him to come again." I then told him I had just killed one of 51lb. He said "Thanks for that: wasn't it two?" I then told him I would go up and kill his big fellow, and should soon be back, as it had begun to rain and I had no mackintosh. Knowing the water for the last forty years, I knew exactly where the big fish was lying. Two casts and I was into him, without a doubt. He immediately rushed across the river and came out twice with a mighty splash; up 40 to 50 yards, back in close to me, off out again, till he was practically rubbing the opposite bank, then into the middle before I could get a pull at him and regain about 40 yards of line. As soon as I got a fair strain on off he went, quite 60 yards down-stream. (I often notice big fish, when getting beat, go down), a quick turn, and then slowly back up. I told my keeper to get down ready, and as he was about beat I would bring him in to him. This I was able to do, and out came a 42½-pounder not more than an hour from the time I had landed the 51. I was now wet through and wanted some lunch, so back to my friend with "his" fish and to lunch. Since this day I have killed another salmon of 46lb. on the same water.

TAKEN THE HARD WAY

R oy Flury, who with Theodor Dalenson wrote *Alten: The Story of a Salmon River* (1991) and *Alten Reflections* (1993), told me about a most extraordinary incident that occurred on the Alten in 1990. A letter from J.T. Grey describing what happened was published in *The Atlantic Salmon Journal* in 1990.

Michael Perron was fishing the Ovre Sierra pool with a large tube fly, which was taken by a salmon. As the fish began to thrash and roll, a coil from his line snared a second fish, which joined battle with the first one as well as the angler. The second fish was landed after a thirty-minute struggle and soon after that the first fish was successfully landed.

The first fish landed weighed 35¼lb and the second fish landed weighed 28¾lb – total weight 64lb. Doubtless two fish have been landed in similar fashion before – perhaps even two salmon have been caught in this way – but I would lay a bet that nobody will have landed a bigger brace of salmon than Perron.

Michael Perron's brace of salmon, landed at the same time and together weighing 64lb

Howel Considine's salmon presented by Phelps Esq. and cast by Frank Buckland

A 44lb SALMON
IN SPAWNING RAIMENT

Sometime during the 1990s I was making enquiries about certain items in the Frank Buckland collection – casts of big fish that were originally housed in what was then called The British Museum (Natural History). My friend the late Alwyn Wheeler of the Fish Department told me that some had been removed to the Scottish Fisheries Museum at Anstruther in Fife.

Much later I contacted the curator of the museum, Linda Fitzpatrick, for permission to look over these items. In the event I paid a visit and duly inspected several plaster casts that were waiting to be restored, if and when funding became available. The most interesting item was a plaster cast of a 44lb Irish salmon caught with a fly by Howel Considine on 20 October 1869 at Hermitage on the River Shannon.

This fish is of particular interest for several reasons. Not only is it a link with the great fishing that was justly famous on the beats near Castleconnell on the Shannon, but it demonstrates the disfiguration of a cock salmon in full-spawning raiment – with jaws designed to grab a rival by the tail and drag it upstream (see page 15). Also, it is a reminder – for me anyway – of certain chapters in what I consider to be one of the greatest angling books of all time, O'Gorman's *The Practice of Angling* (1845).

GILFRED HARTLEY'S
52lb NORWEGIAN SALMON

Gilfred Hartley's *Wild Sport and Some Stories* (1912) includes some accounts of struggles with portmanteaux salmon in Norway.

> A good many years ago the writer of this paper was fortunate enough to kill a 40-lb. salmon, with fly, in a Scotch river. Then, long after, the Fates put almost into his very hands a much greater gift, and when the eager hands were just closing on it they ruthlessly snatched it away. This second fish had taken its temporary owner a mile down a Norway river: its strength was all but exhausted: it could be seen, was seen, for minutes at a time in the clear green water – its fins, its markings, the cast leading to its mouth, perfectly plain and distinct. But when all danger seemed over, and nothing was left but to gently tow the huge hulk into an ideal landing-place, the worn tackle parted, and a great prize was lost for ever. It may be that the fisherman's rejoicings at the first capture were too loud and immodest, that he took too much credit to himself for what he had accomplished, and therefore he was punished; and if this was the case, it is permissible perhaps to suggest that the cruel chastening which he received on this second occasion was borne with a fitting amount of meekness, more in utter dejection and grief than with furious denunciation, because two short years later [in July 1905] the memory of the lost salmon became bearable, and a new joy took the place of the old deep sorrow.

Hartley made a very interesting comment about fishing in Norway, which was so different from fishing in Scotland:

> ... in Scotland; no doubt chiefly because in a big spate our salmon do not take a fly or spoon: they cannot see the lures in thick dark flood; but in Norway you may have a rise of even four or five feet, and yet the water remains perfectly clear.

Hartley got his second chance with a 50-pounder and his account of playing the fish (on pages 11 to 24 of his book) is inspiring. After the fish was gaffed and safely landed, Hartley wrote:

An hour after its capture, and with the loss of a good deal of blood, it weighed an honest 52lb. This latter steelyard had been recently shop-tested and found accurate. The fish was weighed on another scale, and finally with Norwegian weights, and all corresponded.

And – that there should be no flaw, for once, in the doing, no fly this time in the ointment – the fish was perfectly fresh run: there were sea-lice on his tail.

'Sea-lice on its tail!' Imagine any human being made happier by such a thing as this!" So may some exclaim who only know salmon boiled or fried. Yet that little detail gives satisfaction now, and will do so, strange as it may appear to such critics, for long afterwards. They perhaps imagine that the triumph of capture is a mere momentary sensation, soon forgotten, dimmed by the next success, or even sooner, when the appetite has been satisfied with the slain. It is one of the greatest charms of all kinds of the higher sports that this is not so.

Hartley made a point of recording that he killed his biggest Scottish salmon on a fly, and he had tried the fly, albeit without success, prior to hooking his 52-pounder on a prawn – could it be that, despite his protestations, he would have been a happier man had he taken it on a fly?

Gilfred Hartley's gillie, Mons Gjörven, with the 52lb salmon

AN EXCEPTION THAT
PROVES THE RULE*

Peter O. Behan, Professor Emeritus of Clinical Neurology at Glasgow University, is devoted to fly fishing for salmon, but like many of us, when water conditions have demanded a catholic approach he has used other methods to obtain sport. In 1987 when he was a guest of a Norwegian colleague, he fished the Vosso River and caught a huge salmon. His host, Professor Johan A. Aarli, Department of Neurology of the University of Bergen, kindly sent me the following note, dated 11 August 2005.

> Professor Peter Behan fished the Vosso, Norway, on the 4th July 1987 and caught a large salmon. The salmon was caught on worm and he used a 25lb breaking strain with a multiplier. The beat where the salmon was caught on the Vosso was at Larshølen. The fish weighed 25 kilograms (55 lbs) and was weighed on the local farmer's scale. He kindly gave the salmon to me and I had it smoked and can testify to its size and condition. I trust this information is of help to you.

Including all the salmon weighing between 50lb and 60lb in this book would have doubled its size and made it unmanageable – but I hope somebody else will pick up the challenge and produce a companion volume. I include Peter's salmon because he is a friend of mine and was a close friend of my late lamented sporting companion Hugh Falkus.

---

*Another great friend, the late Richard Walker, used to get hot under the collar if anyone used this expression because, as he said, 'An exception never proved any rule.'

APPENDICES

APPENDIX 1

SALMON FISHING IN NORWAY

Exceptional salmon fishing was discovered in Norway in the 1820s and for decades anglers visited that country each year in search of peace, quiet, clean air, challenging rivers and big fish. This interesting episode was well documented for readers of the *Fishing Gazette* by one of their regular correspondents from Norway, who signed himself 'Rugde' (see Appendix 1).

Visitors often used to take over a farmhouse vacated by the owner of the fishing rights. For the sake of convenience, the farmer would move his family into a suitable barn for the duration of the let. On a visit to one of these farmhouses, Malcolm Greenhalgh found that one tenant, an Englishman by the name of Shelton, had left his mark. Shelton had fished the Tana River from 1882 to 1891, and duly engraved his name and listed his visits on the wooden walls of the house. Moreover, he adorned the walls with silhouettes of the larger salmon by tracing round the outlines of the fish.

Keen anglers who regularly leased salmon beats on Scandinavian, mostly Norwegian, rivers included members of the British aristocracy. Successive Dukes of Roxburghe, for example, took a beat on the Alten River to complement those they owned on the middle reaches of Scotland's River Tweed. The various Dukes would invite friends and colleagues to join them, often for the duration of the season – as described by Rugde, it took considerable time and effort to reach Norway in those days, let alone somewhere off the beaten track. No doubt the guests were carefully selected for their ability to live and enjoy the simple life as much as for their prowess with rod and line. To help in that respect, local gillies and boatmen were a necessity. The Alten boatmen were especially renowned then, as they are now. Here's what Roy Flury has to say about the current incumbents:

> The Alten boatmen are one of the great assets of the river and are a part of
> the whole experience of fishing there. Their knowledge and traditions are

This is one of Shelton's wall engravings – it has survived for well over a century

passed from father to son and they are experienced fishermen themselves. The fishing in June and for much of July is almost all from the boat. As the river falls, so wading and bank fishing become possible. The boats, or rather canoes, originally came from Karasyok. They are made of wood, are about 27ft in length and today many are made by the boatmen themselves. There are two men in each canoe, the man in the stern is the captain who uses the outboard between pools and directs the bowman. The latter's job is to row slowly and keep the canoe steady as it is backed down the pool. Everything is watched intensely. I would describe the first few casts in the canoe when first visiting Alten as intimidating. If you hear a knocking sound, it's your knees.

Modified versions of the canoes made at Karasyok in the nineteenth century – like this one – are still used on the Alten River

Another member of the aristocracy to fish in Norway was the Russian Count Denissoff. One of the most colourful figures in European salmon fishing history, Count Denissoff was an émigré who left Russia for Britain before the revolution. Before the First World War, Denissoff had been Tsar Nicholas II's minister of finance, and had made his fortune through some involvement with the building of the Trans Siberian Railway.

Details of Denissoff's private life would fill a book but, in his defence, it should be noted that when, in 1921, he leased a beat on the Aaro around Sogn and Fjordane that was owned by the Sogndal community, he invited many people to share the fishing on this marvellous piece of water. Invitations were sent out every year from May until September. Charles Ritz once arrived thinking that he might have abused Denissoff's hospitality by almost inviting himself, only to find that he was most welcome. He described his host in his book *A Fly Fisher's Life* (1959) as one of the *seigneurs* of the *ancien régime*.

Denissoff probably caught more portmanteau salmon than any other fisherman. There is a photograph of cardboard copies of four of them in Ritz's book – 53lb, 54lb, 54lb and 58lb – together with a graphic description of the river:

Fishing for Aäro salmon is not the kind of sport one usually associates with any other river, be it in Scotland, Norway, Iceland or Canada. This fierce stream – an unbelievably fast and dangerous water – is only half a mile long and the current is such that its salmon are exceptionally broad, heavy and powerful. They provide the most exciting sport imaginable.

Unfortunately, several mistakes seem to have been made in the reporting of Denissoff's catches. For instance, Ritz mentions a so-called world record fish of 76lb that was taken on the Aäro but this appears to be fictitious. A mistake in interpreting a weight of 31 kilos as 65½lb by the usually careful J. Arthur Hutton in a letter that was published in the *Fishing Gazette* of 2 August 1922 was probably the start of a story of another fictitious fish attributed to Denissoff through no fault of his own. However, his 68lb 4oz fish taken from the Aäro in 1921 is not in doubt (No. 415).

In 1965, when Denissoff was told that his lease was not going to be renewed, he left in anger, collecting all his chattels and fishing equipment and decamping to France, but not before burning down his house and fishing hut. He never went back. Most owners and lessees of fishing rights on salmon beats kept records of catches and of fishing days. The Roxburghe Records, for example, contain extensive details of fishing on the Tweed as well as on the Alten over many years. I feel sure that Denissoff's catch records are still extant and I for one would love to study them.

Malcolm Thorne, a noted collector of angling books and angling memorabilia, owns many pieces that once belonged to Denissoff, and is presently engaged in writing a pen portrait of this famous Russian, who incidentally, had a long-term friendship with L.R. Hardy, probably the best known of the Hardy family of tackle makers.

Confusingly enough, the names of many Norwegian rivers have changed over the years. For instance, the Alta was for many years known as Alten, and the Aaro was known as the Aroy or Aro among other variations. The Gaula was the Guul, Laugen was Lougen, Pasvik was Passvig and the Vosso was called Vos, Vosa and Vossa. The Vosso is also referred to by the names of its two main sections – Bolstad and Evanger. The distance from the mouth of the Vosso at Bolstad fjord to Lake Evanger is just over two miles and this stretch is frequently referred to as the Bolstad River. Lake Evanger is about four miles long and the distance between the top of the lake and Lake Seim is four miles. This section of the Vosso is frequently named Evanger.

FLY-CAUGHT RIVER ALTEN SALMON

Tormod Leinan of Alta in Norway responded to Roy Flury's request for details of salmon weighing 50lb or more caught on fly on the Alten River since the Second World War by compiling the following list. Tormod, who has spent most of his life working as a boatman on the Alten, insists that his list is incomplete, but the thirty-four fish he has documented will make salmon anglers aware that the River Alten is, or was, the premier river in the world for producing mighty salmon on the fly.

Although some of these salmon appear in my own lists (marked * because I already knew about them), I have included Tormod's list in full as a tribute to him and to the Alten River.

Tormod Leinan's list of big River Alten salmon

LB	ANGLER	POOL	DATE/YEAR
60	Hans Kjeldsberg	Gønges	17.06.48
60*	Ole A. Mosesen	Forbygningen	06.48
60*	Earl of Dudley	Sandiakoski	24.06.49
58	Torleif Leinan	L. Stengelsen	16.06.47
58*	Admiral W. A. Read	Steinfossnakken	09.07.68
58	Kåre Bull	L. Sierra	08.08.80
57*	Agnar Johnsen	Bollo	30.07.82
56	Åge Helgesen	Saarikoski	01.08.75
56	Frode Danielsen	U. Sorrisniva	26.07.92
55*	Antti Parkinen	U. Sorrisniva	25.07.85
54	Mr. Black	Ronga	18.07.54
54	Gunnar Kristensen	Svartfossnakken	01.07.84
54	Alistar Ballantine	Kista	16.08.92
54	Einar Anthonsen	Forbygningen	30.06.00
53*	Mrs Clare De Burgh	Svartfossnakken	09.07.68
53	Kåre Jørgensen	L. Sierra	25.08.80
53	Odd Hansen	U. Sierra	18.07.83
53	Olaf Lampe	Goddaniemi	02.08.89
53	Bill Caine	Væliniva	13.07.98
52	Didrik Heitmann	Saarikoski	03.07.76
52	Geir Zakariassen	Brattstrømmen	07.07.83
52	Morton Seaman	Langstilla	09.07.94
51	Hans Kjeldsberg	Langstilla	20.06.45
51	Jens Jensen	Steinfossnakken	20.07.78
51	Odd Hansen	Harestrømmen	06.07.83
51	Hans Lie	Brattstrømmen	30.07.84
51	Morton Seaman	L. Sierra	11.07.92
51	Espen Ottem	Brattstrømmen	15.08.96
50	Hans Kjeldsberg	L. Detsika	26.07.47

Tormod Leinan sent me the list of salmon weighing more than 50lb caught on the Alten River. The photograph shows how intimidating the rough waters of the Alten in its faster sections can be

LB	ANGLER	POOL	DATE/YEAR
50	Torleif Leinan	Åkergjerdet	26.07.76
50	Dagfinn Storvann	Bahtakoskinakken	03.07.81
50	Ted Dalenson	Sandiakoski	30.06.84
50	Peter Stroh	Vinakorva	20.08.99
50	Tor Arne Olaussen	Gammelplassen	30.06.00

50LB VOSSO RIVER SALMON

The information about Tod Corbett's list comes to me via George Miskin, an acquaintance of long standing and a renowned collector of angling memorabilia. His collection is not only comprehensive but also of extreme interest.

George Miskin has fished for salmon at Skorvelien in Norway, as a guest of Colonel D. Beard, for many years. Skorvelien is a seven-mile long beat at Voss Evanger, just upstream of the Bolstad beat on the Vosso River, and the house, also called Skorvelien, overlooks the famous Skorve pool. All the fishing here remained in the hands of the Barlow family from 1880 until the last war, when three miles were lost because the leases could not be taken up during the German occupation. Many famous fishermen have fished at Skorvelien, including Tod Corbett and Arthur Hutton. Corbett was a local legend but his fame was almost universal in salmon-fishing circles. It was common knowledge that 'The old gillies, who knew him well, would point out every spot where he would catch fish.' Hardy's named a rod after him, specially designed to handle big fish in heavy waters.

During regular visits, Hutton did much research on fish-scale reading and condition factor data to the extent that his findings frequently became a feature of big-fish reports in contemporary fishing magazines. Tod Corbett kept records of the fishing at Skorvelien, and noted that between 1921 and 1931, sixty-nine fish of over 40lb were killed, and that eleven fish of 50lb or more were killed between 1900 and 1932. Colonel Beard referred to Corbett's records in a letter to George Miskin:

> Up until 1932 the records were kept in great detail in Tod Corbett's amazing book and after that in the 40lbs books and in my records. These are now held by the twins (probably at Skorvelien). Just to wet your appetite I enclose the record of 50lb fish caught between 1900 and 1932 from Tod's book. One of the 57½ lb fish was caught by my grandmother [Mrs P. Barlow, No. 297] and is probably the second biggest fish caught by a lady (after Miss Ballantine).* It was stuffed and used to hang in the hall of her house and frightened us all when we were children. The stuffed fish was given to the Acton Museum, who threw it away quite recently, because it got the moth!! Another of the 58½ lb fish was caught by the famous Wye fisherman J. Arthur Hutton, who presented some butcher's scales to Skorvelien, which you may remember. The scales had a box but would only fit into it if the scales were set to 58½ lbs!!

Todd Corbett's list of 50-pounders 1900–1932

WEIGHT	SEX	LENGTH	GIRTH	YEAR
58.08	Male	49¾	3081	1902
58.08	Male	49¾	2983	1911
58.08	Male	51¾	30	1920
58.08	Male	52	29	1922
57.08	Male	52¾	29	1923
54	Male	49	29	1923
53	Male	51		1900
	Male	49	27¼	1920
52	Male	49	25½	1923
51.08	Male	48½	27½	1930
50.12	Male	51½	29½	1932

The method used to catch the above fish is not included in the data.

*In fact, the sequence is as follows: 1. Miss Ballantine 64lb, 2. Miss D. Davey 59½lb, 3. Lady Haworth 58½lb, 4. Mrs Perry Barlow 57½lb

APPENDIX 2

FISHING IN NORWAY BY 'RUGDE'

This article by 'Rugde' appeared in the *Fishing Gazette*.

The Exploitation of Norwegian Salmon Rivers by Englishmen.
From the Norwegian Point of View

Amongst the interesting articles contained in the Jubilee Number of the *Bergen Jaeger og Fisker Forening's* magazine, there is one which tells the story from the Norwegian point of view of the English salmon anglers' discovery and exploitation of the Norway rivers from the very beginning.
The following is a summary thereof: -

"The first Norwegian handbook on angling which I know of came out in 1839. It bears the title 'Fluefiskerirt's Arrvendelse I Norge.' I have never seen this book. I do not even know whether any copies of it still exist. According to the statement of a contemporary, it contained good drawings and explanations with regard to everything pertaining to fly fishing and trolling. It also contained designs of flies in every stage of manufacture. The book is, characteristically enough, published by an Englishman, Robt. D. Hutchinson, who had long resided in Drammen. It was written with the distinct intention of instructing the natives, and, says my informant – William Bilton, author of 'Two Summers in Norway' – 'there is no doubt that this little work will contribute to make a special English art familiar to such good students thereof as the Norwegians, with the opportunities they have of practising it.'
"It is no mere chance that the first Norwegian handbook upon angling was published by an Englishman. The first anglers who threw a fly on Norwegian rivers were certainly visitors from our neighbour land to the West. From them we have learnt the art, and the development which has taken place since has been markedly under English influence. The mere fact that English names and terms are prevalent among Norwegian fishermen for nearly all the articles employed, for every kind of fly, etc., is sufficient evidence of this. The first English anglers came here probably in the 'twenties;

that is to say, about 100 years ago. They came singly, and as explorers in a foreign land, looking for good sport, and above all salmon fishing. They brought into many of our remote valleys, the first breathe of foreign life. With wondering eyes they were met, but with real Norsk hospitality were they received. And they took back with them vivid impressions of our wonderful scenery and the democratic conditions and state of existence in which Norwegians lived.

"As our country and its sporting possibilities became better known, the number of those who were attracted by these glowing accounts increased. Below I will give some extracts from them in order to show the conditions under which sport was then conducted.

"A journey to Norway in the first half of the nineteenth century was no easy matter. Some few English anglers reached the West Coast in sailing craft which were employed in carrying freight across the North Sea. Others came by the steamers which plied between Hull and Gothenburg, and which occasionally, at any rate, called at Christiansand (1840). But most of them travelled *via* Hamburg, Copenhagen, and Gothenburg to Christiania. Thence they drove with horse and carriole along the country roads northwards to Trondhjem, or westwards through Valders to the West Country, and through Gudbrandsdal to the Romsdal and the Nordmore water system. The outfit was always a light one. It consisted of clothing and the inevitable bacon and tea, and a bottle case suspended underneath the vehicle. The fishing rods were lashed to one of the carriole shafts.

"There were a great many difficulties, with the language, the food and lodging, the horses, the state of the roads etc., and there was a want of comfort which must have been very trying for such cultivated men as those were. But according to all accounts, the difficulties were met with good humour and eventually overcome.

"The first rivers experimented upon were the large ones. Perhaps the Laagen was the very first; but the one that was best known and which became the objective of so many of the first salmon anglers was the Namsen – 'the King of all Salmon Rivers,' as it is called in a description written about the end of the thirties. By that time, moreover, practically all the large rivers along the extensive coast of Norway were known to, and had been fished by, Englishmen.

"One of the first English anglers who came over was William Bilton, author of 'The Angler in Ireland' and 'Two Summers in Norway'. He fished the Namsen in 1837 and 1839, and also tried other rivers on his various

journeys. In the book above-mentioned he gives much interesting information in regard to the life of our people at that time and the travelling
conditions. On his way to and from the Namsen he made many detours.
Thus in June, 1839, he travelled through Valders down to Laerdalsören,
tried the Laerdal, which he considered almost impossible as a salmon river
as it was too shallow and rapid, and proceeded off to Skjolden. From thence
he returned through Baeverdal before the road was traversable for wheeled
vehicles. When coming back from Namsos he went from Trondhjem to
Molde, partly by land, visited the Romsdal, and got back to Christiania *via*
Gudbrandsdal.

"I will not dwell at greater length on Bilton's travelling performances
although the subject is attractive enough, but will refer to what he says in
regard to the salmon fishing on the Namsen and the conditions he found
there. He was not the first English sportsman who fished that river, nor was
he without competitors: nevertheless, he had a very good time. There was
no such thing as rent to pay for the river, the fishing was free; but he
adhered to the plan that the fish he caught should be divided between the
riparian owners on the one side, and the boatman, his host, and himself on
the other. To mutual satisfaction! In this connection it is interesting to learn
that the riparian owners on the lower part of the river where he fished least
were dissatisfied because he did not pay more attention to their water, and
he was obliged to spend several days there in order that they should get a
share of the fish. The pay which the boatmen received was very small, but
in addition they got 'one speci-daler' for every salmon caught over 30lb. in
weight; hence these were termed 'specie lax.' The fishing was splendid. One
day he hooked 25 fish, of which he landed six; he lost many, his gear not
being equal to playing such heavy salmon in so large a river. In 27 days he
got 100 fish weighing 1,558lb., besides a number of grilse and sea trout.
Nine of the salmon were over 30lb. When Bilton returned in 1839 the competition on the river had become very perceptible, both from English and
Norsk fishermen. Of the latter he remarks that they were quick to imitate,
and that if their interest in the fishing continued to increase the best days of
the Namsen would soon be over. He himself, however, would seem to have
had little to complain of. One day he rose 16 salmon in one pool and landed
10; and on another he got 11 weighing 216lb. Altogether, from July 12 to
August 23, he captured 147 salmon weighing 1,800lb., besides grilse and
sea trout.

" 'Two Summers In Norway' contains information also in regard to other Norwegian rivers then known to Englishmen. Thus the Alten, which was already fished by an Englishman attached to an English company which worked the copper mines in the neighbourhood, is mentioned, and so too nearly all the rivers in the Trondhjem Amts. Those of the Romsdal too are referred to, but more specifically in the Bergen country, except the Laerdal; the author merely says that salmon had been caught in a couple of rivers in the neighbourhood of Bergen – probably the Bolstad and Dalelverre. The rivers in the extreme south – at Mandal, Christiansand and Arendal – were fished by Sir Humphrey Davy.

"William Bilton's accounts of his travels undoubtedly contributed greatly to induce English anglers to visit Norway; it is at any rate certain that the number increased very considerably in the succeeding years. As a direct outcome thereof there was published ten years later the first English handbook on salmon fishing in Norway, the well-known 'Jones' Guide to Norway and Salmon Fishers' Pocket Companion'. It came out in 1848, and was written by Frederic Tolfrey, Esq., author of 'The Sportsman in France', 'The Sportsman in Canada', etc. The book was dedicated to Sir Hyde Parker, who by general consent, says the Foreword, bears the title of honourable 'Father of Norwegian Salmon Fishers'.

"As the title implies, it is a travelling hand-book with information regarding routes and quarters; but it also contains a quantity of information of a purely sporting character, coloured illustrations of a number of well-known salmon flies, etc. In real English fashion the writer asserts his nation's superiority as a sporting one. 'England,' he says, 'is unquestionably a forcing-house for sportsman.' 'The sportsman is a being sui generis; he is a plant, so to speak of purely English growth, for in no other country is there to be found a corresponding specimen of the genus homo. Frenchmen,' he says, 'are not, and never will be, sportsmen; of fly-fishing they know nothing; they are ignorant of the very rudiments of the art.' In this connection Norwegians are not mentioned; probably they were looked upon as ignoramuses. In this book travellers to Norway are still advised to journey by way of Hamburg, while the carriole routes from Christiania northwards and westwards are recommended. Amongst these is the one viâ Laerdal to Bergen. Of that town the author does not speak in flattering terms. 'As a town,' he says, 'Bergen is about as uninteresting a place as can be imagined. It does not contain a single thing of interest, and it rains there eleven months of the year and three-fourths of the twelfth; it may therefore be justly termed Norway's "pot de chambre".'

"The angler is advised to betake himself as quickly as possible to Evanger or Bolstadören. Here the fishing is stated to belong to Mr. Stirling, from whom permission to fish can easily be obtained. No other rivers in the Bergen region are named in 'Jones' Guide'. It would seem that at that time the Laerdal, since then so famous, was not a salmon river of any importance. Alterations in its bed have no doubt produced greater depth and made it more attractive for large fish. The book also gives a long list of Norwegian rivers, the greater number of which would seem even thus early to have been let to Englishmen. Thus most of the Namsen is stated to be taken up already, and that chance anglers run the risk of being disappointed.

"When we come to the middle of the sixties we find our whole country, so to speak, occupied by English fishermen. About that time (1864) a new handbook made its appearance, which applied to shooting as well as fishing It is dedicated to Professor Rasch, is called 'Sport in Norway and Where to Find It', and is written by the Rev. M. R. Barnard. It contains descriptions of all the known salmon rivers – 125 of them – and at the same time mentions shooting possibilities. Of the conditions with us the preface to this book gives a very good idea.

"It says: - 'Hitherto a mystery, so to speak, as hung over the Norwegian salmon rivers, and false statements have in consequence been spread in regard to them. These statements have taken two opposite forms – the one that every yard of river is let and in the hands of Englishmen, and that a man can easily get a seat in Parliament as a Norwegian salmon river; and the other that he has nothing more to do than to step ashore and he will find salmon waiting for him to catch in every river. I need not say that these opposite poles of authenticity are false. The first has, I imagine, its origin from those who, well knowing the splendid sport which in some places is to be had, have adopted this plan in order to keep such knowledge to themselves and their own circle of friends; whilst the latter is a natural reaction against the other. There is no doubt, however, that the best parts of the best rivers are taken for shorter or longer periods; but that a man blessed with a good constitution, who is not afraid of exercise and a little roughing it, should not find very fair sport, experience has shown me to be absolutely untrue.'

"Barnard's book also contains information with regard to our first attempts at the artificial hatching of salmon spawn. It is stated that during the last ten years the Government has been taking steps in that connection, and that the English fishermen were aware of its importance.

"Amongst the books on Norway more recently published may be named the following: 'Wild Norway' by Abel Chapman, contains a series of descriptions of salmon fishing and shooting, accompanied by many illustrations. Fraser Sandeman's 'Angling Travels in Norway' contains, amongst other matter, a very detailed account of the fishing on the Voss and Evanger River, where the celebrated 'Saghang' Pool awoke the author's admiration. Major Mockler-Ferryman's book (1896), 'Travel, Sport and Folklore on the Hardanger Fjord and Fjeld'; and the River Gaula in Søndfjord is specially described in Stanford's book 'A River in Norway'.

"In 1907 General Burton published a book on 'Trouting in Norway': his experiences being mostly from the Søndfjord and Nordfjord (Bredheim Sandal, Førde, Gloppon, Loen, Skei, and Jølster). Most interesting, perhaps, of all, however, is Sir Henry Pottinger's delightful work, 'Flood, Fell and Forest', in which he set down the adventures, doings and experiences of an old hunter and fisherman throughout a period of nearly 50 years in all parts of Norway from the wastes of Finmarken to 'Sørlomdet.'

"The above few lines will, I hope, convey some idea at any rate with regard to Englishmen's fishing here in the country from its first commencement and onwards as it has developed. Our own development in the art of angling has progressed at the same time, and, so to speak, alongside it. The English skimmed off the cream by obtaining control of our best salmon rivers; what has been left to us is the spring and late autumn fishing, a kind of sport which is conducted under different conditions, and which requires, to a certain extent, other lures than the fly.

"But we have had one field of action to ourselves – rod fishing for trout among the mountains and in the small streams. Here we ourselves have had control, and have made progress even although English influence has been strong.

"Norwegian anglers will always, however, be grateful to our friends from the West for the example they have shown, for the implements they have brought us, and for their meaning of the term 'fair sport' which has also become our own."

RUGDE

It is interesting to compare Rugde's first-class historical roundup of Norway's salmon fishing and the English influence with a brief taste of Norwegian fishing eighty years on, as provided by Charles F. Holden in *The Game Fishes of the World* (1973).

A few years ago the fishing in Norway was difficult to reach and there were few comforts; but to-day good steamers cross the North Sea, and every convenience is to be had in the way of houses and food. Some idea of the angling here can be had by selecting the river Alten, which has about thirty miles of good fishing water, well adapted to casting a fly. The fish average about twenty pounds, and four rods can take in the season about ten thousand pounds of salmon. The river is controlled by one Englishman.

The river Namsen is divided into eight beats and affords its owners magnificent sport, occasional fishes making fifty pounds. The fishing here is done from a boat, which is worked in a zig-zag fashion across the stream, so that the fly or spoon reaches every part of it. In rivers of the second class, each rod is supposed to take from eight hundred to one thousand pounds of salmon. Nearly all the rivers here differ or have some peculiarity: thus the Aarö is famous for its large fish, sixty pounders having been taken. The river Laerdal is not a 'boat river' and can be forded, or the angler may cast from the banks.

Charles Holden manages to get the Chief Fisheries Inspector to grade Norwegian rivers from the point of view of their rental value, which is a pretty 'useful way to reflect their fishing quality'.

As to the angling rank of Norwegian rivers, I am indebted to Inspector Herr Landmark for the following: He estimates the value of the salmon and sea-trout in an average year as 1,462,000 kr. The Tana ranks first with an average of 59,945 kr., then the order is Laogen River, Gula, Orkla, Namsen, Mandel, Nisser, Topdal, Laerdal, Drammen, Voss, Vefsen, Stjordal, Figgen and Haa. The richness of this country in salmon streams can be realized when, eliminating the purely trout streams, there are one hundred and sixty salmon rivers.

The *Fishing Gazette* of 4 June 1927 published a table detailing the size of the annual net-catch of salmon in Norway (sea and river) for the period 1899 to 1923. Over a million fish were killed in nine out of the twenty-four years including the first and last years.

APPENDIX 3

BIG SALMON CAUGHT IN FINLAND AND SWEDEN

FINLAND

Although by June 2006 I had managed to accumulate data for nine entries relating to Finland's portmanteaux salmon, I was aware that obtaining details of other big fish from this country was going to be difficult. Jan Eggers came to my rescue with the news that he had contacted Matti Kettunen, who not only volunteered to do the necessary research but also, most importantly, would be directly contactable because he spoke English.

Matti Kettunen noticed that in March 1993 the hunting and shooting magazine *Metsastys ja Kalastus* published a list of 'The Known Biggest Salmon From Finland', which I am privileged to reproduce:

94lbs 14oz	1904 or 1905	TORNIO RIVER
79lbs 6oz	1928	TANA RIVER
77lbs 2oz	1896	KYMI RIVER
68lbs 6oz	1924	KEMI RIVER
67lbs 4oz	1915	OULU RIVER

Another huge salmon weighing 83lb 12 oz was netted in 1943. The 79lb 6oz fish in the above list is the well-documented salmon that was caught by Henrik Henriksen. According to the website arcticangler.no-history Henriksen was fishing with a lure bought in Finland that he 'had hammered and mended several times to make it move the right way throught the water'. We are also told that Henriksen was boat fishing when he hooked the fish and that it took many hours to land. An illustration of Henriksen's spoon, which looks quite like the modern Salmo spoon, was shown in *Villmarksliv* magazine in January 1983. Per Gubransen, a notable Norwegian fishing historian, commented in a letter:

> Courtney Williams and 'Jock Scott' etc. etc. all have the postmaster Henriksen's thirty-six kilo salmon caught on a spoon under Storfossen in the Tana, end of August 1928. The Postmaster wrote himself, to the magazine

Fiskesport (1936, p.86) in answer to enquiries, that he had been unaware that his capture would have caused such a stir. He had taken no measures, and no photograph – the weight would be confirmed by members of his family.

Matti Kettunen has kindly collected a lot of data on large salmon many of which were caught on bait, not knowing, because I failed to advise him properly, that this book does not provide the scope for recording salmon caught on bait unless their weight exceeds 60lb.

As already mentioned, the Tana River separates Finland from Norway for part of its course. Whereas it is usually conceded that Norway's Alten is the finest river in the world for big salmon that are regularly caught on fly, it is also recognised that the Tana River has unquestionably produced more fish in the 60lb to 70lb range. Here is a short extract from one of Jan Eggers' many letters to me.

Outdoor writer Matti Kettunen sent me a letter with the above Finnish big salmon information and he has written several books, in Finnish, about salmon fishing in his country. In his letters to me Matti Kettunen mentioned no less than 52 salmon over 25 kilos, but no less than 23 of these weighed over 28 kilos. So without any doubt I think we can say that the Tana river is the best river for very big Atlantic salmon in Western Europe at the moment.

Catches of big Finnish salmon over a long period have not been picked up to the extent that Norwegian catches have. Thanks to Matti Kettunen and other writers, this situation is changing rapidly, particularly with the advent of the internet. Here's Jan Eggers again:

Searching in Google I find no less than 617,000 items with River Tana information on the Internet and feel sure there will be pictures and salmon info.

SWEDEN

When an author makes a list of anything for the first time he is bound to discover something about the subject that he had never previously noticed. While making my list of big salmon I became aware that I was not getting as many citations for big Swedish salmon as I had expected. When the list was nearing completion (there has to be a last entry if a book is ever to be published), I checked up and found eleven entries for Swedish salmon with an average weight of 63lb, most of which were bait-caught fish originating from details supplied by Jan Eggers. It was extraordinary that there was only one entry between 50lb and 60lb, so I decided to see if Roy Flury could wring out some more information from his Swedish contacts. I was in luck. Roy Flury wrote to Nils-Erik

Tornquist, who very kindly obtained information for a list of fly-caught fish from Anders Sörensson. All of these fish were taken from the Mörrum River. Similarly, Göran Ulfsparre gave details of three more fly-caught fish from the River Em.

Anders Sörensson's List

50lbs 8oz	P. BJÖRKLUND	22.06.1991
51lbs 6oz	R. JOHNSSON	26.04.1992
51lbs 14oz	O. ANDREASSON	29.09.1995
52lbs 10oz	K. HÄKKANSSON	10.05.2000
52lbs 10oz	M. SVENSSON	6.05.1995
53lbs 3oz	C. PALM	13.07.1992
54lbs 7oz	M. BJÖRKMAN	27.05.1992
55lbs 6oz	E. NEDERGAAR	26.07.1994
58lbs 13oz	P. BRUGMANN	31.05.1992

Göran Ulfsparre's List

54lbs 3oz	L. POSTONEN	29.09.1992	From Sea Pool
53lbs 10oz	J. DEREHED	05.10.1992	From Home Pool
53lbs 12oz.	L. P. GUSTAFSSON	21.05.2000	From Sea Pool

Mats Svensson's 52lb 10oz Mörrum River salmon   *M. Björkman's 54lb Mörrum River salmon*

Kent Häkkansson's 52lb 10oz salmon (left side) that he took from No. 4 pool on the Mörrum

Peter Brugman's 58lb 13oz Mörrum River salmon

A pristine salmon taken from the Sea pool on the Morrum River, with its captor

This is the Sea pool, where Gustafsson hooked and killed his salmon

APPENDIX 4

DECLINE OF THE RIVER RHINE

The Rhine must once have been the queen of European salmon rivers, and in those days could have produced at least a hundred entries for this book. Approaching the new millennium, it had no runs of salmon whatsoever, although due to considerable improvement in water quality, Rhine salmon are now once again a fact of life.

Just how productive of big fish the Rhine was, even when the runs were in decline, can be estimated from an extract of a letter sent by Henry Fennell and published by the *Fishing Gazette* on 24 May 1902, when no less than three 50lb Rhine salmon were on the slab of one London fishmonger at the same time!

It may be interesting to note here that in 1889 I had the opportunity of taking one day at Mr. Grove's the dimensions of three Rhine salmon which formed a trio little less notable. They were all male fish and were in excellent condition. The heaviest nearly turned the scale at 55lb. In length it measured 51½in.; in girth 28in. The largest of the two other fish scaled just under 4½oz. under the 50lb. It measured 47½in. in length and 27½in. in girth. The other salmon was 6oz. under the 50lb., and measured in length 47in., and in girth 27in. I remember that at the time I saw these fish I remarked a great similarity in appearance between the two latter, and, for the nonce, I dubbed them "twin brothers." It should be remembered that salmon lose considerably in weight during transit.

Doubtless the river suffered a series of strokes that brought about its demise, but looking back to the late nineteenth century, it appears that the main damage was caused by the difficulty of policing the river, so that commercial netting interests on the lower reaches were allowed practically to exterminate the runs of fish. The following piece culled from *The Angler's Notebook and Naturalist's Record* (1888), page 77, published by William Satchell, London, illustrates the decline of this once great salmon river.

The same sad tale of decrease in the salmon supplies comes from the Rhine, but the cause there is different. Evidently protection is urgently required if salmon-hatching operations are to be of any use to their projectors. *Land and Water* says –

"This year's salmon fishery in the Upper Rhine, between the falls of Schaffhausen and Strasburg will prove the most insignificant known for a long number of years. The yield from last season was bad enough, the catches having been considerably below the average of many preceding years, but this season, in consequence of the pernicious methods of salmon catching at the lower parts of the Rhine, and the wholesale taking of salmon ready for spawning, the catches have proved the smallest and most indifferent ever effected. From the beginning of January to the end of May only some fifteen salmon had been caught between Bâle and Schaffhausen, as it found useless to carry on any regular operations; whilst from June to the present date the total of catches have been considerably below the average number of previous seasons, and extraordinarily small, considering the millions of salmon fry deposited by the Governments of Switzerland, Bavaria, Wurtweberg, and the Grand Duchy of Baden at various parts of the Upper Rhine, and all in spite of the exceptionally favourable state of the water. No fishing or netting of salmon was attempted at the otherwise favourably-situated salmon fishery stations near Rheinfelden and Lauffenburg, in Switzerland. On the other hand, it is stated, that the Dutch fishermen have caught as many as 12,000 salmon in one week, making 2,000 fish taken daily, or as much as the 120 salmon fishermen stationed at Bâle and Schaffhausen had been taking during the entire extent of the season. It seems, therefore, quite clear that all young salmon deposited into the Upper Rhine are caught up upon their return journey from the sea by the Dutch fishermen; a few specimens, perhaps, manage to evade their big salmon nets, and escape to their place of birth."

APPENDIX 5

NUMBER OF SALMON CAUGHT
WEIGHING OVER 60lb SINCE 1700

PERIOD	NUMBER OF FISH CAUGHT
1700–1800	8
1801–25	3
1826–50	2
1851–75	9
1876–1900	24
1901–25	54
1926–50	28
1951–75	21
1976–2000	20

APPENDIX 6

THE TOP TWELVE GIANT SALMON CAUGHT FLYCASTING SINCE THE END OF WORLD WAR II

CAPTOR	WEIGHT lbs oz	RIVER	YEAR	PLACE
1 Wiljo Saaristo	61 12	Tana	?	Finland
2 Kalle Karhunen	60 10	Tana	1966	Finland
3 Ole Andreas Mosesen	60 8	Alten	1948	Norway
4 Lord Dudley	60 0	Alten	1949	Norway
5 Hans Kjeldsberg	60 0	Alten	1948	Norway
6 Kristian Stiemstrom	59 4	Indalsalven	1999	Sweden
7 Per Brugmann	58 13	Mörrum	1992	Sweden
8 Kare Bull	58 0	Alten	1980	Norway
9 Admiral W.A. Read	58 0	Alten	1962	Norway
10 Torlief Leinan	58 0	Alten	1947	Norway
11 Jurgen Reppening	57 6	Alvkarlaby	1991	Sweden
12 Agnar Johansen	57 0	Alten	1982	Norway

N.B. Major Ivar Hauge caught a 70lb salmon in 1952 on the Tana. The fish was caught on a Jock Scott but he was harling as opposed to casting.

APPENDIX 7

STURDY'S TABLE

Weight to Length Salmon

INCHES	LB	INCHES	LB
30	11.574	43	34.082
31	12.770	44	36.516
32	14.046	45	39.063
33	15.404	46	41.725
34	16.848	47	44.506
35	18.379	48	47.407
36	20	49	50.432
37	21.713	50	53.584
38	23.522	51	56.864
39	25.428	52	60.274
40	27.435	53	63.819
41	29.544	54	67.500
42	31.759	55	71.320

Length taken from end of snout to the end of the middle rays of the tail fin, measured straight.

BIBLIOGRAPHY

TITLE	AUTHOR	PUBLISHER	DATE
The Driffield Angler	Alexander Mackintosh republished by the Flyfisher's Classic Library	Published privately (Yorkshire);	1806 1994
Two Summers in Norway	Reverend W. Bilton	Saunders & Otley, London	1840
The History of British Fishes (Volumes I and II)	William Yarrell	John Van Voorst, London	1841
Days and Nights of Salmon Fishing in the Tweed	William Scrope	John Murray, London	1843
Sport	Sir W. Bromley-Davenport	Chapman & Hall, London	1845
The Practice of Angling (Volumes I and II)	James O'Gorman	William Curry & Co. Dublin and Longmans, Brown & Co. London	1845
The Oxonian in Norway	Reverend Frederick Metcalfe	Edward Arnold, London	1846
Jones's Guide to Norway	Frederic Tolfrey	Longman, Brown, Green & Longman, London	1848
The Erne, its Legends and its Fly Fishing	Reverend Henry Newland	Chapman & Hall, London	1851
Natural History of Ireland (Volume IV pages 69-268)	Thompson		1856
The Angler Naturalist	H. Cholmondeley-Pennell	John Van Voorst, London	1863
British Fishes (Volume IV)	Jonathan Couch	George Bell & Sons, London	1877
The Fishes of Great Britain and Ireland (Volume I)	Francis Day	Williams & Norgate, Edinburgh	1880-1884
The Natural History of British Fishes	Frank Buckland	Unwin Brothers, London	1881
Notes and Jottings on Animal Life	Frank Buckland		1882
Field Sports of Northern Europe	Capt. L. Lloyd	Hamilton, Adams & Co., London	1885
British and Irish Salmonidae	Francis Day	Williams, London	1887
The Angler's Notebook and Naturalist's Record	Edited by William Satchell	William Satchell & Co., London	1888
Off The Mill	G.F. Browne, Bishop of Stepney	Smith & Elder	1895
The Salmon	Edited by A.E. Gaythorne Hardy	Longmans Green, London	1898
British Freshwater Fishes	Sir Herbert Maxwell	The Standard Art Book Co., London	1904
Salmon Fishing on the Grand Cascapedia	Edmond W. Davis	Privately published	1904

Flood, Fell and Forest	Henry Pottinger	Edward Arnold, London	1905
Reminiscences of Halsten Muri	J. Arthur Hutton	Sherratt & Hughes, London	1907
Salmon Rivers and Lochs of Scotland	W.L. Calderwood	Edward Arnold, London	1909
Wild Sport and Some Stories	Gilfrid W. Hartley	William Blackwood & Sons, Edinburgh & London	1912
The Salmon Rivers of England and Scotland (second edition)	Augustus Grimble	Kegan Paul Co. Ltd, London	1913
The Salmon Rivers of Scotland (third edition)	Augustus Grimble	Kegan Paul Co. Ltd, London	1913
Great Hours in Sport	Edited by John Buchan	Thomas Nelson & Sons, London	1921
Observations on a Salmon River	Frank Griswold	Published privately (Massachusetts, USA)	1922
Fishing for Salmon	Dr Cyril Marson	A. & C. Black	1929
Fifty Years and More of Sporting Scotland	Duke of Portland	Faber & Faber, London	1933
Game Fish Records	Jock Scott	H.F. & G. Witherby Ltd, London	1936
Where to Fish	Edited by H.D. Turing	The Field, London	1923, 1926, 1937, 1952
Great Angling Stories	Edited by John Dickie	W. & R. Chambers, London	1941
Angling Diversions	A. Courtney Williams	Herbert Jenkins, London	1945
The Fisherman's Bedside Book	'BB'	Eyre & Spottiswoode	1945
Thoughts on Angling	J.C. Mottram	Herbert Jenkins, London	c.1945
A Salmon Fisher's Notebook, A Fishing Fantasy	J. Hughes-Parry	Eyre & Spottiswoode	1949
Wye Salmon and Other Fish	J. Arthur Hutton	John Sherratt, Altrincham	1949
Salmon Fishing in Norway	Peter Prag	Norway Travel Association London	1953
Salmon Fishing	Richard Waddington	Faber & Faber, London	1959
Angler's Cavalcade	Eric Horsfall Turner	A. & C. Black, London	1966
Out of the Mainstream	Philip Crowe	Charles Scribner's & Sons, New York	1970
A Fly Fisher's Life (revised edition)	Charles Ritz		1972
Life-History and Habits of the Salmon Sea-Trout, Trout and Other Freshwater Fishes (third edition)	P.D. Malloch	Original edition 1910 published by Malloch's of Perth and London; second edition 1912	1975
The Great Salmon Rivers of Scotland	John Ashley-Cooper	Victor Gollancz Ltd, London	1980
Trout and Salmon Flies	Douglas Sutherland and Jack Chance	Pelham, London	1982
The Salmon Book	Douglas Sutherland	Collins, London	1982

A Salmon Fisher's Odyssey	John Ashley-Cooper	H.F. & G. Witherby Ltd, London	1982
Salmon Stories	Jack Chance	Debrett's Peerage Ltd., London	1983
A Line on Salmon	John Ashley-Cooper	H.F. & G. Witherby Ltd, London	1983
An Irish Salmon Gilly	Bill Hammond	Litho Press, Middleton, Co. Cork	1984
Teno – Saamen ja Lehen Virta	Raimo O. Kojo	W. S. øy	1984
Atlantic Salmon and the Fly Fisherman	Gary Anderson	Doubleday	1985
Fly Fishing for Salmon and Sea Trout	Arthur Oglesby	The Crowood Press, Marlborough	1986
Guinness Angling Records	L. Cacutt	Guinness Publishing, Enfield	1988
Salmon and Women	Wilma Paterson and Prof. Peter O.Behan	H.F. & G. Witherby Ltd, London	1990
The Flyfisher's Companion	John Buckland	Octopus Publishing, London	1990
Alten: The Story of a Salmon River	Roy Flury and Theodor Dalenson	Laurence Viney, Berkhampstead	1991
The Big Fish	Edited by Arthur Oglesby and Lucy Money-Coutts	Robinson, London	1992
Alten Reflections	Roy Flury and Theodor Dalenson	Laurence Viney, Berkhampstead	1993
A Century of Sport	Sylvain Gingras	Les Edition Rapides Blanc Inc., Quebec	1994
Med Karjolog Laksestenger ('With Carriole and Salmon Rod')	Per Gulbrandsen	Lokalhistorisk Forlag	1994
The Complete Salmon Fisher	Malcolm Greenhalgh	Blandford, London	1996
Salmon Netting in North Devon	A. Grant and P. Waters	North Devon Museum Trust	1998
Tenon Tarinat ('Stories of Tana')	Tero Ronkainen, Jamatti, J. Sãrömaa	Ajatus Books	1998
Vigeland i Vennesla	Arne Krogstad	V. G. & V. M. R. [?]	1999
Lohiyõ Tenolla ('Salmon Nights on Tana')	Matti Kettunen	Karisto øy	2000
The River Ewe, Reminiscent River Recollections of a Ross-shire	Kenneth Mackenzie	Stuart MacKenzie, Poolewe	2000
Guardian of the Salmon	G.H. Bielby	Halsgrove, Tiverton, Devon	2001
Storlaksens Rike ('A Big Fish Empire')	Eikeset, Heitmann and Nielsen	Alta Laksefiskeri interessentskap	2001
Grand Cascapedia Giants	Ronald S. Swanson	Meadow Run Press, New Jersey, USA	2005
Atlantic Salmon, An Illustrated Natural History	R. Sutterby and Malcolm Greenhalgh	Merlin Unwin Books, Ludlow	2005

Laksefisket í Namsen och de andere Elvene í Namdalen
('Salmon Fishing in the Namsen and Other Rivers in the Nam Valley')

PHOTOGRAPHIC CREDITS

All illustrations are copyright the author, with the following exceptions, which are kindly provided by these individuals or institutions:

A. Sörrenson 467, 468; The Alta Association 141; Alta Museum 380, 453; from *An Irish Salmon Gillie* (Litho Press, Cork) 34; Antti Parkkinen 139; Arne Krogstad 250, 329; from Arthur Oglesby and Lucy Money-Coutts, *The Big Fish* (Robinson, 1992) 226, 296, 320, 326; ASJ/Editions Rapides Blanc 126; Atholl Estates 416, 417; Atlantic Salmon Federation 244; Bill Read 168, 187; courtesy of Blair Castle Estate 204–5, 209; Bozo Ivanovic 81; The Bulman Inn, County Cork 233; from C. D. Marson, *Fishing for Salmon* (A & C. Black, 1929). 213; David Beazley 107; David Hatwell/courtesy Topsham Museum Society 273; David R. Cowan/David James 441; Debrett's Peerage 173, 241, 249; Duke of Roxburghe Records 74, 93, 99, 183, 185, 192; Dumfries and Galloway Libraries, Information and Archive 84; E. Krogh 201, 384; from Edmond Davis, *Salmon Fishing on the Grand Cascapedia* (New York, 1904) 87; Eget Forlag-Harran/Roy Flury 356; Fiske Journalen Yearbook 158, 241, 276; Flyfisher's Journal 263, 301; Gloucester City Museum 291, 312; Hans Hatle, Barents Sea Safaris 392; Haraldsen Tours of Oslo 217; Hoddom Castle Estate 83; from J. A. Campbell, *A Century of Sport* (Editions Rapides Blanc) 123; J. Waddington 96; from Jack Hughes-Parry, *Fishing Fantasy* (Eyre & Spottiswoode, 1949) 212; Jan Eggers 246, 332, 363; Jesper Fohrmann 12; from Jock Scott, *Game Fish Records* (1936) 258; from Joseph Adams, *Salmon and Trout Angling* (Hutchinson, 1923) 175; Karl Magne 270; Karl Magne/David Hatwell 331; MacCleary 214; Malcolm Greenhalgh 21, 22, 104, 163, 230, 269; Martha Coigney 77; Metsastys ja Kalastus 401; Michael Kitchen 189; Mike Crosby 2; Mrs Andersen, Edinburgh 290; National Library of Scotland 178–9; North Devon Museum's Trust 280; Odd Haraldsen 221, 234, 255; P. Klippinger 438, 468; Per G. Gulbrandsen 137; Per Olav Moum 300, 302; Ron Swanson 337; Roy Flury 44, 61, 79, 82, 92, 108, 110, 118, 119, 157, 164, 169, 186, 194, 261, 269, 371, 414, 446, 456; Sir Richard Hyde Parker, Melford Hall, Suffolk/Roy Flury 176; Sylvain Gingras/Editions Rapides Blanc 140; T. Millington Drake 79; courtesy of Topsham Museum Society (front jacket), 274; Tormod Leinan/Roy Flury 265; Urheilu Kalastus 241, 307; Wilfred Kennedy 339; from William Cavendish-Bentinck, *Fifty Years and More of Sport in Scotland* (Faber & Faber, 1933) 292.

The author and publishers have endeavoured to trace the copyright holders, where necessary, for the images reproduced. This has not been possible in all cases and they apologize for any unwitting infringement of copyright.

INDEX

Page numbers in *italics* refer to illustrations, those in **bold** indicate main discussion.

Aaro River 95–7, 337–41, 343–50, 357
Aarven, Johann 357
Aas, Paul 272
Aberdeen Journal 406–8
Alaollitervo, Väinö 400, *401*
Allen, Thomas 193
Alston, Major W.H.S. 263, 299–301
Alta River *see* Alten River
Alten River 446; boatmen *92, 93, 167*; salmon over 50lbs 74, 75, 79–81, 82, 92, 98, 108, 116, 117, 118–20, 139, 141, 155–6, 157–8, 164–7, 168, 183–4, 186–7, 192, 194; salmon over 60lbs 265, 272, 371, 380; Steinfoss pool *169*; Upper Kista *178–9*
Angler's News 277, 410
Annan River 83–5, 214, 228, *229*, 259
Arthur, General C.A. 62
Ashley-Cooper, John 72–3, 90, 91, 101, 125, 128, 136, 143, 181, 235, 238, 239, 242, 252–3, 283, 287, 402
Athole, Dukes of **203–9**, 416, 417
Awe Loch 425–7, 433
Awe River 67, 94, 105, 124–5, 129, 144, 145–51, 155, 195–6, 226

bag (lave) net 290–1, 378–9
Bainbridge, Mr. G.B. 104, 163
Bainbridge, Mr. Jr. 104
Ballantine, Miss Georgina 115, 116, 196, **317–19**
Baltic Sea 266, 268, 332, 386, 395–6; Laxfestivalen Trolling Tournament 304

Bandon River 233–4
Barnes, Charles B. 114
Bates, E.P. 231–2
Beauly River 68–70
Bennett Lawe, Sir John 129
Bergesen, Charles 303
Bergsche Maas River 246
Berriedale River 292–3
Billingsgate 357, 366, **381–2**
Bjørge, Karl Jørgen 220, *221*
Blackwater River *210*, 218–19, 222–5, 228, 389
Blythswood, Lord 111–12
Border Esk River 420–1
Bostock, Neville 71
Bradley Martin, Esmond 140
Brereton, Mr 130
Bromley-Davenport, Sir W. 136, *137*, 266
Browne, Bishop 364–9
Buckland, Frank 170, 236, 279, 313, 322, 324, 353, 355–6, 365, 366–7, 368, 395, 447
Bush Fishery, Co. Antrim 405

Calderwood, W.L. 63, 261–2, 283, 287, 290, 379, 402, 426–7
Campbell, Duncan 433
Canada *see* Grand Casapedia River; Margaree River; Matapedia River; Restigouche River
Chance, Jack 118–20, 128, 172, 225, 240, 249, 263, 299–301, 330
Charrington, H.C. 270–1
Childs, Dr C. 67
Cholmondeley-Pennell, H. 321, 394–5, 399
clamp-foot reel *203*
Clarke-Jervoise, Commander H. 62
Coates, Sir Stuart 90, 115–16
Coigney, Dr. Rodolphe 76–8
Considine, Howel 447
Cook, Reverend A. 259
Corbet, Major B.D. 74, 116, 117
Corbett, E.M. 251

Cotter, Captain 174
Courtney Williams, A. 321–2, 333, 364–5, 373, 396, 402, 434
Covington, Hannah 159–60
Craven, W.G. 112–14
Crerar, John (gillie) 208, *209*
Crowe, Philip Kingsland 180, 201–2, 244
Crump of New Bond Street (fishmonger) 333, 373
Cumberland Derwent River 104, 220

Davenport, Lord 266
Davey, Miss D. 258
Davis, Edmond W. 87–8, 105–7
Day, Francis 351, 370, 376, 405
de Burgh, Clare 118–20
de Pass, Harold 226
Dee River 242, 407, 408
Denissoff, Count **343–50**, 357
Derwent River 104, 220
Devereux, R.G. 235
Deveron River 143, *188*, 189–91
Devon River 410–13
D.J.W. 214
Drammen River 387–8
drift net 285–6
Dudley, Earl of 186
Duff, Willie (gillie) 416–17
Dun, Robert 123
Dungarvan, Viscount 110

Earn River 440–1
Eden River 142–3, 181–2, 396–8
Eggers, Jan 86, 154, 163, 175, 307
Eira River 71, 172
England 399–400; *see also* Billingsgate; Border Esk River; Derwent River; Eden River; Exe River; North Esk River; Severn River; South Esk River; Spittal Beach, Berwick; Taw River; Thames River;

Tyne River; Usk River; Wye River
Erne River 231–2
Esk River *see* Border Esk River; North Esk River; South Esk River
Evanger River 358–62 *passim*
Ewe River 63, 66, 428–32; Ladies' Pool 58, *63, 66*
Exe River **273–6**, 280

Ferguson, L. **104**, 220
The Field 94, 317–18, 389, 396, 397–8, 425–6, 433
Finland 409; Tano River 400, *401*
Fishing Gazette (including editor's correspondence): fly-caught salmon over 50lbs 66, 67, 109, 114, 115–16, 121, 125, 133–5, 136, 142, 145–6, 149–50, 159–60, 161, 196–7, 203; lost fish 416, 419–20, 435–7; record brace 443, 444–5; salmon between 50lbs and 60lbs 217, 219, 228, 242, 248, 251; salmon over 60lbs 261–2, 264, 265, 267–8, 273–5, 279, 280, 282, 283–4, 285–6, 290, 292–4, 295, 297, 299, 308–11, 313, 315–16, 325–8, 333, 336, 337–8, 339, 340, 343–8 *passim*, 356–7, 358–62, 365–6, 372, 377–9, 381–5, 386, 387, 388, 394, 395–6, 399, 402, 404–5, 409, 412
Fison, Dr E. 102, *103*
Floors Castle Estate 98, 117, 161–2, 192
Flury, Roy 75, 108, 110, 117, 120, 156, 157–8, 177–80, 186–7, 244, 269, 272, 341, 348–50, 372, 390–1, 446; and Dalenson, 98, 183, 194

Flyfishers' Journal 76–8,
195–6, 288–9, 387–8,
409
Flynn, Billy (gillie) 222–3,
224, 225
Foged, Krono 382, 384, 385
Forth Estuary 290–1
Frank, Russell (keeper) 85
Fraser, Pipe-Major 68–70
Fusta River 137, 156

Galloway News 334–6
Galway 351–4
*Game and Gun and Anglers'
Monthly* 146–9
Garry River 129–30
Germany 395–6; Rhine River
355–6
Gordon, Mr C. (gillie) 242
Gore Booth, Sir Henry 295
Grand Casapedia River 62,
71, 87–8, 89, 105–7,
107, 114, 123, 126,
131–2, 140; Lorne
Cottage 71, 114, 126
Grant, Alexander 129–30
Grant, Duncan 60–1
Grant (Pool House keeper) **63**,
66
Green, Major 242–3
Grimble, Augustus 64–5, 67,
105, 111–12, 121,
124–5, 143, 155,
161–2, 278–9, 287,
312–13
Grimestad, Jens 358–62
Grove, Messrs., of Bond Street
(fishmongers) 279, 333,
364–5, 373, 399–400,
404–5
Guest, Merthyr 314

Haggart, J. 277–9
Hägglund, George 363
Haig, Colonel Douglas 422–3,
424
Hamilton, Colonel N.
Dalrymple 108, 155–6,
164–7, 183–4, *185*
Hammond, Admiral 435–7
Haraldsen, Odd 240, *241*,
255
Harrison, James (gillie) *87*, 88
Hartley, Gilfred 448–9
Hatwell, David 68, 69, 78,

270–1, 275, 276, 301,
330, 399, 442
Hauge, Major Ivor 201–2
Hegan, Colonel 265
Heia, Odd 240, *241*
Henriksen, Henrik 393
Hill, Jimmy *281*
Holland, Bergsche Maas River
246
Home, Colonel W. 100–1
Home, Earl of 196–201
Humphreys, Mr. J.H.
(fishmonger) 325–7
Huntington, Major A.W. 94,
144
Hutton, Arthur 71, 146, 170,
171, 213, 216, 219,
248, 258, 264, 275,
285, 305, 310–11,
327–8, 337, 345–7,
356–7, 359, 360,
378–9, 381–2, 419–20,
443, 444
Hyde Parker, Sir *176*, 177–80

Ianetta, V. 239
Indalsälven River 175
Ireland 351–4, 389; *see also*
Bandon River; Blackwater
River; Bush Fishery, Co.
Antrim; Erne River;
Shannon River; Suir
River
Islamouth 215
Ivanovic, Bozo 79–81

Jamieson, Ken 442
Johansen, Agnar 157–8

keepers **63**, 66, 85, 147–8,
149, *188*, 189–90
Kennedy, Wilfred 337–41
Kidson, W.A. 136
Kjolstad, Svein 356–7
Klerck, Magnus 390–2

Larsen, Egil 234
Latham, J. 218–19
Laxfestivalen Trolling
Tournament 304
Laycock, General Joseph 192
Leardal River 216
Leigh, Hon. D. 110
Lewis, James 296–7
Lindsay, Dr Alexander 212

Loch Awe 425–7, 433
Loudon, Peter 83–5
Lowther Bridger, Mr 181–2
Lulea River 333
Lundquist, Christer 86
Lyon River 283–4

McKenzie, Cecil 109
Mackenzie, George 142–3
Mackintosh, Alexander
127–8
Maher, Michael 152–4
Mannsverk, Bjarne 265
Margaree River 109
Marshall, Dr 217
Marson, Dr Cyril 213
Marston, R.B. (editor) *see
Fishing Gazette*
Matapedia River 76–8
Maxwell, Sir Herbert 66,
100–1, 130, 152–4,
260, 337, 422–3
Merton, Professor T.R. 216
Mikklesen, Bjorvlff (boatman)
92
Milburn, Fred 125
Miller, Mr. T. 297
Mørch, Per 245
Moonen, Raymond J. 217
Moray Firth 404–5
Morison, Mrs Clementine
(Tiny) *188*, 189–91
Morrison, Major 92
Mörrum River 86, *332*, *438*
Mosesen, Ole 75, 194
Mosesen, Ole Andreas 75,
168, 186–7, 194
Mosesen, Tormod (gillie) *119*,
120, 168, 187
Moums, Erik and Svein 302

Nadeau, Henry 126
Namsen River *414*; fly-
caught salmon over 50lbs
104, 110, 154, 159–60,
163, 177–80; salmon
between 50lbs and 60lbs
230, 237, 240, 242–3;
salmon over 60lbs 261,
269, 302, 307, 308–11,
314, 342, 356–7
Neiden River 372
Ness, J.T. 238
nets: bag (lave) 290–1, 378–9;
drift 285–6; stake 374–6

Nith River 334–6
North Esk River 114, 434
Norway 378–9, 387–8,
448–9; *see also* Aaro
River; Alten River;
Drammen River; Eira
River; Evanger River;
Fusta River; Leardal
River; Namsen River;
Neiden River; Olden
River; Otra River; Pasvik
River; Rauma River; Sand
River; Sødal River; Tana
River; Torridal River;
Vipen River; Vosso River
Norwegian salmon at
Billingsgate 381–2

Oglesby, Arthur 115; and
Money-Coutts, Lucy 86,
95, 98, 136, 220, 226,
296, 320, 326
Olden River 288–9
Oldfield, Miss Annie 230
Oldham, J.M. 114
Olsson, Kenneth 268
O'Mahony, Mr 228
Otra River 245

Parkkinen, Antti 139
Parsons, J. Graham 244
Pasvik River 295, 386,
390–2
Pedersen, Anton 194
Perron, William 446
Phipps, Henry C. 89, 107
Portland, Dukes of 292–3
Prichard, O.M. 117
priest 298
Pryor, Arthur 161–2
Pullar, Major F. 215

Rauma River 136, 266
Read, Admiral William A. 75,
168, *169*
Reece, Richard 296–7
Remes, Martin *306*, 307
Restigouche River 442
Rhine River 355–6
Roxburghe, Dukes of 74, 98,
99, 117, 120, 156, 162,
167, *192*, 392
Roxburghe Records 92, 116,
117, 192
'Royal Ascot' salmon 325–7

Rudd, J.D. 86
Russia *see* Tana River
Ruthven, Lord 121–2
Rutuna, Pekka 409

Sagmo, Fridgeir 342
St George, Howard 91
Sand River 240, *241*, 303, 418–19
Schwabe, Misses Phyllis and Evelyn 216
Scotland 406–8, 410–13; *see also* Annan River; Awe River; Beauly River; Berriedale River; Dee River; Deveron River; Devon River; Earn River; Ewe River; Forth Estuary; Garry River; Loch Awe; Lyon River; Moray Firth; Nith River; Stinchar River; Tay River; Tweed River; Ythan River
Scott, Colonel A.E. 143
Scott, Jock 83, 114, 121, 129, 235, 258, 259, 270, 305, 334, 379, 410–12, 433
seal bites 393
Seaman, Morton 98
Seem, Ola 307
Sepponen, Pirkko 240, *241*
Severn River 193, 312–13, 370
Shannon River 66, 125, 174, *174*, *175*, 247, 293–4, *295*, 374–6, 447
Sødal River 328, *329*

Somerville, D.K. 252–4
South Esk River 252–4
Southesk, Earl of 253–4
Sowerby, Murray 330, *331*
Spaulding, J.T. 71
Spey River 60–1, 64–5, 97, 112–14, 260, 406–8
Spittal Beach, Berwick, England 393
stake nets 374–6
Stanley, Hon. Victor 131–2
Stephens, Mr *281*
Stewart, Thomas 282–3, 298
Stewart, W. 298
Stiemström, Kristian 175
Stinchar River 287
Stromme, Georg 320
Struik, Gijsbert 246
Sturdy, Mr. (scale) 248, 251, 294, 333, 442
Suhr, Einar 141
Suir River 152–4
Swanson, Ron 71, 89, 107, 114, 122, 123, 235
Sweden 363; *see also* Baltic Sea; Indalsälven River; Lulea River; Mörrum River

Tana River 138–9, 201–2, 240, 276, 307, 373, 382–5, 393
Tano River 400, *401*
Taw River 280, *281*
Tay River: fly-caught salmon over 50lbs 62, 72–3, 90, 111–12, 115–16, 117, 121–2, 127–8, 133–5,

203–9; lost fish 416–17; salmon between 50lbs and 60lbs 215, 217, 236, 238, 239, 243, 247; salmon over 60lbs 260, 277–9, 282–3, 286, 298, 313, 315–16, 317–19, 324, 333, 364–9, 373, 394–5, 402, 410
Thames River 227, 321–3
Thornton, Mr H.G. 145–51
Thorpe, Colonel James 105
Torridal River 250
Towy River 212
Tweed River 261–2, 422–4; Floors Castle Estate 98, 117, 161–2, 192; fly-caught salmon over 50lbs 60–1, 86, 91, 100–1, 102, 130, 136, 161–2, 196–201
Tyne River 285–6

Ugland, Halvor 250
Usk River 265, 296–7

Valle, Nils 373
Vane-Tempest-Stewart, Lord 237
Varrie, John 228, *229*
Vassenden, Jakob 372
Vernes, Jaqueline 82
Vipen River 267–8
Vosso River 170; salmon between 50lbs and 60lbs 217, 220, 234, 240, 244, 248, 249, 251,

255; salmon over 60lbs 263, 270–1, 299–301, 320, 330, 358–62, 372, 377–8
Voysey, Richard 273–6

Waddington, Richard 91, **95–7**
Wales, Towy River 212
Walker, Wullie 402
Wallace, Jock 334–6
Walle, Per 276
Walthall, Brigadier General E.C. 222–5
Ward, Miss Lettuce 72–3
Waud, G.C. 248
Wells, C.M. **249**, 271, 299–301, 330
Westminster, Duke of 156, 186, 192
Wheen, Miss 154
White, Major H.H.R. 137, 156
Willes, Henry 195–6
Winterton, Lord 64–5
Wye River: lost fish 419–20; record brace 443–5; salmon between 50lbs and 60lbs 213, 216, 235; salmon over 60lbs 258, 264, 297, 305, 370, 371
Wyndham Smith, J. 443–5

Yarrell, William 177, 198–201, 381, 400, 404
Ythan River 407

Zetland, Marquis of 133–5